Computer Networks and Communications

Computer Networks and Communications

Edited by
Lewis Price

www.willfordpress.com

Published by Willford Press,
118-35 Queens Blvd., Suite 400,
Forest Hills, NY 11375, USA

ISBN: 978-1-68285-766-3

Cataloging-in-Publication Data

Computer networks and communications / edited by Lewis Price.
   p. cm.
Includes bibliographical references and index.
ISBN 978-1-68285-766-3
1. Computer networks. 2. Telecommunication. 3. Digital communications. 4. Communication.
5. Network computers. I. Price, Lewis.
TK5105.5 .C66 2020
004.6--dc23

For information on all Willford Press publications
visit our website at www.willfordpress.com

Contents

Permissions

List of Contributors

Index

Preface

A computer network is a digital telecommunications network. It involves computing devices that exchange data with each other using connections between nodes. Wireless media such as Wi-Fi or cable media like optic cables or wires are used to establish these data links. Interpersonal communications are facilitated by computer networks, which allow users to communicate easily and efficiently through different means. Shared use of application and storage servers, use of email and instant messaging, access to the World Wide Web, etc. are some of the applications and services supported by computer networks. The wired technologies used for networking include coaxial cable, optical fiber and twisted pair cabling. The wireless technologies include terrestrial microwave communication, radio and spread spectrum technologies, communication satellites and free-space optical communication. This book studies, analyzes and upholds the pillars of computer networks and communication and its utmost significance in modern times. It is a valuable compilation of topics, ranging from the basic to the most complex advancements in this field of study. It will help new researchers by foregrounding their knowledge in this branch.

After months of intensive research and writing, this book is the end result of all who devoted their time and efforts in the initiation and progress of this book. It will surely be a source of reference in enhancing the required knowledge of the new developments in the area. During the course of developing this book, certain measures such as accuracy, authenticity and research focused analytical studies were given preference in order to produce a comprehensive book in the area of study.

This book would not have been possible without the efforts of the authors and the publisher. I extend my sincere thanks to them. Secondly, I express my gratitude to my family and well-wishers. And most importantly, I thank my students for constantly expressing their willingness and curiosity in enhancing their knowledge in the field, which encourages me to take up further research projects for the advancement of the area.

Editor

Selective Route based on SNR with Cross-Layer Scheme in Wireless Ad Hoc Network

Istikmal, Adit Kurniawan, and Hendrawan

School of Electrical Engineering and Informatics, Institut Teknologi Bandung, Jl. Ganesha 10, Bandung 40132, Indonesia

Correspondence should be addressed to Istikmal; istikmal@telkomuniversity.ac.id

Academic Editor: Sandra Céspedes

In this study, we developed network and throughput formulation models and proposed new method of the routing protocol algorithm with a cross-layer scheme based on signal-to-noise ratio (SNR). This method is an enhancement of routing protocol ad hoc on-demand distance vector (AODV). This proposed scheme uses selective route based on the SNR threshold in the reverse route mechanism. We developed AODV SNR-selective route (AODV SNR-SR) for a mechanism better than AODV SNR, that is, the routing protocol that used average or sum of path SNR, and also better than AODV which is hop-count-based. We also used selective reverse route based on SNR mechanism, replacing the earlier method to avoid routing overhead. The simulation results show that AODV SNR-SR outperforms AODV SNR and AODV in terms of throughput, end-to-end delay, and routing overhead. This proposed method is expected to support Device-to-Device (D2D) communications that are concerned with the quality of the channel awareness in the development of the future Fifth Generation (5G).

1. Introduction

Ad hoc network is expected to have a more significant role in the implementation of future 5G. Ad hoc network also provides the inclusion of D2D communication, a technology which becomes one of the key enablers for several advance communication techniques such as critical communication [1]. Ad hoc network also supports the development of Mobile-to-Mobile (M2M) communication [2, 3]. In D2D and M2M communication, the successful data transmission is influenced by the mechanism of the routing protocol. This protocol is responsible for seeking routes as the delivery path and has to be able to adapt to different situations, such as the movement of the users and the channel quality. Various routing mechanisms have been proposed for D2D [4, 5] but are restricted to the route discovery efficiency due to the fully distributed network [6]. The keys to improve the efficiency in route discovery are reducing the overhead and finding the route with good quality connection to improve the throughput performance.

Efficient communication must offer the capability to support application with rapid bandwidth requirement [7]. With this requirement, the path to deliver the data should have good quality. Moreover, to achieve intelligent D2D communication with resource constraint and intermittent connectivity, the devices require intelligent protocols which the conventional routing protocols cannot solve [8].

The conventional routing protocol that uses hop count as a metric for determining the path is perceived no longer appropriate for applications that require a good quality communication path. The protocol should be more adaptive and has to consider the link quality being used as the path to deliver the data [9, 10]. The routing algorithm that helps network find a reliable path will improve the network resilience against path break and packet loss. The cross-layer scheme is one of promising methods that has become popular in recent research to achieve maximum network utility [11]. This method shares information between layers and joint cooperations to increase network performance with general or specific solutions.

Previous studies had proposed some new methods with more attention to the quality of path. These methods were based on the quality of service (QoS) and the quality of the channel (QoC). In the case of QoS, one of such research was quality awareness with effective estimated throughput [12]. Another related research is a mechanism to find high throughput path by taking the expected total number of Medium Access Control- (MAC-) layer transmissions into account [13]. This research is further enhanced using cooperative transmission [14]. On the other hand, [15] and [16] proposed a routing metric that considered the expected transmission time and high throughput route selection with medium time metric, respectively. In the case of QoC, a mechanism to improve multihop routing using SNR by adding the SNR information into Route Request (RREQ) was proposed in [9, 17]. The use of SNR and Receive Power (RP) to find the route was proposed by [18, 19] by adding up the SNR information into Route Reply (RREP) mechanism. In [20] and [21], routing selection was improved using minimum summation of inverse SNR and weighted SNR average of all links in the path, respectively. Moreover, a study reported in [22] proposed a routing protocol for wireless sensor networks through SNR-based dynamic clustering, while that reported in [23] used cooperative Automatic Repeat reQuest (ARQ) system to minimize total network energy consumption while delivering a minimum required SNR. Routing protocol based on streamlines of potential field where data rate depended on SNR was studied in [24], and cluster routing protocol considering the SNR and residual energy of the nodes with cross-layer design was proposed in [25]. However, previous work that used SNR in routing protocols had some issues in the methods. To solve these issues, we proposed new methods. Details on the issues and the proposed method are discussed in Sections 2 and 4, respectively.

The paper is organized as follows. Section 2 describes the related work and the contributions of this research. Section 3 describes the network model and throughput formulation. Section 4 describes the weakness of earlier methods and the design of selective route based on SNR with cross-layer scheme. Section 5 describes the routing protocol performance and analysis. Finally, Section 6 is the conclusion and future research opportunities.

2. Related Work

A mechanism to improve multihop routing using SNR by adding the SNR information into RREQ was proposed in [17]. This scheme used the average route quality as the ratio between the overall path quality and the number of hops. The result showed improvement in network throughput and reduced packet error rate. However, adding SNR information in the broadcast of RREQ mechanism had caused increasing overhead and complexity of the route discovery process.

Study in [9] discussed the important of SNR as link quality to use in routing protocol. The paper suggested cross-layer mechanism with SNR information to obtain better routing. This mechanism added SNR information in each RREQ packet; the destination node then determined the best route and replied by sending a RREP packet. Since the RREQ and the RREP frame carried the new extension field, this method had caused higher overhead and complexity in both way mechanisms.

Authors in [18] used SNR and RP as valuable information for routing protocol. The proposed scheme added two extra fields in RREP packet to store SNR and RP information. The

source node selected the route based on any best available values of SNR or RP. The performance results with cross-layer design improved their performances with respect to service quality.

The same method with addition of SNR information in RREP mechanism was proposed by [19]. In this method; the authors applied lower to upper layers scheme, where SNR information from physical layer was utilized in routing protocol. From the simulations, the proposed method achieved higher throughput than the conventional routing protocol that used hop count as routing metric. In [20], routing selection was improved using minimum summation of the inverse SNR. The metric was equivalent to this method of all the links in the path. Through simulation, the proposed method claimed gain for better performance in terms of amount of delivered packet and end-to-end delay. Although this method is used to find the path with good channel quality, the selection of the path with this method may have one or more links with very low quality.

Authors in [21] used SNR as channel-aware routing metric. The proposed scheme utilized the weighted signal-to-noise ratio average. The best route was selected based on the minimum accumulated SNR average. The algorithm had resulted in higher throughput, better packet delivery ratio, and less average delay. However, this method had similar weakness to previous method using minimum summation of the inverse SNR.

In summary, earlier methods that used SNR information as metric in channel-aware routing had two main schemes. First, the proposed scheme used routing discovery process, such as RREQ and RREP, to collect SNR information from the node. Second, to select the appropriate route, the earlier methods used average of SNR or summation of SNR of all the link. However, the use of SNR in earlier research, namely, by using the sum or the average of SNR, has a weakness because one or more links can have a very low SNR even though the average is high. This weakness will be explained further in Section 4. Furthermore, the use of SNR information in early researches on the route discovery process RREQ and RREP has increased overhead and complexity which should be avoided.

To overcome above problems, we propose an improved method which collaborates the cross-layers information, that is, the cooperation between the network and physical layer. In this scheme, we used same existing methods that employed SNR and cross-layer design to improve routing protocol performance. The most important aspects in our proposed methods, which have not been addressed in previous work and become our contributions, are as follows. Instead of adding SNR information to the RREQ or RREP process, we propose a selection of links for the reverse route mechanism based on SNR. This mechanism avoids additional overhead. Furthermore, selection route with a SNR threshold mechanism also improves the route choice compared to the previous minimum summation or average of the SNR methods. We additionally describe this cross-layer performance in network model and throughput formulation model based on SNR to give more explanation and analysis.

3. Network Model and Throughput Formulation

3.1. Network Model. Since distributed network will influence its performance [6], in this subsection, we obtain and give explanation on the correlation between SNR of connection through propagation model and the expected number of hops as well as the average number of connections. Through this model, we can analyze the correlation between node density, node distribution, and the SNR connection. The performance of the network will be influenced by SNR connection, as described later in Section 3.2. For network model, we use an N-node network uniformly distributed over an area of a square with length of $2d$. Based on [26, 27], we can calculate the expected number of hops and the average number of connections as follows. If the node density is $\delta = N/(2d)^2$ and the node transmission range is τ, then the number of average neighbors is $g = (N/(2d)^2)\pi\tau^2 - 1$. The average distance between a node pair is given by $(d/3)(\sqrt{2} + \ln(1 + \sqrt{2}))$ and the average number of hops is $E_{hc} = (d/3\tau)(\sqrt{2} + \ln(1 + \sqrt{2}))$.

We can calculate the total number of network links as $gN/2$. If we assume the number of connections is Q, then we approximate the average number of connections by $N_{cl} = 2Qk/(g + 1)N$. For two-ray ground propagation model [28, 29], with the transmit power (P_t), the system loss (L), the separation distance between transmitter and receiver (d_s), the gain transmit (G_t), and the gain receiver (G_r), thus we can calculate the power received in the receiver node given by $P_r(d) = P_t G_t G_r h_t^2 h_r^2/(d_s)^4 L$, with the height transmitter node (h_t) and the height receiver (h_r). If the SNR node is γ, with $G_t = G_r = L = 1$, and $h_r = h_t = 1.5$ meters from the ground, then we can calculate the expected number of hops per connection, E_{hc}, and also the average number of connections over a given link, N_{cl}, by

$$E_{hc}(\gamma) = \frac{2d\left(\sqrt{2} + \ln\left(1 + \sqrt{2}\right)\right)\sqrt[4]{\gamma}}{9\sqrt[4]{P_t}},$$

$$N_{cl}(\gamma) = \frac{4Qd\left(\sqrt{2} + \ln\left(1 + \sqrt{2}\right)\right)\sqrt[4]{\gamma}}{9N(g + 1)\left(\sqrt[4]{P_t}\right)}. \tag{1}$$

The SNR value of each connection will affect the expected number of hops per connection. The higher the SNR value, the better the ability of the network to have number of hops per connection. Figure 1 shows the SNR impact to expected number of hops per connection, with the difference of side length (d), which are 250 m, 500 m, and 1000 m. We observed that increasing the side length of the network area also increased the expected number of hops per connection, especially in high SNR. The path connection consisting of links with high SNR has improved the ability of the network in obtaining better average number of connections, as shown in Figure 2 for fixed side length area. The links with high SNR provide a network to have better capability to create a path to deliver the data.

We observed that, with high SNR in the connection, the network could offer a big capability in terms of the average number of connections and the expected number

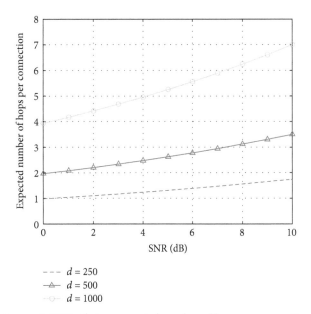

FIGURE 1: SNR effect on expected number of hops per connection with a different area length.

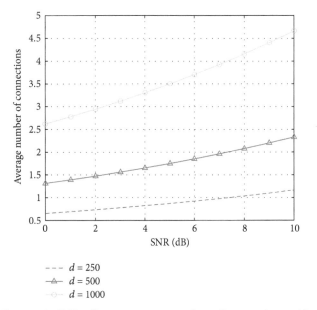

FIGURE 2: SNR effect on average number of connections with different area length.

of hops per connection, especially over wider area (d). This capability can improve network performance. AODV SNR-SR that considers SNR connection in the network will have opportunity to gain better average number of connections and the expected number of hops per connection to improve network performance.

3.2. Throughput Formulation. Throughput can be obtained by calculating the average number of successful data transmitted during the observation interval. Denote B as the throughput, the average number of packets that successfully transmitted is $E[A]$, and the average duration of time required to transmit the data is $E[T]$; then

$$B = \frac{E[A]}{E[T]}. \qquad (2)$$

If R is average rate for delivery of the data and $\overline{K}$ is average of the data transferred, then the total average time to send $\overline{K}$ is $\overline{K}/R$ seconds. If t_p represents the average propagation time and t_a is the average time of the process at all nodes, then we can calculate $E[T]$ as

$$E[T] = \frac{\overline{K}}{R} + 2\left(t_a + t_p\right). \qquad (3)$$

The quality of channel link and the mobility of node will have immediate effect on the probability of bit error. Let P_r be the average probability of bits successfully delivered in the transmitted data. This probability of success is influenced by the probability of error in a connection and the number of hops. So we can rewrite $E[A]$ by

$$E[A] = \overline{K}P_r, \qquad (4)$$

while the throughput as function of P_r and R can be written as

$$B = \frac{\overline{K}P_r}{\overline{K} + 2R\left(t_a + t_p\right)} R. \qquad (5)$$

If p is the probability of error and p_i is the probability of error on connection i, then the probability of success transmitting data on a connection i is $(1 - p_i)$. The total probability of success in sending the data for a path delivery that consists of N links connection can be written as follows:

$$P_r = \prod_{i=1}^{N}\left(1 - p_i\right). \qquad (6)$$

To analyze the correlation between the quality of the channel SNR with the throughput performance, we use the probability of error as bit error rate (BER) function [30], which is given by

$$p = 1 - \left(1 - \beta\right)^n, \qquad (7)$$

where β is the bit error rate and n is the number of bits. We can calculate BER based on SNR and modulation technique. If Binary Phase Shift Keying (BPSK) modulation is used, the corresponding BER [31] is

$$\mathrm{BER} = Q\left(\sqrt{2\frac{E_b}{N_o}}\right), \qquad (8)$$

where $Q(\cdot)$ denotes the Q-function and E_b/N_o denotes the energy per bit to the noise power ratio. If the signal bandwidth is approximately equal to the bandwidth of the noise or similarly equal to the receiver using a matched filter to get the maximum value of SNR, we can estimate $E_b/(N_o/2) \approx S/N$.

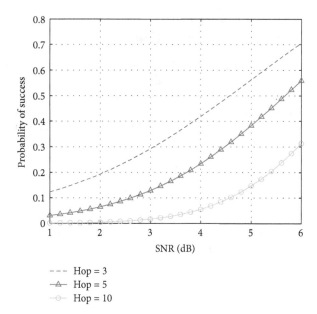

FIGURE 3: Probability of success with increasing SNR and different number of hops.

So, we can write the probability of error as a function of SNR as follows:

$$p = 1 - \left(1 - Q\left(\sqrt{\frac{S}{N}}\right)\right)^n. \qquad (9)$$

If we denote $\gamma = S/N$, then the throughput a function of γ can be rewritten as

$$B(\gamma) = \frac{\overline{K}\prod_{i=1}^{N}\left(1 - Q\left(\sqrt{\gamma}\right)_i\right)^n}{\overline{K} + 2R\left(t_a + t_p\right)} R. \qquad (10)$$

Equation (10) shows the throughput as a function of the probability of bit error as influenced by the SNR of the link connection. The probability of success to deliver the data will increase with higher SNR, as shown in Figure 3 with different number of hops scenario. To improve the throughput, the routing protocol should choose the link that has good SNR with a minimum probability of error. The simulation in Figure 4 shows that the throughput can gain higher performance by increasing SNR of the link connection with different transmission rate scenario. We observed that the probability of success and the throughput performance showed a significant improvement when the SNR connection increased.

Based on this fact and the mathematical model, we propose a selective algorithm with SNR as the parameter to choose the link as the path. To obtain a path that has a good SNR, the routing protocol must be well informed from the physical layer. For that purpose, we used cross-layer scheme as the method for routing protocol to get SNR information from the physical layer. We used SNR threshold (γ_{tr}) for the algorithm. A link can be selected by the routing protocol as a transmission line if $\gamma \geq \gamma_{tr}$. With this algorithm, the routing protocol AODV SNR-SR will select link as the path, based on

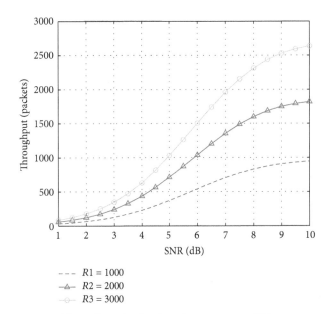

FIGURE 4: Throughput (packets) performance over different transmission rate (packets) with increasing SNR of link connection.

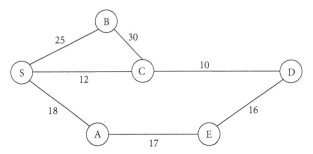

FIGURE 5: Illustration of network path.

SNR values that meet the criteria. This routing algorithm can improve the network resilience against path break and low throughput by helping the network to find a reliable path base on SNR. The details of this method will be explained further in Section 4.

4. SNR-Based Selective Reverse Route with Cross-Layer Scheme

Generally, routing protocols select the path by minimizing the number of hops. However small number of hops usually corresponds to the selection of links with long transmission range and less capacity than the best paths that exist in the network. This long transmission range corresponds to low value of SNR. In ad hoc network, this poor SNR selection of link often produces the link-break, thus degrading overall network performance.

In previous researches, to get SNR information, the algorithm uses route discovery process, by adding the information in RREQ and RREP mechanism. Since RREQ mechanism broadcasts to all the neighbors and RREP unicasts, these methods increase the routing overhead and the complexity. Moreover, the algorithm used the minimum summation of the inverse SNR or the average of SNR value of the path. We call it AODV SNR.

This implementation could be inappropriate and cause the selected path to perform not as expected. It has weakness as one or more links can have a very low SNR even though the average is high. In this study, we use reactive routing protocol AODV [32] as the rule model, which is widely used. To show the importance of this issue, we illustrate this problem as shown in Figure 5.

The solid line represents the connection between nodes. The link channel quality is represented by SNR value, next

to the node, with node S as the source and node D as the destination. For example, link S-A has SNR = 18 dB and link E-D has SNR = 16 dB. These values are estimated at receiver nodes A and D, respectively. In this case, to make a connection, a minimum SNR of 10 dB is required to get the maximum transmission range.

The routing protocol with hop count metric will choose the smallest number of hops as the path to deliver the data, which is S-C-D, with 2 hops. We can see that these hops consist of link that has low SNR to get the smallest hop. From (10), the throughput performance will decrease in connection with low SNR. Moreover, the mobility will cause this connection with low SNR to become vulnerable to the link-break, particularly if the nodes move to directions that decrease the SNR among them.

In AODV SNR, the routing protocol chooses the path that has the largest sum or largest average of the SNR. In this case, the AODV SNR will choose the path S-B-C-D, with the total of SNR being 65 dB or in the average 21.7 dB. When we use minimum summation of inverse SNR, the routes' metric for routes (1) (S-B-C-D), (2) (S-C-D), (3) (S-A-E-D) is equal to 0.1733, 0.1833, and 0.1768, respectively. Therefore, the routing with minimum of inverse SNR metric will select route 1 as the best route, same with the average SNR metric. Unfortunately, although it has an average of the largest SNR or the minimum summation of inverse SNR, the path may include link with low SNR, which is link C-D. The path with long trajectory with larger hops may have more links with very low SNR. In this situation, the link with low SNR will cause degradation of the throughput. Similar situation also occurs in hop count method, especially in mobility circumstances.

In this study, to solve the problem, we propose a new method, which is selective route based on SNR. We enhanced the reactive routing protocol AODV, and we call it as AODV SNR-SR. Link selection is done in the reverse route process, which will be used by the RREP. Figure 6 shows the proposed cross-layer design in AODV SNR-SR.

When the source needs to transmit the data, RREQ is generated. Reverse route is created when an intermediate node receives a RREQ. This reverse route is stored in the node for RREP path. After RREQ arrived at the destination, the RREP will be generated by the destination. Using reverse route, a destination node can send RREP to the source. Reverse route entry consists of source IP address, source sequence number, number of hops to the source node, and

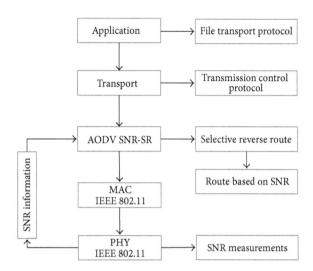

FIGURE 6: Cross-layer scheme AODV SNR-SR.

the IP address of the node from which RREQ is received. With this mechanism, when there is change on one of the links in reverse route, that is, path break, the RREP cannot be sent through this path and therefore uses another path. In cases where there is no available reverse route, then the source will generate new RREQ, after the time out. In AODV mechanism, source begins transmitting data when it receives the RREP, which has arrived first. The source will send the data to the destination using this reverse route.

With those mechanisms, it is important to select the appropriate reverse route based on SNR to get the best route. In AODV SNR-SR, selective route is conducted in the reverse route process. To avoid undesired small SNR selection in route path, we use minimum SNR threshold, which is γ_{tr}. We define SNR threshold as the minimum requirement of the SNR received by a node, so that a given connection or path can be selected as a route by the routing algorithm. This SNR threshold needs to be set in all nodes. When a node receives a RREQ, it calculates the SNR (γ) and compares it with SNR threshold; if the results meet the criteria $\gamma \geq \gamma_{tr}$, the reverse route will be made and saved as route cache. When there is no available reverse routes that meet the criteria, the source will enter new discovery process.

If SNR (γ) criteria are not met, the reverse route is not created by the node, so the RREP cannot use this link. This filter makes RREP only use the reverse routes that meet the criteria; therefore, the sender only receives RREP with the route that has good SNR. In this case of AODV SNR-SR, the scheme will choose path S-A-E-D, where γ_{tr} = 15 dB. SNR is a measure for determining the quality of a signal as it is disturbed by noise. The calculation can be done by determining the value obtained from the power of information signal and noise signal. The connection between nodes will have SNR value that depends on the mobility of both nodes. In this model, the SNR values are calculated with SNR = $10 \log(P_{rss}/N_0)$, where P_{rss} is the received signal strength and it is assumed that the noise value is constant and same on all nodes. We used noise floor (N_o) $2.512e - 13$ corresponding to thermal noise of the system [33]. In

this study, we use two-ray ground propagation model to calculate the power at receiver, as described in network model section. The two-ray ground reflection model considers both the direct path and ground reflection path as multipath component. In our model, we assume that link qualities in both directions are identical. The reason is that, in ad hoc network, distribution of nodes within service area would have a direct path as well as a reflected path from the ground when the distance between nodes is short. In this propagation model, the forward and the reverse links would have the same characteristics in terms of path loss. In our model, nodes would have the same antenna height, located closely one to another, so we use two-ray ground propagation model.

The motivation of using SNR selection in reverse path mechanism is to avoid overhead, whereas other modifications on AODV generally use RREQ and RREP to gather SNR information, that would increase the size and complexity of the routing packet control. SNR threshold is used to avoid selection of one or more link with very low SNR as a part of the route. The mechanism of the route discovery process and implementation of selective reverse route algorithm in AODV SNR-SR can be seen in Figure 7. Route recovery mechanism works when there is a link-break at the transmission path, with Route Error (RERR) notification to the sender as depicted in Figure 8. When the intermediate node fails to deliver the data to the next hop due to path break and there is no other available paths, this node will generate RERR and send it to the source through the reverse path. After receiving this RERR, the source will create a new route discovery process to find a new path to transmit the data.

5. AODV SNR-SR Performance and Discussion

We evaluated the performance of AODV, AODV SNR, and AODV SNR-SR with Network Simulator (NS). The NS version for this particular simulation is version 2.35 [34]. In networks simulator, we enhanced the wireless-phy.cc to get power reception based on propagation model and then computed the SNR value. This SNR information is used by AODV SNR-SR to select appropriate route. We set the SNR threshold in route process by enhancing the aodv.cc. We varied the number of nodes and velocity in simulation scenario. We evaluated throughput, end-to-end delay, and routing overhead performance. The mobility model was random waypoint with simulation area of 1,000 m × 1,000 m. The data packet was 512 bytes, with channel bandwidth 2 Mb/s, noise floor (N_o) $2.512e - 13$, and simulation time 300 seconds. Maximum node speeds were 5 m/s, 10 m/s, 15 m/s, and 20 m/s and numbers of nodes were 20, 70, 120, and 170, respectively. Table 1 shows the simulation parameters. For single connection between two nodes, the correlation between the received SNR and the distance in two-ray ground propagation model is shown in Figure 9. The deployment of D2D in ad hoc network can use Wireless Fidelity (WIFI) with range up to more 100 m or WIFI direct as new technology with the range up to 200 m [35, 36]. Based on these facts, we found the distance that satisfies the D2D with WIFI direct technology and is adequate to set as the SNR threshold. We used SNR threshold 35 dB in the simulation,

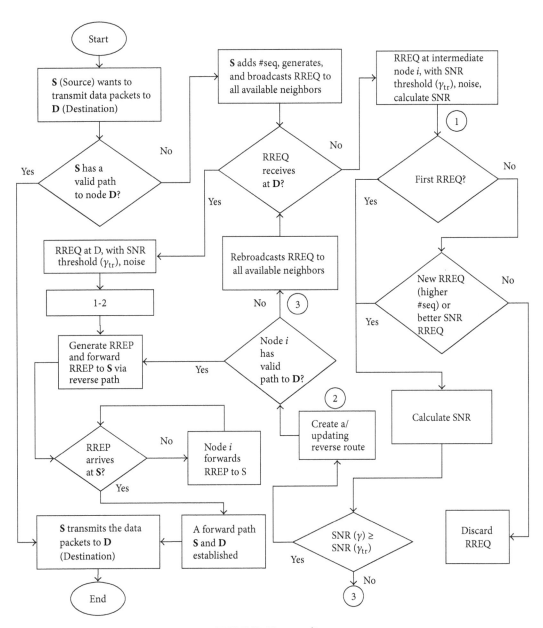

FIGURE 7: AODV SNR-SR route discovery process.

TABLE 1: Simulation parameters.

Mobility model	Random waypoint
Propagation model	Two-ray ground
Simulation duration	300 seconds
Number of nodes	20, 70, 120, 170 nodes
Simulation area	1000 m × 1000 m
Max node speed	5 m/s, 10 m/s, 15 m/s, 20 m/s
Antenna	Omni antenna
Modulation	BPSK

within the distance range of 150 m. This proposed method expected to support D2D communication in the environment that considers a ground-reflected propagation path between transmitter and receiver, in addition to the direct LOS (Line of Sight) path.

In Figure 10, we display the advantage of the proposed method compared to AODV and AODV SNR. In small number of nodes, the proposed method has a small advantage average throughput. However, the proposed method showed significant improvement of average throughput when the number of nodes increased. For example, in 170 nodes, the advantage of proposed method in average throughput was about 36% and 80% higher as compared to AODV SNR and AODV schemes. AODV SNR-SR also gained advantage when the number of nodes increased; the average end-to-end delays were about 30% and 20% smaller as compared to AODV and AODV SNR, respectively, as presented in Figure 11.

We analyzed the reasoning of results that appeared in Figures 10 and 11 as follows. The increasing number of nodes will correspondingly increase both the density of nodes and the average number of neighbors. If the area of side length is

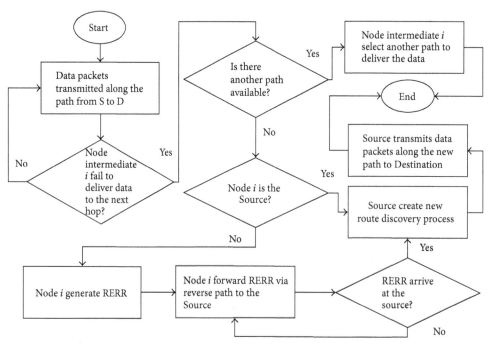

FIGURE 8: AODV SNR-SR route recovery.

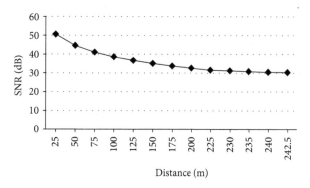

FIGURE 9: Received SNR in single connection with two-ray ground propagation model.

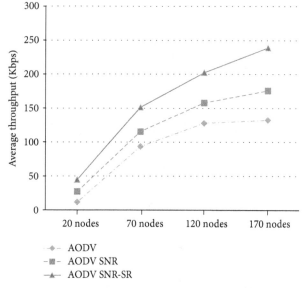

FIGURE 10: Average throughput comparison between AODV, AODV SNR, and AODV SNR-SR with increasing number of nodes.

fixed, then such increasing number of nodes will also increase the total number of network links that can be created, as described in network models in Section 3.1. This situation makes the routing protocol easier to find possible routes, especially connection with high SNR. When the path consists of connections with high SNR, the throughput performance will increase as described in (10). The path with good quality connections will reduce the path breaks and allow more stability in sending the data, therefore decreasing the average end-to-end delay.

Simulation results for routing overhead per received data packet are shown in Figure 12, where AODV SNR-SR outperformed AODV SNR and AODV, with smallest routing overhead. We observed that, in small number of nodes, routing protocol produced small overhead; however, with the increasing numbers of nodes, the overhead rapidly became larger. The proposed method showed a big advantage which

was about 59% and 36% smaller overheads as compared to AODV and AODV SNR.

We also compared AODV SNR-SR, AODV SNR, and AODV with respect to node velocity. The AODV SNR-SR outperformed the AODV SNR and AODV in terms of smaller overhead per received data packet in node velocity scenario as shown in Figure 13. We observed that the proposed scheme was about 44% and 59% more efficient in routing overheads compared to AODV SNR and AODV, respectively. These results show good agreement with (14), where routing

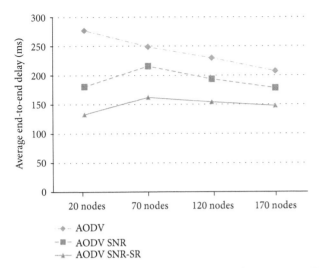

FIGURE 11: Average end-to-end delay comparison between AODV SNR-SR, AODV SNR, and AODV with increasing number of nodes.

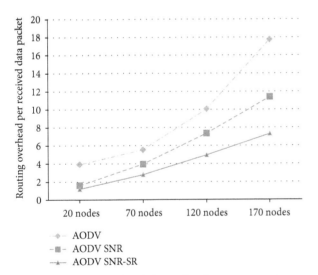

FIGURE 12: Routing overhead (normalized) comparison between AODV, AODV SNR, and AODV SNR-SR with increasing number of nodes.

overhead will have immediate effect on the network efficiency based on SNR. The analysis and the reasoning of the results in Figures 12 and 13 can be described as follows. Normalized routing overhead is calculated as the ratio of the total routing control packets to deliver data packets. Routing control packets included RREQ, RREP, and a RERR. This RERR is triggered by link-break to give notification to the sender. If the sender does not have alternative route, it will broadcast RREQ again and enter the route discovery process.

The routing overhead corresponding to network performance can be analyzed as follows. We can evaluate the efficiency of the network (η) for a single link by calculating the average total number of bits being transferred during time T, which is α. The total bits to process forward route RREQ are β_{RREQ}.

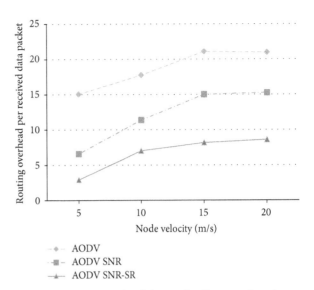

FIGURE 13: Routing overhead (normalized) comparison between AODV, AODV SNR, and AODV SNR-SR with increasing node velocity.

Denote φ_{RREP} to be the total number of bits as the acknowledgment route process RREP and ε_{RERR} to be the total bits notification of route failure, RERR. If the effective rate transmission is R_{eff} and transmission rate is R, then we can express the efficiency as $\eta = R_{eff}/R$. If the probability of error p for x transmission can be expressed as

$$p(x) = p^{x-1}(1-p),\qquad(11)$$

then the mean of this probability of error ψ can be expressed as

$$\psi = \sum_{X=1}^{\infty} xp^{x-1}(1-p) = \frac{1}{1-p}.\qquad(12)$$

If we use a model approach in selective ARQ [30], then we can find the efficiency of the network-based routing overhead which is related to probability of error by

$$\eta = \frac{\alpha - \beta_{RREQ}}{(1/(1-p))(\alpha + \varphi_{RREP} + \varepsilon_{RERR})},\qquad(13)$$

and as an SNR function we derive efficiency as

$$\eta(\gamma) = \frac{(\alpha - \beta_{RREQ})(1 - Q(\sqrt{\gamma})_i)^n}{(\alpha + \varphi_{RREP} + \varepsilon_{RERR})}.\qquad(14)$$

We can conclude from (13) that the increasing routing overhead will reduce network efficiency and throughput. From (14), the route with link that has better SNR is also more efficient. SNR on link connection will have an impact on the probability of error and link failure. This will influence the amount of RERR and the path break will trigger RERR. Accordingly, if the source does not have any routes, it will start route discovery process and generate RREQ. This mechanism will increase the routing overhead.

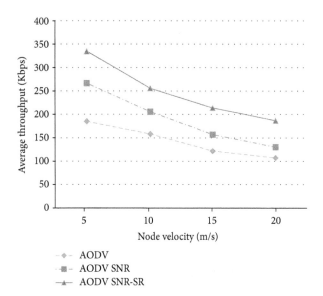

FIGURE 14: Average throughput comparison between AODV, AODV SNR, and AODV SNR-SR with increasing node velocity.

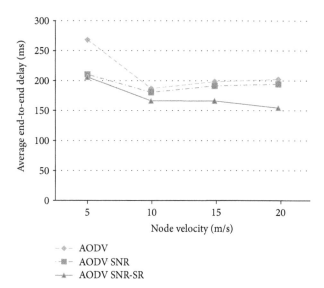

FIGURE 15: Average end-to-end delay comparison between AODV SNR-SR, AODV SNR, and AODV with increasing node velocity.

Simulation results for the throughput are shown in Figure 14 with increasing node velocity. The throughput decreased along the increase of node velocity, with AODV SNR-SR outperforming AODV SNR and AODV. We observed that the proposed method yielded significant improvement of throughput when the velocity increased, in average about 45% and 78% higher compared to AODV SNR and AODV.

The simulation results for the end-to-end delay with respect to node velocity are shown in Figure 15. The proposed AODV SNR-SR again outperformed AODV SNR and AODV. We observed that, in slow velocity, the end-to-end delay performance varied less between AODV SNR and AODV SNR-SR. However, in high velocity, the AODV SNR-SR got advantages with smaller end-to-end delay about 31% and 26% compared to AODV and AODV SNR.

From the results in Figures 14 and 15, we analyzed the following. When the node velocity increases, the distribution of the network becomes more dynamic. This situation leads the SNR connection to be more unstable, and often path break occurs. Consequently, the throughput will decrease and end-to-end delay becomes higher. To analyze correlation between end-to-end delay and the SNR connection in Figures 11 and 15, we can use (3), (9), and (12). For single connection with the average probability of error ψ for x transmission, we calculate the end-to-end delay (D_{e2e}) for one-way delay by

$$D_{e2e} = \frac{\overline{K} + R\left(t_a + t_p\right)}{R\left(1 - Q\left(\sqrt{\gamma}\right)_i\right)^n}. \tag{15}$$

From (15), we can see that higher SNR connection will produce smaller end-to-end delay; this is the reason why network performance increases. AODV SNR-SR is capable of maintaining performance due to higher SNR connection in the route. We analyzed the correlation between the velocity of nodes and the network performance as follows. The

average duration of the path connection (ρ) depends on the transmission range (R), number of hops (s), and the velocity of the node (V). If we use mobility models which are exponentially distributed with parameter σ for the average duration of the path connection [37], then we can get

$$\rho = \frac{1}{\sigma} = \frac{1}{\sigma_0} \frac{R}{sV}, \tag{16}$$

and the probability density function is given by

$$f\left(x\right) = \frac{\sigma_0 sV}{R} e^{-(\sigma_0 sV/R)x}, \tag{17}$$

where σ_0 is the constant of proportionality and is independent from R, s, and V. From (16) and (17), we can see that velocity of node will decrease the average duration of connection path and induce the degradation of network performance. The higher average of connection path with better SNR connection is, the lower end-to-end delay and improved throughput will be produced. Transmission range will depend on both the distribution and the density of nodes as described in Section 3, that SNR of connection will have direct effect on the throughput performance. The reasoning of velocity effect on routing overhead with results shown in Figure 13 is described as follows. From (16), we also can approximate the routing overhead that is influenced by the velocity of the node, which is T_s/ρ, where T_s is time simulation. When the velocity increases, it will result in lower average duration of the path connection and higher routing overhead.

In this proposed mechanism, the performance will depend on the network model as mentioned in Section 3.1 and the SNR threshold. The density and distribution of the network will have an impact on the SNR connection. Since the distribution and the mobility of the node in network are difficult to predict, there is situation where SNR connection cannot meet the SNR threshold. This situation makes the

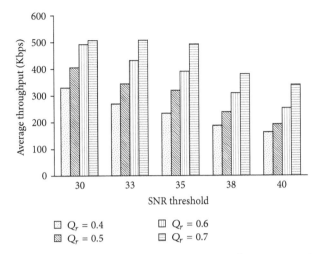

FIGURE 16: Average throughput as minimum and maximum SNR ratio (Q_r) with different SNR threshold.

routing protocols unable to find the suitable routes that agree with channel quality requirement. Another situation is the node fail to deliver the data to the next hop due to the path break or there are no available paths. When this situation happens, a new route discovery process must be undertaken.

We analyzed the impact of the SNR threshold and the distribution of SNR connection to the network performance as follows. Figure 16 shows the correlation between SNR threshold, the Q_r factor, and the average throughput performance. The Q_r factor is defined as the ratio of minimum SNR compared to maximum SNR on the distribution of the SNR connections, which is $Q_r = \mathrm{SNR_{min}/SNR_{max}}$. We set maximum SNR connection to 50 dB and minimum SNR connection to 20 dB, 25 dB, 30 dB, and 35 dB. For the distribution of SNR connection between 20 dB ($\mathrm{SNR_{min}}$) and 50 dB ($\mathrm{SNR_{max}}$), we get $Q_r = 0.4$. We generated 100 random SNR connections using five different SNR thresholds, which were 30 dB, 33 dB, 35 dB, 38 dB, and 40 dB. In this scenario, the SNR connection that complies with the SNR threshold was assigned as route and the throughput of this connection are calculated. We observed that higher Q_r factor improved the throughput of the network. When $\mathrm{SNR_{min}}$ has wider gap to the SNR threshold, it will reduce the performance. On the other hand, it will increase the performance when $\mathrm{SNR_{min}}$ is close to the SNR threshold. When the SNR threshold is close to $\mathrm{SNR_{max}}$, the increasing Q_r factor will not greatly influence the throughput performance, also causing the routing protocol hard to find suitable path that meets the requirement. Although lower SNR thresholds seem to gain higher throughput, they can produce connection with lower SNR and cause degradation of network performance, especially in lower Q_r factor. For example, SNR threshold 30 dB with $Q_r = 0.4$ will produce throughput smaller than the SNR threshold 33 dB with $Q_r = 0.5$.

In summary, AODV SNR-SR outperforms AODV SNR and the conventional AODV, because it gains more throughputs with better algorithm mechanism as described in Sections 3 and 4, respectively. The proposed scheme can also improve the route discovery efficiency and make routing

protocol more adaptive with channel-aware for D2D requirement as mentioned in [6, 8–10], where the conventional schemes cannot solve.

6. Conclusion and Future Research Opportunities

In this study, we developed throughput formulation and network model. We proposed new algorithm in routing protocol to increase the network performance. We proposed this algorithm by enhancing the AODV routing protocols with a cross-layer scheme based on SNR, termed as AODV SNR-SR. This proposed scheme employed selective route based on the SNR threshold in the reverse route process. These mechanisms avoid high routing overheads and low SNR selections in the route path. With these techniques, AODV SNR-SR outperforms AODV SNR and AODV in terms of throughput, end-to-end delay, and routing overhead. The AODV SNR-SR shows a significant advantage in throughput, end-to-end delay, and routing overhead when the number and the velocity of nodes increase. This algorithm can improve network resilience against path break and high throughput performance to support D2D development. For future work, SNR threshold mechanism has to be considered along with the application and the type of the data, especially for adaptive data rate.

Acknowledgments

This work is supported by Ministry of Research Technology and Higher Education of the Republic of Indonesia, Telkom University, and Yayasan Pendidikan Telkom.

References

[1] M. Riaz, N. M. Khan, and S. J. Nawaz, "A generalized 3-d scattering channel model for spatiotemporal statistics in mobile-to-mobile communication environment," *IEEE Transactions on Vehicular Technology*, vol. 64, no. 10, pp. 4399–4410, 2015.

[2] A. Attwood, M. Merabti, and O. Abuelmaatti, "IoMANETs: mobility architecture for wireless M2M networks," in *Proceedings of the IEEE GLOBECOM Workshops, GC (Wkshps '11)*, pp. 399–404, Houston, TX, USA, December 2011.

[3] S. Mumtaz, K. M. Saidul Huq, and J. Rodriguez, "Direct mobile-to-mobile communication: paradigm for 5G," *IEEE Wireless Communications*, vol. 21, no. 5, pp. 14–23, 2014.

[4] S. Riaz, H. K. Qureshi, and M. Saleem, "Performance evaluation of routing protocols in energy harvesting D2D network," in *Proceedings of the 1st International Conference on Computing, Electronic and Electrical Engineering, (ICE Cube '16)*, pp. 251–255, Quetta, Pakistan, April 2016.

[5] B. Kaufman, J. Lilleberg, and B. Aazhang, "Spectrum sharing scheme between cellular users and ad-hoc device-to-device users," *IEEE Transactions on Wireless Communications*, vol. 12, no. 3, pp. 1038–1049, 2013.

[6] Y. Wu, S. Wang, W. Liu, W. Guo, and X. Chu, "Iunius: a cross-layer peer-to-peer system with device-to-device communications," *IEEE Transactions on Wireless Communications*, vol. 15, no. 10, pp. 7005–7017, 2016.

[7] R. Edirisinghe and A. Zaslavsky, "Cross-layer contextual interactions in wireless networks," *IEEE Communications Surveys & Tutorials*, vol. 16, no. 2, pp. 1114–1134, 2014.

[8] O. Bello and S. Zeadally, "Intelligent device-to-device communication in the internet of things," *IEEE Systems Journal*, vol. 10, no. 3, pp. 1172–1182, 2016.

[9] A. L. Beylot, R. Dhaou, V. Gauthier, and M. Becker, "Cross-layer simulation and optimization for mobile ad-hoc networks," in *Mobile and Wireless Communication Networks*, E. M. Belding-Royer, K. Al Agha, and G. Pujolle, Eds., vol. 162 of *IFIP International Federation for Information Processing*, pp. 13–22, Springer, Boston, Mass, USA, 2005.

[10] J. Zuo, C. Dong, S. X. Ng, L. L. Yang, and L. Hanzo, "Cross-layer aided energy-efficient routing design for ad hoc networks," *IEEE Communications Surveys & Tutorials*, vol. 17, no. 3, pp. 1214–1238, 2015.

[11] A. Zhou, M. Liu, Z. Li, and E. Dutkiewicz, "Joint traffic splitting, rate control, routing, and scheduling algorithm for maximizing network utility in wireless mesh networks," *IEEE Transactions on Vehicular Technology*, vol. 65, no. 4, pp. 2688–2702, 2016.

[12] K. Kunavut, "Link quality aware routing based on effective estimated throughput for mobile ad hoc networks," in *Proceedings of the 21st International Symposium on Intelligent Signal Processing and Communication Systems, (ISPACS '13)*, pp. 487–492, Naha, Japan, November 2013.

[13] D. De Couto, D. Aguayo, J. Bicket, and R. Morris, "A high-throughput path metric for multi-hop wireless routing," in *Proceedings of the 9th Annual International Conference on Mobile Computing and Networking (MobiCom '03)*, pp. 134–146, San Diego, Calif, USA, September 2003.

[14] B. Sen, J. Guo, X. Zhao, and S. Jha, "ECTX: a high-throughput path metric for multi-hop wireless routing exploiting MAC-layer cooperative retransmission," in *Proceedings of the 13th IEEE International Symposium on a World of Wireless, Mobile and Multimedia Networks, (WoWMoM '12)*, pp. 1–9, San Francisco, CA, USA, June 2012.

[15] R. Draves, J. Padhye, and B. Zill, "Routing in multi-radio, multi-hop wireless mesh networks," in *Proceedings of the 10th Annual International Conference on Mobile Computing and Networking (MobiCom '04)*, pp. 114–128, September 2004.

[16] B. Awerbuch, D. Holmer, and H. Rubens, "The medium time metric: high throughput route selection in multi-rate ad hoc wireless networks," *Mobile Networks and Applications*, vol. 11, no. 2, pp. 253–266, 2006.

[17] R. Agüero, J. A. Galache, and L. Muñoz, "Using SNR to improve multi-hop routing," in *Proceedings of the IEEE 69th Vehicular Technology Conference (VTC Spring '09)*, pp. 1–5, Barcelona, Spain, April 2009.

[18] F. Alnajjar, "SNR/RP aware routing model for MANETs," *Cyber Journals: Multidisciplinary Journals in Science and Technology, Journal of Selected Areas in Telecommunications*, pp. 40–48, 2011.

[19] M. K. Islam and R. K. Liu, "Cross-layer optimization of AODV routing protocol for mobile ad-hoc network (MANET)," in *Proceedings of the 2nd International Conference on Computer Science and Electronics Engineering (ICCSEE '13)*, pp. 1834–1837, 2013.

[20] B. Amiri, H. R. Sadjadpour, and J. Garcia-Luna-Aceves, "Outage optimum routing for wireless networks," in *Proceedings of the 7th International Wireless Communications and Mobile Computing Conference, (IWCMC '11)*, pp. 1–6, Istanbul, Turkey, July 2011.

[21] M. Elshaikh, M. F. M. Fadzil, N. Kamel, and C. M. N. C. Isa, "Weighted signal-to-noise ratio average routing metric for dynamic sequence distance vector routing protocol in mobile ad-hoc networks," in *Proceedings of the IEEE 8th International Colloquium on Signal Processing and Its Applications, (CSPA '12)*, pp. 329–334, Melaka, Malaysia, March 2012.

[22] S. Ganesh and R. Amutha, "Efficient and secure routing protocol for wireless sensor networks through SNR based dynamic clustering mechanisms," *Journal of Communications and Networks*, vol. 15, no. 4, pp. 422–429, 2013.

[23] A. M. Akhtar, A. Behnad, and X. Wang, "Cooperative ARQ-based energy-efficient routing in multihop wireless networks," *IEEE Transactions on Vehicular Technology*, vol. 64, no. 11, pp. 5187–5197, 2015.

[24] Y. B. Nechaev and A. V. Stromov, "Interference aware routing in massively dense wireless networks based on streamlines of potential field," in *Proceedings of the 39th International Conference on Telecommunications and Signal Processing (TSP '16)*, pp. 79–82, Vienna, Austria, 2016.

[25] A. Ben Ammar, A. Dziri, M. Terre, and H. Youssef, "Multi-hop LEACH based cross-layer design for large scale wireless sensor networks," in *Proceedings of the International Wireless Communications and Mobile Computing Conference (IWCMC '16)*, pp. 763–768, Paphos, Cyprus, 2016.

[26] X. Chen, H. M. Jones, and D. Jayalath, "Channel-aware routing in MANETs with route handoff," *IEEE Transactions on Mobile Computing*, vol. 10, no. 1, pp. 108–121, 2011.

[27] S. Panichpapiboon, G. Ferrari, and O. K. Tonguz, "Optimal transmit power in wireless sensor networks," *IEEE Transactions on Mobile Computing*, vol. 5, no. 10, pp. 1432–1447, 2006.

[28] A. Goldsmith, *Wireless Communications*, Cambridge University Press, 2005.

[29] T. Rappaport, *Wireless Communications: Principles and Practice*, Prentice Hall, 2001.

[30] J. D. Spragins, J. L. Hammaond, and K. Pawlikowski, *Telecommunications: Protocols and Design*, Addison-Wesley Publishing, 1991.

[31] M. Khosroshahy, *Study and Implementation of IEEE 802.11 Physical Channel Model in YANS (NS3 prototype) Network Simulator*, INRIA-Sophia Antipolis-Planète Group, 2006.

[32] C. E. Perkins and E. M. Royer, "Ad-hoc on-demand distance vector routing," in *Proceedings of the 2nd IEEE Workshop on Mobile Computing Systems and Applications (WMCSA '99)*, pp. 90–100, New Orleans, La, USA, February 1999.

[33] J. Kim and J.-M. Ahn, "Aggressive spatial reuse scheme for the 802.11 wireless LAN," *The Journal of Korean Institute of Communications and Information Sciences*, vol. 41, no. 2, pp. 222–228, 2016.

[34] Network Simulator, NS 2.35, http://www.isi.edu/nsnam/ns/ns-build.html.

[35] A. Pyattaev, K. Johnsson, S. Andreev, and Y. Koucheryavy, "3GPP LTE traffic offloading onto WiFi Direct," in *Proceedings of the IEEE Wireless Communications and Networking Conference Workshops (WCNCW '13)*, pp. 135–140, Shanghai, China, April 2013.

Enabling LTE and WiFi Coexisting in 5 GHz for Efficient Spectrum Utilization

Hongyu Sun,[1,2] **Zhiyi Fang,**[1] **Qun Liu,**[3] **Zheng Lu,**[1,2] **and Ting Zhu**[2]

[1]*College of Computer Science and Technology, Jilin University, Changchun, China*
[2]*Computer Science and Electrical Engineering, University of Maryland, Baltimore, MD, USA*
[3]*Network Center, Jilin University, Changchun, China*

Correspondence should be addressed to Qun Liu; liuqun@jlu.edu.cn and Ting Zhu; zt@umbc.edu

Academic Editor: Kyandoghere Kyamakya

Due to the increasing mobile traffic demands in cellular network, researchers have proposed the coexistence of LTE and WiFi technologies in 5 GHz unlicensed bands. Therefore, how to efficiently utilize the spectrum in 5 GHz becomes extremely important. To avoid the channel access conflicts, current LTE Unlicensed (LTE-U) technology introduces the duty cycle of LTE, while License-Assisted Access (LAA) technology introduces Listen-Before-Talk (LBT) mechanism. While these two technologies improve the spectrum utilization by using time division access schema, we believe that more efficient spectrum utilization can be achieved by enabling simultaneous transmissions from LTE and WiFi. In this paper, we propose a novel method (i.e., *Low Amplitude Stream Injection (LASI) method*) to enable the simultaneous transmissions of WiFi and LTE frames in the same channel and recover the data from the conflicts. To further utilize the *LASI* method, we introduce the *Conflict-Tolerant Channel Allocation (CTCA)* algorithm to optimize the channel allocation and achieve more efficient spectrum utilization in 5 GHz. Extensive simulation results show that our approach achieves lower latency and higher throughput. Compared with the state-of-the-art LTE-U and LAA technologies, our approach can improve the spectrum efficiency 2.9 times.

1. Introduction

As the number of mobile devices (e.g., smartphones and tablets) increases, mobile traffic demand is increasing significantly in recent years. According to the global traffic forecast by Cisco Visual Networking Index (VNI) [1], global mobile data traffic reached 3.7 exabytes per month by the end of 2015, up from 2.1 exabytes per month by the end of 2014. Furthermore, the mobile data traffic will continue to grow and reach 30.6 exabytes per month by 2020 at a compound annual growth rate (GAGR) of 53%. However, the spectrum utilized to offload these mobile traffic is scarce resource according to the regulations of ITU (International Telecommunication Union) [2]. Therefore, it is urgent for the research communities to look for new solutions to solve the increasing mobile traffic.

One of the most promising solutions for increasing capacities is utilizing *ISM* spectrum in 5 GHz. Currently, IEEE developed 802.11ac [3] and also extent 802.11n to 5 GHz

to offload the increasing mobile traffic, while there has been a recent push by many major companies, such as Qualcomm, Huawei, Nokia, Ericsson, T-Mobile, and NTT, to deploy LTE devices in 5 GHz [4–7] as the addition of the existing licensed spectrum. The first standard has been published by 3GPP in 2014 [8].

How to efficiently assign channels between LTE and WiFi devices comes to a key challenge to achieve the coexistence and collaborations between multiple WiFi access points and LTE eNodeBs. The existing channel management works such as [9–13] only focus on how to allocate channels in the homologous WiFi networks.

The most related works used to manage channels between LTE and WiFi are LTE Unlicensed (LTE-U) proposed by Qualcomm in [14] and License-Assisted Access (LAA) proposed by 3GPP in release 13 [8]. These two methods could achieve the coexistence of LTE and WiFi devices when they share the same spectrum. However, both LTE-U and LAA are time division multiple access methods by which LTE and

WiFi must use the spectrum alternatively in time domain. However, the time division only allows LTE and WiFi devices use the channel alternatively, which could not optimize the spectrum utilization and also introduce time delay. Therefore, we propose *Low Amplitude Stream Injection (LASI)* and *Conflict-Tolerant Channel Allocation (CTCA)* to enable the coexistence of LTE and WiFi with high performance and better channel utilization. Specifically, our contributions are as follows.

(i) Compared with state-of-the-art LTE-U/LAA or LTE-U/LAA based works, we propose enabling LTE and WiFi devices to allocate the channel simultaneously in time domain and apply *Low Amplitude Stream Injection (LASI)* method for resolving interference between them when they transit together. We also proved the correctness of *LASI* method in theoretical level. Theoretically, *LASI* could increase the channel utilization efficiency especially in dense deployed scenarios since it has great probability that LTE and WiFi devices allocate the same channel in these scenarios.

(ii) In order to further improve the channel utilization between LTE and WiFi devices in both low and high-density deployed scenarios, we further propose *Conflict-Tolerant Channel Allocation (CTCA)* to adaptively choose channel for optimizing both interference and network performances. *CTCA* defines a parameter to help APs decide which channel to allocate for transmission according to current topologies. Theoretically, *CTCA* could adaptively optimize interference and performance in both low and high-density deployed scenarios.

(iii) Extensive simulation results show that our approach achieves lower latency and higher throughput. Compared with state-of-the-art LTE-U and LAA technologies, our approach can improve the spectrum efficiency 2.9 times.

The rest of this paper is organized as follows: Section 2 discusses the related work. Section 3 introduces the background of LTE and WiFi coexistence researches. Section 4 presents the motivation behind the work. Section 5 defines the network model and assumptions. Section 6 introduces our main design, followed by the evaluation in Section 7. Section 8 concludes the paper.

2. Related Work

We classify related work into (i) spectrum sharing between homogeneous technologies, (ii) spectrum sharing between heterogeneous technologies, and (iii) the current spectrum sharing methods between LTE and WiFi in unlicensed 5 GHz bands.

(i) Spectrum Sharing between Homogeneous Technologies. The current spectrum sharing methods between the devices with the same technology (such as WiFi/ZigBee) are to isolate spectrum across different time, frequency, and space. Examples of coarse frequency-based isolation include [9,

10, 12, 15, 16]. Examples of fine-grained frequency-based fragmentation include [11, 13, 17–19]. Several approaches use time-domain isolation based on centralized scheduling or distributed carrier senses such as [20, 21]. LTE uses space division method to isolate the interference between different devices. The spectrum sharing between homogeneous technologies is easy to manage since they have the same PHY/MAC protocols. Compared with current homogeneous technologies spectrum sharing methods, our method focuses on cross technologies spectrum sharing for optimizing the spectrum utilization in 5 GHz unlicensed bands.

(ii) Spectrum Sharing between Heterogeneous Technologies. TIMO [22] is the pioneer work to manage the spectrum between cross technologies (WiFi and other technologies in 2.4 GHz); TIMO uses nulling to let the interferer decode its signal. ZIMO [23] decodes both WiFi and ZigBee signals. However, in [22, 23] the ZigBee and cordless phone occupy a much narrower channel and have lower power than WiFi signals; in this paper we propose solving the spectrum sharing problem between LTE and WiFi with the similar bandwidth and power.

(iii) Spectrum Sharing between LTE and WiFi in Unlicensed Bands. The current works related to the coexistence of WiFi and LTE are classified into three categories, LTE Unlicensed (LTE-U) based work, License-Assisted Access (LAA) based work, and simultaneously transmission work.

LTE-U was firstly proposed by Qualcomm and maintained by LTE forum [24]; the main principle of LTE-U is isolating the access of LTE and WiFi devices by the duty cycle of LTE. Reference [25] analyzed the performance of coexistence of LTE and WiFi by which WiFi allocated the channel when the duty cycle of LTE is in the "off" status; the results show that LTE-U based methods are unfair for WiFi devices. To improve LTE-U method, [26–30] make a more careful design of LTE-U to increase the throughput of WiFi devices. Reference [31] proposed a novel distributed algorithm for opportunistic sharing of unlicensed bands among LTE and WiFi devices (more details related to LTE-U are discussed in Section 3).

LAA was proposed and maintained by 3GPP as the first standard to achieve the coexistence of WiFi and LTE technologies; the main principle of LAA is introducing carrier sensing mechanism to LTE PHY layer [8]. Reference [32] analyzed the downlink performance of LAA with a simple Listen-Before-Talk mechanism and [33] tested the throughput of LAA based schema. The most original LAA methods are described in [6, 7, 34, 35]. Channel switch is considered in LAA to achieve a harmonious coexistence with WiFi in [36–38] which investigated the energy efficiency of LAA system. References [39, 40] designed and implemented LAA system in practical (more details related to LAA are discussed in Section 3).

However, LTE-U and LAA based schema are all time division spectrum sharing methods preventing the further improvement of the spectrum utilization.

To further optimize the spectrum utilization between LTE and WiFi devices, [41, 42] proposed enabling the

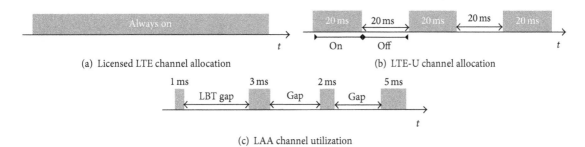

(a) Licensed LTE channel allocation

(b) LTE-U channel allocation

(c) LAA channel utilization

FIGURE 1: Current LTE and WiFi coexistence methods. (a) shows the channel utilization of LTE in licensed bands; LTE is a kind of scheduled networks in licensed bands; therefore, LTE always allocates the channel if there exists mobile traffic; (b) shows the channel utilization of LTE-U, which uses duty cycle to free channel to WiFi in fixed time domain; (c) shows the channel utilization of LAA, in which LTE shares the channel with WiFi by using Listen-Before-Talk (LBT) mechanism.

simultaneous transmission between LTE and WiFi coexisting networks. Reference [41] could enable the simultaneous transmission between LTE devices while our work aims to enable the simultaneous transmission between LTE and WiFi devices; the smartphone could receive he LTE and WiFi signals simultaneously by using the method proposed in [42]; however, it could receive the signals from only one LTE base station and WiFi access point from downlink. Our work aims to solve both the downlink and uplink problems with multiple LTE and WiFi devices.

3. Background

To achieve the coexistence of LTE and WiFi in 5 GHz with efficient spectrum utilization, LTE forum and 3GPP propose using LTE Unlicensed (LTE-U) and LTE License-Assisted Access (LAA) separately. Most of the work introduced in Section 2 is LTE-U or LAA based work. In this section, we will describe the principles of LTE-U and LAA briefly and explain how to further improve the spectrum utilization by our method.

The main differences among traditional Licensed LTE, LTE-U, and LAA are described in Figure 1. Their main principles and differences are detailed as follows.

(i) Licensed LTE channel allocation: traditional Licensed LTE occupies the channel all the time if there is mobile traffic to be delivered. There are no other cross technologies such as WiFi or ZigBee sharing the same channel with LTE in the traditional licensed bands of LTE; therefore, Keep LTE in the "on" status for data delivery. However, offloading the traffic to unlicensed bands is avoidable since the licensed bands are scarce resource which is hard for managing the increasing global traffic (detailed in Figure 1(a)).

(ii) LTE-U channel allocation: LTE Unlicensed was first proposed by Qualcomm and promoted by LTE-U forum. LTE-U introduces duty cycle to coordinate the channel utilization between LTE and WiFi devices. Figure 1(b) is a simple example showing how LTE shares the channel with WiFi devices when LTE duty cycle is 50%. In Figure 1(b), LTE allocates and frees the channel during every 20 ms alternatively. Therefore,

WiFi could allocate the channel when LTE is in the status of "off."

(iii) LAA channel allocation: LAA was proposed by 3GPP. LAA introduces Listen-Before-Talk (LBT) to coordinate the channel utilization between WiFi and LTE devices. Figure 1(c) shows that LTE devices listen to the channel first before sending or receiving the data. Therefore, both WiFi and LTE devices could allocate the channel to sending data if the channel is idle.

In summary, both LTE-U and LAA are time division multiple access-like (TDMA-like) schedule method for channel utilization between LTE and WiFi devices though they defined different channel management methods (detailed in Figures 2(a) and 2(b)). LTE-U and LAA could achieve the coexistence of WiFi and LTE. However, the TDMA-like channel allocation methods introduce transmission time delay; therefore, it is urgent to find new channel management methods to further improve the channel utilizations. In this paper, we propose using the parallel channel utilization method (detailed in Figure 2(c)) to optimize the channel utilization between WiFi and LTE devices in 5 GHz unlicensed bands.

4. Motivation

How to solve the conflicts is the key issue to achieve coexistence of LTE and WiFi. Previous studies focus on avoiding these conflicts, such as LTE-U schedules WiFi frames with the duty cycle of LTE, and LAA adds LBT mechanism to avoid conflicts with WiFi. In summary, both of them assume that LTE and WiFi should allocate the channel in different time slots to avoid conflicts. However, time division utilization hardly achieves further improvement of spectrum efficiency and it also would cause time delay especially in dense deployment scenarios. To enable LTE and WiFi coexisting with lower transmission delay and higher spectrum efficiency, this section initializes a new conflict dealing method to motivate efficient channel allocation method in LTE and WiFi coexisting networks. In order to describe this easily, some definitions used in the remaining parts of this paper are defined in Abbreviations.

4.1. The Need for New Conflict Resolving Method. Spectrum utilization efficiency would be significantly improved if we are

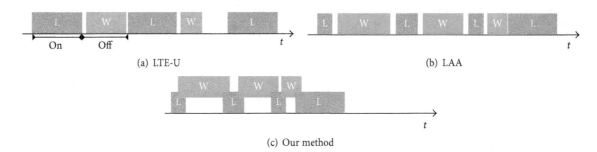

FIGURE 2: Channel utilization of our method, LTE-U and LAA. LTE-U and LAA are TDMA-like channel allocation methods which can not further improve channel utilization efficiency; our method introduces parallel transmission method to enable the concurrent transmission between WiFi and LTE devices.

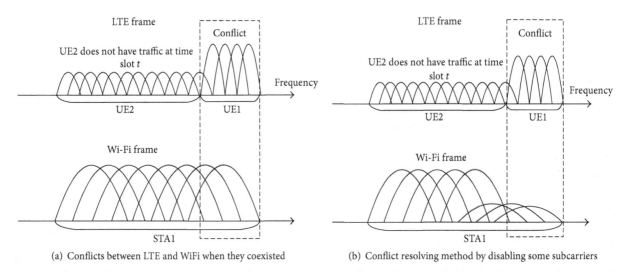

FIGURE 3: Conflicts in LTE and WiFi coexisting networks and a promising conflict resolving method by disabling some subcarriers of WiFi frames.

able to enable LTE and WiFi transmit simultaneously in the same channel. As we know WiFi APs only communicate with a single client in one time slot while LTE could communicate with multiclients by using Orthogonal Frequency-Division Multiple Access (OFDMA) method. A simple example shown in Figure 3(a) introduces this difference. When eNB connects with client UE1 and client UE2, AP connects with client STA1 only. But only UE1 and STA1 are in the conflict region; therefore, UE2 could receive the message correctly while UE1 and STA1 are certain to encounter the conflicts if they are transmitting in the same time slot. However, the spectrum utilization efficiency would significantly improve if LTE and WiFi transmit simultaneously and the data could recover from the conflicts.

One of the promising solutions which could make the data survive from the conflicts is shown in Figure 3(b). If the subcarriers in WiFi which interfere with STA1 are disabled, then the data transmitted UE2 could survive from the conflicts while the remaining subcarriers of WiFi which are not disabled also could survive. In order to evaluate how much spectrum efficiency would be increased by this subcarrier disabling method, we do a simple one AP and one eNodeB experiment, with the details in the *Observation*.

Observation. Spectrum utilization efficiency of *parallel channel utilization schema* is better than traditional time division method.

Experiment Setup and Results. One eNodeB with multiclients is deployed firstly; then, we deploy one eNodeB with multiclients in the conflict region with eNodeB. We think about an extreme situation that each client want to send message in every time slot for both LTE and WiFi.

The spectrum efficiency we observed is shown in Figure 4. If we use the subcarrier disabling method as channel parallel utilization schema, we can figure out that by utilizing this schema the spectrum utilization efficiency of this coexisting network is 1.6 times that utilizing time division schema.

4.2. The Need for New Channel Allocation Method to Achieve Efficient Spectrum Utilization in 5 GHz. Besides the channel allocation mechanisms, many works should be researched to achieve the coexistence of WiFi and LTE networks, such as network architecture, protocol design, and QoS balancing. However, as a basic technology, channel allocation mechanism is an essential part to achieve high efficiency coexistence of cross technologies.

Since 2.4 GHz unlicensed band is too crowded, we should enable LTE and WiFi coexisting in 5 GHz; the new features of

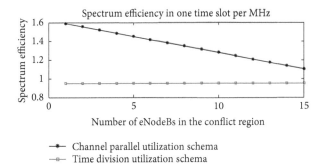

FIGURE 4: Spectrum efficiencies of time division channel utilization method and parallel channel utilization method.

the channels in 5 GHz cause new challenge for allocation as follows.

(i) Nonoverlapped Channel Used in 5 GHz for the Dense Deployment. Until this paper, there are only 9 nonoverlapped 20 MHz channels used in 5GHz in United States. The nonoverlapped feature in 5 GHz is much different from the overlapped channel in 2.4 GHz. Clients would face a serious conflict once they can not choose an exclusive channel especially in dense deployment scenario. If LTE is offloading their traffic in 5 GHz, the scarcity of these nonoverlapped channels would be more obvious.

(ii) Most Operators Want to Deploy eNodeBs and Get a Full Coverage in the Deployed Scenarios. These competitions between operators make the nonoverlapped channel in 5 GHz more scarce, because we should assign different channels to each operator for avoiding interference interoperators. As far as we know, there are six main operators in United States that provide LTE services. They are AT&T, Claro, T-Mobile, Sprint, Open Mobile, and Choice Communications. From the competition view, each company wants to offload their traffic into 5 GHz, which makes the nonoverlapped 20 MHz channel get more inefficient.

(iii) Different Media Access Methods of LTE and WiFi Networks Make the Negotiation between LTE and WiFi More Difficult. Carrier Sensing Media Access (CSMA) was used in WiFi network to schedule channel access, while LTE utilizes Orthogonal Frequency-Division Multiple Access (OFDMA) to schedule different resource belonging to different clients.

In summary, new channel allocation mechanism is urgent for LTE and WiFi coexisting networks to manage the spectrum utilization. To fill this gap, in this paper we present *Conflict-Tolerant Channel Allocation (CTCA)* (in Section 4) to achieve efficient spectrum utilization.

5. Preliminaries

This section introduces the assumptions and the network model related to the rest of our work.

5.1. Assumptions. The assumptions behind our works are as follows.

(1) The WiFi networks are isomorphic, running 802.11ac protocols in 5 GHz band, the channel width is 20 MHz, and they only use 9 channels in 5 GHz. This assumption is reasonable because in US only 9 channels are used in 5 GHz for WiFi network. Our work aims to resolve channel sharing problem among these 9 channels while it is also easy extend to other channels.

(2) The eNodeBs from different operators deployed Pico nodes in 5 GHz. We assume Picos could get the location information of its clients. This assumption is also reasonable because LTE can recognize the clients in the edge for handover. We could just use this function to get the clients location information.

(3) eNodeBs from different operators allocate different channels to avoid interferences. Definitely, there may exist some mechanisms to avoid the conflicts between eNodeBs from different operators when they share the same channel, but it is out of our research scope in this paper.

In LTE and WiFi coexisting networks, there are more conflicts when AP and eNodeB allocate the same channel. However, the current time division channel utilization schema is limited for further efficient spectrum utilization and also caused a transmission delay. To resolve this problem, in Section 4, we propose *Low Amplitude Stream Injection (LASI)* to deal with these conflicts and motivate a new *Conflict-Tolerant Channel Allocation (CTCA)* method to increase the spectrum utilization and guarantee the transmission time delay in LTE and WiFi coexisting network.

5.2. Network Model. Under these assumptions, we define the network model. Suppose most of the operators want to deploy their eNodeBs and provide LTE service in a dense deployment scenario such as a stadium or music concert with thousands of audiences. WiFi service providers also want to deploy access points in these scenarios. The network architecture of LTE and WiFi coexisting networks is as shown in Figure 5, where n represents the number of WiFi access points in the network model; that is, $AP = \{AP_1, AP_2, \ldots, AP_n\}$. m represents the number of eNodeBs from different operators. We assume that different operators utilize different channels to avoid interference in assumption (3). Therefore, it does not need to distinguish eNodeBs from different operators; the total number of eNodeBs is $eNB = \{eNB_1, eNB_2, \ldots, eNB_m\}$.

We suppose there are multiclients connected with AP_i, and we define client j connected to AP_i as STA_{ij}. Similarly, we also define UE_{ij} as client j which connects to eNB_i.

6. Main Design

Depending on the network model defined in Section 5, the overall design of our approach is presented in this section. We first propose *Low Amplitude Stream Injection (LASI)* method to enable data recovery from conflicts. To further utilize the *LASI* method, we introduce the *Conflict-Tolerant Channel Allocation (CTCA)* and its detailed steps secondly.

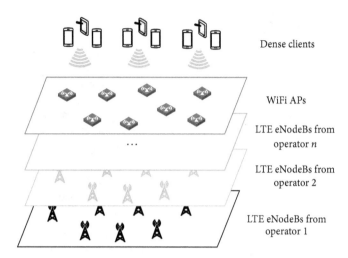

FIGURE 5: Architecture of LTE and WiFi coexisting network in 5 GHz band.

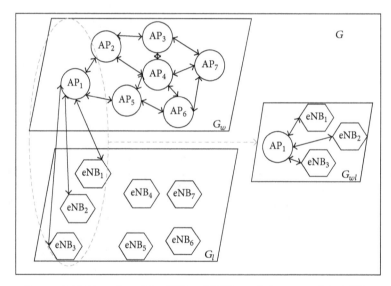

FIGURE 6: Multigraph model of LTE and WiFi coexisting network in 5 GHz.

6.1. Design Overview. Based on the network model, eNodeBs would get a fixed channel first while eNodeBs from the same operator share the fixed channel. APs would allocate channels in three steps: (i) choosing an idle channel which has not been allocated by neighbor nodes (including APs and eNBs); (ii) choosing a channel which is allocated by neighbor APs and sharing the channel with time division schema; and (iii) choosing a channel which is allocated by the neighbor eNodeBs from one operator.

Due to the different types of nodes (APs and eNodeBs), we model this problem as a multigraph coloring problem. Graph $G = G_l \cup G_w \cup G_{wl}$. The relationship of these three subgraphs is shown in Figure 6, where $G_l = (V_l, E_l)$ represents the conflicts in LTE network. In subgraph G_l, $V_l = \{eNB_1, eNB_2, \ldots, eNB_m\}$, and $E_l = $ NULL since we do not consider the interference between eNodeBs in this paper (see assumption (3)). $G_w = (V_w, E_w)$ represents the conflicts in WiFi networks. In subgraph G_w, $V_w = \{AP_i \mid i \in (1, 2, \ldots, n)\}$, and we add an edge between AP_i and AP_j if they

have potential to interfere with each other. $G_{wl} = (V, E_{wl})$ represents the conflict between LTE and WiFi networks. In subgraphs G_{wl}, $V = V_l \cup V_w$, and we add an edge between AP_i and eNB_j if they have potential to interfere with each other.

There are two design goals of *Conflict-Tolerant Channel Allocation (CTCA)* method presented in this section: (i) optimizing spectrum utilization and (ii) decreasing network latency in this coexisting networks. To achieve the first design goal, AP should first allocate idle channels for information transmission and decide which channel to allocate once no idle channel left. To achieve the second design goal, AP should try best to avoid time division channel access method. If there exist cochannel utilization situations between APs and eNodeBs, we explore *LASI* method to enable data to recover from conflicts. In summary the overall design is shown in Figure 7.

The CTCA in Figure 7 consists of three parts; the first part is *LASI* method shown in Figure 7(a). The second part is nonoverlapped channel allocation in G_w shown in

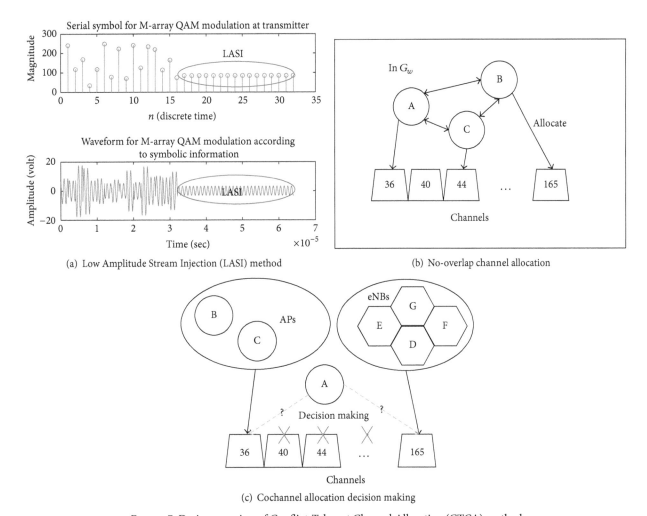

(a) Low Amplitude Stream Injection (LASI) method

(b) No-overlap channel allocation

(c) Cochannel allocation decision making

FIGURE 7: Design overview of Conflict-Tolerant Channel Allocation (CTCA) method.

Figure 7(b). The last part is the cochannel allocation decision making part shown in Figure 7(c).

6.1.1. LASI Conflicts Resolving Method. LASI shown in Figure 7(a) is applied for resolving conflicts between APs and eNodeBs in LTE and WiFi coexisting networks. *LASI* is a practical implementation of subcarrier disabling method (see Section 2) to achieve channel parallel utilization. *LASI* method makes data recover from the conflicts. The details of LASI will be introduced in Section 6.2.

6.1.2. Nonoverlapped Channel Allocation in G_w. APs apply this step to allocate an idle channel from the remaining channels after eNodeBs finishing their fixed channels. Each AP allocates the channel and optimizes the conflict to zero (i.e., choose different channels from their neighbors). If no such channels left, jump to the cochannel allocation decision making part.

6.1.3. Cochannel Allocation Decision Making in G. APs apply this step to decide which channel to utilize once there are no idle channels to choose according to their neighbors. In this paper, we collect the client information of the neighboring

nodes for this decision making. The details of this method will be introduced in Section 6.3.

By applying these three steps, CTCA algorithm enables LTE and WiFi to allocate proper channels for increasing spectrum utilization and decreasing network latency.

6.2. LASI Conflict Resolving Method. We first present the *Low Amplitude Stream Injection (LASI)* method in this section. secondly we proved the correctness of LASI and also discussed the additional delay by utilizing LASI method in LTE and WiFi network.

6.2.1. Procedure of LASI. LASI is proposed to resolve conflicts between LTE and WiFi frames in MAC layer. LASI utilizes both the features of OFDMA in LTE and CSMA in WiFi network. As we described in Figure 3 (see Section 2), we can protect both part of WiFi frame and some LTE subframes (e.g., subframes belonging to UE2) by disabling some subcarriers in the conflict region.

However, disabling some subcarriers is hard to implement; therefore we propose the practical Low Amplitude Stream Injection method, short for *LASI* method to enable data to recover from conflicts. LASI injects some lower

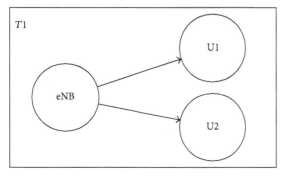

(a) *T1*: eNodeB sense clients in conflict region

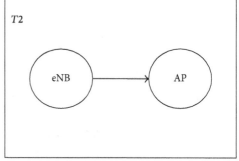

(b) *T2*: eNodeB exchange injected stream information to AP

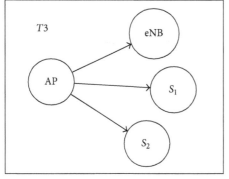

(c) AP notifies its client and eNodeB about the injected stream information

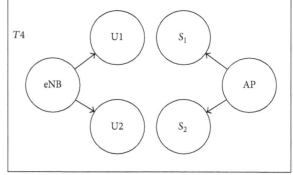

(d) eNodeB and WiFi begin to communicate with their clients

FIGURE 8: Negotiation and synchronization procedure for LTE and WiFi to communicate with subcarrier to be injected by Low Amplitude Stream.

amplitude stream in the subcarriers of WiFi frames which affects LTE clients in the conflict region. Figure 7(a) introduces the key principles of *LASI*. *LASI* could be easily implemented by quadrature amplitude modulation (QAM).

In order to negotiate which and how many subcarriers should be injected in WiFi frames, LTE should exchange control information with the APs sharing the same channel. The negotiation procedure is shown in Figure 8. From Figure 8, four time slots are needed to negotiate which and how many subcarriers to be injected into WiFi frames. The details of the four steps are as follows.

  (i) *T1*: eNodeB first senses the clients in conflict region. Figure 8(a) describes this activity of time slot *T1*. If eNodeB sensed some clients in conflict region, procedure goes to *T2*.

 (ii) *T2*: eNodeB tells WiFi access point which and how many subcarriers should be injected by Low Amplitude Stream to avoid the conflicts between eNodeBs in the conflict region (see Figure 8(b)).

(iii) *T3*: WiFi broadcasts the injected stream information to its clients and the eNodeB that sent the information in *T2* (see Figure 8(c)). Therefore, the WiFi clients could decode the information correctly, and eNodeBs also could get ready to exchange messages with their clients.

(iv) *T4*: WiFi access point and LTE transmit information to their own clients, respectively (see Figure 8(d)). This is the normal transmission after the negotiation.

6.2.2. Theoretical Analysis. We prove the correctness of LASI and also analyze the latency caused by LASI method.

Theorem 1. *LASI is correct from the theoretical level by utilizing quadrature amplitude modulation (QAM) and orthogonal frequency-division multiplexing (OFDM) technology.*

Proof. Consider that a conflict occurs between LTE frame and WiFi frame in the same channel. We define the signal S_1 in physical layer of LTE frame in (1), and we also define the signals of WiFi frame as S_2 in (2):

$$S_1 = \sum_{j1=1}^{m1} a_{j1} * f_i + \sum_{j2=m1}^{m2} a_{j2} * f_i + \sum_{j3=m3}^{m} a_{j3} * f_i, \quad (1)$$

$$S_2 = \sum_{i1=1}^{n1} A_{i1} * F_i + \sum_{i2=n1}^{n2} A_{i2} * F_i + \sum_{i3=n2}^{n} A_{i3} * F_i. \quad (2)$$

In (1) and (2), we assume that $\sum_{i2=n1}^{n2} A_{i1} * F_i$ and $\sum_{j2=m1}^{m2} a_{j1} * f_i$ are in the conflict region. If we inject the lowest amplitude stream in case the modulation is 256 QAM, the amplitude of the injected stream is calculated by the formula

$$a_k \atop \forall k \in [j_2 \to m_2] = |(1 \pm i)| \approx 1.41, \qquad (3)$$

where a_k is 63% of the second lowest amplitude and only eight percent of the highest amplitude; thus the injected stream could avoid the conflicts in a promising degree. Besides this a_k ($k \in (j_2$ to $m_2)$) are equal and in the same frequency which almost could not affect other signals transmitting in the same channel. Thus LSAI is correct from the theoretical level. $\square$

Theorem 2. *There exists 1 time unit delay when one pair of eNodeBs and APs are running LASI method.*

Proof. In $T1$, eNodeBs always sense their clients and calculate the locations of the clients; thus the first $T1$ phase does not introduce additional time delay. In $T2$, eNodeB should send a notification to AP; this introduces an additional time delay. For $T3$, WiFi always uses CSMA to sense channels before they transmit; we just utilize this CSMA carrier to notify the client and eNB about the information of injected subcarriers; therefore $T3$ is not the additional time delay, so $T3$ does not introduce additional time delay. In $T4$, it also does not introduce additional time delay because it is a normal transmission between eNodeB/AP and their clients. $\square$

6.3. Nonoverlapped Channel Allocation in G_w. APs first allocate channels from the remaining ones when eNodeBs finish their channels setting. Allocating the remaining nonoverlapped channel could minimize the conflicts in the network. this section introduces the nonoverlapped channel allocation algorithm first followed by its theoretical analysis.

6.3.1. Nonoverlapped Channel Allocation Algorithm. G_w presents the graph of WiFi network; in order to minimize the conflicts, WiFi APs first allocate the nonoverlapped channels with 20 MHz width after eNodeBs had allocated their channels. The nonoverlapped channel assignment problem for WiFi network can be modeled as a graph coloring problem of graph G_w in which the APs are the vertices of a graph. A conflict between two APs is represented by an edge in the graph. The goal of this graph coloring problem is to assign a set of distinct colors. To enable the most efficient use of these channels the objective of this issue is to color graph G_w with minimum number of colors and avoid any conflicts.

The nonoverlapped channel allocation problem in G_w is stated as follows. A channel assignment $C(AP_i)$, $AP_i \in V_w$, is a mapping $C : V_w \to \{1, 2, \ldots, k\}$ from the set of vertices to the set of colors. We say that an edge (AP_i, AP_j) is conflict-free edge when AP_i and AP_j allocate different nonoverlapped channel (all the 20 MHz channels in 5 GHz used in United States are nonoverlapped channels); otherwise if they share the same channel we say edge (AP_i, AP_j) is a conflict edge.

The interference of AP_i and AP_j is serious once they share the same channel. Since there is no overlapped channel in 5 GHz, if the conflict occurs, it occurs on the whole channel,

not partially described in [13]. So in order to minimum the conflicts between APs in G_w, we define conflict factor of WiFi network as CF_w, and CF_w is presented as

$$CF_w \left(AP_i, AP_j, c \right) = \begin{cases} 0, & \left(C \left(AP_i \right) \neq C \left(AP_j \right) \right), \\ 1, & \left(C \left(AP_i \right) = C \left(AP_j \right) \right). \end{cases} \qquad (4)$$

$CF_w(AP_i, AP_j, c)$ presents the total effect of conflict in an edge, c represents the color of node AP_j, and the objective in this phase is to optimize the conflicts between APs. If we can not achieve this goal, we just let the APs try the third phase in Section 6.4. So the objective in this phase is shown as (5) when we find a mapping C for graph G_w.

$$\max \sum_{\forall e = (AP_i, AP_j) \in E_w} CF_w \left(AP_i, AP_j \right) = 0. \qquad (5)$$

6.3.2. The Detailed Algorithm. The nonoverlapped channel allocation algorithm in G_w is shown as Algorithm 1, which has two steps according to the algorithm.

Initialization Step. Line (1) to Line (7) introduce the initialization step; in Line (2), all the APs points are assigned an initial color, and in Line (5)$CF_w(AP_i, AP_j) \in E_w$ was initialized.

Optimization Step. In this step, we begin to optimize the conflicts in Lines (9), (10), (11), (12), and (13). The objective functions are shown in (1), and we should make sure the value of this function is zero; if we can not guarantee this value the algorithm breaks in Line (15) and is called cochannel allocation algorithm proposed in Section 6.4.

6.3.3. Complexity Analysis. In *assumption* (1) we assume that we discuss the channel reuse in 5 GHz and share the 9 nonoverlapped WiFi channels with a width of 20 MHz. Thus the maximum number of the colors is 9; therefore $C = 1, 2, \ldots, 9$. We also assume that the network is connected when in dense deployment.

So the complexity of nonoverlapped channel allocation part depends on the number of reminding channels after LTE allocate the channels. The details are analyzed below. We assume that k is the remaining channel, and we have the following theorems.

Theorem 3. *Nonoverlapped channel allocation is polynomial time solvable problem when $k \leq 2$.*

Proof. Given a graph $G = (V, E)$, (1) coloring graphs are the empty graphs and (2) coloring problem is equivalent to bipartite graph determining problem. We divided V into two disjoint sets V_1 and V_2; that is, V_1 and V_2 are independent sets, and every edge connects a vertex in V_1 to one in V_2, we assume $|V_1| = m$ and $|V_2| = n$, we set different colors to the vertexes connected by edge in sets V_1 and V_2, and the complexity is $O(m \times n)$, which is polynomial time solvable problem. $\square$

Theorem 4. *Nonoverlapped channel allocation is an NP-hard problem when $k \geq 3$.*

```
        Initialize:
 (1)  for i = 1 to n do
 (2)     C(AP_i) = 1
 (3)     for j = i − 1 to n do
 (4)        if (AP_i, AP_j) ∈ E_w then
 (5)           CF_w(AP_i, AP_j, C(AP_j)) = 1
 (6)        else
 (7)           CF_w(AP_i, AP_j, C(AP_j)) = 0
 (8)        end if
 (9)     end for
(10)  end for
        Optimize:
(11)  if (AP_i, AP_j) ∈ E_w & C(AP_j) = c then
(12)     if CF_w(i, j, c) == 1 then
(13)        for p = 1 to k do
(14)           if CF_w(i, j, p) == 0 then
(15)              C(AP_j) = p
(16)           else
(17)              Call co-channel allocation algorithm in Section 4.2
(18)           end if
(19)        end for
(20)     end if
(21)  end if
```

ALGORITHM 1: Nonoverlapped channel allocation in G_w.

Proof. Consider the general problem of coloring an undirected graph: given a graph $G = (V, E)$, does there exist k-coloring $C(k \geq 3) : v \rightarrow \{1 \cdots k\}, 1 \leq k \leq |V|$, such that $\forall e = (v_i, v_j) \in E \Rightarrow C(v_i) \neq C(v_j)$? We formulate our nonoverlapped channel allocation as this general problem with the objective function $\forall e = (AP_i, AP_j) \, CF_w(AP_i, AP_j) = 0$; thus nonoverlapped channel allocation is an NP-hard problem since the general coloring problem is NP-hard problem. □

6.4. Cochannel Allocation Decision Making in G. There may be some APs that did not allocate any channel after the nonoverlapped channel allocation phase since the design goal of nonoverlapped channel allocation is to optimize the conflicts in G_w; if there are no idle channels to allocate in G_w, the procedure would move to cochannel allocation decision part. The most important challenge in this part is how to decide which channel to allocate.

6.4.1. Parameters Design for Cochannel Allocation Decision Making. If there are no exclusive channels to allocate, AP has to share the same channel with other APs or other multi-eNodeBs from one operator, and these two types of decisions are analyzed as follows.

Type 1: Cochannel with Another AP. WiFi uses CSMA to isolate data transmission between different APs, which is a time division method, and the transmission time delay will also increase when waiting to allocate the channel.

Type 2: Cochannel with Multi-eNodeB from One Operator. More conflicts are confronted when APs share the same channel with eNodeBs. However, LASI method can resolve this kind of conflicts.

So, AP should make a decision whether to choose to have cochannel with another AP or multi-eNodeBs. And this selection should consider the spectrum efficiency and transmission time delay since we can utilize LASI method to solve conflicts between LTE and WiFi. For the cochannel decision between Type 1 and Type 2, we define $N_c(i)$ as a parameter to make this decision $N_c(i)$ present the number of clients that can be solved per time slot and per MHz. $N_c(i)$ is calculated by

$$N_c(i) = \frac{\sum_{\forall (AP_i \in G_w) \& C(AP_i) = c} n_i + \sum_{\forall (eNB_j \in G_{wl}) \& C(eNB_j) = c} N_j}{T * B_w}, \tag{6}$$

where n_i presents the number of clients served by AP_i and N_j represents the number of clients served by eNB_j, while T is the time we measured and B_w is the width of the channels shared by AP and eNodeB. From (6), we can easily deduce the average number of clients that can be solved by two APs sharing the same channel in (7) and APs sharing the channel with multi-eNodeBs from a specific operator in (8).

$$N_w(i) = \frac{N(AP_i) + \sum_{j=1}^{m} N(AP_j)}{B_w * t_{slot} * \sum_{j=1}^{m} N(AP_i)}, \tag{7}$$

```
            Initialize:
(1)  for i = 1 to n + m do
(2)    for j = 1 to n + m do
(3)      if (AP_i, AP_j) ∈ E_w then
(4)        N_w(i)+ = N(AP_j)
(5)      else
(6)        if (AP_i, eNB_j) ∈ E_wl then
(7)          N_l(i)+ = N(eNB_j)
(8)        end if
(9)      end if
(10)   end for
(11) end for
            Decision making:
(12) a = 5/16; b = 11/16.
(13) for i = 1 to n do
(14)   N_w(i) = N_w(i)/(B_w * t_slot * N_w(i))
(15)   N_l(i) = a * (N_l(i)/(B_w * t_slot * N_w(i))) + b * (N_l(i)/(B_w) * t_slot)
(16)   if N_w(i) ≤ N_l(i) then
(17)     C(AP_i) = C(AP_j){(AP_i, AP_j) ∈ E_w}
(18)   else
(19)     C(AP_i) = C(eNB_j){(AP_i, eNB_j) ∈ E_w}
(20)   end if
(21) end for
```

ALGORITHM 2: Cochannel allocation decision making algorithm in G.

$$N_l(i) = \alpha * \frac{N(AP_i) + \sum_{j=1}^{m} N(eNB_j)}{t_{slot} * B_w * \sum_{i=1}^{m} N(eNB_j)} + \beta$$

$$* \frac{N(AP_i) + \sum_{j=1}^{m} N(eNB_j) - M}{t_{slot} * B_w}.$$

$$(8)$$

6.4.2. The Detailed Algorithm.
The cochannel allocation algorithm is shown as Algorithm 2. There are two phases in Algorithm 2, and the details are as follows.

Initialization. Line (1) to Line (10) are initialization phase; in this phase AP and eNode exchange the clients information with each other and utilize this information to calculate $N_l(i)$ and $N_w(i)$ in Line (4) and Line (7) separately.

Decision Making. AP makes the decision according to value of $N_l(i)$ and $N_w(i)$; if $N_l(i) \geq N_w(i)$, AP_i choose to have cochannel with multi-eNodeBs; otherwise AP chooses to have cochannel with other APs.

6.4.3. Complexity Analysis of Cochannel Allocation Decision Making Algorithm.
This section introduces the complexity of cochannel allocation decision making algorithm.

Theorem 5. *The complexity of cochannel allocation decision making is $O(m * n)$.*

Proof. Consider that in a graph $G = V, E$, finding a mapping $C : v_i \rightarrow 1 \cdots k$ ($1 \leq k \leq |V|$), the problem could be formulated as $\forall e = (v_i, v_j) \in E \Rightarrow C(v_i) = C(v_j)$; we assume $|V| = n$, and the complexity is $O(n)$. Cochannel allocation

decision making algorithm is a two-step $v_i \rightarrow 1 \cdots k$. The first step is searching in $G_w = (V_w, E_w)$ and calculating the decision parameter $N_w(i)$, and secondly search in $G_wl = (V_wl, E_wl)$ and calculate $N_l(i)$; we assume that $|V_w| = n$ and $|V_wl|$; thus the complexity of cochannel decision making problem is $O(m \times n)$. □

7. Evaluation

We evaluate LTE and WiFi coexistence using multiple threads simulators which are implemented by Python. We set the channel bandwidth to 20 MHz, which is compatible to 802.11n/ac and LTE in licensed bands. LTE and WiFi allocate totally 8 channels in 5 GHz (channels 36, 40, 44, 48, 149, 153, 157, and 161). For WiFi, we implemented one kind of server (sender) and client (receiver) according to 802.11ac. For LTE, we implemented four kinds of servers and clients: LTE Control-free (LTE-C), LTE-U, LAA, and our approaches (CTCA); LTE-C, LTE-U, and LAA are three baselines; the main principles are detailed in Section 7.3.

7.1. Experiment Setup.
We randomly deploy APs and LTE eNodeBs in a 200-meter square region, and we assume that the APs and eNodeB share the same transmission range of 35 meters, and the eNodeBs are Picos which provide indoor services. Six operators want to deploy their Picos in this region. The modulation of both APs and eNodeBs is QAM-256, which is modulated by OFDM method. We fixed 36 APs and 36 eNodeBs in this region, the eNodeBs come from 6 operators, each operator deploys 6 eNodeB, and the eNodeBs from the same operator occupy the same channel (e.g., channel 48). The clients of the WiFi APs and LTE

eNodeBs could be changed with different settings if required in the experiments. The transmission data rate is fixed, each operator gets fixed channel for transmission from other operators, and each AP should allocate a channel according to the standards defined in LTE-C (see Section 7.3), LAA, LTE-U, and CTCA methods.

7.2. Performance Metrics. To evaluate the efficiency of spectrum utilization when LTE and WiFi coexist in 5 GHz, we evaluate average transmission number, average transmission delay, and spectrum efficiency. The specific definitions are as follows.

Average Transmission Number. The average transmission number indicates how many packets could be transmitted/second/link (links include the WiFi links and LTE links). Therefore, the average transmission number could be calculated by

$$ATN = \frac{\sum_{i=1}^{n} TN_i + \sum_{j=1}^{m} TN_m}{n + m}, \tag{9}$$

in which *ATN* represents the average transmission number, *n* represents *n* WiFi links, and *m* represents *m* LTE links. TN_i and TN_j represent the transmission number of WiFi link *i* and LTE link *j*. Therefore, $ATN * (m + n)$ indicates the total throughput of the LTE-WiFi coexistence system.

Average Transmission Delay. Average transmission delay is the number of time units cost when transmitting one packet.

Spectrum Efficiency. Spectrum efficiency measured in this paper is defined as the ratio of transmission number and spectrum bandwidth.

7.3. Baseline. We compared our approach with the following baselines.

Baseline I: LTE Control-Free (LTE-C). LTE-C lets LTE and WiFi run in the same band without any channel management control. In LTE-C, LTE devices transmit as scheduled in the assigned channel, and WiFi devices utilize CSMA to access the channels when there is traffic to be resolved.

Baseline II: LTE-U. As described in Section 3, WiFi devices control their transmission by the duty cycle of LTE devices. WiFi devices transmit when the status of LTE devices is "off," while LTE devices transmit when the status is "on." Therefore, they use the channel alternatively but LTE has higher priorities.

Baseline III: LAA. LAA adds LBT mechanism to share the same channel with WiFi devices. In LAA method, both LTE and WiFi sense the channel before sending packets. The transmission delay of LTE and WiFi devices would be longer in dense deployed scenarios.

7.4. Performance Comparison. This section compares CTCA with LTE control-free (LTE-C), LTE Unlicensed (LTE-U), and License-Assisted access (LAA) methods. Average transmission number, average transmission delay, and spectrum efficiency are evaluated separately in this section.

7.4.1. Average Transmission Number. Firstly, the average transmission number was evaluated with different network parameters. And the results are shown as in Figures 9, 10, and 11.

Figure 9 describes the average transmission number of one link including WiFi and LTE links in a fixed transmission period with the change of the number of LTE clients. Figure 9(a) shows that the average transmission number decreases with the number of UE clients; the reason why we got the experimental results is that each individual LTE client could get less and less time slot for transmission with the increasing number of the total clients. However, the total transmission number increases in LTE-WiFi coexisting systems, and the average transmission number of CTCA increased by 24% of that LTE-C, 109%, and 26% of LAA and LTE-U separately. As the number of UE clients increases, both WiFi and LTE devices will be "back off" since the Listen-Before-Talk mechanism. Therefore, the average transmission number of LAA method is the lowest one.

Figure 9(b) shows the average transmission number of LTE clients and WiFi clients separately. This kind of data could reveal some details of the LTE-WiFi coexistence system. We can see that CTCA and LTE-C algorithms could keep the average transmission number of LTE devices in a stable level with the increasing UE clients because LTE devices do not need to be back off when coexisting with WiFi devices, while the transmission numbers of LTE-U and LAA decrease sharply with the number of UE clients since the Listen-Before-Talk mechanism causes more conflict and back-off when the UE number increases.

Figure 9(b) also shows that the average transmission number of WiFi devices decreased with the number of UE clients. However, the average transmission number of our CTCA method is greater than those of LTE-C, LTE-U, and LAA since our method could utilize the channel simultaneously with LTE devices.

Figure 10 shows the trends of average transmission number with the increasing number of WiFi clients (STAs). With similar reason to the result in Figure 9, the average transmission number slightly decreases with the increasing number of STAs, while the total transmission of the LTE-WiFi coexistence system increases. Figure 10(a) shows that the average transmission number of CTCA increased by 21%, 124%, and 25% of those LTE-C, LAA, and LTE-U. Figure 10(b) shows CTCA can keep the average transmission number of LTE despite the increasing number of WiFi clients while the average transmission number equals that of LTE-C and is greater than LAA and LTE-U. Figure 11 shows that the average transmission number of CTCA is greater than the baselines when the duty cycle of LTE is larger than 20%, while the average transmission number of CTCA is less than LTE-U and LTE-C when LTE duty cycle is less than 20%. The main reason is that when LTE in a low duty cycle, there is nearly no parallel utilization of LTE and WiFi devices.

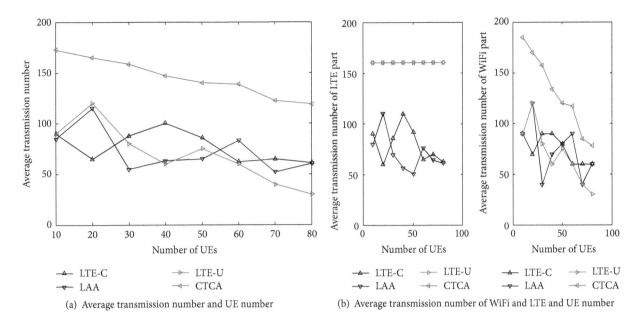

(a) Average transmission number and UE number

(b) Average transmission number of WiFi and LTE and UE number

FIGURE 9: Results of transmission number with different UE number.

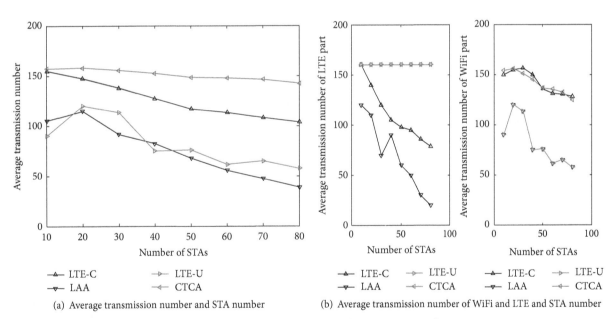

(a) Average transmission number and STA number

(b) Average transmission number of WiFi and LTE and STA number

FIGURE 10: Results of transmission number with STA number.

7.4.2. Average Transmission Delay. We also evaluate average transmission delay of CTCA, LTE-C, LAA, and LTE-U with different parameters. The results are shown in Figures 12, 13, and 14.

Figure 12 shows that the transmission delay of CTCA decreases by 10%, 39%, and 29% compared with those of LTE-C, LAA, and LTE-U. The reason why our algorithm could decrease the average transmission time delay is that relying on both LTE and WiFi devices could transmit the data if the traffic is demanded, while LTE-C, LAA, and LTE-U would cost some time units to get the right of the channel which causes additional time delay.

To further analyze the average transmission delay for WiFi and LTE part separately, we get the results which are

showed in Figure 12(b). The average transmission delay of LTE devices increases with the number of UE clients since more UEs share the same resource, which can not guarantee that each of them could transmit in time. However, our approach is even better than LTE-C, LTE-U, and LAA.

We also evaluated the average transmission delay when the number of WiFi clients increases; the results are showed in Figure 13; the average transmission delay of CTCA decreases by 39%, 45%, and 21% of those LTE-C, LAA, and LTE-U. Figure 13(b) also shows that the transmission time delay of LTE-C and LTE-U increases with the number of STAs.

Figure 14 shows that the transmission delay of CTCA is always lower than those of LTE-C, LAA, and LTE-U. This is because CTCA lets WiFi and LTE transmit together in

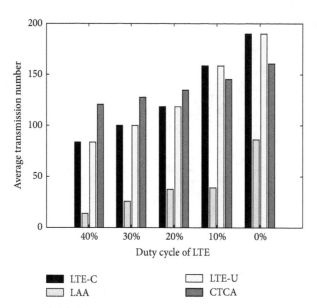

FIGURE 11: Results of transmission number with different duty cycle of LTE.

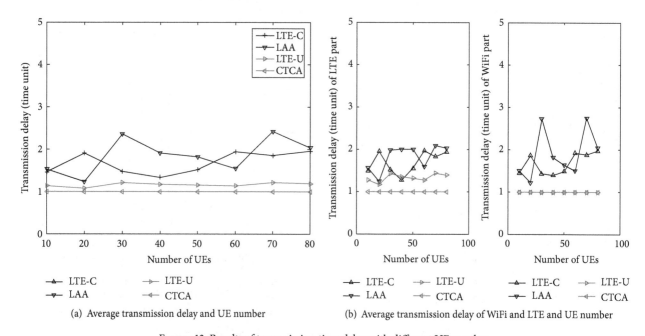

(a) Average transmission delay and UE number

(b) Average transmission delay of WiFi and LTE and UE number

FIGURE 12: Results of transmission time delay with different UE number.

the same channel which could decrease the time delay for channel allocation. We also get another useful result that the average transmission delay could keep stable when the duty cycle of LTE is lower than 40%.

7.4.3. Spectrum Efficiency. We evaluate the spectrum efficiency of CTCA in three scenarios; (i) UE is more denser than STA, (ii) STA is more denser than UE, and (iii) we also evaluate the average spectrum utilization when LTE duty cycle equals 40%; Figure 15 shows that in scenario (i), the spectrum efficiency of CTCA is nearly 2x of LTE-C, LAA, and LTE-U; in scenario (ii), spectrum efficiency of CTCA is 1.2x, 2.3x, and 2.2x of LTE-C, LAA, and LTE-U; in scenario

(iii), spectrum efficiency is 1.3x, 3.4x, and 2.9x of those LTE-C, LAA, and LTE-U.

8. Conclusion

In this paper, we present *Conflict-Tolerant Channel Allocation (CTCA)* method in LTE and WiFi coexisting 5 GHz band, especially for resolving the increase conflicts in dense deployment scenarios. To the best of our knowledge, this is the first Conflict-Tolerant Channel Allocation method for LTE and WiFi coexisting network aiming at efficient spectrum utilization and low time delay consideration. This work for the first time proposes *Low Amplitude Stream Injection*

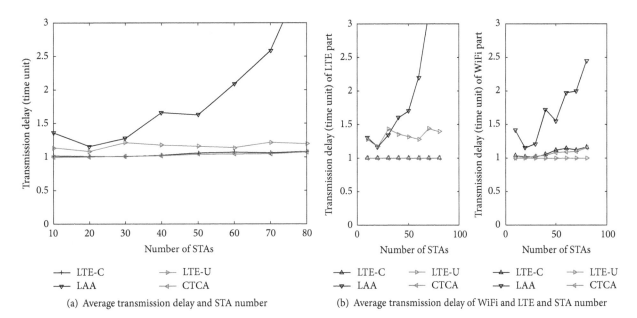

(a) Average transmission delay and STA number

(b) Average transmission delay of WiFi and LTE and STA number

FIGURE 13: Results of transmission time delay with different STA number.

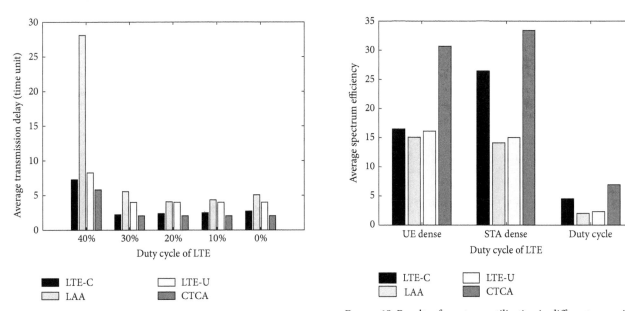

FIGURE 14: Results of transmission delay with different duty cycles of LTE.

FIGURE 15: Results of spectrum utilization in different scenarios.

(LASI) to deal with the increasing conflicts between LTE and WiFi especially in dense deployment scenarios. *LASI* method enables LTE and WiFi to transmit simultaneously by allocating the same channel with low transmission time delay and high spectrum efficiency. Cochannel allocation decision making of CTCA method defines a parameter to help AP decide whether to choose to have cochannel with another AP or other LTE base stations, by which the spectrum utilization efficiency could be further improved. In the future, we shall extend this work to achieve the fairness utilization of spectrum.

Abbreviations

AP_i: Access point i providing WiFi services in LTE/WiFi coexisting networks

eNB_i: eNodeB i providing LTE services in LTE/WiFi coexisting networks

STA_{ik}:   Client k belonging to AP_i

UE_{ik}:   Client k belonging to eNB_i

G_w: Conflict graph between APs

G_l: Conflict graph between eNodeBs

G_{wl}:   Conflict graph between APs and eNodeB

G: $G_w \cup G_l \cup G_{wl}$.

Competing Interests

The authors declare that they have no competing interests.

Acknowledgments

This project is supported by NSF Grants CNS-1503590 and CNS-1539047.

References

[1] Cisco, "Cisco Visual Networking Index: Global Mobile Data Traffic Forecast Update, 2015–2020," 2016.

[2] "Spectrum monitoring," http://www.spectrummonitoring.com/standards/#LTE

[3] L. A. N. Man, S. Committee, and I. Computer, Wireless LAN Medium Access Control (MAC) and Physical Layer (PHY) Specifications, 2013.

[4] "Qualcomm wants LTE deployed on unlicensed spectrum," 2015.

[5] "U-LTE: Unlicensed Spectrum Utilization of LTE," 2015.

[6] "Ericsson first to give smartphone users indoor boost with License Assisted Access," 2015.

[7] Ericsson, T-Mobile push unlicensed LTE into limelight as '4.5G' technology for IoT, 2015.

[8] "Overview of 3GPP Release 13 V0.0.6," 2014.

[9] M. Arunesh, B. Vladimir, and B. Suman, "A client-driven approach for channel management in wireless lans," in Proceedings of the 25th IEEE International Conference on Computer Communications (INFOCOM '06), Barcelona, Spain, April 2006.

[10] A. Mishra, S. Banerjee, and W. Arbaugh, "Weighted coloring based channel assignment for WLANs," ACM SIGMOBILE Mobile Computing and Communications Review, vol. 9, no. 3, pp. 19–31, 2005.

[11] K. Tan, J. Fang, Y. Zhang et al., "Fine-grained channel access in wireless lan," in Proceedings of the ACM SIGCOMM Conference (SIGCOMM '10), pp. 147–158, New Delhi, India, August 2010.

[12] T. Moscibroda, R. Chandra, Y. Wu, S. Sengupta, P. Bahl, and Y. Yuan, "Load-aware spectrum distribution in wireless lans," in Proceedings of the IEEE International Conference on Network Protocols (ICNP '08), IEEE, Orlando, Fla, USA, 2008.

[13] S. Rayanchu, V. Shrivastava, S. Banerjee, and R. Chandra, "FLUID: improving throughputs in enterprise wireless LANs through flexible channelization," in Proceedings of the 17th Annual International Conference on Mobile Computing and Networking (MobiCom'11) and Co-Located Workshops, pp. 1–12, Las Vegas, Nev, USA, September 2011.

[14] Qualcomm, "A comparison of LTE advanced HetNets and WI-FI," 2014.

[15] S. Souvik, R. Božidar, L. Jeongkeun, and K. Kyu-Han, "Cspy: finding the best quality channel without probing," in Proceedings of the 19th International Conference on Mobile Computing & Networking (MobiCom '13), pp. 267–278, Miami, Fla, USA, October 2013.

[16] R. Chandra, R. Mahajan, T. Moscibroda, R. Raghavendra, and P. Bahl, "A case for adapting channel width in wireless networks," in Proceedings of the ACM SIGCOMM 2008 Conference on Data Communication (SIGCOMM '08), ACM, Seattle, Wash, USA, 2008.

[17] L. Yang, W. Hou, L. Cao, B. Y. Zhao, and H. Zheng, "Supporting demanding wireless applications with frequency-agile radios," in Proceedings of the 7th USENIX Conference on Networked Systems Design and Implementation (NSDI '10), p. 5, San Jose, Calif, USA, April 2010.

[18] H. Yu, O. Bejarano, and L. Zhong, "Combating Inter-cell Interference in 802.11ac-based multi-user MIMO networks," in Proceedings of the 20th ACM Annual International Conference on Mobile Computing and Networking (MobiCom '14), pp. 141–152, Maui, Hawaii, USA, September 2014.

[19] L. Yang, W. Hou, L. Cao, B. Y. Zhao, and H. Zheng, "Supporting Demanding Wireless Applications with Frequency-agile Radios Multimedia Streaming in Home/Office," pp. 1–21, 2010.

[20] E. Ziouva and T. Antonakopoulos, "Reprint CSMA/CA performance under high traffic conditions: throughput and delay analysis throughput and delay analysis," Computer Communications, vol. 25, no. 3, pp. 313–321, 2002.

[21] J. Herzen, A. Banchs, V. Shneer, and P. Thiran, "CSMA/CA in time and frequency domains," in Proceedings of the International Conference on Network Protocols (ICNP '15), San Francisco, Calif, USA, 2015.

[22] S. Gollakota, F. Adib, D. Katabi, and S. Seshan, "Clearing the RF smog: making 802.11n robust to cross-technology interference," in Proceedings of the ACM SIGCOMM Conference, Toronto, Canada, August 2011.

[23] Y. Yan, P. Yang, X.-Y. Li, Y. Tao, L. Zhang, and L. You, "ZIMO: building cross-technology MIMO to harmonize ZigBee Smog with WiFi flash without intervention categories and subject descriptors experiment rationale and setup," in Proceedings of the 19th Annual International Conference on Mobile Computing and Networking (MobiCom '13), Miami, Fla, USA, 2013.

[24] "Lte in unlicensed spectrum: Harmonious coexistence with wi-fi," 2015.

[25] A. M. Cavalcante, E. Almeida, R. D. Vieira et al., "Performance evaluation of LTE and Wi-Fi coexistence in unlicensed bands," in Proceedings of the IEEE 77th Vehicular Technology Conference (VTC Spring '13), Dresden, Germany, June 2013.

[26] B. Jia and M. Tao, "A channel sensing based design for LTE in unlicensed bands," in Proceedings of the IEEE International Conference on Communication Workshop (ICCW '15), June 2015.

[27] C. Cano and D. J. Leith, "Coexistence of WiFi and LTE in unlicensed bands: a proportional fair allocation scheme," in Proceedings of the IEEE International Conference on Communication Workshop (ICCW '15), pp. 2288–2293, IEEE, London, UK, June 2015.

[28] O. R. Fitness, F. O. R. Any, P. Purpose, A. L. L. Such, and I. Is, "Coexistence Study for LTE-U SDL V1.0 (2015 -02)," Tech. Rep., 2015.

[29] F. M. Abinader, E. P. L. Almeida, F. S. Chaves et al., "Enabling the coexistence of LTE and Wi-Fi in unlicensed bands," IEEE Communications Magazine, vol. 52, no. 11, pp. 54–61, 2014.

[30] M. G. Sriyananda, I. Parvez, I. Güvene, M. Bennis, and A. I. Sarwat, "Multi-armed bandit for LTE-U and WiFi coexistence in unlicensed bands," in Proceedings of the IEEE Wireless Communications and Networking Conference (WCNC '16), Doha, Qatar, April 2016.

[31] Z. Jiang and S. Mao, "Inter-operator opportunistic spectrum sharing in LTE-unlicensed," IEEE Transactions on Vehicular Technology, no. 99, 2016.

[32] C. Chen, R. Ratasuk, and A. Ghosh, "Downlink performance analysis of LTE and WiFi coexistence in unlicensed bands with

a simple listen-before-talk scheme," in *Proceedings of the 81st IEEE Vehicular Technology Conference (VTC Spring '15)*, pp. 1–5, IEEE, May 2015.

[33] A. Bhorkar, C. Ibars, and P. Zong, "On the throughput analysis of LTE and WiFi in unlicensed band," in *Proceedings of the 48th Asilomar Conference on Signals, Systems and Computers (ACSSC '15)*, pp. 1309–1313, Pacific Grove, Calif, USA, November 2014.

[34] J. Jeon, H. Niu, Q. Li, A. Papathanassiou, and G. Wu, "LTE with listen-before-talk in unlicensed spectrum," in *Proceedings of the IEEE International Conference on Communication Workshop (ICCW '15)*, pp. 2320–2324, June 2015.

[35] P. Xia, Z. Teng, and J. Wu, "How loud to talk and how hard to listen-before-talk in unlicensed LTE," in *Proceedings of the IEEE International Conference on Communication Workshop (ICCW '15)*, pp. 2314–2319, London, UK, June 2015.

[36] H. Li, Y. Chang, F. Hao, A. Men, J. Zhang, and W. Quan, "Study on dynamic channel switch in license-assisted-access based on listen-before-talk," in *Proceedings of the 13th International Symposium on Wireless Communication Systems (ISWCS '16)*, pp. 506–510, Poznań, Poland, September 2016.

[37] Q. Chen, G. Yu, R. Yin, A. Maaref, G. Y. Li, and A. Huang, "Energy efficiency optimization in licensed-assisted access," *IEEE Journal on Selected Areas in Communications*, vol. 34, no. 4, pp. 723–734, 2016.

[38] T. Yang, C. Guo, S. Zhao, Q. Zhang, and Z. Feng, "Channel occupancy cognition based adaptive channel access and back-off scheme for LTE system on unlicensed band," in *Proceedings of the IEEE Wireless Communications and Networking Conference (WCNC '16)*, pp. 1–6, IEEE, Doha, Qatar, April 2016.

[39] S. Han, Y. C. Liang, Q. Chen, and B. H. Soong, "Licensedassisted access for lte in unlicensed spectrum: a mac protocol design," *IEEE Journal on Selected Areas in Communications*, vol. 34, no. 10, pp. 2550–2561, 2016.

[40] E. Chai, K. Sundaresan, M. A. Khojastepour, and S. Rangarajan, "LTE in unlicensed spectrum: are we there yet?" in *Proceedings of the 22nd Annual International Conference on Mobile Computing and Networking (MobiCom '16)*, pp. 135–148, ACM, New York, NY, USA, 2016.

[41] L. Li, A. H. Jafari, X. Chu, and J. Zhang, "Simultaneous transmission opportunities for LTE-LAA smallcells coexisting with WiFi in unlicensed spectrum," in *Proceedings of the IEEE International Conference on Communications (ICC '16)*, pp. 1–7, May 2016.

[42] S. Yun and L. Qiu, "Supporting WiFi and LTE co-existence," in *Proceedings of the IEEE Conference on Computer Communications (INFOCOM '15)*, pp. 810–818, IEEE, Hong Kong, May 2015.

3

Energy Efficient Clustering Protocol to Enhance Performance of Heterogeneous Wireless Sensor Network: EECPEP-HWSN

Santosh V. Purkar ⑩[1] **and R. S. Deshpande** ⑩[2]

[1]*Department of Electronics and Telecommunication Engineering, Matoshri College of Engineering and Research Center, Nashik Eklahare odhagaon, Affiliated to Savitribai Phule Pune University, Pune, India*
[2]*S.C.S.M.CO.E, Ahmednagar Nepti, Affiliated to Savitribai Phule Pune University, Pune, India*

Correspondence should be addressed to Santosh V. Purkar; svpurkar@kkwagh.edu.in and R. S. Deshpande; raj.deshpande@yahoo.co.in

Academic Editor: Youyun Xu

Heterogeneous wireless sensor network (HWSN) fulfills the requirements of researchers in the design of real life application to resolve the issues of unattended problem. But, the main constraint faced by researchers is the energy source available with sensor nodes. To prolong the life of sensor nodes and thus HWSN, it is necessary to design energy efficient operational schemes. One of the most suitable approaches to enhance energy efficiency is the clustering scheme, which enhances the performance parameters of WSN. A novel solution proposed in this article is to design an energy efficient clustering protocol for HWSN, to enhance performance parameters by EECPEP-HWSN. The proposed protocol is designed with three level nodes namely normal, advanced, and super, respectively. In the clustering process, for selection of cluster head we consider different parameters available with sensor nodes at run time that is, initial energy, hop count, and residual energy. This protocol enhances the energy efficiency of HWSN and hence improves energy remaining in the network, stability, lifetime, and hence throughput. It has been found that the proposed protocol outperforms than existing well-known LEACH, DEEC, and SEP with about 188, 150, and 141 percent respectively.

1. Introduction

Remote event sensing is possible by wireless sensor network, which is composed with certain number of small size sensor nodes with capabilities such as advanced processing, support for communication protocol, transceivers, and sensor with better sensitivity. As wireless sensor nodes or network is easy to deploy and manage, deployment may be uniform, linear, or random based on objectives. To record a real time event, large number of sensor nodes needs to be arrange systematically, such that information collection is possible for low intense and large threshold events for longer span of time. This indicates that the wireless sensor network (WSN) is a cost-effective networking solution for information updating in the coverage radius or in the sensing region. But, the main problem faced by WSN or wireless sensor node is its limited resources. Normally resources available are low storage, less processing power compared to complex instruction set computer, antenna system with limited gain, low energy backup or battery, and low bandwidth for communication. Depending on the application, WSN has its own respective constraints other than low energy backup. Some of the popular applications supported by WSN are in surveillance, forestry, weather forecasting, habitat monitoring, monitoring volcano activity, tracking target in military, machine health updating, inventory systems, and biomedical applications [1–3]. Very different classified applications of WSN are in geoinformatics system (GIS) and intelligent transport system (ITS) [3]. With these examples, applications can be categorized into social, industrial, medical, military, GIS and research field. As WSN is not only composed with wireless sensor nodes, but one of the most important element contributed for WSN is base station (BS) or sink node. To prolong the activity of event monitoring and information updation, it is very necessary to utilize the available energy from the network systematically. Hence, there is high demand to design and implement an energy efficient scheme to prolong the performance parameters. Design and implementation of an energy efficient scheme is the commonly suggested solution by researchers in the form of local and global energy saving such as sleep and wake-up strategy, data aggregation, overload reduction, single hop communication, multihop communication, and transmission power control inside WSN. Different approaches proposed by researchers are like data updating at BS through query, threshold, and time based approach [1–4]. Clustering based routing is the most suitable approach to support for load balancing, fault tolerance, and reliable communication and hence to prolong performance parameters of WSN. The clustering scheme has three elements as the cluster head (CH); one of the sensor nodes from respective area works as an intermediate node to transfer concise report of activity from the network in the form of aggregated data to the controller of system that is, BS. Finally, sensor nodes or cluster members (CM) collect and report the event information to CH regularly or as and when it is required. Indirectly, CH manages all CMs locally and utilizes the available resources systematically. CH also contributes for different responsibility towards the cluster such as channel allocation, intimation of power related information, relay information from lower level to higher level CH if needed, as well as reforms the cluster and controls the activity of routing based on distance from BS or CM. Finally, clustering scheme is the well-organized routing framework in the sensory system for the sake of energy conservation in WSN. However, clustering scheme provides better energy conservation in WSN, but at run time, there is variation in energy level at sensor nodes of WSN. Hence, network with different energy level nodes is formed. This type of network is referred as heterogeneous WSN and has no longer support to traditional designed clustering protocol, which is based on assumptions of equal energy capability nodes (homogeneous WSN). HWSN is synonymous to real time sensor system, which is composed with different capability nodes for monitoring different parameters. Hence, researchers turn their focus to design and develop clustering protocol for HWSN. Main components of HWSN are same as WSN like sensor nodes and BS, but in this sensor, nodes have different capability such as varied energy backup level, varied antenna system, high processing, and link capability. On the outset, high energy capability nodes is the best choice of all the varied features, as battery energy level controls all the varied features of sensor node. A higher energy backup node is the best choice from the available capabilities, as energy contributes for varied features of sensor nodes. There are the different approaches suggested by researchers to work with clustering scheme as mentioned in [1, 2]. All those approaches have their respective merits and demerits. In real time, application node whose battery energy level is lower than energy required for sensing accurately or processing is termed as dead node. Thus, energy optimization scheme is also being demanded because it minimizes the death of nodes from WSN. Metaheuristic approach is the preferable optimization scheme to enhance performance parameter. Although heuristic approaches support to extract the full

benefit of local energy saving and are greedy in nature for communication establishment, they are found to be less suitable for saving global energy as depicted in [5]. However, the metaheuristic approach is a full proof solution for energy efficiency and finding the best for global. We try to follow the metaheuristic approach for selecting the cluster head for HWSN with three different energy level nodes such as normal, advanced, and super as given in [6, 7]. In the proposed work, we present a distributed clustering approach in the form of hybrid of energy and communication cost. A novel protocol named Energy Efficient Clustering Protocol to Enhance Performance of HWSN (EECPEP-HWSN) is proposed here with different objectives: (i) select the best possible node to be the CH based on real time information, and (ii) enhance stability period and lifetime by reducing energy consumption in the form of reducing internal overhead and cost of processing energy. In the proposed clustering protocol, there is an assumption of random deployment or distribution of nodes, with the considerations that nodes in remote applications are randomly deployed. All nodes are location aware at the time of deployment. The issue we highlighted here is for the sake of load balancing and minimizing energy consumption of the network by dividing the network initially in four subsections called as zones based on population [8]. All the nodes have to work for the role of CH or CM but only one at particular cluster round. A certain amount of clusters and hence the CH generated inside the network at a time and there location is also known to the other member of network. In the proposed network model, everybody gets an opportunity to work as the CH or intermediate CH rather than the role of cluster member. The sensor node or member node plays its role of transferring collected data to respective zone CH, which is in the coverage range. It is well assured that the selected temporary CH and final CH are less likely in the or on the vicinity of network.

The proposed work is presented here in the following subsections as second section presents literature survey based on published literature and follow the energy consumption model from the same. Third section offers network details acquired for the proposed work in the form of network model, proposed work in the form of explanation of mathematical base is presented in the form of proposed protocol in fourth section, and proposed work simulation and performance parameters are explained in fifth section. Simulated work and its validation with existing well-known protocol is elaborated in section six, and final outcome of proposed work is presented in the form of conclusion with future scope in last section.

2. Literature Survey

Though the design and implementation of energy efficient clustering protocol are demanded, there are number of issues raised during real time working. Designing an energy efficient routing based on the cluster scheme to support heterogeneity, scalability, and hierarchy in topology are the main goals of researchers in the area of wireless sensor network to prolong the lifetime [1, 2]. Energy efficient clustering is possible by initiating load balancing among the nodes and must keep scheme excursion free in terms of energy. To prolong the lifetime of WSN or heterogeneous WSN, researchers put a lot of effort to design energy-efficient clustering scheme with a varied approach than clustering with hierarchical topology as presented in [3]. In this protocol, CH selection is based on calculating routing energy cost required by node with reference to BS from the respective group. Authors used the Gaussian elimination method to select the most feasible low-loss route with reference to node for the role of CH. The second point is that the CH node near to BS is selected as the first-level CH and CH node at longer distance as lower level CH. This offers the best suitable route discovery scheme to avoid loossy path (the path which have weak or lower energy nodes) and hence enhance energy efficiency, improves stability, and lifetime of the network. But this scheme has less consideration of selected CH position and less curious about energy consumption rate adopted by particular node. Hence there is high possibility of abrupt breakage in stability and hence reduced lifetime of the network. This is one of the best examples of multihop routing but it also possesses the limitations of multihop routing. In scalable environment, routing table was found to be huge and it imposed higher energy load on the respective node. To achieve greater energy efficiency and to reduce internal overhead, a different approach of dividing the available network into multiple clusters is proposed by Rana and Zaveri in the form of [9].

In this scheme, less loss energy path is selected with reference to nodes for the role of CH. Updation of energy information is needed regularly for selecting best suitable routing path, but it imposes extra load in case of scalable network. Sometimes the CH node may be at longer distance from BS, which increases energy consumption. To support load balancing and efficient resources, utilization in the form of single hop cluster routing for homogeneous WSN is initiated by Heinzelman et al. [10]. This is one of best protocols to support the objective of load balancing by providing chance to each and every node to become the CH over a life of network. But, the node which is elected as CH for particular round would never be CH again in the next $1/p$ round with probability of cluster head p. CH election is based on random number generation by nodes within the range of 0 to 1. The node whose values are less than the threshold $T(n)$ has been elected as cluster head for particular round. Once the node is elected as CH, then it publishes its identity and associated parameter in the form of advertise ADV message to the CM in the coverage zone. The CM replied to ADV with associated parameters like time slot acquired, energy level available, hop count, and so on. Based on the reply received from the CM nodes of its coverage, the CH prepares TDMA and publishes it on air. With this, everybody comes to know the time slot on which to participate for communication. Other than this slot period, a particular node can be in sleep state, to save energy. A merit from this work is that the CH role is rotated among available sensor nodes such that load balancing is achieved. With single-hop approach, considerable energy saving is possible. But, there are a higher number of demerits to compensate for merits as no basis of residual energy for the

selection of CH and rotation of CH impose possibility that the node elected as the CH is on the vicinity of network or in the vicinity. Lastly, as basis of centralized clustering approach is utilized for design, it is less suitable for scalable network. Minimizing this problem by the support of optimum number of cluster and using available energy faithfully is initiated by Wang et al. [11]. This protocol works on the principle of LEACH as per random approach, but with the consideration of residual energy and death toll calculation from BS. Decision based on the available time period before the complete energy depletion helps in CH selection. This improves the stability period and hence the lifetime of the network. This approach enhances the energy utilization with sacrifice of increased internal overheads, which requires high processing energy and impose load on network performance.

Extension of Low Energy Adaptive Clustering Hierarchy (LEACH) work is presented by Li and Liu [12]. The main objective of this work is to design an energy efficient clustering protocol to improve energy remaining in the network and prolong the lifetime of the network. This is to compensate for the assumptions of all equal energy nodes available inside the network during different clustering cycles. Hence, this protocol considers residual energy of the node and distance with respect to BS, and the other cluster member is considered for the selection of CH. The CH node with lower distance with respect to BS is treated as second level CH and the node with higher distance as level-1 CH. In this level-1, the CH transfers collected data on behalf of cluster to level-2 for further communication to BS. Hence the burden of communication (transmission) is reduced for level-1 CH and considerable energy saving in case of level-2 is achieved. Hence, energy utilization is systematic. But, to continue for next cycle, parameters need to be updated at the end of every cluster cycle. In this case, also CH selection threshold probability for both levels is different from normal LEACH, which results in energy excursion between two different CH selections. But, this scheme was unable to incorporate initial energy value in CH selection process. This scheme is less supportive in case of different capability nodes. To resolve the said issue, a solution in the form of Hybrid, Energy-Efficient, Distributed Clustering (HEED) protocol is proposed by Younis and Fahmy [13]. In this scheme, CH selection is based on node degree and residual energy with one addition parameter in the form of relative distance. The selected CH was found to be more faithful than earlier explained protocol. But, the selected node is less assured in network premises and hence results in higher energy dissipation. This leads to stability breakage, and hence lifetime is affected badly; designed protocol is not suitable for heterogeneous WSN and unable to explore average energy utilization.

Stable Elections Protocol (SEP) is introduced to enhance stability and lifetime of heterogeneous WSN by Smaragdakis et al. [14]. Two level energy nodes are introduced in this protocol namely, normal and advanced nodes. Basically in HWSN, nodes those are heterogenite in resources are less in percentage fraction. In this scheme, CH selection is based on available initial energy with nodes. Normally, the advanced node has higher energy level backup than its follower node. The probability of node to be the CH is different for both types of node, but mostly the advanced node has more chance to get selected as CH than normal node. In the study, increasing percentage factor of advanced nodes and hence probability of CH selection improves performance in the form of stability and lifetime, which also improves throughput of the network. Demerits of the said system are advanced node get punished badly as there is no reference of distance between selected CH node and BS, they have more chance to get selected as CH and hence reduce the network survival time of network. To reduce the possibility of selecting mostly one type of node (e.g.,advanced nodes) for the role of CH, a new approach called Distributed Energy- Efficient Clustering (DEEC) protocol is proposed by Qing et al. in [15]. Distributed energy efficient clustering (DEEC) is another HWSN clustering protocol having different approach of selecting CH. In DEEC, CH selection is based on ratio of residual energy to average energy of the network. By varying the epoch period, we can have a well-balanced scheme of CH selection for different types of node. The node whose energy level, initial or residual energy, is higher gets more chance to become CH than the node with low energy level. But, DEEC have the constraints as network lifetime is recorded and helping in computing reference energy available for further activity. DEEC have the same problem as SEP protocol as to punish advanced node badly and need to kept global knowledge of network. Elbhiri et al. presents a different approach from DEEC in the form of Developed Distributed Energy-Efficient Clustering protocol in [16]. In the study, they uses initial and residual energy to select CH. But, for the said selection, all the nodes must have global knowledge of the network. This scheme also uses the concept of computing reference energy for cluster round. This protocol has different probability of CH selection for different types of nodes. To resolve this up to certain level author of Enhanced Developed Distributed Energy-Efficient Clustering (EDDEEC) suggest CH selection criteria based on residual energy and average energy of the network, and change the probability of CH selection for different type of node [17]. As this protocol accounts for three different types of nodes, probability of CH selection is based on respective weights. This nonprobabilistic approach gives less importance to relative and average distance in selecting the CH node. This scheme also has lower association with other members; this can be improved by adding distance parameter in CH selection.

Other approach based on LEACH for HWSN with three different kinds of nodes is proposed by Kumar et al. [18]. In the study, CH selection is based on residual energy and relative distance in hierarchical clustering network. With hierarchical network, multilevel clusters are formed in case of scalable network. This creates unequal size of clusters inside the network. Hence, it affects the performance parameters supported by the protocol. Large numbers of clusters affect network survival time and hence reduce the stability and lifetime from the network.

Finally, one of the different approaches presented by author for exclusive network arrangement is given in [19]. In the study, clustering of multiple profile nodes are presented by the author and their structure topology is proposed in the form of multiple cluster. Nodes from different clusters communicate differently and form a virtual network of same type of nodes to initiate communication of event data updation. In this, nodes with smallest distance and better node degree will be selected as CH. But, selected CH may be at the vicinity and creates unnecessary energy dissipation. Hence, stability and lifetime get affected badly. A novel scheme of energy-efficient event driven hybrid routing protocol proposed by author in [20]. A main objective of this scheme is to distribute available heavy traffic evenly over the clustered network by offering unequal size cluster environment. Selected CH offers better node degree and hence achieves better energy efficiency. Cluster near the sink is normally of smaller size than moderate size cluster in the middle of the network. The approach of CH selection is based on available energy on routing path, nodes with higher energy on path selected as the best suitable node for the role of CH. This scheme enhances energy efficiency of the network and hence improves lifetime, but less assurance for selected node in the premises of network. Follow the strategy of multihop communication for information transfer. To enhance energy efficiency in HWSN with the feature of scalability taken into account, a new protocol was proposed by author in [21]. In this scheme, original hybrid energy efficient distributed (HEED) work is explored through the base of fuzzy logic with three different types of nodes. CH selection is based on node density, residual energy, and the distance between node and sink. Fuzzy logic is used to calculate the most probable node to be CH for further activity of network. About 27 different combinations are evaluated for best suitable node selection. But, again control heads for network management are higher and consume greater energy for CH calculation. Probability function value changed for every iteration imposes burden on network energy. Though there are multiple schemes available to prolong performance parameters of HWSN, all those are somehow are less faithful to really enhance the energy efficiency of WSN without considering their CH selection criteria and network model support.

Hence to design and implement energy efficient clustering with heterogeneous WSN, a novel approach of CH selection is proposed in this article such that energy utilization of the network is improved. Hence, all respective performance parameters get improved.

2.1. Motivation. There are certain issues found in the abovementioned clustering protocols in terms of faithful CH selection, energy-efficient cluster formation, and network management. There is the CH selection criteria indirectly linked with probabilistic approach or connected to threshold $T(n)$ with probabilistic approach. By varying the CH selection criteria it is possible to select most promising node to be CH, but it increases internal overhead. Sometimes, the node selected as CH is at the vicinity or in the vicinity, which increases the energy consumption in the network and hence reduces the performance of network. So, the node with this position is not suitable for the role of CH. Hence, the nodes must have better internal parameter and better connectivity with nodes and mainly situated in the premises of network. Hence, a better CH selection approach enhances the performance parameters of the network.

2.2. Energy Consumption Model. Communication section consists of transmitter and receiver; transmitter section of sensor nodes consumes energy to run radio electronics and amplifier circuit. On the contrary, the receiver section consumes energy only in the receiving packet at radio electronics over communicating distance [5, 14]. If the communication entities separated by distance d is less than a threshold distance, then free space energy consumption model is used for energy expenditure calculation else multipath model is utilized. Data aggregation feature is incorporated for CH to BS delivery is same as [5, 14]. While transmitting a packet of length L to a distance d, energy expenditure is calculations are presented in (1).

Here, parameters involved have their respective significance as E_{elec} is the energy consumed by transmitting or receiving electronics circuitry to process single bit information. E_{tx} and E_{rx} are the energies consumed by transmitting and receiving section to process data packet of length L, which also depend on digital coding and on digital modulation scheme utilized. E_{fs} and E_{mp} are the amount of transmitter amplifier expenses in the form of energy required for free space model (free space energy loss) and for multipath model, respectively. Main classified information about amplifier (power amplifier) is to control the setting of power such that if communication distance d between sender and receiver is less than d_0, then free space power loss model is to be considered for energy calculation.

The energy required at transmitter side with free space model is

$$E_{tx}(L, d) = LE_{elec} + LE_{fs}d^2 \quad d \ll d_0. \tag{1}$$

If the distance d is greater than threshold distance, then multipath model is utilized for energy expenses calculation as

$$E_{tx}(L, d) = LE_{elec} + LE_{mp}d^4 \quad d \gg d_0. \tag{2}$$

Energy consumption at receiver side is

$$E_{rx}(L, d) = LE_{elec}, \tag{3}$$

where L is the length of data packet in number of bit for communication. Calculation of d_0 is

$$d_0 = \frac{\sqrt{E_{fs}}}{\sqrt{E_{mp}}}. \tag{4}$$

3. Network Model

In the proposed network model, we use three-level node energy heterogeneity. The network model consists of n randomly deployed sensor nodes on $M \times M$ sensing layout. It is predefined as all the nodes including BS are static on postdeployment. Communication links between each other are assumed to be symmetric [14]. The CH on behalf of

sensing network is responsible to forward collected data directly to BS. All supervisory and unsupervisory data messages are transacted through wireless links.

Initially, network layout is divided in four zones based on population, and BS is at the center of network field. Every node has the capability to sense, aggregate, and forward the data. It is a prime consideration that the node always have data for transfer. Nodes namely normal, advanced, and super with increasing order of energy level as presented in [14]. For our simulation, we are using energy increment factor of about twice the former. Hence, in the proposed protocol, we have three-level energy value of heterogeneity as E_0, E_{Adv}, and E_{Super} for energy of normal, advanced, and super nodes, respectively. Nodes with percentage population factor as a for advanced nodes with total n nodes, which is equipped with energy factor greater than m times than normal node. Super nodes are equipped with energy incrementing factor as m_0, with percentage population factor a_0 with respect to total n nodes. Individual node details in the form of equation are presented as follows.

Initial energy for normal nodes is E_0 with population count as $n(1 - a - a_0)$. Subsequently, advanced and super node populations are na and na_0, respectively. Energy available with advanced and super node is E_{Adv} and E_{Super}, respectively.

Energy calculations for respective nodes are as follows:
Energy contributed by the normal node is

$$E_{normal} = nE_0(1 - a - a_0). \tag{5}$$

Energy by the advanced node is

$$E_{Adv} = nE_0(1 + m)a. \tag{6}$$

Energy due to the super node is

$$E_{Super} = nE_0(1 + m_0)a_0. \tag{7}$$

Equations (5–7) present energy available with all three types of nodes. Total initial energy proposed in the network model is calculated as E_{Tot}:

$$E_{Tot} = E_{normal} + E_{Adv} + E_{Super}, \tag{8}$$

$$E_{Tot} = nE_0 - naE_0 - na_0E_0 + naE_0 + nE_0ma \\ + na_0E_0 + na_0m_0E_0. \tag{9}$$

In (9), it is found that the second and fourth terms are of equal magnitude and are out of phase. Terms third and sixth are of the same magnitude and are out of phase. Hence, (9) is rewritten as

$$E_{Tot} = nE_0 + nE_0ma + na_0m_0E_0 = nE_0(1 + ma + m_0a_0). \tag{10}$$

Hence, from (10), we hereby conclude that if we add heterogeneity level up to level-2, available energy increased by factor $(1 + ma)$, and if it is increased to level 3, then energy increased by factor $(1 + ma + m_0a_0)$. If we would like to improve heterogeneity to "N" level greater than 2, then the equation is modified as given below:

$$E_{\text{Tot}} = nE_0 \left(1 + ma + \sum_{i=0}^{N} (m_i a_i) \right), \quad i = 0, \ldots, N, \quad (11)$$

where N can be any integer number.

It means that the network with N level heterogeneity has energy level $(1 + ma + \sum_{i=0}^{N} (m_i a_i))$ times greater than normal nodes involved in network (Homogeneous Wireless Sensor Network), but the constraints of node energy heterogeneity level is greater than 2.

In the proposed scheme, the CH selection approach is nonprobabilistic rather than probabilistic. We can very well calculate other supporting parameters involved in clustering processes as follows.

Number of rounds supported by the network before complete death can be calculated as

$$R = \frac{E_{\text{Tot}}}{E_{\text{Round}}}, \quad (12)$$

where R is denoted as total number of rounds supported by network before death of all nodes. E_{Round} is the energy dissipated by the network for completing one round and can be calculated as

$$E_{\text{Round}} = K \left(2nE_{\text{elec}} + nE_{\text{DA}} + LE_{\text{mp}} d_{\text{to BS}}^4 + nE_{\text{fs}} d_{\text{to CH}}^2 \right), \quad (13)$$

where K is the optimal number of clusters generated, E_{DA} is the data aggregation energy for CH, $d_{\text{to BS}}$ is the distance between CH to BS, and $d_{\text{to CH}}$ is the distance between cluster members to CH.

$d_{\text{to BS}}$ and $d_{\text{to CH}}$ are calculated as

$$d_{\text{to CH}} = \frac{M}{\sqrt{2\pi K}},$$
$$d_{\text{to BS}} = 0.765 \frac{M}{2}. \quad (14)$$

Taking the derivative of E_{Round} with respect to k and equating it zero gives optimum number of cluster heads K_{opt} and is calculated as

$$K_{\text{opt}} = \frac{\sqrt{n}}{\sqrt{2\pi}} \times \frac{\sqrt{E_{\text{fs}}}}{\sqrt{E_{\text{mp}}}} \times \frac{M}{d_{\text{to BS}}^2}, \quad (15)$$

$$P_{\text{opt}} = \frac{K_{\text{opt}}}{n},$$

where $P_{\text{opt}} = 0.1$ is the optimum probability of number of clusters.

4. Proposed Protocol

Main objectives of proposed energy efficient clustering protocol are to reduce internal overheads of network management, reduce the possibility of selected CH on the vicinity, and support scalability. Select the node for the role of CH such that the CM is able to communicate to BS in a fair way, without introducing extra load on other nodes. Selection of CH must be with run time parameter. At the end

of every cluster cycle, all nodes update their parameter information to BS. Design clustering protocol must support scalability features. With all these objectives, we are presenting here a novel scheme of energy efficient clustering protocol to enhance performance metrics of HWSN. Initially, all the nodes are deployed randomly in equal percentage over the network; the network is divided into four sections based on population density in the form of zone A, Zone B, zone C, and zone D as given in [8].

$$\text{Total network area} = \text{area } (A + B + C + D). \quad (16)$$

This scheme reduces the internal overhead for network management; this improves the energy utilization and enhances energy remaining in the network at run time. Some of the issues of existing clustering protocol are such as cluster size is arbitrary, selected CH is located towards the boundary of the network and hence energy depletes at faster rate. This affects the network survival time and network performance. In the proposed work, we are selecting the node for the role of CH is based on real time parameter available with the sensor node. We introduce a very new profile parameter named as Node Quality Index or Node Index (NI), which is a fusion of node real-time parameters. Node Quality Index is the devised parameter based on initial energy, residual energy, and the hop count required by particular node with respect to base station. As for CH selection based on energy, there are some of the criteria such as initial energy with node must be high enough to handle the role of CH for cluster management activity such as advertisement, frame formation, and data packet transaction with respect to BS (energy greater than or equal to this is expected), after cluster round, energy remaining with the node must be high enough to handle the responsibility of sensor node (higher energy level is expected such that node can be CH in upcoming rounds), and the assurance of aliveness and finally node must be moderately or nearly situated from the base station. The selected CH will be able to support scalable network for multihop communication. Mathematical representation of the proposed scheme is presented in the form of mathematical model given below.

4.1. Protocol Explanation. In this proposed work, we are presenting a new approach of CH selection by introducing a very new parameter named as Node Quality Index (Q_{ni}). Node Quality Index is the fusion of initial energy of the node, current available energy at run time, and hop count with respect to base station. For devising node index, we are using index modelling from the available different modelling approaches of database system.

Before the execution of the above-mentioned steps, one of the important phases needs to execute for faithful execution of complete algorithm as for some clustering cycle, and it is found that most of the nodes have equal value of NI. So filtering phenomenon is found to be complex, and to minimize the complexity, we incorporate LEACH policy for selecting CH for small number of rounds (e.g., 50 rounds). With this approach, we initially have the approach of load

Prerequisites:
  (i) All nodes are location aware and updated with neighbor information.
  (ii) Nodes always have data ready to transfer at every cluster cycle.
  (1) Start
  (2) Nodes from each zone send their respective attributes to BS
  (3) BS collect and update it in database
  (4) BS calculate NI for each node for every zone
  (5) BS list number of nodes with NI
  (6) Calculate the average value of NI
  (7) BS compare calculated NI with Average NI
  (8) Number of nodes whose value greater than average NI are listed
  (9) Nodes those are about ±10% of boundary are sorted zone wise
  (10) Nodes those are on the verge are filtered if other member is available from the zone
  (11) Intimate nodes from each zone as selected temporary CH for that zone
  (12) Node whose value greater than average NI of competitive nodes selected as Final CH on behalf of network
  (13) Temporary CH updated with final CH
  (14) Before transferring data packet to BS, temporary CH has to check distance with respect to BS and final CH
  (15) If distance between final CH is greater than BS, then send collected data packet to BS directly
  (16) Final CH send only collected data packets from others to BS
  (17) Again back to step 2.

ALGORITHM 1

balancing; with initial network division, we achieved improved energy utilization (in the form of reduced internal overheads), and the size of formed cluster is controllable than the arbitrary size of network [8]. We target the applications with proposed protocol are such as in surveillances, weather forecasting, home automation, traffic management, habitat monitoring, in machine health analysis, and inventory management.

The fundamental CH solution applied for proposed work is

$$CH_i = \begin{cases} Q_{ni} > Avg_i, & \text{for } i > 50 \\ Q_{ni}\dfrac{P_i}{1 - P_i\,(rmod)\,(1/P_i)} & \text{for } i = 0 \text{ to } 50, \end{cases} \quad (17)$$

where $Avg_i = \left(\sum_{i=0}^{n} Q_{ni}/|Q_{ni}|\right)$.
Boundary = boundary of network layout ±10%.

$$CH_i = [\text{boundary} \cap (Q_{ni} > Avg_i)]. \quad (18)$$

5. Simulation Parameters

This section highlights the parameters set for implementation and performance validation for simulation work. Some of those are explained as follows:

  (i) *Stability period*: The time period before the death of very first node from available sensor nodes of operating WSN (HWSN).

  (ii) *Number of alive nodes per cluster round*: Number of nodes alive from the network for every cluster round, which indirectly presents the available energy remaining in the network.

  (iii) *Number of dead nodes per cluster round*: Number of nodes dead per cluster round against changing

energy level inside the network during network survival time. This factor indirectly presents death rate of nodes over cluster cycle. Which indicate possible lifetime remains with network in the form of cluster round.

  (iv) *Throughput*: Number of data packets sent from the sensor nodes towards base station over the cluster round presents amount of throughput per cluster round. Amount of throughput signifies energy efficient utilization of available network resources. Throughput presents quality of the network.

Parameter set utilized for the purpose of simulation is presented in the form of Table 1.

6. Discussion

This section focuses on implementation strategy and results of our simulated work and its validation with well-known published protocol such as LEACH, SEP, and DEEC.

With reference to parameter set given in Table 1, we randomly deploy the network in 200 m × 200 m form. Divide the network into four zones based on population; placement of BS is at the center of the network with position (100 × 100). Total node population over the network is 200, with percentage fraction factor $a = 0.2$ and $a_0 = 0.1$. With advanced node energy value about to double the normal node energy, super node energy value is also about twice of advanced node.

6.1. Validation with LEACH Protocol. As we know LEACH strategy is best suitable for improving lifetime of WSN by offering an equal opportunity to everybody to become a CH and balance the energy consumption as proposed in [10]. But it is a random selection of CH; there is no reference of residual energy as well as hop count of selected CH with reference to

TABLE 1: Simulation parameter.

Serial Number	Parameter symbol	Name	Value
1	$M \times M$	Network area	$200\,\mathrm{m} \times 200\,\mathrm{m}$
2	N	Number of nodes	200
3	E_0	Initial energy of nodes	0.5–1.5 J
4	L	Data packet size	4000 bits
5	E_{elec}	Radio electronics energy	50 nJ/bit
6	E_{efs}	Free space energy	$10\,\mathrm{pJ/bit/m^2}$
7	E_{mp}	Amplification energy	$0.0013\,\mathrm{pJ/bit/m^4}$
8	E_{DA}	Data aggregation energy	5 nJ/bit/signal
9	d_0	Threshold distance	87–87.7 m
10	BS	Sink node	(100, 100)

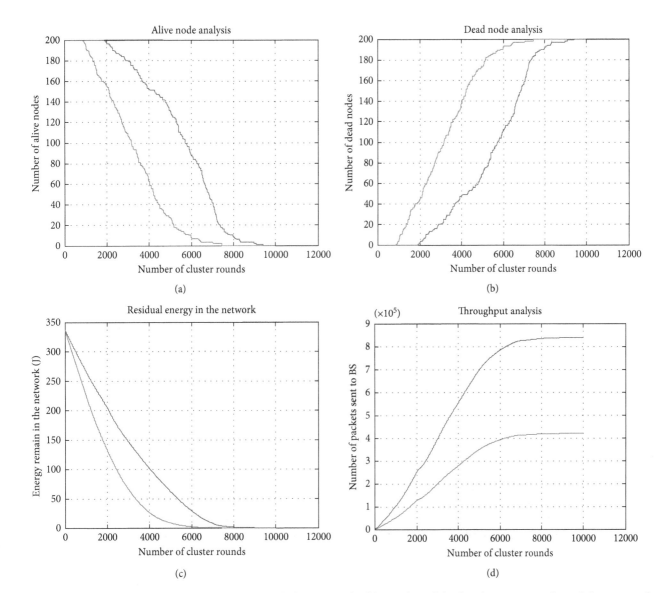

FIGURE 1: (a) Number of alive nodes versus number of cluster rounds. (b) Number of dead nodes versus number of cluster rounds. (c) Energy remaining in the network versus number of cluster rounds. (d) Number of data packets sent to BS versus number of cluster rounds.

BS. Hence, our protocol outperforms than the LEACH with this aspect in the form of stability period and lifetime presented in Figures 1(a) and 1(b). Colour used for presentation is blue for the proposed protocol and red colour is used for the former protocol. As per LEACH, there is less guarantee that the selected node is inside the network premises and not on the verge of vicinity or in the vicinity. Assumption of single hop and arbitrary cluster size decreases the energy efficiency of the

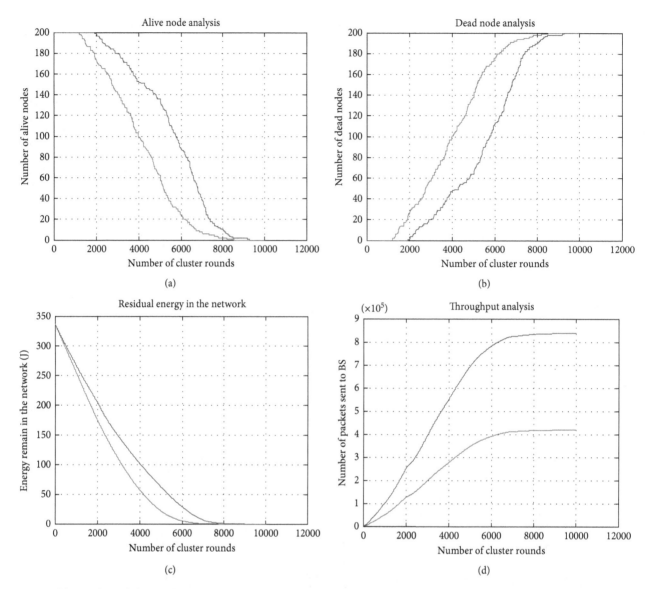

FIGURE 2: (a) Number of alive nodes versus number of cluster rounds. (b) Number of dead nodes versus number of cluster rounds. (c) Energy remaining in the network versus number of cluster rounds. (d) Number of data packets sent to BS versus number of cluster rounds.

network. The proposed protocol solves this issue with reduction in internal overhead packets, well assured selected CH, and in the network premises. Hence, controlled energy utilization results in improved energy remaining in the network than LEACH protocol as shown in Figure 1(c). Finally, available energy is utilized efficiently and systematically for longer span of time improves throughput from the network shown in Figure 1(d).

6.2. Validation with SEP Protocol. As selection of CH is based on energy rather than the random selection of LEACH, it offers best suitable node to be CH. In LEACH, probability of node to be CH is equal for all nodes, but in SEP, probability of CH selection is different for two different nodes. Hence, it offers better performance than LEACH protocol in heterogeneous WSN. Basically SEP is proposed to introduce energy heterogeneity in WSN, that is, in the form of advanced nodes other

than normal node as per [14]. But in the SEP protocol, there are two levels of probability function to differentiate between advanced and normal node for the role of CH. This varies energy level excursion and hence energy remain in the network fluctuate greatly. Finally, depleting the energy faster results in reduced performance parameters of the network. It normally punishes the high energy node and results in reduction of stability period and lifetime. As shown in Figure 2(a), lifetime Figure 2(b) and energy remaining in the network Figure 2(c) are compared with the proposed protocol. The graph is presented with two colours as red is used for former protocol and blue is used for proposed protocol. As the proposed protocol is free from the varying probability function and changing energy level utilization, it improves energy remaining in the network or residual energy in the network and enhances the stability period, lifetime, and hence number of data packets sent towards base station in the form of Figure 2(d).

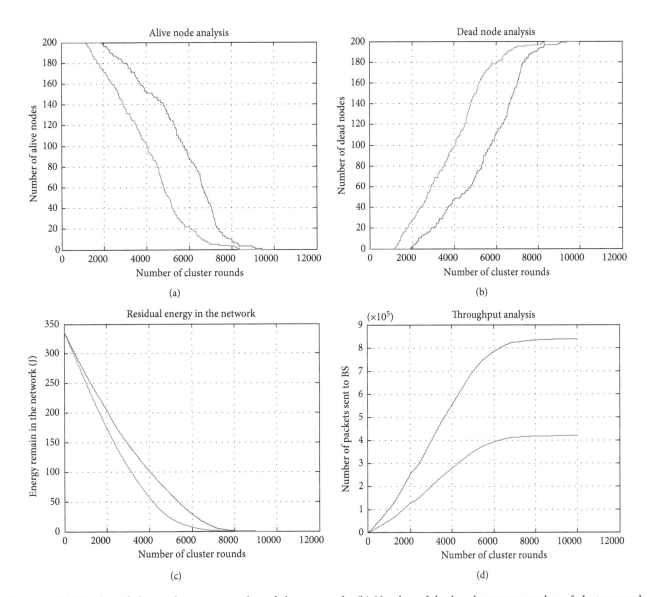

FIGURE 3: (a) Number of alive nodes versus number of cluster rounds. (b) Number of dead nodes versus number of cluster rounds. (c) Energy remaining in the network versus number of cluster rounds. (d) Number of data packets sent to BS versus number of cluster rounds.

TABLE 2: Performance validation table.

Serial Number	Name of the protocol to be simulated					% enhancement on		
	Performance parameter	LEACH	SEP	DEEC	Proposed	LEACH	SEP	DEEC
1	First node death (stability)	874	1206	1136	1931	221	160	170
2	Tenth node death	1345	1903	1710	2896	215	152	170
3	All nodes death (lifetime)	7254	8199	8375	9284	128	113	110
Overall performance parameter improvement with proposed protocol						**188**	**141**	**150**

6.3. *Validation with DEEC Protocol.* DEEC protocol proposed by author with the approach of average energy in the network and initial lifetime calculations in the form of number of round are given in [15]. In this protocol, global knowledge of the network needs to be updated, and probability threshold function also plays an important role for CH selection. As there is variation in energy level during real-time operation inside the network, computing the average energy reference for the CH selection for subsequent cluster round calculation is affected by energy balancing inside the network. One more point needed to be highlighted is that different probability functions incorporate inside the protocol, which has bad effects on energy remain in the network. Hence, reduce the lifetime of sensor network as depicted in Figures 3(a) and 3(b) in the form of blue and red colour. Energy unbalancing of DEEC is depicted in the form of energy remaining in the network as in Figure 3(c). Throughput of the former protocol is also getting reduced, presented in Figure 3(d). However, the proposed protocol does not have any varying probability function, and the criteria for CH selection are deterministic. Hence, the proposed protocol outperforms than the former DEEC.

Some of the figures in Table 2 are recorded from the simulation based on the parameter set given in Table 1. Here, the first value represents stability that is nothing, but first sensor node death occurred during operation. Second value is for tenth dead node, which is the death of 10th working node from network field to estimate death rate with working protocol and to find maximum possible lifetime remain with network. Finally, Lifetime is the parameter which depicts the death of all deployed sensor nodes from the network. Table 2 shows statistics for validating the proposed protocol simulation based on performance parameters such as stability, death of tenth node, and lifetime in the form of cluster round, which depicts that the proposed design outperforms for HWSN, which is based on energy heterogeneity. Hence, the proposed clustering protocol supports load balancing, and also it improves stability and lifetime of network than the former well-known protocols.

7. Conclusion

In the proposed clustering protocol of HWSN, selection of CH is based on newly devised parameter in the form of node index depending on current available energy, initial energy, and hop count from the base station. The node selected for the role of temporary CH of each zone is situated off the vicinity and at a limited distance from BS. This approach assures available energy utilized for the sake of data manipulation and communication, it leads to improved energy remaining in the network and enhance the throughput from the network. Finally, the node which has a better value of NI than temporary selected CH and of the vicinity can be the final CH. Other achievement with proposed approach is internal overheads getting reduced to greater extent with the initial division of network in sections. Due to this, formed clusters have controlled size than arbitrary size cluster of the earlier protocols. All these approaches contribute to improve energy efficiency; force to enhance stability period and lifetime; and improve residual energy of the network and hence throughput than existing protocol.

We try to explore our proposed work with a different mechanism as spanning tree for route finding, try to use the mobile sink scheme to enhance the performance of the proposed design and finally try to use weight calculation method based on different parameters associated with sensor node for finding the best possible node as the CH for the role of CH.

References

[1] A. A. Abbasi and M. Younis, "A survey on clustering algorithms for wireless sensor networks," *Computer Communications*, vol. 30, no. 14–15, pp. 2826–2841, 2007.

[2] S. V. Purkar and R. S. Deshpande, "A review on energy efficient clustering protocols of heterogeneous wireless sensor network," *International Journal of Engineering and Technology*, vol. 9, no. 3, pp. 2514–2527, 2017.

[3] S. A. Nikolidakis, D. Kandris, D. D. Vergados, and C. Douligeris, "Energy efficient routing in wireless sensor networks through balanced clustering," *Algorithms*, vol. 6, no. 1, pp. 29–42, 2013.

[4] G. Abdul-Salaam, A. H. Abdullah, M. H. Anisi, A. Gani, and A. Alelaiwi, "A comparative analysis of energy conservation approaches in hybrid wireless sensor networks data collection protocols," *Telecommunication Systems*, vol. 16, no. 1, pp. 159–179, 2016.

[5] S. Singh, A. Malik, and R. Kumar, "Energy efficient heterogeneous DEEC protocol for enhancing lifetime in WSNs," *Engineering Science and Technology an International Journal*, vol. 20, no. 1, pp. 345–353, 2017.

[6] A. Kashaf, N. Javaid, Z. A. Khan, and I. A. Khan, "TSEP: threshold-sensitive stable election protocol for WSNs," in *Proceedings of the 10th International Conference on Frontiers of Information Technology*, pp. 164–168, Islamabad, Pakistan, December 2012.

[7] P. Saini and A. K. Sharma, "E-DEEC-enhanced distributed energy efficient clustering scheme for heterogeneous WSN," in *Proceedings of the 1st International Conference on Parallel, Distributed and Grid Computing (PDGC 2010)*, pp. 205–210, Solan, India, October 2010.

[8] B. Manzoor, N. Javaid, O. Rehman et al., "Q-LEACH: a new routing protocol for WSNs," in *Proceedings of the International Workshop on Body Area Sensor Networks (BASNet-2013), SciVerse Science Direct 2013*, vol. 19, pp. 926–931, Halifax, NS, Canada, June 2013.

[9] K. Rana and M. Zaveri, "Synthesized cluster head selection and routing for two tier wireless sensor network," *Journal of Computer Network and Communications*, vol. 2013, Article ID 578241, 11 pages, 2013.

[10] W. R. Heinzelman, A. Chandrakasan, and H. Balakrishnan, "Energy-efficient communication protocol for wireless microsensor networks," in *Proceedings of the Hawaii International Conference on System Sciences*, pp. 1–10, Maui, HI, USA, January 2000.

[11] M. Y. Wang, J. Ding, W. Chen, and W. Guan, "SEARCH: a stochastic election approach for heterogeneous wireless sensor networks," *IEEE Communications letters*, vol. 19, no. 3, pp. 443–446, 2015.

[12] H. Li and J. Liu, "Double cluster based energy efficient routing protocol for wireless sensor network," *International Journal of Wireless Information Networks*, vol. 23, no. 1, pp. 40–48, 2016.

[13] O. Younis and S. Fahmy, "HEED: a hybrid, energy-efficient, distributed clustering approach for ad-hoc sensor networks," *IEEE Transactions on Mobile Computing*, vol. 3, pp. 366–379, 2004.

[14] G. Smaragdakis, I. Matta, and A. Bestavros, "SEP: a stable election protocol for clustered heterogeneous wireless sensor network," in *Proceedings of the Second International Workshop on Sensor and Actuator Network Protocols and Applications (SANPA'04)*, pp. 1–6, Boston, MA, USA, August 2004.

[15] L. Qing, Q. Zhu, and M. Wang, "Design of a distributed energy-efficient clustering algorithm for heterogeneous wireless sensor network," *Computer Communications*, vol. 29, no. 12, pp. 2230–2237, 2006.

[16] B. Elbhiri, R. Saadane, S. E. Fkihi, and D. Aboutajdine, "Developed distributed energy-efficient clustering (DDEEC) for

heterogeneous wireless sensor networks," in *Proceedings of the 5th International Symposium on I/V Communications and Mobile Network (ISVC)*, pp. 1–4, Rabat, Morocco, September–October 2010.

[17] N. Javaid, M. B. Rasheed, M. Imran et al., "An energy-efficient distributed clustering algorithm for heterogeneous WSNs," *EURASIP Journal on Wireless Communications and Networking, Springer*, vol. 2015, p. 151, 2015.

[18] D. Kumar, T. C. Aseri, and R. B. Patel, "EEHC: energy efficient heterogeneous cluster scheme for wireless sensor networks," *Computer Communication*, vol. 32, no. 4, pp. 662–667, 2009.

[19] J. Lloret, M. Garcia, D. Bri, and J. R. Diaz, "A cluster-based architecture to structure the topology of wireless sensor networks," *Sensors*, vol. 9, no. 12, pp. 10513–10544, 2009.

[20] M. Faheem, M. Z. Abbas, G. Tuna, and V. C. Gungor, "EDHRP: energy efficient event driven hybrid routing protocol for densely deployed wireless sensor networks," *Journal of Network and Computer Applications*, vol. 58, pp. 309–326, 2015.

[21] S. Chand, S. Singh, and B. Kumar, "Heterogeneous HEED protocol for wireless sensor networks," *Wireless Personal Communications*, vol. 77, no. 3, pp. 2117–2139, 2014.

4

Wormhole Detection based on Ordinal MDS using RTT in Wireless Sensor Network

Saswati Mukherjee,[1] **Matangini Chattopadhyay,**[1]
Samiran Chattopadhyay,[2] **and Pragma Kar**[1]

[1]*School of Education Technology, Jadavpur University, Kolkata, India*
[2]*Department of Information Technology, Jadavpur University, Kolkata, India*

Correspondence should be addressed to Saswati Mukherjee; saswatimuk@gmail.com

Academic Editor: Gianluigi Ferrari

In wireless communication, wormhole attack is a crucial threat that deteriorates the normal functionality of the network. Invasion of wormholes destroys the network topology completely. However, most of the existing solutions require special hardware or synchronized clock or long processing time to defend against long path wormhole attacks. In this work, we propose a wormhole detection method using range-based topology comparison that exploits the local neighbourhood subgraph. The Round Trip Time (RTT) for each node pair is gathered to generate neighbour information. Then, the network is reconstructed by ordinal Multidimensional Scaling (MDS) followed by a suspicion phase that enlists the suspected wormholes based on the spatial reconstruction. Iterative computation of MDS helps to visualize the topology changes and can localize the potential wormholes. Finally, a verification phase is used to remove falsely accused nodes and identify real adversaries. The novelty of our algorithm is that it can detect both short path and long path wormhole links. Extensive simulations are executed to demonstrate the efficacy of our approach compared to existing ones.

1. Introduction

Security issues of a Wireless Sensor Network (WSN) are a significant concern since sensors are deployed in a hostile environment. Sensor nodes are vulnerable to both external and internal attacks. Wormhole attack is a type of external attack initiated by pairs of colluding attackers as shown in Figure 1. These pairs of colluding attackers are connected by low latency links, namely, wormhole links. In this paper, the phrase "wormhole links" is synonymously used as "wormhole tunnels". High frequency or wired links are used to establish these low latency links. At one end of the link the attacker captures the packets, tunnels them via wormhole link, and replays the packets at the other end once the link is established [1]. Thus, the distant sensor nodes around the two ends of wormhole links consider each other as neighbours although they are far from each other. Each wormhole node is capable of faking a route that is shorter than the original route. By building this high speed tunnel, a wormhole attack can disrupt the routing mechanism, attract a large amount of traffic, and also launch selective forwarding attack. Moreover, the wormhole links also exploit some sophisticated attacks like man-in-the-middle attack, cipher breaking attack, and denial of service attack.

Several solutions have been proposed to repulse wormhole attack in the literature. However, most of the techniques have their own limitations like requirements of synchronized clock [2], positioning device, or directional antenna [3], which increase the hardware cost of the system. Some existing solutions use neighbour mismatch method [1], Round Trip Time (RTT) calculation with message encryption using hash function [4], and topological comparison using new packet type [5]. But these solutions have certain limitations like wormholes remaining undetected in sparse network, increased message overhead, and so forth. In addition, some localization-based approaches are proposed to relax these limitations. However, most of them have some restrictions. For example, node labelling scheme requires neighbour

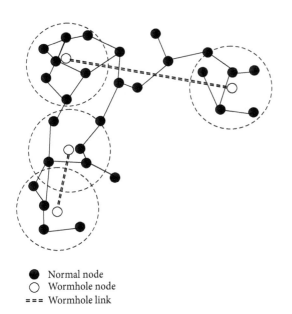

● Normal node
○ Wormhole node
=== Wormhole link

FIGURE 1: Wormhole attack scenario.

finding approach, which restricts its efficiency in large scale networks. In short, the severity of effects of wormhole attack in WSN, countermeasures, and their limitations motivate us to propose a novel efficient scheme to defend against wormhole attacks.

Wormhole tunnels can be of two types: long path and short path. In long path wormhole tunnel, the colluding pair of wormhole nodes is positioned far away from each other whose distance is equivalent to k hops where k is greater than a sufficiently large constant. Long path wormhole tunnels have diverse and significant effect on the network topology since it partitions the network into two or more subnetworks. On the other hand, in short path wormhole tunnels, the wormhole nodes at both ends of the tunnel are relatively shorter than 2 hops distance. Although short path wormhole tunnels do not partition the network, they increase packet dropping and, hence, network traffic is affected. Short path wormhole tunnels may have interferences or overlapping ranges which makes them even more difficult to be identified by normal range-based detection techniques.

Long path wormholes have been studied in [6–8]. In this paper, we have proposed algorithms for detection of long path as well as short path wormhole tunnels.

In this work, we propose a novel range-based topology comparison method for wormhole detection in WSN. Behaviour of wormhole attackers in the network disrupts the network connectivity; so, an abnormal network structure is introduced by the wormholes which needs to be explored. Each node gathers the RTT of a message and measures the distance from its neighbours. Based on this distance, a neighbourhood subgraph is generated. Then, by using shortest path algorithm, an estimation distance matrix is constructed between all node pairs. Next, we apply the ordinal Multidimensional Scaling (MDS) on the estimation distance matrix to restructure the subgraph and embed it on a plane. Ordinal MDS takes this estimation distance matrix as input and produces a spatial configuration of nodes by assigning

virtual node positions (i.e., node coordinates). The estimated distances between the node pairs are ranked and are compared with the virtual distance for monotonicity relation. The disparity caused by the disagreement of the rank order is reduced via iterative computation of node coordinates and the corresponding virtual distance is updated until the virtual distance agrees with the rank order of the estimated shortest distance. The underlying observation of our wormhole detection is as follows. If i is a wormhole then a deviation can be observed between the virtual distance and the estimated distance even after iterative computation of virtual coordinates of the nodes. Otherwise, if i is a normal node, the virtual distance is a mere approximation of the estimated distance. The nodes which are violating the monotonic property are put to the suspect node set. Then, a filtering technique is used to determine the real wormhole link from the suspect node set.

It is well studied in [9] that the wormhole nodes hide the tunneling/propagation delay when radio transmission is used. So, this characteristic can be used to detect short path wormhole tunnel instead of relying solely on topological features of the network. Hence, we consider using the RTT of a message. We assume that the wormhole nodes connected by short path are present in the network if RTT of a message between two ends of a short wormhole path is abnormally less than the $1/k$ times of the average RTT of all normal links.

The main contributions of this work are as follows.

(i) We propose a wormhole detection algorithm that can defend both the long path and the short path wormhole links. For long path wormholes, there are almost no false positives but, for short path wormhole tunnels, some false positives do exist.

(ii) Our approach does not require any deterministic threshold to generate probable wormholes.

(iii) We adopt a method to eliminate the true nodes which are initially suspected.

(iv) Our proposed method has been compared with the state-of-the-art TRM method [1], WORMEROS [4], and MDS-based local connectivity [7]. Our method can detect all wormhole nodes with fewer false positives.

The rest of the paper is organized as follows. Section 2 presents the previous research efforts that contribute to our approach. In Section 3, the model definition of our work is introduced. Section 4 presents the detailed outline of our approach. Three principal modules of the proposed mechanism: efficient network reconstruction, suspicion phase, and verification phase, are described in detail. In Section 5, influence of several parameters and time complexity of our approach are discussed. Section 6 presents the experimental results obtained through simulation. Section 7 concludes the paper and discusses the future extensions.

2. Related Work

2.1. Wormhole Detection in Wireless Networks. There are several approaches for wormhole attack detection based on the symptoms introduced by wormhole links.

The first line of defence is based on special hardware devices that use geographical leashes and temporal leashes [2]. Leash is information added to the packet in order to defend wormhole attack. In geographical leashes, GPS technology is required to capture the node location included in the packets and all the nodes require loosely synchronized clock. Temporal leash ensures that each packet transmitted between source and destination nodes has packet expiration time which limits the maximum travel distance. All the nodes need to have tightly synchronized clock. However, to protect the leash, authentication data is added to the packet which increase the communication and processing overhead. In [3], directional antennas are used to locate the infeasible communication; however, it mitigates wormhole problems partially and degrades network connectivity by rejecting legitimate neighbours. Čapkun and others [10] proposed mutual authentication with distance-bounding algorithm to detect wormhole attacks without requiring any clock synchronization. But this approach uses special hardware for accurate time measurements. All these countermeasures increase the hardware cost of the system and are impractical in resource constraint devices.

The second line of defence relies on RTT of the packets and topology comparison [5]. Clock synchronization is an issue for distance estimation between source and destination for every packet but topology comparison eliminates this limitation. However, the scheme in [5] uses special packet type which increases the communication overhead. WORMEROS [4] detects and eliminates wormholes in two consecutive phases. Firstly, RTT-based neighbour finding method is applied without intermediate node cooperation. A deterministic threshold value is used to compare the RTT values between the source and destination and RTT values higher than the threshold is considered as suspect wormhole link. Secondly, encrypted message exchange with different frequency confirms the wormholes. This algorithm detects all wormholes but has more false positives. In [11], authors gather the hop count value and delay associated with the disjoint paths and calculate the propagation delay per hop to detect wormhole attacks. It considers that the delay per hop of the path under attack is much larger than the normal path. Flooding mechanism is used to calculate and compare the delay per hop.

The third line of defence is based on neighbour mismatch which exploits the local neighbourhood information based on expanding the transmission range [1]. Although the scheme is lightweight and requires no additional hardware, the algorithm efficiency drops in case of sparse network as the entire method depends on neighbour set comparison. In [12], the RTT between two successive nodes is considered for wormhole detection and the neighbour set of each node is compared with other successive nodes. The scheme does not require any specific hardware but it suffers from increased memory overhead since each node needs to store the neighbour list. LiteWorp [13] introduces a notion called guard nodes which overhear the transmission of two neighbouring nodes and determines the malicious behaviour of one of its neighbour. However, in sparse network, finding a guard node is not always feasible for a particular link. MobiWorp [14]

is an extension of LiteWorp which assumes availability of location information. Choi and others [15] use neighbour node monitoring of each node and detect fake neighbours that are beyond the transmission range.

The fourth line of defence uses graph mismatch under connectivity models. Poovendran and Lazos [16] present a location-based solution by using guard nodes that have extra communication range to deal with wormhole attacks. Establishing multihop pairwise keys is not properly handled in the said graph-based framework.

The fifth line of defence considers statistical mismatch in traffic flow to detect the presence of wormhole links. In split multipath routing (SMR) protocol [17], a statistical analysis and time constraint algorithm rely on a drastic deviation in the routing statistics stored in the sink node under wormhole attack. It is unable to detect multiple wormholes in the network. PWORM [18] introduces packet marking scheme to gather routing information against packet drop. It calculates the frequency of a node appearing in the path because wormhole attack attracts more traffic and appears more frequently than normal nodes. Path length variations are calculated to localize the wormhole.

In the last line of defence, abnormality in the network topology due to wormhole tunnels is studied. In [8], wormhole attack is detected by identifying some prohibited substructures in the network connectivity that are not generally observed in normal connectivity graph. This method works well in Unit Disk Graph (UDG) connectivity model but is inaccurate for non-UDG model. In [19], authors propose MDS visualization of wormholes (MDS-VOW) that detects wormholes by visualizing anomalies in the reconstructed network formed by using the MDS technique. This scheme uses a centralized approach and it is suitable if one malicious node resides at both ends of the wormhole links. For large scale network, Wang and Lu [9] enhance the MDS-VOW and propose an interactive wormhole detection method, which monitors the topology changes based on real time visualization approach known as interactive visualization of wormholes (IVoW). However, this detection requires domain knowledge and expertise to solve visual analysis problems. Another connectivity-based approach is proposed in [6] that uses bipartite subgraph theory to remove wormholes. The algorithm is robust in different communication models but suffers from many false positives. Dong and others [20] propose a wormhole detection method that relies on network connectivity information. It detects wormholes in a distributed manner by observing topology deviations. It is suitable for both continuous and discrete geometric terrain where each node maintains connectivity with neighbouring nodes on the surface. However, increased node density is an issue in the detection performance. Chen and others. [21] propose DV-hop localization scheme which calculates hop count between the anchor nodes and estimates the average size for one hop. Location of each unknown node is estimated by using maximum likelihood estimation. In [22], mobile beacon and positioning scheme are used for wormhole detection. The mobile beacon can localize the attacker by estimating the center of the attackers' communication area. In [7], MDS is executed to reconstruct the local subgraph of each

TABLE 1: Summary of different techniques to detect wormholes.

Defense	Basic method	Pros	Cons
Wu et al. [1]	Local neighbourhood information	Lightweight	Less efficient in sparse networks
Hu et al. [2]	Leashes	Authentication protocol using symmetric cryptography	Communication and processing overhead
Hu and Evans [3]	Cooperative protocol using directional antennas	Uses one hop neighbour information	Detects partial wormholes and degrades network connectivity
Vu et al. [4]	RTT calculation and encrypted message exchange	High detection rate	High False positives and computation overhead
Alam and Chan [5]	RTT calculation and topology comparison	Topology comparison reduces false positives	Communication overhead
Ban et al. [6]	Bipartite subgraph theory	Robust in different communication models	High false positives
Lu et al. [7]	Connectivity-based approach	Less false positives	Short path wormholes remain undetected
Maheshwari et al. [8]	Graph connectivity	Efficient in UDG model	Inaccurate in non-UDG models
Wang and Lu [9]	Interactive visualization of wormholes (IVoW)	Improves detection efficiency	Requires domain knowledge and expertise to solve visual analysis problems
Čapkun et al. [10]	Distance-bounding algorithm	No additional clock synchronisation	Special hardware needed for time measurement
Chiu and Lui [11]	Hop count and delay calculation	High detection rate	Memory overhead
Tun and Maw [12]	RTT and number of neighbours calculation	No hardware required	Memory overhead
Khalil et al. [13]	Local monitoring using guard nodes	Lightweight and suitable for resource constraint networks	Not efficient in sparse networks
Khalil et al. [14]	Isolate attackers by secure central authority (CA)	Isolate attackers with increased scalability; low detection latency	Increased message exchange between CA and mobile nodes
Choi et al. [15]	Neighbour node monitoring	Timer prevents wormhole attacks without requiring clock synchronization	Does not support DSR optimization
Poovendran and Lazos [16]	Location-based and decentralized	Time synchronization not required	Packet transmission overhead
Zhao et al. [17]	Statistical analysis of routing detect wormholes	Lightweight	Detection rate declines in presence of multiple wormholes
Lu et al. [18]	Real time secure packet marking algorithm	Detects both active and passive attacks	Wormholes remain undetected in less traffic scenario
Wang and Bhargava [19]	MDS-visualization of wormholes	Efficient in case of single wormhole; less false positives	Centralized approach
Dong et al. [20]	Distributed approach using network connectivity information	Suitable for contiguous and discrete geometric terrain	Increased node density affects detection performance
Chen et al. [21]	DV-hop localization	Range-free localization	Intolerant to packet loss
Chen et al. [22]	Mobile beacon and positioning scheme	Energy efficient and high detection probability	Require GPS enabled beacon node to detect wormholes

node based on its neighbour information. The reconstructed network is then validated and verified for detecting probable wormhole nodes. A refinement technique is used to exclude suspect nodes and remove false positives.

Different techniques of wormhole detection along with their pros and cons are summarized in Table 1.

In this work, we propose a novel wormhole detection mechanism with almost no false positives and improved detection performance in both sparse and dense networks.

2.2. Ordinal MDS and Its Applications. MDS is a collection of techniques which embed dissimilar data for a given dissimilarity matrix in a selected dimension space. The embedding is often used to visualize and analyze exploratory data [23]. MDS is applied on the dissimilarity matrix which produces a position of objects in a small dimensional space as output. The basic objective of MDS is to find the coordinates of objects in a p dimensional space so that there is a good agreement between the observed dissimilarity and the interobject distances. Traditional MDS techniques are categorised into metric and nonmetric MDS. In metric MDS, the dissimilarities between objects are linear to Euclidean distances whereas, in nonmetric or ordinal MDS, the dissimilarities exhibit a monotonic transformation with the Euclidean distances. Ordinal MDS nevertheless finds a good embedding in Euclidean space by monotonic regression. It gains better performance since it demands less rigid relationship between dissimilarities and distances. For the last few years ordinal MDS has widely been applied for node localization issues in WSN [24–28]. Miao and others [25] propose a RI-MDS localization algorithm that combines metric and nonmetric MDS and use affine transformation to translate relative coordinates to absolute ones. Nhat and others [24] propose NMDS-TOA localization algorithm that combines TDOA and MDS-map and uses sufficient number of anchor nodes to form the final estimated map. The significance of applying ordinal MDS over metric MDS is as follows.

(1) Ordinal MDS gains better performance by matching the disparity as closely as possible with the virtual distance having the restriction that the disparity maintains a monotonic relationship with the estimated distances between node pairs.

(2) The scaling is based on the rank order of the disparity. Ideally, the ranks of the nodes based on estimated distance are monotonic with their ranks based on true Euclidean distance.

(3) Ordinal MDS computes the node coordinates iteratively and updates the virtual distance to improve rank order agreement between estimated distances and virtual distances of node pairs.

(4) Ordinal MDS compensates the distortion caused by distance measurement errors via iterations.

In our approach, we have used ordinal MDS to reconstruct the local subgraph of each node.

3. Model Definition

In this section, we define the proposed model along with reasons for choosing this model. For the purpose of wormhole detection, we have considered two types of nodes: normal and wormhole.

3.1. Network Model.
The network model is structured with N sensor nodes deployed in a planar region and is denoted by a communication graph $G = (V, E)$. In this graph G, vertices V denote the nodes and edges E denote the communication bidirectional links. We have considered UDG as the connectivity model and the deployment environment is assumed to be random. The sensor nodes do not require any special hardware or globally synchronized clock. Moreover, nodes are considered to be static and initially none of the nodes is compromised. Initially, the transmission range of every node is assumed to be identical, that is, r, since each node is modelled as a UDG. But for the purpose of justifying our wormhole detection method, we have expanded the transmission range of each normal node to $R = 2r$, which

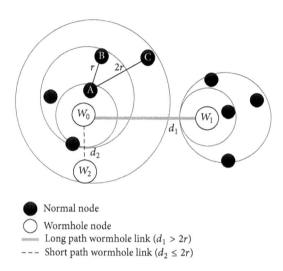

Normal node
Wormhole node
Long path wormhole link ($d_1 > 2r$)
Short path wormhole link ($d_2 \leq 2r$)

FIGURE 2: Illustration of proposed model.

means that each node is capable of collecting its neighbour information when $d \leq 2r$. Consider a node i in graph G; the neighbour of node i is denoted as $N_G^{2r}(i)$. Since our work is primarily range-based, we measure distance based on RTT denoted as Ω of a message between each node i and its neighbours $N_G^{2r}(i)$. We use $\Omega_G^{2r}(i, j)$ to denote the RTT between the nodes i and j in the network G.

3.2. Adversary Model

3.2.1. Wormhole Definition.
Under wormhole attack, the malicious nodes generally work in pairs and establish a high speed, long distance tunnel between them. This tunnel or high frequency links create an illusion to the sensor nodes around the two ends of the link as direct neighbours. Wormhole nodes advertise a false short route to a destination, capture packet from one location, and transmit them to its paired wormhole node through the high speed tunnel.

In this work, we assume that the attacker can launch a wormhole attack without modifying any packet or compromising any node. Moreover, the cryptographic mechanisms and encryption keys that are shared between the nodes for secure communication remain unaware of the attacker.

Figure 2 depicts our model. In this figure, d_1 and d_2 represent the length of long path and short path wormhole links, respectively. In the network G, the path of the wormhole link e is assumed to be either long or short. In the long wormhole link, the wormhole peer(s) are placed far apart, so that the communication regions of the two ends do not overlap with each other. Nodes at the two ends of an edge e are denoted by $i(e)$ and $j(e)$. The shortest distance between $i(e)$ and $j(e)$ is denoted by $d_G(i(e), j(e))$. We have assumed that long path wormhole tunnel is present in the network if $d_G(i(e), j(e)) > 2r$, where $2r$ denotes the maximum transmission range of normal nodes. In addition, we have further assumed that wormhole attack prevails in the network even when the length of the wormhole tunnel is short; that is, the distance between the wormhole nodes is $d_G(i(e), j(e)) \leq 2r$.

4. RTT-Based Iterative MDS for Wormhole Detection

In this section, we put forward the detailed design and analysis of our wormhole detection approach based on ordinal MDS.

4.1. Outline. For the detection of the wormhole attack, range-based distance estimation and topological comparison are used to identify the wormhole links. The overview of our scheme is as follows. In the network, each node i gathers the RTT value of a message from its direct neighbours that are within the transmission range $2r$. In other words, a link is established between the node pairs if their distance is $d \leq 2r$. Based on the RTT measure, distances between node i and its direct neighbours are estimated and stored in a sparse matrix. This sparse matrix is used to construct the shortest distance matrix between all node pairs. Then, on this internode shortest distance matrix, ordinal MDS is applied which generates virtual node positions. Considering this estimated node position, Euclidean distance between the node pairs is calculated which generates virtual distance matrix.

However, the presence of wormhole link causes a disparity between estimated shortest path matrix and the reconstructed distance matrix. Ordinal MDS reduces this disparity via iterative computation of node position (i.e., node coordinates) and thereafter updating the Euclidean distance between the node pair. Then, the monotonic property is checked in the updated Euclidean distance matrix in relation to the RTT-based shortest distance matrix. Kruskal's Stress1 [29] measure is applied to check whether the updated node position fits the estimated dissimilarities, that is, the shortest path matrix. But, due to wormhole placement in the network, distance measurement errors cannot be compensated by mere approximation. On the other hand, absence of wormhole nodes results in a reconstruction which is a mere approximation of the estimated shortest distance matrix. The disparity between the reconstructed distance matrix and the estimated shortest path matrix affects the network reconstruction. The validity of the network reconstruction is very crucial in identifying the adversaries. In our approach, ordinal MDS is executed on each node to reconstruct the network and detect the probable wormholes on the basis of distortion in the reconstruction. The disparity generated via iterative MDS produces some false alarm and so filtering mechanism is adopted to remove the falsely accused nodes and identify the real wormhole links.

In the light of the above discussion, our detection approach mainly involves two modules: (a) applying ordinal MDS on shortest distance matrix for network reconstruction and (b) executing filtering techniques to identify the real adversaries. In the first module, the suspect node list is generated. The verification phase in the second module filters the normal nodes from the suspect list and final wormhole nodes are presented.

In the following section, these two modules are described in detail.

Input: A network graph $G(V, E)$
Output: Shortest distance matrix/Dissimilarity matrix $[P_{i,j}^{\Omega}]$
(1) **for** each node $i \in V$ **do**
(2)   Each node i collects RTT values from its neighbours whose $d \leq 2$ and forms sparse matrix
(3)   Construct neighbourhood subgraph $\Gamma_G^{\Omega}(i)$ of node i
(4)   Apply ordinal MDS on $[P_{i,j}^{\Omega}]$ to reconstruct the subgraph
(5) **end for**

ALGORITHM 1: Floyd-Warshall shortest distance algorithm for shortest distance matrix.

4.2. Ordinal RTT-Based Reconstruction. In this section, the first module is divided into three phases for better understanding.

4.2.1. RTT-Based Distance Estimation. Two nodes are considered to be neighbours if $d \leq 2r$. Each node i in the network G collects the RTT, Ω, of a message from its neighbours and estimates the distance based on the travel time. We measure RTT, Ω, by sending ICMP PING packets from node i to its neighbour and receiving an acknowledgment back for the same packet. Theoretically, in a wireless environment, the RTT, Ω, of a message can be related to the distance d between nodes assuming that the wireless signal moves at a speed of light c. So we calculate the distance by the following formula:

$$d = c \times \frac{(\Omega)}{2}. \tag{1}$$

This measured distance d between every pair of sensor nodes that can hear each other is stored in a sparse matrix. Thus, each node i generates a neighbourhood subgraph denoted by $\Gamma_G^{\Omega}(i)$. Then, Floyd-Warshall shortest path algorithm is applied to calculate the shortest distance between all node pairs in $\Gamma_G^{\Omega}(i)$. The shortest distance matrix is denoted as $[P_{i,j}^{\Omega}]$. Algorithm 1 presents the Floyd-Warshall shortest path algorithm.

4.2.2. Network Reconstruction. In this section, nonmetric MDS technique is applied on the shortest distance matrix $[P_{i,j}^{\Omega}]$ which is also known as dissimilarity matrix to rebuild a network $\overline{\Gamma}_G^{\Omega}(i)$. In this network $\overline{\Gamma}_G^{\Omega}(i)$, a virtual position (i.e., node coordinates) is assigned to each node to calculate the Euclidean distance between each node pair (i, j) in $\overline{\Gamma}_G^{\Omega}(i)$. Thus a virtual distance matrix $[D_{i,j}^m]$ is generated. Each value in the matrix $[D_{i,j}^m]$ is denoted as $D_{i,j}^m$.

For ease of understanding, we subdivide the steps of ordinal MDS as follows.

(a) In nonmetric MDS, the disparity between each node pairs is related to Euclidean distance by some monotone function $d_{i,j} = f(\delta_{i,j})$. That is, in nonmetric MDS or ordinal MDS, for two pairs of nodes (i, j) and (k, l), if the shortest path distance of node pairs (i, j) is less than (k, l), then the

Euclidean distance of node pairs (i, j) is also less than (k, l) and vice versa.

Let (i, j) and (k, l) denote the two node pairs in network G, respectively. The distance between all the node pairs in the shortest distance matrix $[P_{i,j}^{\Omega}]$ is ranked from the smallest to the largest. The shortest path distances between two node pairs (i, j) and (k, l) are compared with the virtual distances of the corresponding node pairs in Euclidean distance matrix in $[D_{i,j}^{m}]$ to check the monotonic relationship. If there is any disparity in the distances of the two node pairs (i, j) and (k, l), that is, if $P_{i,j}^{\Omega} < P_{k,l}^{\Omega}$ and $D_{i,j}^{m} > D_{k,l}^{m}$, then Pool Adjacent Violators (PAV) algorithm [30] is applied to obtain a distance estimator $\overline{D}_{i,j}^{m}$. PAV algorithm works by averaging the distance of node pairs $D_{i,j}^{m}$ and $D_{k,l}^{m}$ which has violated the monotonic property with the distance of the preceding nonviolator. It is expressed by the following condition:

If $(P_{i,j}^{\Omega} < P_{k,l}^{\Omega})$ and $(D_{i,j}^{m} > D_{k,l}^{m})$, then

$$\overline{D}_{i,j}^{m} = \overline{D}_{k,l}^{m} = \frac{\left(D_{i,j}^{m} + D_{k,l}^{m}\right)}{2}. \tag{2}$$

Otherwise,

$$\overline{D}_{i,j}^{m} = D_{i,j}^{m}$$
$$\overline{D}_{k,l}^{m} = D_{k,l}^{m}. \tag{3}$$

(b) Based on this average distance estimator, new coordinate x_i^m for each node $i \in G$ is computed by the following formula:

$$x_i^m = x_i^{m-1} + \frac{a}{n-1} \sum_{i \neq j} \left(1 - \frac{\overline{D}_{i,j}^{m-1}}{D_{i,j}^{m-1}}\right)\left(x_j^{m-1} - x_i^{m-1}\right), \tag{4}$$

where n = number of nodes, m = iteration counter, and a = iteration increment of steepest descent method.

Thereafter, the Euclidean distance $D_{i,j}^{m}$ is updated in the virtual distance matrix $[D_{i,j}^{m}]$.

(c) Then, Kruskal's Stress1 [29] measure is applied to test how well the reconstructed distance matrix or the new spatial node configuration fits the shortest distance matrix. In particular, value of Stress1 decreases if rank order agreement improves between shortest distance matrix and the reconstructed distance matrix. Ordinal MDS always aims to minimize the stress. Stress1 measure is denoted by the following formula:

$$\text{Stress1} = \sqrt{\frac{\sum_{i=0, j=0, i \neq j}^{n} \left(\overline{D}_{i,j} - D_{i,j}\right)^2}{\sum_{i=0, j=0, i \neq j}^{n} \left(D_{i,j}\right)^2}}. \tag{5}$$

The Stress1 measure is executed until the stress value is satisfied. That is, Stress1 < threshold ε. This threshold, ε, is obtained by observing how well the new configuration of nodes matches the shortest distance matrix, such that ε becomes constant after iterative computation of nodes' coordinates. If Stress1 > ε, the process is repeated; otherwise, it is terminated. The steps of ordinal MDS are presented in Algorithm 2 which generates the suspect node set.

4.2.3. Suspicion Phase. In this phase, a mechanism has been adopted to find which nodes can be suspected or challenged. We have observed in our simulation that after repeated iterations, the threshold, ε, becomes almost a constant value of 0.17. We are considering those nodes as suspect wormhole nodes which violate the monotonic property even after Stress1 < ε. We add those nodes in the suspect node set. As discussed in the adversary model, wormhole nodes introduced disparity between the shortest distance and the reconstructed distance. Since wormhole nodes are placed far apart, there is a significant mismatch between the shortest path distance and the virtual distance. However, there are some normal nodes which show such type of disparity too after the network reconstruction. After implementing this phase, all the suspect wormhole nodes are produced.

4.3. Verification Phase. In suspicion phase, some normal nodes may be mistakenly identified as suspect wormhole nodes which introduce false positive results. Removal of too many false positive nodes breaks the normal links and disrupts the network functionality. So, we use a filtering technique to verify and confirm real wormhole nodes and remove nodes involved in false positive.

4.3.1. Long Path Wormhole Link Detection. The wormhole nodes create a local structure; so, for detection of long path wormhole links, we use the theory of complete bipartite graph. Let W_1 and W_2 be two sets that contain wormhole nodes w_1 and w_2, respectively, in network G. Let the edge set be denoted by $W_1 \times W_2$ between the node pair $w_1 \in W_1$ and $w_2 \in W_2$. Considering the node sets W_1 and W_2 that contain nodes at the two ends of the wormhole, each node i is given the illusion that all the nodes in set W_2 are its direct neighbours. Thus, all edge sets $W_1 \times W_2$ share a node from both the set W_1 and the set W_2 and there are no edges formed between two nodes in the same set either in W_1 or in W_2. Thus, a complete bipartite subgraph G' of G is constructed.

Under wormhole-free environment, for each node pair $(w_1 \in W_1, w_2 \in W_2)$, the shortest distance is $d_{G'}(w_1(e), w_2(e)) \leq 2r$. Therefore, for any node pair (w_1, w_2), either there exists an edge e between w_1 and w_2 or there is a common neighbour between them. This happens iff $N_{G'}^{2r}(w_1) \cap N_{G'}^{2r}(w_2) \neq \phi$.

By carefully studying the behaviour of long path wormhole links, we can guarantee that there is no common element or node between the two ends of a wormhole tunnel. Thus, we arrive at Theorem 1.

Theorem 1. *There exists a long path wormhole between the node pair $(w_1 \in W_1, w_2 \in W_2)$ if the distance between them is much greater than twice the transmission range, that is, $d_{G'}(w_1(e), w_2(e)) > 2r$, and there is no common neighbour between w_1 and w_2 which is denoted by $N_{G'}^{2r}(w_1) \cap N_{G'}^{2r}(w_2) = \phi$.*

Theorem 1 is used to filter the suspect wormhole nodes using complete bipartite subsets. Firstly, all the connected components in this suspect nodes set S are identified. Let N be the set of such connected components. For detection of a wormhole pair, we consider only the connected component

Input: Shortest distance matrix/Dissimilarity matrix $[P_{i,j}^{\Omega}]$
Output: Suspect node set S
(1) Each node $i \in V$ is assigned an arbitrary initial location as (x_i, y_i)
(2) Set the threshold value $\varepsilon = 0.17$ for Stress1 measure
(3) Set iteration counter $m = 0$
(4) Compute Euclidean distance between each node pair $(i, j) \in V$ to generate virtual distance matrix $[D_{i,j}^{m}]$
(5) Apply monotone regression using PAV algorithm on $[P_{i,j}^{\Omega}]$ and $[D_{i,j}^{m}]$ to calculate disparity and get intermediate matrix $[\overline{D}_{i,j}^{m}]$
(6) **if** $(P_{i,j}^{\Omega} < P_{k,l}^{\Omega})$ and $(D_{i,j}^{m} > D_{k,l}^{m})$ **then**
(7) $\quad\quad \overline{D}_{i,j}^{m} = \overline{D}_{k,l}^{m} = (D_{i,j}^{m} + D_{k,l}^{m})/2$
(8) $\quad\quad$ Add node i to the suspect node set S
(9) **else**
(10) $\quad\quad \overline{D}_{i,j}^{m} = D_{i,j}^{m}$
(11) $\quad\quad \overline{D}_{k,l}^{m} = D_{k,l}^{m}$
(12) **end if**
(13) Calculate new coordinate (x_i^m, y_i^m) for each node i_m using steepest descent method
(14) Set $a = 0.2$ as proposed by Kruskal [29]
(15) $x_i^m = x_i^{m-1} + (a/(n-1)) \sum_{i \neq j} (1 - \overline{D}_{i,j}^{m-1}/D_{i,j}^{m-1})(x_j^{m-1} - x_i^{m-1})$
(16) $y_i^m = y_i^{m-1} + (a/(n-1)) \sum_{i \neq j} (1 - \overline{D}_{i,j}^{m-1}/D_{i,j}^{m-1})(y_j^{m-1} - y_i^{m-1})$
(17) Recalculate the Euclidean distance of each node pair $D_{i,j}^{m}$ to update distance matrix $[D_{i,j}^{m}]$
(18) Calculate the Kruskal's Stress1 measure
(19) **if** Stress1 $> \varepsilon$ **then**
(20) $\quad\quad$ Set $m = m + 1$
(21) $\quad\quad$ Go to step (5)
(22) **else**
(23) $\quad\quad$ Terminate
(24) **end if**

ALGORITHM 2: Steps of ordinal MDS algorithm for suspect node set.

and, hence, exclude isolated nodes. Then, we apply complete bipartite subgraph algorithm [31] for each connected component $C \in N$. The algorithm in [31] generates several complete bipartite subgraphs denoted as $(c_0, c_1, c_2, \ldots, c_x \in N)$. Let each node pair be denoted as $(w_1, w_2) \in C$ such that $w_1 \in W_1$ and $w_2 \in W_2$, where W_1 and W_2 are the two partitions of the bipartite subgraph. On each bipartite subgraph, we test the condition given in Theorem 1. For each C, we check $d_{G'}(w_1(e), w_2(e)) > 2r$. If $c_0 \in N$ is a complete bipartite subgraph that satisfies the condition $N_{G'}^{2r}(w_1) \cap N_{G'}^{2r}(w_2) = \phi$ then we have detected all the wormhole nodes connected by long path. Moreover, the basic aim of detecting the wormhole attack is to nullify them without disrupting the network functions. Since the wormhole nodes attract large volume of traffic, it is necessary to discard the increased network traffic passing through the wormhole link while retaining the functionalities of the nodes. We do this by removing the edges $W_0 \times W_1$ in the complete bipartite subgraph. The detection of long path wormholes is presented in Algorithm 3.

4.3.2. Short Path Wormhole Link Detection.

When two wormholes at two ends are very close to each other, those wormhole nodes are connected by short path. Thus, the shortest distance between the wormhole peer connected by short path is $d_G(w_1(e), w_2(e)) \leq 2r$. Eventually, these nodes get filtered out when wormholes connected by long path are detected.

Input: Suspect node set S
Output: Long path wormhole nodes
(1) Identify all connected components N from S
(2) **for** each $C \in N$ **do**
(3) $\quad\quad$ Find Complete Bipartite Set W_1, W_2 for node pair $(w_1, w_2) \in C$ such that $w_1 \in W_1$ and $w_2 \in W_2$
(4) $\quad\quad$ **for** each $w_1 \in W_1$ and $w_2 \in W_2$ **do**
(5) $\quad\quad\quad$ **if** $d_{G'}(w_1(e), w_2(e)) > 2r$ **then**
(6) $\quad\quad\quad\quad$ **if** $N_{G'}^{2r}(w_1) \cap N_{G'}^{2r}(w_2) = \phi$ **then**
(7) $\quad\quad\quad\quad\quad$ Discard the edges $W_1 \times W_2$
(8) $\quad\quad\quad\quad$ **end if**
(9) $\quad\quad\quad$ **end if**
(10) $\quad\quad$ **end for**
(11) **end for**

ALGORITHM 3: Long path wormhole detection algorithm.

So, merely relying on RTT-based distance estimation for detecting short path wormholes is not the right approach. We use RTT for detecting wormhole nodes connected by short path. The RTT between two ends of a short path wormhole tunnel is much less than the RTT between normal nodes since the wormhole nodes hide the propagation delay in radio transmission.

Input: Suspect node set S
Output: Short path wormhole nodes
(1) Each node i calculate RTT of each link
(2) Node i calculates average RTT of all its neighbours $\chi_G^{N(i)}$
(3) **if** $\Omega_G^{2r}(w_1', w_2') \leq \chi_G^{N(i)}/2$ **then**
(4)   Confirm the link $\Omega_G^{2r}(w_1', w_2')$ as wormhole links
        connected by a short path
(5) **end if**

ALGORITHM 4: Short path wormhole detection algorithm.

According to Theorem 1, all possible node pairs are identified from the suspect list by applying the algorithm of complete bipartite subgraph. Let (w_1', w_2') be one such connected node pair that belongs to C (set of complete bipartite subgraphs) whose $d \leq 2r$. As mentioned in the adversary model, RTT between the wormholes connected by short path is abnormally less than average RTT of all normal links. Thus, the RTT between short path wormhole links is at most $1/k$ times of average RTT of all normal links as shown in Algorithm 4. In the following section, we analyze this condition.

5. Discussion on Parameters

In this section, we discuss how different parameters influence the performance of the detection method. Moreover, we also justify the value chosen for RTT.

Effect of r. In our experimental set up, we set $r = 2$. There are primarily two reasons. Typical length of a long path wormhole tunnel is set to 6 to 8 hops. The value of r is chosen so that $2r$ is just more than the length of the wormhole tunnel. If the value of r is increased such that $2r$ is much greater than the length of the wormhole tunnel, a larger neighbourhood subgraph will be generated due to which number of false positives will increase.

Effect of ε. The computation of Stress1 measure determines how smoothly the reconstructed network can be embedded on a plane. Setting the optimum threshold of Stress1 measure helps in identifying the suspect nodes in our approach. In particular, setting lower threshold fails to capture all wormhole nodes although it reduces the overhead of the verification phase. On the other hand, higher threshold captures all wormhole nodes but may introduce false positives and may increase overhead of the verification phase. It has been observed experimentally that $\varepsilon > 0.2$ induces false positives. So, $\varepsilon = 0.17$ is considered as optimum value where all the suspect wormhole nodes are included in the suspect set for further filtering that results in few false positives.

Effect of k. For short path wormhole tunnel detection, let the RTT between (w_1', w_2') be $\Omega_G^{2r}(w_1', w_2')$. We require that $\Omega_G^{2r}(w_1', w_2')$ is at most $1/k$ times of average RTT of all normal links. In normal links, let RTT between each node pair (i, j) be p. Let the RTT between the wormhole peer be $p/2$ as wormhole nodes hide the tunneling delay. Therefore, we can

say $p > p/2$. Let, for each node i, the average RTT with all its neighbours whose $d \leq 2r$ be denoted as $\chi_G^{N(i)}$, where $N(i)$ is the neighbours of node i in network G. Substituting $p/2$ with $\Omega_G^{2r}(w_1', w_2')$ and setting $k = 2$, we check the condition $\Omega_G^{2r}(w_1', w_2') \leq \chi_G^{N(i)}/2$ for the detection of short path wormhole links. When $k = 2$, the attacker connected by short path is very likely to be detected.

This parameter is used to detect short path wormhole tunnel. Let the RTT between the normal node pair (i, j) be p. Since the wormhole nodes hide the tunneling delay while propagating the packet, we may assume that the time to tunnel the packet between wormhole nodes connected by short path is less than p. Hence, RTT between the wormhole pair is considered to be p/k, where $k = 2$. Setting $k > 2$ will reduce the tunneling delay to such an extent that it may not be practical in a real short path wormhole tunnel scenario.

5.1. Time Complexity Analysis. Range-based ordinal MDS method for detecting wormholes has several steps: Floyd-Warshall shortest path algorithm, ordinal MDS method, and wormhole detection using complete bipartite subgraph. The time complexity has been analyzed as follows.

(i) The time complexity of Floyd-Warshall shortest path algorithm is $\mathcal{O}(v^2)$.

(ii) The time complexity of ordinal MDS is $\mathcal{O}(v^3)$.

(iii) Algorithm 3 comprises two parts. In the first part, we consider finding connected components in the set of suspect nodes. Let us consider the suspect nodes to be $w_0, w_1, w_2, \ldots, w_i \in S$. The time complexity for finding a connected component in the suspect node set S, that is, a path/edge from node w_1 to w_2, is $\mathcal{O}(we)$ since each path or edge is obtained in $\mathcal{O}(e)$ time [32]. Thus, the time complexity for finding each complete bipartite subgraph is $\mathcal{O}(we)$.

In the second part, Algorithm 3 needs to find a common neighbour of (w_1, w_2) for each connected node pair (w_1, w_2). Since the search is restricted to only one common neighbour for each wormhole pair, the number of common neighbour is a constant c. Thus, the time complexity of finding common neighbour is $\mathcal{O}(cn)$, that is, $\mathcal{O}(n)$.

6. Experimental Analysis

To verify the efficacy and performance of our method, experiments are conducted under different node distributions, radio models, and positions of wormholes.

6.1. Simulation Environment

6.1.1. Node Deployment. We have chosen two node deployment models: random deployment and perturbed grid deployment. In perturb grid model, the nodes are deployed on a grid $a \times b$. Each node in the network is perturbed with a perturb ratio p with the node's initial position. Each cell is a square grid with edge length l. Then, nodes having coordinate (x, y) are perturbed with $p = 0.2$ and are placed in the region

$[x - pl, x + pl] \times [y - pl, y + pl]$. In random deployment, nodes are placed randomly in the network field. It has been observed that in perturbed grid deployment the nodes' positions show more uniformity than the random deployment.

6.1.2. Communication Model. In our method, we have adopted UDG as the connectivity model. In UDG model, each pair of nodes i and j has bidirectional link if and only if their distance is no larger than r, where r is the communication radius.

6.1.3. Wormhole Placement. The first pair of wormhole node is placed randomly in the network. The other pairs are placed at uniform distances from the first pair. We have observed that if all wormhole nodes are placed randomly, they do not attract much traffic due to isolation. We have considered varying number of wormhole nodes with varying node density.

6.2. Simulation Results. We conduct experiments under various node densities and compare them with TRM [1], WORMEROS [4], and MDS-based local connectivity [7] methods and present the results. We use ns-2 simulator to implement our algorithm for performance evaluation. We deploy 100 nodes over a square field considering three network dimensions 10×10, 500×500, and 1000×1000. The initial transmission range of each node is set to 250 m. But, later, it is expanded to 500 m. The average node degree varies from 4 to 20. The maximum number of wormhole nodes is 20. For long path wormholes, our detection algorithm considers the fact that the colluding wormholes are not less than 6 hops apart from each other.

6.3. Detection Rate. Figures 3(a), 3(b), and 3(c) depict the relationship between varying number of wormholes and detection performance under three network distribution fields considering the UDG connectivity model and random deployment.

The results in Figures 3(a), 3(b), and 3(c) show that our method has almost 100% detection rate under different network field size with varying wormhole nodes and varying node density. In Figure 3(a), TRM method has slightly better detection rate when the network is dense. But Figures 3(b) and 3(c) show a sharp decline in detection performance of around 71% and 63%, respectively, when the network changes from dense to sparse. As TRM method solely relies on neighbour mismatch, the detection rate fails when the node density decreases. On the other hand, our approach uses the complete bipartite subgraph algorithm to clearly identify all the adversaries and, hence, the method of detection is suitable for both sparse and dense networks.

Figure 3(d) shows that perturbed grid deployment introduces some isolated wormholes which remain undetected and hence leaves an impact on the wormhole detection rate. It can be observed, from Figure 3(d), that the percentage of isolated wormholes gradually reduces to zero when the number of wormholes increases. Moreover, reduction in the number of isolated wormholes improves the detection efficiency because increasing number of wormholes establish

pairwise wormhole links which are identified easily using the complete bipartite subgraph methods.

6.4. False Positive and False Negative. We conduct this experiment to examine the false positive and false negative rate with varying network density ranging from 20 to 100 nodes distributed randomly and in perturbed grid in a constant field size of 1000×1000. Figures 4(a) and 4(b) show the false positive rate in relation to the average node degree for random distribution and perturbed grid distribution, respectively. Figures 4(a) and 4(b) indicate that the number of false positives decreases as the node degree increases. Figure 4(a) shows that our method has greatly surpassed WORMEROS method and MDS-based local connectivity method in random deployment. In Figure 4(b), for perturbed grid distribution, the number of false positives in our method is less than MDS-based local connectivity method. However, we observe that initially when there are a less number of nodes, say 20 to 40, with average node degree from 4 to 8, our method shows few false positives. The reason is that some true nodes are suspected as probable wormholes while detecting short path wormhole links. As the node size increases, there is almost no false positives.

The result obtained in Figure 5 shows that in our approach the false negative is reduced to zero thus achieving detection rate of almost 100% in both sparse and dense networks while WORMEROS method has a detection rate of 92% only in dense networks with few false negatives.

6.5. Cost Analysis. The proposed long path wormhole link detection method comprises three algorithms, namely, Algorithms 1–3. We have calculated the number of iterations that take place in these three algorithms and computed their total. This total number is considered to be the cost, c, of our detection method. We have considered random deployment. We have executed our detection method a number of times by varying number of nodes and number of wormholes. For a fixed number of node and a fixed number of wormholes, the detection method is run a number of times over random deployments. The cost plotted in Figure 6 is the average of cost of all such runs. Figure 6 shows the cost of detecting wormholes with respect to the number of nodes and the number of wormholes in the network. When the number of nodes increases, detection cost becomes higher. If we keep the number of nodes fixed and vary the number of wormholes, cost increases but the rate of increase is less. When the number of wormhole nodes is 4, then the curve for cost, c, versus number nodes, n, may be approximated by a function $c = \mathcal{O}(n^{1.6})$. Thus, the solution is scalable.

6.6. Observation on Node Degree. Figure 7 shows that the presence of wormholes increases the average node degree by creating false neighbours. It is observed that wormhole-free environment shows a lower average node degree ranging from 4 to 15 while perturbed grid shows a relatively medium average node degree ranging from 10 to 25. However, random deployment shows high range of average node degree of 15 to 27. Thus, it could be inferred that wormhole attack creates an

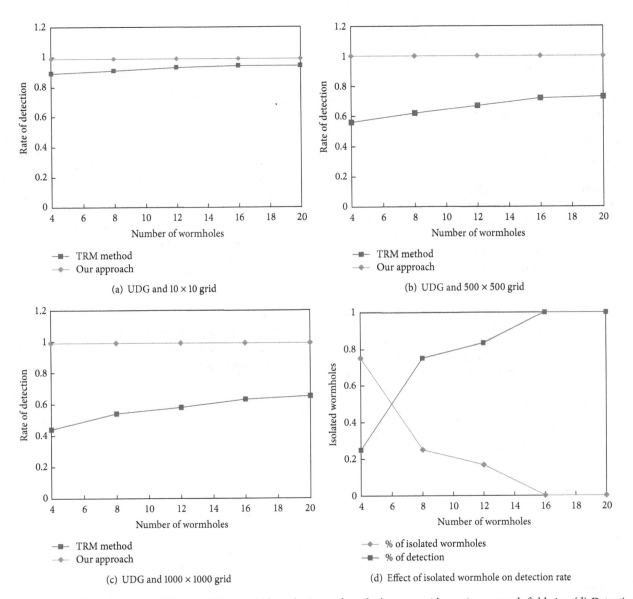

FIGURE 3: (a)–(c) show detection efficiency of 20 wormhole nodes in random deployment with varying network field size. (d) Detection efficiency of 20 wormhole nodes in perturbed grid deployment in 1000 × 1000 grid.

illusion of false neighbours in the network in order to attract large volume of traffic.

6.7. Multiple Wormholes. Figure 8 presents three scenarios of multiple wormholes placed at different position of the network. Figures 8(a) and 8(b) show the wormhole links which are far away from each other. Our method can detect all wormhole nodes connected by long path with almost no false positives. Figure 8(c) depicts a scenario where both ends of a wormhole pair are connected by a long path. One end of such wormhole pair is adjacent to one of the ends of another wormhole pair. These adjacent wormhole nodes eventually establish a short path wormhole link between each other. In our approach, such wormholes which are closely positioned to each other can be detected but with some false positives. The reason is that there might be some normal node pair

(i, j) which is closely positioned. The RTT of such node pair is much less than the average RTT value of the network due to its proximity. The RTT value between such normal node pair is very close to abnormally low RTT value and, thus, this node pair (i, j) gets enlisted as wormholes too. As the sensor nodes generally maintain a distance from each other, such closely placed nodes are rare.

7. Conclusion

For the past few years, wormhole attacks have drawn more attention since they partition the network in two sets and disrupt the normal network functionalities. However, in earlier works, many countermeasures are proposed but those methods may require special hardware and/or suffer from high overhead. In this work, we analyze the topological differences

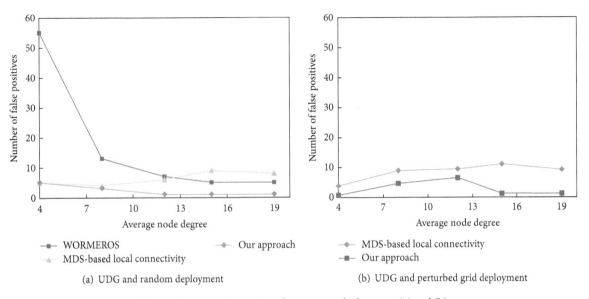

(a) UDG and random deployment

(b) UDG and perturbed grid deployment

FIGURE 4: False positive rate with average node degree in (a) and (b).

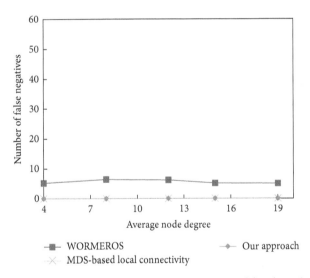

FIGURE 5: False negative rate with average node degree in UDG model with random deployment.

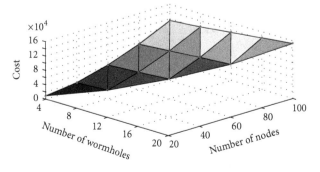

FIGURE 6: Detection cost in random deployment.

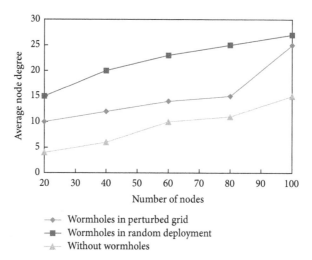

FIGURE 7: Effect of wormholes on average node degree.

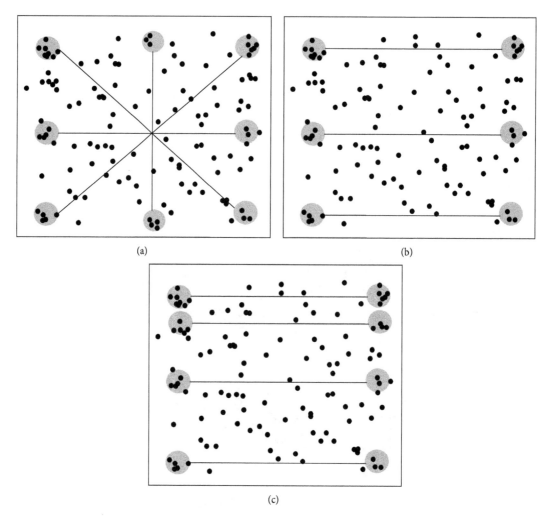

FIGURE 8: Multiple wormholes are placed at different positions of the network. (a) and (b) show wormhole links connected by long paths. Wormhole links connected by short path are shown in (c).

induced by wormholes and propose ordinal MDS-based network reconstruction using RTT to detect wormhole links. Our method can detect multiple wormhole links connected by short path and long path. The simulation results demonstrate that our approach can detect all wormhole nodes in dense as well as in sparse networks with perturbed grid and random deployment. Detection of long path wormhole links with almost no false positives has been achieved. Detection of wormholes connected by short paths introduces some false positives. So, in future, the issue of false positive for short path wormhole links remains open for further investigations.

Competing Interests

The authors declare that there are no competing interests regarding the publication of this paper.

References

[1] G. Wu, X. Chen, L. Yao, Y. Lee, and K. Yim, "An efficient wormhole attack detection method in wireless sensor networks," *Computer Science and Information Systems*, vol. 11, no. 3, pp. 1127–1141, 2014.

[2] Y.-C. Hu, A. Perrig, and D. B. Johnson, "Packet leashes: a defense against wormhole attacks in wireless networks," in *Proceedings of the 22nd Annual Joint Conference on the IEEE Computer and Communications Societies (INFOCOM '03)*, vol. 3, pp. 1976–1986, April 2003.

[3] L. Hu and D. Evans, "Using directional antennas to prevent wormhole attacks," in *Proceedings of the Network and Distributed System Security Symposium*, pp. 1–11, San Diego, Calif, USA, February 2004.

[4] H. Vu, A. Kulkarni, K. Sarac, and N. Mittal, "Wormeros: a new framework for defending against wormhole attacks on wireless ad hoc networks," in *Proceedings of the International Conference on Wireless Algorithms, Systems, and Applications*, pp. 491–502, Springer, 2008.

[5] M. R. Alam and K. S. Chan, "RTT-TC: a topological comparison based method to detect wormhole attacks in MANET," in *Proceedings of the 12th IEEE International Conference on Communication Technology (ICCT '10)*, pp. 991–994, IEEE, Nanjing, China, November 2010.

[6] X. Ban, R. Sarkar, and J. Gao, "Local connectivity tests to identify wormholes in wireless networks," in *Proceedings of the 12th ACM International Symposium on Mobile Ad Hoc Networking and Computing (MobiHoc '11)*, ACM, Paris, France, May 2011.

[7] X. Lu, D. Dong, and X. Liao, "MDS-based wormhole detection using local topology in wireless sensor networks," *International Journal of Distributed Sensor Networks*, vol. 2012, Article ID 145702, 9 pages, 2012.

[8] R. Maheshwari, J. Gao, and S. R. Das, "Detecting wormhole attacks in wireless networks using connectivity information," in *Proceedings of the IEEE 26th IEEE International Conference on Computer Communications (INFOCOM '07)*, pp. 107–115, May 2007.

[9] W. Wang and A. Lu, "Interactive wormhole detection in large scale wireless networks," in *Proceedings of the IEEE Symposium on Visual Analytics Science and Technology (VAST '06)*, pp. 99–106, November 2006.

[10] S. Čapkun, L. Buttyán, and J.-P. Hubaux, "SECTOR: secure tracking of node encounters in multi-hop wireless networks," in *Proceedings of the 1st ACM Workshop on Security of Ad Hoc and Sensor Networks*, pp. 21–32, ACM, Washington, DC, USA, October 2003.

[11] H. S. Chiu and K.-S. Lui, "DePHI: wormhole detection mechanism for ad hoc wireless networks," in *Proceedings of the 2006 1st International Symposium on Wireless Pervasive Computing*, pp. 1–6, IEEE, Spa Phuket, Thailand, January 2006.

[12] Z. Tun and A. H. Maw, "Wormhole attack detection in wireless sensor networks," *International Journal of Electrical, Computer, Energetic, Electronic and Communication Engineering*, vol. 2, no. 10, pp. 2184–2189, 2008.

[13] I. Khalil, S. Bagchi, and N. B. Shroff, "LITE WORP: a lightweight countermeasure for the wormhole attack in multihop wireless networks," in *Proceedings of the International Conference on Dependable Systems and Networks (DSN '05)*, pp. 612–621, Yokohama, Japan, July 2005.

[14] I. Khalil, S. Bagchi, and N. B. Shroff, "MOBIWORP: mitigation of the wormhole attack in mobile multihop wireless networks," *Ad Hoc Networks*, vol. 6, no. 3, pp. 344–362, 2008.

[15] S. Choi, D.-Y. Kim, D.-H. Lee, and J.-I. Jung, "WAP: wormhole attack prevention algorithm in mobile ad hoc networks," in *Proceedings of the IEEE International Conference on Sensor Networks, Ubiquitous, and Trustworthy Computing (SUTC '08)*, pp. 343–348, Taichung, Taiwan, June 2008.

[16] R. Poovendran and L. Lazos, "A graph theoretic framework for preventing the wormhole attack in wireless ad hoc networks," *Wireless Networks*, vol. 13, no. 1, pp. 27–59, 2007.

[17] Z. Zhao, B. Wei, X. Dong, L. Yao, and F. Gao, "Detecting wormhole attacks in wireless sensor networks with statistical analysis," in *Proceedings of the WASE International Conference on Information Engineering (ICIE '10)*, vol. 1, pp. 251–254, August 2010.

[18] L. Lu, M. J. Hussain, G. Luo, and Z. Han, "Pworm: passive and real-time wormhole detection scheme for WSNs," *International Journal of Distributed Sensor Networks*, vol. 2015, Article ID 356382, 16 pages, 2015.

[19] W. Wang and B. Bhargava, "Visualization of wormholes in sensor networks," in *Proceedings of the 3rd ACM Workshop on Wireless Security*, pp. 51–60, ACM, October 2004.

[20] D. Dong, M. Li, Y. Liu, X.-Y. Li, and X. Liao, "Topological detection on wormholes in wireless ad hoc and sensor networks," *IEEE/ACM Transactions on Networking*, vol. 19, no. 6, pp. 1787–1796, 2011.

[21] H. Chen, W. Lou, Z. Wang, J. Wu, Z. Wang, and A. Xi, "Securing DV-Hop localization against wormhole attacks in wireless sensor networks," *Pervasive and Mobile Computing*, vol. 16, pp. 22–35, 2015.

[22] H. Chen, W. Chen, Z. Wang, Z. Wang, and Y. Li, "Mobile beacon based wormhole attackers detection and positioning in wireless sensor networks," *International Journal of Distributed Sensor Networks*, vol. 10, no. 3, Article ID 910242, 2014.

[23] M. C. Van Wezel and W. A. Kosters, "Nonmetric multidimensional scaling: neural networks versus traditional techniques," *Intelligent Data Analysis*, vol. 8, no. 6, pp. 601–613, 2004.

[24] V. D. M. Nhat, D. Vo, S. Challa, and S. Lee, "Nonmetric MDS for sensor localization," in *Proceedings of the 3rd International Symposium on Wireless Pervasive Computing (ISWPC '08)*, pp. 396–400, IEEE, Santorini, Greece, May 2008.

[25] C. Miao, G. Dai, K. Mao, Y. Li, and Q. Chen, "RIMDS: multidimensional scaling iterative localization algorithm using RSSI in wireless sensor networks," in *Proceedings of the China*

Conference on Wireless Sensor Networks, pp. 164–175, Springer, 2014.

[26] B. Li, W. Cui, and B. Wang, "A robust wireless sensor network localization algorithm in mixed LOS/NLOS scenario," *Sensors*, vol. 15, no. 9, pp. 23536–23553, 2015.

[27] V. K. Chaurasiya, N. Jain, and G. C. Nandi, "A novel distance estimation approach for 3D localization in wireless sensor network using multi dimensional scaling," *Information Fusion*, vol. 15, no. 1, pp. 5–18, 2014.

[28] X. Zhang, Y. Wu, and X. Wei, "Localization algorithms in wireless sensor networks using nonmetric multidimensional scaling with RSSI for precision agriculture," in *Proceedings of the 2nd IEEE International Conference on Computer and Automation Engineering (ICCAE '10)*, vol. 5, pp. 556–559, Singapore, February 2010.

[29] F. Groenen, J. Patrick, and M. Velden, *Multidimensional Scaling*, Wiley Online Library, 2005.

[30] W. Härdle and L. Simar, *Applied Multivariate Statistical Analysis*, vol. 22007, Springer, Berlin, Germany, 2007.

[31] D. Eppstein, "Arboricity and bipartite subgraph listing algorithms," *Information Processing Letters*, vol. 51, no. 4, pp. 207–211, 1994.

[32] Y. Zhang, C. A. Phillips, G. L. Rogers, E. J. Baker, E. J. Chesler, and M. A. Langston, "On finding bicliques in bipartite graphs: a novel algorithm and its application to the integration of diverse biological data types," *BMC Bioinformatics*, vol. 15, no. 1, article 110, 2014.

5

Managing Hierarchically Structured DTN-Like Networks

Riku Luostarinen ⓘ and **Jukka Manner** ⓘ

Aalto University School of Electrical Engineering, Department of Communications and Networking, Espoo, Finland

Correspondence should be addressed to Riku Luostarinen; riku.luostarinen@aalto.fi

Academic Editor: Jemal H. Abawajy

Network management in Delay/Disruption Tolerant Networks (DTNs) is an active research topic and covers topics such as system architecture, roles of actors, and management protocol. The existing solutions either expect a flat management hierarchy or do not address the hierarchical structure used in management. However, in many real-world DTN use cases, particularly in emergency and military contexts, the actors using the DTN system are a part of an organizational or operational hierarchy, and the network design and topology follow the hierarchical structure. This paper introduces a DTN management scheme that is based on that hierarchy. The paper presents a node categorization that is based on the hierarchy, the characteristics of the hierarchical management, roles and responsibilities of the managed and managing nodes in the hierarchy, and the related concept of *management responsibility stack*. Further, the paper discusses the characteristics of the messaging and configurability of the nodes in a hierarchical network, and introduces a problem called *DTN management trilemma*. The paper also presents a use case where the concepts of this paper are applied to network management of a hierarchical organization in a reference scenario, and the performance of the hierarchical management methods is compared to an equivalent nonhierarchical solution.

1. Introduction

The modern Internet is heavily built upon the TCP/IP protocol stack, and the connections are characterized by a low latency, end-to-end connectivity, and low packet loss. The services are typically expected to be always-available and always-on. However, also a large number of other kinds of networks exist. For example, in the military, and in emergency and crisis management operations and environments, fixed network infrastructure may not be available. In these contexts, the organization structure of the operators is typically highly hierarchical, and the network topology follows the structure and patterns of the organization. Further, the network consists of different temporarily set up fixed, vehicular, or mobile nodes that may communicate with each other over various homogeneous wired and wireless links. Due to mobility and the characteristics of the network, the connections are intermittent, and delays and packet losses are high. In these kind of disconnected, intermittent, low-bandwidth (DIL) environments [1], as they are often referred to particularly in the military domain and in

context, the communication is based on, or has a lot of similarities to, Delay/Disruption Tolerant Networking (DTN) [2, 3].

In traditional IP networks, there must be an end-to-end connectivity between the nodes that want to communicate. In DTNs, no such requirement exists. In DTN architecture [4, 5], a bundle layer is used to form a message-oriented routing overlay on top of the transport layer of the OSI model. The bundle layer uses Bundle Protocol [6] to communicate with other DTN nodes through the underlying heterogeneous link technologies. The messaging is based on *store-carry-and-forward* paradigm and allows nodes to communicate in an intermittently connected network with high delays, high packet loss, and low link capacities.

To monitor, control, and guarantee the operability of the network, network management is needed. In traditional IP-based networks Simple Network Management Protocol (SNMP) [7] is a de facto standard for the management. SNMP runs on top of User Datagram Protocol (UDP) and is supported by a wide range of network devices. In SNMP, the entities that perform management operations are called managers and those entities that are managed are called agents. The basic functionality of SNMP consists of synchronous queries from managers to agents, query responses from agents to managers, and asynchronous SNMP trap messages that agents send to notify managers of occurred events and condition changes of the managed entity.

IP-based network management tools do not perform well in all networks. In its basic form, SNMP heavily relies on the use of *get*, *get-next*, and *get-bulk* requests from managers to agents and on responses to these requests that are sent from the agents back to the managers. However, when operating in DTNs or other challenged networks, continuous end-to-end connectivity may not exist or cannot be guaranteed. Requests may get lost or they may be so delayed that the response gets outdated before it reaches the manager. Thus, SNMP and other network management protocols that use synchronous messaging and request-response model perform poorly in DTN environment [8]. Instead, the management should use asynchronous mechanisms that are based on intelligent push of management data from agents to managers and on configurable autonomous behaviour of agents.

In this paper, we study the network management of hierarchically structured organizations that operate in challenging environments and in which the network topology follows, or is based on, the organizational hierarchy and patterns. This is typical especially to the military, emergency response agencies, and to crisis management operations. The network management of these organizations significantly differs from management of a flat well-connected network. This paper aims to show how to manage networks of these hierarchical organizations that operate in DTN environment, how the hierarchy affects the management, and what is the performance of the proposed hierarchical management methods compared to an equivalent nonhierarchical solution.

This paper approaches the network management in DTNs from the perspective of a hierarchical network. The paper presents the impact of the hierarchy to (1) management centralization, (2) network quality in different parts of the network, (3) roles and responsibilities of the managing and managed nodes, and (4) configurability and messaging between the nodes. The paper also introduces a use case that shows how network management can be done in a hierarchical military organization in a given reference scenario using the exiting technical solutions and the concepts introduced in this paper. Based on the use case, a performance comparison of hierarchical and nonhierarchical management solutions is presented.

The rest of the paper is organized as follows: In the next section, we go through related work. In Section 3, we discuss the characteristics of hierarchical network management, present a node categorization, and show how the categories are tied to an organizational hierarchy. The next section presents the roles and responsibilities of the nodes and introduces a concept of *Management responsibility stack*. Section 5 is focused on the messaging and configurability, and Section 6 presents a use case that applies the concepts of this paper to a hierarchical organization of

a reference military scenario. In Section 7, we provide summary and conclusions.

2. Background and Related Work

Various solutions to network management in DTN environment have been studied and proposed. Peer-to-peer (P2P) technologies, that have been used in management of traditional networks [9, 10], have been applied to DTN context as well [11, 12]. The solutions aim at distributed management and autonomous self-management. Peoples et al. have studied DTN self-management of deep space network [13]. The solution is based on the use of the context-aware broker (CAB) middleware that makes decisions based on policies and contextual data that is autonomously gathered by the managed node. However, the aforementioned solutions do not address management hierarchy.

Pierce-Mayer and Peinado have implemented the DTN-O-Tron node management system [14, 15] for DTN Interplanetary Overlay Network (ION) environment where Contact Graph Routing (CGR) [16, 17] is used. Their approach is similar to the case study presented in Section 6 of this paper in the sense that it is based on DTN management drafts and on-going work in IETF, namely, on DTN Management Protocol (DTNMP) that is a former version of Asynchronous Management Protocol [18] that we use in our use case. However, DTN-O-Tron is nonhierarchical, focused on CGR context, uses additional middleware, and relies on a centralized database that is not applicable in our context.

Papalambrou et al. have implemented a shell script based DTN monitoring solution on the DTN2 reference implementation in a network of three nodes [19]. The implementation is based on static topology with predefined routing tables and a fixed set of monitoring parameters. Thus, the solution is not scalable and cannot be used in a network with mobile nodes. Torgerson has focused on Network Monitor and Control (NM&C) system and management tools in Interplanetary Overlay Network (ION) context [20]. Kumar et al. have studied DTN configuration management and defined Configuration Network Management Protocol (CNMP) [21] that experiments extending NETCONF [22] to DTN environment. However, the results are very preliminary, and the solution does not tackle the fundamental problems of DTN management as it relies on concepts, such as resource locking and acknowledgments of operations, that require bidirectional message exchange.

Ferreira et al. have studied [23, 24] the usage of SNMP in Vehicular Delay-Tolerant Network (VDTN) architecture [25]. Unlike in traditional DTN stack, in the VDTN architecture, the bundle layer resides below the transport and network layers of the OSI model. Also, the bundle layer consists of separate control and data planes. In the study, the IP packets that contain SNMP messages in UDP datagrams were encapsulated into DTN bundles, i.e., the approach is based on carrying IP packets over DTN. SNMPv3 with a customized MIB and out-of-band signaling for the connection establishment was used. The approach was demonstrated in laboratory environment with a manager and a set of static relay nodes and moving vehicles but does not tackle the fundamental problem related to request-response messaging of SNMP in DTNs. Similarly, the monitoring and management tool of Dias et al. [26] is based on control plane data of the out-of-band signaling of the VDTN architecture.

Another approach is to use in DTNs a management protocol that is tailored to the environment with high delays and packet loss and to guarantee interoperability with Internet management protocols, such as SNMP. Salvador, Macedo, and Nogueira present the HiErarchical MANagement (HE-MAN) architecture [27, 28] for Vehicular Delay-Tolerant Network (VDTN) environment. In the architecture, nodes that are close to each other are clustered together and managed locally using SNMP. For remote monitoring, SNMP over the Bundle Protocol is used in publish-subscribe fashion. The solution is targeted for VDTN applications with very strict delay constraints and requires high-speed and low-delay communication links between the nearby nodes. Thus, it is not suitable for environments where such links do not exist.

Campbell has studied [29] the possibility of using an SNMP gateway on the edge of high and low latency parts of the network. In the study, the gateway gathers data from the DTN to a local database. At the same time, the gateway acts as an SNMP agent towards the low latency network so that the data can be queried from the gateway using SNMP messages. Further, the gateway sends asynchronously SNMP *trap* notification messages to selected SNMP managers in the low latency network. However, the solution has problems with addressing, and it assumes that all the manageable nodes in the DTN network are manually preconfigured to the setup. Thus, it is not scalable or applicable in dynamically changing networks. In the study, the management protocol used on the DTN side of the gateway is Diagnostic Interplanetary Network Gateway (DING).

DING [30] is a network management protocol for environments where traditional IP-based solutions, such as SNMP, do not perform well. In the DING protocol *subscribers* receive information from *providers* based on *subscription requests*. A *subscription request* defines the content that the subscribers want to receive from the providers, and a time interval and possibly a condition for the delivery. The specification of DING is on draft level and, as such, incomplete but can be seen as a predecessor for work related to DTN management that has been done later in IRTF and IETF.

In Section 4, we present the requirements and responsibilities related to network management of hierarchically structured DTN-like networks. Ivancic has written in 2009 an IETF draft [31] that describes requirements for DTN management. The requirements listed in the document are on high level and can be seen as general guidelines and good practices to apply for suitable parts of the specific task at hand. According to the requirements, a DTN system must be manageable both locally (through physical or real time access to the device) and remotely (over DTN). The management must be incremental and support configuration validation and rollback. The nodes must be capable of autonomous behaviour. The document also lists the parameters related to bundle and convergence layer that administrators must be able to monitor and configure and mentions administrative tools that the system should

contain. A milestone for updated network management requirements has been set to February 2017 in IETF DTN working group (https://datatracker.ietf.org/wg/dtn/charter/) but has not been finished at the time of writing (5/2018) and is according to IETF mailing list (https://mailarchive.ietf.org/arch/msg/dtn/x-EMgP539vjaN7t10fROkVy2PSg/?qid=be9a200d95c97f7d332bdece1fd9d432) being moved to IRTF NMRG for a reboot.

Besides the DTN management requirements, there are several draft papers and work in progress in IETF related to the network management in DTNs. According to the documents, the network consists of actors that can implement either a role of a managing device (*manager*), managed device (*agent*), or both of them. In this paper, we use the same terminology for consistency. The IETF documents cover the architecture called Asynchronous Management Architecture (AMA) and the roles and responsibilities of its actors [32], data model used by the agents [33], the management protocol called Asynchronous Management Protocol (AMP) that is used between the actors [18], and an interface for applications to interact with the protocol [34]. The management use case shown in Section 6.1 of this paper uses AMA and AMP.

DTN management has adopted a lot of concepts, such as self-configuration, self-healing, and self-optimization, from autonomic computing (AC) [35] and autonomic management [36] of traditional IP networks. In the AMA document [32], four services that must exist in a DTN management system are defined. These services are configuration, autonomous parameterized control, reporting, and administration. The configuration service updates the data of the managed application and is used, e.g., to create new data definitions and reports on the agent. The autonomous parameterized control provides managers with an asynchronous way to change the autonomous behaviour of an agent according to predefined, preconfigured and preprogrammed functions, and parameters that are provided to agents at the execution time of the procedure. The reporting service sends information from agents to managers based on time-based or state-based conditions that are defined and set using the first two services. The administration service is used to enforce the mapping of the other three services between the managers and agents, e.g., to define the reports that can be delivered to certain managers, or configurations that are accepted by the agents.

To provide the services, the agents must be capable of producing and sending information to managers based on the predefined conditions. In AMA context, this is called *Intelligent Push of Information*. The system must use in management uniquely identifiable data elements which identification is not tied to the system configuration. Also, the system must aim at minimizing the message size instead of the processing time and be able to produce tactical data definitions (such as averages, selected samples, or data fusions) based on the existing data. The agents must be capable of autonomous operation, and the managers should configure the autonomy engine of the agents instead of directly changing the states of the agents.

The actors communicate using AMP. In AMP, all the messaging is done using three message types, namely *Register Agent*, *Perform Control*, and *Data Report* messages.

Register Agent messages are used to notify a manager about the presence of an agent. *Perform Control* messages are used to perform predefined operations on agents such as to add subscriptions or to define variables for which the managed device should gather values from the network. *Data Report* messages contain data that agents send to managers.

Our paper focuses on management of hierarchically structured DTN-like networks that are used, e.g., by the military and many emergency response agencies such as fire departments. The structure of these organizations is based on units of different sizes. Further, organizations of different size and type may have a different number of hierarchical levels. For instance, fire departments have less hierarchical levels than the military. Further, a fire department of a small city has less fire engines and personnel than a fire department of a big city, and thus, less hierarchical levels is needed. For example, the world's largest fire department, New York City Fire Department (http://www.nyc.gov/fdny), is divided to divisions that consist of multiple battalions. Each battalion contains several fire stations that are geographically located in different places and contain varying number of fire companies. Each company is specialized to some particular task. There are, for example, engine companies, ladder companies, and rescue companies and different special units like collapse rescue units and foam units, in different battalions. A company is made up of up to 20 firefighters and led by a captain and (three) lieutenants in his subordination. During a shift, there are three to five firefighters and an officer in a company. Smaller fire departments follow the same structure but may have less hierarchical levels. For example, a fire department of a small town may consist of only one company operating from a single fire station. From the perspective of network management, units of this kind of, or similar, organization can be managed based upon their organizational position as will be shown in the following sections.

3. Node Categorization and Network Management Characteristics

In hierarchically structured organizations, like the military and emergency response agencies, the network topology follows, or is heavily based on, the organizational structure. The users need to communicate and operate in challenging field environments where normal messaging is not possible and thus rely upon DTN or DTN-like concepts. To monitor and control the nodes, and to keep the network up-and-running, network management is needed.

There are characteristics both in hierarchical organizations and in DTNs that heavily influence the network management. On the one hand, a centralized control is wanted. The units higher in the hierarchy want to have a full overview and control over the network. In the parts of the network where they typically operate, the network connections are good and allow exchange of even large amounts of data between the nodes. The good connections together with hierarchical organization structure strongly advocate the centralization of network management to the top of the hierarchy.

On the other hand, on the bottom of the hierarchy, the nodes operate on the field in challenging environments with limited network resources and intermittent connections. In these conditions, no centralized control can be applied. Instead, the network characteristics push the design towards autonomous behaviour and decentralized solutions in the network management.

As the result, we end up with a need for a hybrid that is half-centralized and half-distributed and autonomous. Further, the management and control within the network is highly heterogeneous. In the higher levels of the hierarchy the network consists of static nodes and links with high speed and low packet loss. In terms of network management, the nodes can operate and exchange information the same way as in traditional IP-based networks. However, when the focus is moved down in the hierarchy, the nodes become more mobile, the connection quality and capacity go down drastically, and the concepts of IP network management fade away gradually. On the bottom of the hierarchy, the network is fully intermittently connected, and the network management is decentralized and based on the concepts used in DTNs. That is demonstrated below in Figure 1.

Among a hierarchically structured network with the aforementioned heterogeneous features, groups of nodes with homogeneous characteristics can be found. We have identified four different types of nodes and made a node categorization based on that as follows:

(i) *Core Nodes.* Static infrastructure that is connected to the Delay/Disruption Tolerant Network is used. Characterized by low latency and low packet loss. Suitable for IP traffic. Acts as a gateway to and from the DTN.

(ii) *Transferable Nodes.* Relatively stable nodes that form the core of the DTN. The nodes may be, for example, heavily equipped transferable trailers or vehicles such as trucks with a built-in communication center. Some of the transferable nodes are only deployable, i.e., they are not built to move independently but can be moved when necessary. These nodes are typically set up to, e.g., tents, buildings that reside on the area of operation, or shipping containers (e.g., intermodal containers), and their movement is occasional. Connections to the core network are good and almost always-on. Horizontal connections between the transferable nodes are intermittent, but when a connection between two nodes exists, the delay and packet loss are typically on a tolerable level, and there is enough bandwidth to exchange detailed network management information. Connections downwards in the hierarchy are intermittent, and the connection quality and properties depend on the communication capabilities and the operating environment of the subordinate node. However, when a connection exists, it is typically possible to exchange reports and basic level network management information between the nodes.

(iii) *Vehicular Nodes.* A vehicle, such as a police car/fire truck/ambulance/jeep/tank, with appropriate radio transceivers. In many cases, the vehicles provide

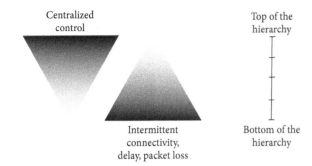

FIGURE 1: Change in the network quality and management centralization in relation to the hierarchical position in the organization.

users a base station which allows the users to connect to the network. Movement of the nodes is regular but not always predictable. Nodes may switch position multiple times a day or move constantly. Vehicular nodes exchange network management information with each other and forward information about each other to nodes higher in the hierarchy. The exchanged data consists of location and reachability information of the nodes that communicate and those nodes that are connected to them.

(iv) *Terminal Nodes.* Personal devices used by the end-users operating on the field, including, e.g., wearable devices and various rugged personal devices (tablets, cell phones, etc.). The devices move along with the users and are thus always on the move. Terminal nodes connect to the network via a base station that is provided by a vehicular node. The connections are almost always wireless. The network management traffic consists of delivering minimal basic data from the terminal node to the base station and receiving simple commands from nodes higher in the hierarchy. Unlike nodes on the higher levels of the hierarchy, terminal nodes do not need to exchange network management data with each other. Further, as the terminal nodes are on the bottom of the hierarchy, they do not need to control or monitor other nodes. Thus, terminal nodes only act as agents, and there are no managers on the bottom of the hierarchy. Notice that in this context, the term "Terminal" only refers to the devices used on the field in aforementioned conditions. The terminals attached to core, transferable, or vehicular nodes are categorized accordingly (based on their network access).

There is a direct relation between the node type and the node's position in the organization hierarchy. As the network topology follows the organizational hierarchy, the nodes of the same type are close to each other, i.e., on the same level or levels in the hierarchy. The core nodes are located in high levels of the organization hierarchy whereas the terminal nodes typically operate in the bottom of the hierarchy.

For example, in the organization hierarchy of the U.S. army (http://www.army.mil/info/organization/unitsand commands/oud/, https://www.thebalance.com/u-s-army-

military-organization-from-squad-to-corps-4053660), the smallest element in the structure is squad (or a section in case of an armor unit) that consists of 8–16 soldiers. The squad may be organized into smaller teams that have an assigned vehicle. 2–4 squads/sections form a platoon. For example, a mechanized infantry platoon consists of 2 sections that together contain four vehicles. A company contains multiple platoons and has a small headquarters element. A company typically consists of 15–25 vehicles. Battalions are self-sufficient units that are composed of four to six companies and are capable of independent operations to a certain extent. The similar kind of hierarchy that nests units further continues with brigades, divisions, and corps. In this kind of organization hierarchy, the soldiers on the field carry their mobile terminal devices. The vehicles have a networking capability, and they provide the users with an access point to the network. The vehicles are controlled by the company headquarter (HQ). The company HQ is connected upwards in the hierarchy to transferable nodes and further to the core network of the battalion. The relation of the node type to the position of the node in the hierarchy is demonstrated in Figure 2 in the context of the military.

4. Roles and Responsibilities in the Management Hierarchy

By definition, there are two types of actors in a management system, namely, managers and agents. An actor that has a role of a manager controls actors with a role of an agent. A node may act as both manager and agent, i.e., a node may control nodes and at the same time be controlled by other node or nodes. Further, in DTN management solutions, such as AMA, the messaging between the nodes consists of control messages sent from managers to agents, reports delivered from agent to managers, and fusions of reports sent between managers. Thus, there is a many-to-many relationship amongst managers and between managers and agents.

There are several requirements for the actors of a system. We identified three fields of requirements, namely *contextual*, *technical*, and *role-based* requirements. The contextual requirements describe the characteristics and way of usage of particular system. The technical requirements define the system-level technical solution needed to enable management in the given context. The role-based requirements define the requirements that depend on the organizational role and the position of the node in the hierarchy in the given context and show how the contextual and technical requirements are reflected to a single node of a system. Based on these requirements, the responsibilities of the actors can be defined in the corresponding fields. The fields are discussed in detail in the following subsections.

4.1. Contextual Requirements and Responsibilities. The contextual requirements are set by the operating environment, the way of usage, the policies, and the various system-level constraints. Thus, the contextual requirements are

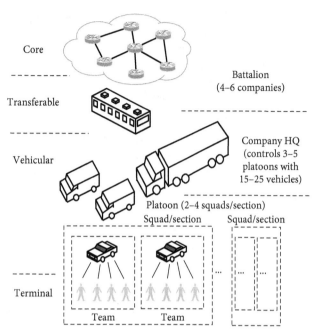

FIGURE 2: Military hierarchy in relation to node categories.

system-wide but may have different effect depending on a node. This difference is described by the role-based requirements. In our study, the contextual requirements are set by the intermittently connected DTN environment, the hierarchical network topology that follows the organization structure, the way the network is used, and the policy that defines how it must be administered. Based on the requirements, the contextual responsibilities can be defined as follows:

(i) The system must provide the administrators with a way to manage the network over intermittently connected and distributed network.

(ii) The management must be suitable for a hierarchically structured organization in which the network topology follows the organization structure, and the network is heterogeneous both in terms of connection quality and management centralization.

These responsibilities are common to all hierarchically structured DTN-like systems. In a specific system, such as the one discussed in the case study of Section 6, the contextual requirements and responsibilities can be defined in more detail based on the details of the organization, the operating environment, and the network equipment and connectivity of the nodes.

4.2. Technical Requirements and Responsibilities. The technical requirements are related to the technical solution that is used to enable the network management service to the administrators. In other words, they define the system-level solution that is needed in order to manage nodes of a system in the context defined by the contextual requirements. The technical requirements contain, for example, the requirements

regarding the management system architecture, the management protocol, and the underlying network and its adapters. Just like contextual requirements, also technical requirements affect nodes differently depending on the role and position of a node in the organization. The role-based requirements and responsibilities describe the way the technical requirements are reflected to a single node.

Various technical solutions for the management of DTN and DTN-like environments have been proposed. Currently, the technical solutions and the roles and responsibilities of DTN management systems are being studied in IETF by Birrane as described in Section 2. In the AMA specification [32], the responsibilities of managers and agents have been defined. The agents must fully support all its Application Data Models (ADM) and locally collect and report all the data defined in them. Further, the agents must provide a configuration service that enables addition, listing, and removal of customized data, reports, macros, and other data definitions. The agents must autonomously execute the controls based on the defined conditions and determine when data must be transmitted to managers. The number of messages sent should be kept as low as possible, e.g., by wrapping multiple reports to a single message. It is allowed for an agent to act as a proxy and perform responsibilities for nodes that do not run an agent software.

The managers must be aware of the ADMs supported by the agents they communicate to and should only refer to information known by the agents. The managers must use controls to define the conditions for data report production in the agents and receive the requested reports asynchronously. Custom data and report definitions should be supported. The managers should also provide an interface to other network management protocols (e.g., SNMP). Managers may produce and exchange fusions of data with other managers.

In hierarchically structured DTN-like networks, data with different granularity are sent in different parts of the network as is described in Section 5. For that, custom data types, data definitions, and reports are needed. Further, fusions of data and relaying of messages are needed in the management. Due to the aforementioned responsibilities of agents and managers, AMA meets these technical requirements and is suitable for network management of hierarchically structured DTN-like networks.

On the protocol level, the system has a responsibility to support the architectural design, i.e., the protocol must implement the functionalities defined in the architecture. In case of AMA, Asynchronous Management Protocol (AMP) [18] is a protocol that meets the requirements of AMA. However, some other compatible protocol could be used as well.

DTN management protocols operate on top of the DTN Bundle Protocol (BP) [6] (or other similar type of protocol) that is capable of transferring management traffic over underlying heterogeneous and intermittently connected network. The BP or its equivalent resides on the Application Layer of the OSI model.

4.3. Role-Based Requirements and Responsibilities. The role-based requirements describe the characteristics of the management that depend on the position and the organizational role of the node in the hierarchy. In other words, they define how the contextual and technical factors are reflected to a single node of the system. Further, they define the difference of two nodes on a same hierarchical level in terms of network management requirements and responsibilities. For example, there can be two completely identical vehicles acting on the same hierarchical level but only one of them acts as a relay node in the organization network. Thus, the management of the vehicles differs from each other and the role-based requirements and responsibilities describe that difference.

The technical requirements and responsibilities change both vertically between the hierarchical levels and horizontally within a level. For example, on the lowest hierarchy level, more lightweight technical solution can be used compared to the higher levels due to the absence of managers. Further, the characteristics of the network vary between the hierarchy levels, and the technical factors tied to the network quality change accordingly. Thus, certain technical solutions, such as request-response based diagnostics, can be used on a certain hierarchy level but not on another. Also, there is variation in networking equipment in the network both vertically and horizontally, which directly affects the management of the nodes. In the vertical manner, higher levels typically use equipment with more capacity due to heavier network load. Horizontally, nodes on the same hierarchical level may use different networking equipment due to their role in the organization hierarchy and network. For example, in a military context, a medic, an artilleryman, and a scout all have completely different roles in the organization even though they may operate on the same hierarchical level. Further, their need for network access and the requirements and limitations regarding that access differ between the nodes due to their roles. The role-based requirements and responsibilities describe these individual characteristics of the network management of the nodes.

In hierarchical organizations, subordinates are responsible for taking care of the tasks given by their superior. The same applies for the nodes in hierarchical network management. In terms of network management, agents are subordinate to managers. Further, the nodes higher in the management hierarchy control the nodes that are below them. Hence, the nodes have responsibilities set by both their role and their relative position in the management hierarchy.

The nodes communicate and exchange network management traffic in the hierarchy both vertically and horizontally. The direction of the communication and the responsibilities of a node depend on the management role (i.e., the actor type) of the node. Further, as a node can act either as a manager, as an agent, or as both of them, the different nodes have different management role-based responsibilities. These management role-based responsibilities in the hierarchy are shown in Table 1.

The managers control, configure, and monitor the nodes below them in the hierarchy. In case of DTNs, monitoring is typically asynchronous, passive, and based on subscriptions [32]. The managers subscribe to data reports from the agents they want to monitor. The agents report their state to the managers based on conditions defined in the subscriptions.

The responsibilities can also be looked from the perspective of the relative position of the node in the hierarchy as illustrated in Figure 3. In the horizontal manner, the managers share the responsibility of monitoring and reporting with other nodes on the same level in the hierarchy. Thus, the managers exchange information with other managers and relay the data of other managers both horizontally and upwards in the hierarchy based on the given policy.

4.4. Management Responsibility Stack. Based on the contextual, technical, and role-based responsibilities, we define the *Management responsibility stack*. The stack has five layers, namely, *Usage and Context*, *Services and applications*, *Architecture*, *Protocol*, and *Network*. The stack resides fully on the application layer of the OSI model. The stack and the relation between the layers are shown in Figure 4.

Similarly to other layered models, each layer of the stack is responsible for certain duties and tasks on its own layer. Further, each layer has a tight relation to the layer below and above it as the characteristics of one layer affect the layers next to it in the stack. From the management point of view, the responsibilities of the layers are as follows.

The *Usage and Context* layer has a responsibility to set the requirements for the system in the given context, to define the way the system must be used, and to set the bounds for the usage. In relation to the *Services and Applications* layer, the *Usage and Context* layer takes care of the contextual requirements and responsibilities by defining how the applications and services must be implemented and which kind of features are needed in the given context. Further, on node level, it defines technical level requirements for the service/application implementation in the particular node.

The *Services and Applications* layer is responsible for enabling the management functions to the administrators of the system and to provide the administrators with a management service. In relation to other layers, it has a responsibility to provide the *Usage and Context* layer a service that is tailored to the given context and use case. Further, the layer guides architecture design by defining downwards in the stack which of the available architectural solutions are feasible or how a new architecture should be designed and built to support the service. In case the architecture is predefined, the *Services and Applications* layer is responsible for adapting the service to the given architecture.

The *Architecture* layer has a responsibility to implement an architecture that enables the management of a system and to provide upwards in the hierarchy an API that makes it possible to build services and applications on top of the architecture. The *Architecture* layer is tightly coupled with the *Protocol* layer that is responsible for implementing the protocol-level presentation of the messages that are needed in the management. The *Architecture* layer defines the functions and operations used in the management architecture, and that way strongly guides the design of the underlying protocol. On

TABLE 1: Management role-based responsibilities in the hierarchy.

Actor	Responsibility	Traffic direction
Agent	Report	Upwards in the hierarchy
Manager	Control, configure, and monitor	Downwards in the hierarchy
	Relay management traffic	Sideways and upwards in the hierarchy

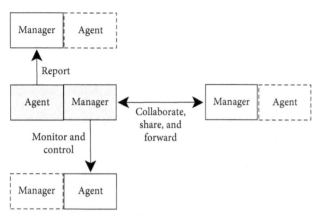

FIGURE 3: Responsibilities set by the management role (i.e., the actor type) and relative position in the hierarchy from the perspective of the highlighted node (in the middle on the left).

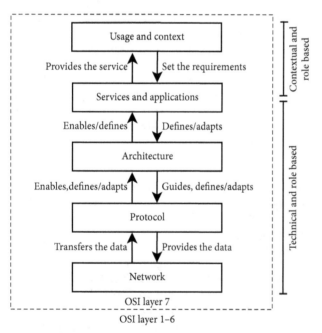

FIGURE 4: Network management responsibility stack and the relations between the layers. The stack resides on the application layer of the OSI model.

the other hand, the architecture also needs to adapt to the limitations set to the protocol implementation. Further, within these limitations, also the protocol design adapts to the given architecture, i.e., the adaptation process works both ways between the layers. Also, in certain cases, the characteristics of the protocol may guide the architectural decisions made. For example, if the protocol does not support

asynchronous messaging, either the architecture must be designed to not rely on it, the underlying protocol must be modified, or the protocol must be changed to one having the support. In summary, the architecture and the protocol go hand in hand and have a strong interconnection so that a change in one usually affects the other.

The *Network* layer is responsible for forming a management network between the actors of a management system. In the management responsibility stack, the term "network" refers to a network on the application layer of the OSI model. Thus, the management network is an application layer logical overlay network on top of the underlying physical network infrastructure. For example, in DTNs, a management overlay network refers to intermittent interconnections between the managing and managed nodes on the DTN bundle layer. Similarly, in case of SNMP, the network consists of those nodes in a UDP/IP network that run SNMP manager or agent software. As the *Network* layer is on the bottom of the stack, it only has an interrelationship upwards in the stack with the *Protocol* layer. The *Protocol* layer must give to the *Network* layer the data of the management protocol in a format that can be carried over the network. In respect of the *Protocol* layer, the *Network* layer has a responsibility to transfer that data between the nodes.

To illustrate the management responsibility stack, the stacks of a hierarchically structured DTN and a non-hierarchical SNMP management network are shown side by side in Figure 5. We can see that, starting from the bottom, the stacks are built on the overlay network of managing and managed nodes, the management protocol, and the architecture that defines the interactions and operations between actors. The actual management service is built on top of the architecture so that it fits in the given context and use case.

5. Messaging and Configurability in Management Hierarchy

Various constraints, requirements, and objectives for DTN management messaging can be identified. In DTN-like networks, bandwidth may be low and transmission window limited, especially in the lower parts of the hierarchical network. When the connections are the bottleneck, the overhead caused by the management must be kept to its minimum. This can be achieved by either keeping the message size really small or by sending slightly bigger messages but with a lower frequency.

Second, from the network manager's point of view, an up-to-date overall picture of the network state is always desired. However, in DTN environment, no timeliness of information can be guaranteed as no status updates can be received from temporarily unreachable or disconnected network nodes. Also, due to disruptions and high packet loss, some of the messages may not be delivered to the managers. Further, too high a sending pace of management traffic may cause congestion and delay the data delivery. However, up to the point of congestion, the higher the frequency of report delivery of the nodes, the more up-to-date information the managers will get from the nodes.

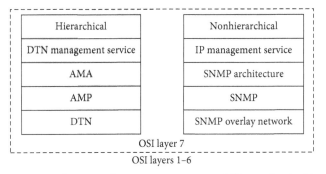

FIGURE 5: The network management responsibility stack of a hierarchically structured DTN (left) and a nonhierarchical SNMP management network (right).

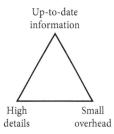

FIGURE 6: DTN management trilemma: only two out of three desired properties of the management messaging can be achieved simultaneously.

In addition to up-to-date information, the network status should be as detailed as possible. Naturally, the more the details are wanted, the more the data must be transferred between the nodes, which leads to bigger packet sizes and increases the proportional amount of network management traffic in the network, i.e., the overhead caused by the management.

Consequently, the network management in DTNs should consist of messages that (1) contain lot of details and information about the nodes and messaging between them, (2) are sent frequently enough to give the managers up-to-date information about the state of the network, and (3) cause minimal amount of overhead to the network. However, the objectives are contradictory, and it is impossible to achieve all the three objectives at the same time. Getting up-to-date status of the network with high details increases the management overhead. If high details with small overhead are wanted, the messages must be sent more infrequently. Further, up-to-date information with small overhead can be achieved only by giving up some details from the messaging. In traditional networks, unlike in the DTN environment, the management is typically not bandwidth-bound, and the constraint for small overhead can be ignored. Thus, the problem is characteristic specifically to DTN system and we have named it the *DTN management trilemma*. The trilemma is illustrated in Figure 6 where the achieved properties of messaging can be presented as a point that is placed inside the triangle.

As opposed to management of a flat DTN, in a hierarchical organization, it is possible to make certain assumptions about messaging in different parts of the network. Within each hierarchical level, the network connections have similar properties. In the higher levels of the hierarchy, connections between the nodes are typically better. This allows more frequent report delivery from agents to managers. Also, as there is more bandwidth available, more details can be added to messages. However, this is done in the expense of increasing the packet size. On the lower levels of the hierarchy, the situation is the opposite. When the link capacity is low and transmission windows possibly short, only very few details can be added to messages to keep the message size small. Also, to keep the overhead caused by the management messages on a moderate level, reports must be delivered fairly infrequently.

In addition to the connection between the hierarchical levels and the properties of DTN management messaging, a connection between the properties, the hierarchy, and the DTN management trilemma exists. When the trilemma is illustrated as a triangle, the properties of messaging on each hierarchical level can be mapped to the triangle as an area, as shown in Figure 7. In other words, the point representing messaging properties of a single node on a certain hierarchical level resides inside the respective area.

In a hierarchical network, the management traffic consists of horizontal message exchange of managers within a hierarchical level, messages that the managers send to agents that are below them in the hierarchy, and upstream data from the agents to the managers above them, as is shown in Table 1 in Section 4. There are four types of messages, namely, *subscriptions*, *reports*, *control messages*, and *diagnostics messages*. Managers send *subscriptions* to receive *reports* from agents and summary reports from other managers of the system. *Control messages* are used to perform operations on the devices. *Diagnostics messages* are used by utility tools like ping and traceroute.

The authors do recognize that the diagnostic tools are typically based on request-response model, and the use of them is in many contexts seen as a bad practice in DTN environment. However, the need for them cannot be omitted. When used correctly, they provide a powerful tool to help administrators resolve problems in the network, especially in well-connected higher layers of a hierarchical network. Yet, the diagnostics tools should be used infrequently, with care, and always manually as they require a deep knowledge about the underlying network, and the usage may easily cause congestion and overload to the low capacity links.

Network management in DTNs is always a trade-off between flexibility and efficiency. As an extreme, all the definitions related to the messaging could be hardcoded to the system. This would be really efficient as all the actors would initially know the recipients, delivery conditions, and contents of all reports, and no messaging for dynamic definitions, such as agent registrations or report subscriptions, would be needed. However, there would be no flexibility. As the other extreme, all the definitions and parameters related to the management could be defined dynamically. That would make the system fully flexible but also inefficient in terms of resource consumption as a lot a management messaging would be required. Also, advanced

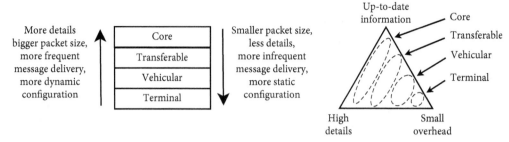

FIGURE 7: Relation of the management trilemma to the hierarchy.

protocol and data definitions that support the complex dynamic definitions would be needed.

In real-world deployments, some kind of compromise should be used to find a balance between flexibility and efficiency. The system should provide suitable data definitions and a protocol to allow dynamic configurability of selected system parts, but set certain things fixed to keep the complexity of the system on a tolerable level, and that way increase the efficiency.

In a hierarchical system, the details and granularity of information that is sent increase from the bottom to the top of the hierarchy as shown in Figure 7. For that, the data definitions in the bottom of the hierarchy are simple and should be fully or almost fully predefined and preconfigured to the system. From the bottom to the top of the hierarchy, the amount of dynamically configured parameters should increase proportionally. On the highest hierarchy levels, the network connections enable dynamic changes to the configurations.

Based on the gradual change of characteristics of messaging and configurability in proportion to hierarchical levels, the network management traffic can be categorized as shown in Table 2. Terminal nodes act only as agents and exchange no management information with each other. They send upwards in the hierarchy only heartbeat signal that contains very small amount of status information of the device (e.g., uptime), or no data at all. The operations performed by the managers to the agents on terminal nodes are small and simple and consist of actions such as subscriptions of reports and basic configuration changes.

Vehicular nodes gather an overview of status reports of the terminal nodes connected to them and report that, along with their own status, upwards in the hierarchy. To keep the size of the report small, only the most important details are added to the message. Due to the high mobility of vehicular nodes, the nodes need to send location and routing related data to each other and to the nodes above them in the hierarchy. Also, vehicular nodes perform basic maintenance operations to terminal nodes.

Transferable nodes move more infrequently than vehicular nodes, and thus, their management traffic contains less routing related data. Transferable nodes exchange with each other more detailed reports about their own status and the nodes below them in the hierarchy. This detailed data are also sent to core nodes upwards in the hierarchy.

Core nodes want to have an overview of the whole network and the nodes below them. The good network connections allow them to exchange all relevant data with other core nodes and that way monitor the overall state of the organization network. Core nodes receive from transferable nodes detailed summaries about the status of the network and nodes below them in the hierarchy. Core nodes may apply major configuration changes to the network, e.g., install or update software patches to the nodes, or affect the routing of the underlying core links. In the core network, both the messaging and the administrative operations highly resemble management of IP network.

Based on the hierarchy level, a default messaging category for each node category has been defined. In normal circumstances, the nodes should communicate using the default messaging category. However, if the quality of connections rapidly decreases, the managers can notify agents to switch temporarily or permanently to a lower category messaging. Also, agents may autonomously identify such a situation and make the switch without manager intervention. If the connection quality later gets improved again, the nodes should switch back to their default messaging category.

In case of a failure in network, a higher-category messaging may be used to troubleshoot the problem. This is typically done both automatically by the nodes and manually by the network administrators. For example, when the problem occurs, a node may automatically send a detailed report to a predefined manager in the network when possible. Moreover, the administrators may decide to manually use diagnostics tools to further investigate the reason and consequences of the problem. However, these diagnostics tools only function in the well-connected parts of the network, as it is difficult to distinguish failures from natural disconnections in the intermittently connected parts of the network.

6. Case Study of Hierarchical Management in a Reference Scenario

In this section, a case study of network management of a hierarchical military organization is shown in an existing reference scenario. The section consists of an introduction of the scenario and the related data set, analysis of the data, description of the management service, the requirements that were set to it, data definitions that it needs, the implementation of the management tasks using AMA and AMP, a performance comparison to a nonhierarchical management solution, and analysis of the results. The paper is concluded by reflecting the implemented management

TABLE 2: DTN management messaging categories.

Node category	Default messaging category	Downwards (manager $\longrightarrow$ agent)	Upwards (agent $\longrightarrow$ manager)	Horizontally (between managers)
Terminal	Minimal	*No traffic*	Heartbeat	*No traffic*
Vehicular	Basic	Subscription of heartbeat	Status update with most important information	Subscriptions and reports related to the status updates of neighbouring vehicular nodes
Transferable	Detailed	Subscription of the status of the vehicular node and a summary of statuses of terminal nodes	Status update with detailed information	Subscriptions and reports related to the status updates of neighbouring transferable nodes
Core	Full	Subscription of the status of the transferable node. Subscription of an overview of the other transferable nodes and the vehicular nodes below	*No traffic*	Subscriptions and reports to exchange all relevant information that is available between the managers of the core

solution against the concepts introduced earlier in this paper.

6.1. Reference Scenario. The Anglova Scenario [37] has been developed in IST-124 task group of NATO Science & Technology organization. In the scenario, a mechanized battalion performs an operation against insurgent forces in a fictitious area and is supported by a naval component and an unmanned aerial vehicle (UAV). The scenario contains a detailed mobility pattern (available at: http://www.ihmc. us/nomads/scenarios/anglova/ (visited 14.5.2018)) for the battalion for over a two-hour period since the start of the operation. The movement pattern has been developed by military experts to match a realistic operation. The positions of the nodes of the battalion are updated once a second. The scenario consists of three vignettes:

(1) Intelligence preparation of the battlefield

(2) Deployment of the forces

(3) Neutralization of insurgent and explosives and medical evacuation

We will focus on the second vignette where the battalion is deployed to the area of Anglova to perform the operation. The headquarters of the battalion is in the area called Fieldmont and the insurgent forces are located in a town called Wellport. In the operation, the battalion moves from Fieldmont to Wellport to "neutralize the insurgents, and to destroy the armaments they have collected."

During the operation, the battalion moves mainly along roads in a hilly terrain that is covered by forests. The battalion comprises four tank companies ($C_1 \ldots C_4$), one command and artillery company (C_5), and one support and supply company (C_6). The tank companies contain 24 vehicles each. The artillery company and the support and supply company contain 22 and 39 vehicles, respectively.

The operation consists of four phases. In the first phase, the battalion moves in a column away from the headquarters. In the second phase, the battalion is split up and starts to move in two separated groups along the two main roads of the area. In the third phase, the both groups are split up to the company level onto the smaller roads on the area. In the fourth phase, the companies are further split up to the

platoons. After the split-up in the beginning of the phase 2, the first half of the battalion moves and splits up further slightly faster than the second half of the battalion.

The battalion Communication and Information System (CIS) is connected to National Operational WAN and the coalition network of NATO Federated Mission Networking (FMN). The vehicles of the companies $C_1 \ldots C_6$ communicate with each other and to the Coalition Headquarters (CHQ) over VHF. As the distance to the CHQ increases during the operation, the VHF connectivity may be poor. Thus, a SATCOM link or communication via UAV can be used as a backup communication channel to the CHQ and also within the battalion that is deployed.

6.2. Data Analysis. In this study, we want to implement a network management service for the battalion of the Anglova scenario. At a given moment of time in the scenario, a connection between some of the nodes does exist and with the others it does not. In this study, we observe the scenario in the time scale of a single phase of the operation. Thus, we are interested in the set of different connections that appear and disappear over time making it possible to communicate in DTN fashion. Further, we are interested in the organizational hierarchy in the different phases and want to identify the connections inside and between different hierarchical levels.

A tank company typically contains three platoons and a headquarters [38]. Depending on the army, there are three to five tanks in each platoon (e.g., in Russia three and in the US army formerly five and nowadays four). In the headquarters, there are additional two tanks and a varying number of other vehicles, such as armored personnel carriers (APC), high-mobility multipurpose wheeled vehicles (HMMWV), and cargo trucks. In addition to that, a maintenance section is normally attached to the company.

No exact information about the vehicles is given in the data set. Yet, based on the node movement and the common structure of army units, relatively precise assumptions about the vehicle types can be made. Further, it is possible to define the positions of the nodes in the organizational hierarchy; we have identified the different companies and roughly divided nodes of each company to platoons.

The data of the Anglova scenario consist latitude and longitude of each of 157 vehicles and a matrix of path losses between every pair of nodes in two different radio frequencies (50 MHz and 300 MHz). In this study, we examine the data set of frequency 50 MHz. The coordinates and the path losses are provided for each second for over two hours from the start of the operation. Based on the given path loss data, we have calculated the connectivity between the nodes during the scenario. Our calculation is based on link budget:

$$P_{RX} = P_{TX} + G - L, \tag{1}$$

where P_{RX} = Received Power (dBm), P_{TX} = Transmitted Power (dBm), G = Gain (dB), and L = Path loss (dB). Based on the information given in the paper [37], we assume the use of NATO Narrow Band Wave Form (NBWF) with the parameters $G = 0\ dB$, $P_{TX} = 37\ dBm$, and $P_{RX} = -100\ dBm$. Thus, we get a receiver's sensitivity threshold S_{RX} for the connectivity between two nodes:

$$\begin{aligned} S_{RX} &\leq P_{TX} + G - P_{RX}, \\ S_{RX} &\leq 137\ dB. \end{aligned} \tag{2}$$

To communicate in traditional IP networks, a full-path connection between the nodes must exist. If the connections are short and intermittent (i.e., they flip-flop), as in the given scenario, IP-based mechanisms perform poorly. However, when the communicating is done in store-carry-forward fashion, even an intermittent connectivity between the nodes is enough to enable messaging.

We have examined each of the four phases of the scenario separately. To take in consideration the DTN nature of the messaging, we look at the connections in each phase in a time window of 10 minutes.

The operation consists of four phases, see Figure 8. In the first phase, the battalion moves in a column away from the headquarters. The tank companies ($C_1 \ldots C_4$) move as a single group in the column. The support and supply company (C_6) is split into two parts and the first of the parts moves in the middle of the column while the remaining part is in the end of the column and leaves the HQ last. The vehicles of the command and artillery company (C_5) are divided along the column already in this early phase of the mission and are in three distinct groups. All the vehicles are on a main road and relatively close to each other and can communicate to each other. The locations of the nodes and the connections between them in the first phase 31 minutes (1860 seconds) after the start of the operation are shown in Figure 8(a).

In the second phase, the battalion is split up and starts to move in two separated groups along the two main roads of the area (Figure 8(b)). The tanks companies stay tightly coupled. The vehicles of the command and artillery company (C_5) are further detached from each other and are joining the tank companies in smaller groups or are being positioned and stopped to some strategic locations in the terrain. The vehicles are still on one of the two main roads of the area and so close to each other that the radio communication between them functions well.

In the third phase, both the main groups are split up to the company level onto the smaller roads on the area. In the fourth phase, the companies are further split up to the platoons. As the vehicles spread on a larger area in a hilly terrain, the path loss between them starts to increase. The split-up takes place at different times in different companies. For example, around 62 minutes after the beginning of the operation Company 1 is already split up to a platoon level, Company 3 is starting to split up, and the rest of the battalion is still formed in companies, as shown in Figure 8(c). In Figure 8(d), the whole battalion is split up to the platoon level.

6.3. Requirements for the Management of the Anglova Scenario.

We have defined a service to manage the nodes during the operation of the Anglova scenario. For clarity, the service focuses only in status monitoring of the nodes in the network. Resolving the possibly noticed failures and problems is not in the scope of the service.

In the scenario, the DTN-like nature of the communications increases as the organization is split up and the nodes get more spread around the area. Figure 9 shows the logical connections used in our network management service 7780 seconds after the start of the operation. From Figure 8(d) the actual DTN connectivity over the links of the data set can be seen. In DTN management, the reports are delivered upwards and horizontally in the hierarchy and the control traffic downwards and sideways, as described earlier in Section 4.

In the scenario, the Coalition Headquarters (CHQ) is the only core level node and acts as the connection point to the core network. Because the data set contains no information about the CHQ, no horizontal management traffic on the core level is included in our management service. On transferable level, there are five central communication points, formed by nodes of command and artillery company (C_5), that are positioned behind the tank companies (to the northern side) and have a functioning network connectivity. Presumably, these nodes are battalion level command points that control the companies below them in the hierarchy. These nodes have an access to the CHQ and act as messaging relay points for transmission, including network management traffic. Two of these transferable nodes, T_1 and T_2, are connected to the nodes below in the hierarchy, and T_3 relays their management traffic upwards in the hierarchy. The nodes $T_2 \ldots T_5$ exchange network management data directly with the CHQ.

Below the transferable nodes, there are 152 vehicular nodes. The vehicular level nodes contain the nodes of tank companies $C_1 \ldots C_4$, nodes of C_6, and those nodes from C_5 that are not on the transferable level. The vehicular nodes of C_5 are divided geographically into two groups that contain 8 and 9 vehicles. Similarly, the vehicles of C_6 are in groups of 19 and 20 nodes. The vehicular nodes of C_5 and C_6 are connected to transferable nodes T_1 and T_2 as shown in Figure 9.

In the data set, there is no information about the terminal level nodes, i.e., the nodes that are in the hierarchy below the

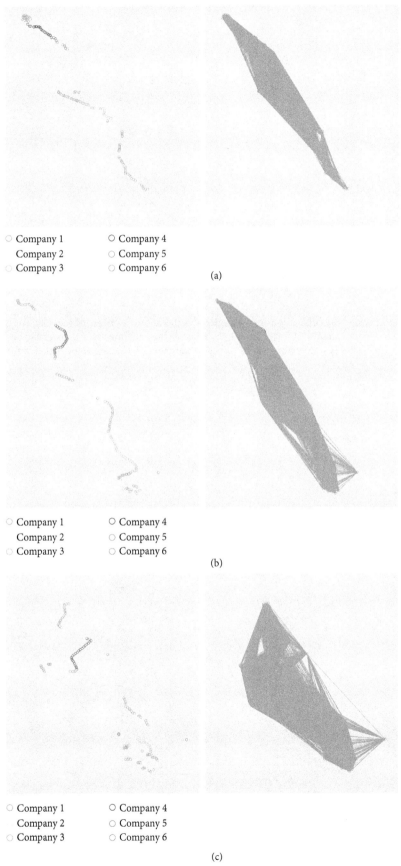

(a)

(b)

(c)

Figure 8: Continued.

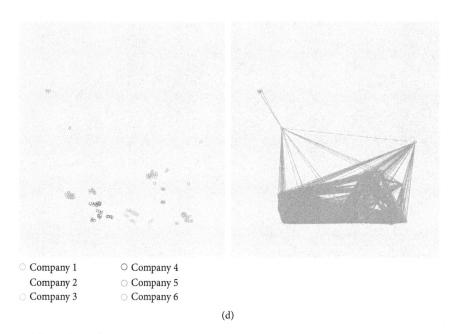

○ Company 1   ○ Company 4
　 Company 2   ○ Company 5
○ Company 3   ○ Company 6

(d)

FIGURE 8: The locations of the nodes and the connections between them in the different phases of the Anglova scenario. (a) Phase 1: the battalion moves in a single column away from the HQ ($t = 1860$ s). (b) Phase 2: the battalion splits up over the two main roads on the area ($t = 2900$ s). (c) Phase 3: the battalion splits up onto many roads grouped in companies. (d) Phase 4: the battalion further splits up to the level of platoons ($t = 7780$ s).

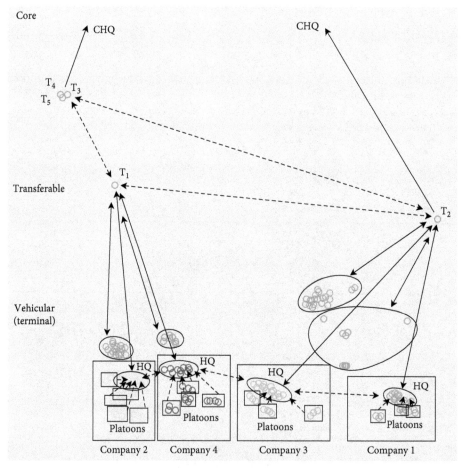

FIGURE 9: Network management traffic through the hierarchical organization of the Anglova scenario at moment $t = 7780$ s. The solid lines show the traffic upwards and downwards in the hierarchy and the dashed line the horizontal data exchange within the organization.

vehicular nodes. For examplificatory purposes, we assume that in each of the tank companies ($C_1 \ldots C_4$), there are 48 terminal nodes that are in the scope of network management. We assume that all these terminal nodes are connected to the company HQ. Further, we assume that in C_5 and C_6, there are two terminal nodes connected to each vehicular level node of the company. Thus, the number of terminal nodes in C_5 and C_6 are 34 and 78, respectively, and the total number of terminal level nodes in the scenario is 304.

We have defined the required outcomes of the management on the different layers of the organization hierarchy as follows:

(i) *CHQ (Core).* An overview of networking of the battalion is wanted as a part of monitoring of the whole operation.

(ii) *Control and Relay Points of C_5 (Transferable).* An overview and status updates of each company is needed to monitor the companies and to make a report to the CHQ. Additionally, horizontal data traffic to exchange status reports between selected transferable nodes (T_1, T_2, and T_3).

(iii) *Tank Company HQ (Vehicular).* Status updates of all the platoons are needed to make sure that the vehicles that belong to the company are reachable and up-and-running. Each company HQ also wants to exchange overview of the company level connectivity with other company HQs in case a backup connection via them is needed, or messages from those companies must be relayed, e.g., due to jamming or loss of certain nodes. All the terminal nodes of the company are monitored by the Company HQ.

(iv) *Platoons of Tank Companies (Vehicular/Terminal).* Reporting responsibility upwards in the hierarchy (to the Company HQ). No horizontal management data exchange.

(v) *Nodes of C_5 and C_6 (Vehicular/Terminal).* The vehicular nodes have a direct reporting responsibility upwards in the hierarchy. No horizontal management data exchange is made. Terminal nodes of the companies are monitored by the vehicular nodes that belong to the same company.

6.4. Definition of Data Types. The management of the defined use case can be performed using Asynchronous Management Protocol. This subsection describes in detail the AMP message structures that are needed to understand AMP messaging used in our management service, to be able to define messages needed in the management, and to calculate the amount of management data sent during the operation.

We have examined the case based on the draft version 3 of the protocol specification [18]. The predefined OIDs of the controls identified by AMP Agent are defined in AMP Agent Application Data Model (ADM). We used version 0.3 of the Agent ADM which is described in [33]. In AMP, all the management is performed using configurations of ADMs,

and communicating with three kinds of messages, namely, *Register Agent*, *Data Report*, and *Perform Control* messages.

In AMP, the messages consist of a one-byte header, a body, and optionally a trailer that contains an access control list. In our implementation, no trailer is attached to the messages. Further, neither positive nor negative acknowledgments (ACK/NACK) for the messages are requested. Messages between the AMP actors are delivered in *Message group* format. *Message group* packs one or more messages together so that they can be delivered as atomic units by an encapsulating protocol used in the communication between the actors. A *Message group* consists of a Self-Delimiting Numeric Value (SDNV) [39] that tells the number of messages in the group, a 5-byte timestamp, and the message data. In our case, only a single message is delivered between the actors at time and the SDNV value takes 1 byte. Thus, the message group and the message header add together an overhead of 7 bytes to each *Register Agent*, *Data Report*, and *Perform Control* message that is sent.

A *Register Agent* message is used to inform a manager about the existence of an agent. The message contains the address of the registering Agent as a Binary Large Object (BLOB), i.e., as the raw bytes of data and its length as an SDNV. If we assume that the system uses 32bit addresses, such as IPv4 addresses or alike, the size of one *Register Agent* message is 5 bytes. Thus, with a message header and message group overhead, the total size of an AMP message containing a registration is 12 bytes.

A *Data Report* message carries report data between the actors. The message consists of a 5-byte timestamp, the recipient address (5 bytes similarly as in case of a *Register Agent* message), number of report entries attached to the message as an SDNV (in this case 1 byte), and the actual report data. On top of that, additional 7-byte overhead of the AMP message group and message headers is added. When each report entry is sent separately, there is 18 bytes of header data, in addition to the actual report data, in each *Data Report* message.

A *Perform Control* message is used to run preconfigured controls on the receiving actor, and can be used, e.g., to create report templates or to add Time-Based Rules to an agent. A *Perform Control* message consists of a timestamp that tells when to run the controls or the macros that are defined in the *Managed Identifier* (MID) collection (MC) of the message. The timestamp is from one to five bytes depending on its value. The controls and macros are identified and parameterized by the Object Identifiers (OIDs) that are defined in the MID of the message. According to the AMP Agent ADM document [33], the Agent ADM Root has a ASN.1 BER-encoded OID 0x2B0601020303 (ID 1.3.6.1.2.3.3) which has a nickname "[8]." Further, Agent Reports (OID 0x2B060102030303) and Agent Controls (OID 0x2B060102030304) have nicknames "[3]" and "[4]," respectively. The nicknames allow the use of compressed parameterized OIDs in the identification of controls and reports. The size of the MID collection of a *Perform Control* message is dependent on the OIDs of the controls that are attached to the message. Thus, each *Perform Control* message consists of 8–12 bytes of fixed data (depending on the given timestamp) and the data of the controls given in the MID collection.

In the Agent ADM, a set of Externally Defined Data (EDD) is defined. The EDD consist of values that the agent must collect from the node and the underlying network and its adapters. Typically, this requires support from the agent application and the firmware of the node where the agent is run. However, the EDD defined in the specification does not consist of all the needed values for the management of a hierarchical organization in DTN or DTN-like environments. Thus, we have defined an AMP Agent ADM EDD extension for hierarchical management (Table 3). The extension must be implemented and included in the agent and its firmware, so that agents can collect the related data for the reports. The defined EDD extension must be known by all the actors of the system.

In the Agent ADM specification, only one report is predefined. However, in the management of a hierarchical organization, reports with different information granularity are used on different levels of the hierarchy. Thus, custom reports for the management must be defined. The reports use the EDD extension of Table 3. The custom reports needed in hierarchical management are shown in Table 4.

Unlike the EDD that must be predefined to all the actors, the reports are defined only to actors who need them by using *Perform Control* messages. The data that a report contains are defined in a report template. Report templates are created by sending a *Perform Control* message that contains a *AddRptTpl* control (OID [4].9) with appropriate parameters. A *AddRptTpl* control consists of an MID that is used to identify the template defined in the message and an MID collection that defines the contents of the template. Size of a *AddRptTpl* control is $9 + N \times 5$ bytes where N is the number of values in the report (definition of each value in the template takes 5 bytes). We have precalculated and attached the size of each custom template to its own column in Table 4. The *AddRptTpl* control is sent inside a *Perform Control* message that increases the overall size by 20 bytes.

After the definition of the report templates, the reports can be subscribed. To subscribe to the reports, a *GenerateRpts* control (OID [4].9) is encapsulated to a *AddTimeRule* control (OID [4].E). The *AddTimeRule* control is sent in a *Perform Control* message, and the total size of the message is 59 bytes including the AMP message header and message group overhead. The reports are delivered as report entries which contain the values that are defined in the template. The size of an entry of each custom report type, i.e., the size of the report data gathered by the agent, is shown in the last column of Table 4.

For consistency, we have defined the EDD and the report templates so that their OID values are under the Agent ADM root (1.3.6.1.2.3.3) but with some gap to the existing value base. However, the OID values shown in the tables should not be used in real-world deployments because there is a chance of collision with values possibly defined in the future versions of AMP specification. Instead, unique OIDs from a namespace that belongs to the deployment should be selected.

6.5. Implementation. The messaging needed in the monitoring can be divided to (1) preconfiguration and (2) the delivery of monitoring data that is sent from the agents to the managers during the operation. The initial preconfiguration can be done before the troops are deployed. In the preconfiguration, the agents register themselves to the managers using *Register Agent* messages. All agents register themselves to the managers above them in the hierarchy. Additionally, some agents need to send another registration horizontally in the hierarchy to allow data exchange with managers on the same level of the hierarchy. After the registration, the managers define the custom reports needed in the monitoring by using *Perform Control* messages. Managers also use *Perform Control* messages to subscribe to the reports they want to receive from the agents by setting *Time-Based Rules* (TRLs) for report delivery. In the TRLs, agents are requested to generate and send reports to managers once in every 10 minutes. The request is sent only once and the reports are delivered as *Data Report* messages from the agents to the managers periodically throughout the operation. The high-level AMP messaging that is needed to implement a monitoring service of our use case is shown in Figure 10.

As described in the previous subsection, there are 304 terminal nodes, 152 vehicular nodes, five transferable nodes, and one core node within the scope of our management service. The core node acts only as a manager, and the terminal nodes only as agents. Also, the transferable nodes T_4 and T_5 communicate only to the CHQ and act only as agents. The transferable nodes T_1, T_2, and T_3 exchange management data both vertically and horizontally in the hierarchy, and act as both managers and agents. Also, the vehicular nodes of the tank company HQs and all the vehicular level nodes of companies C_5 and C_6 have both the role of a manager and an agent. The rest of the vehicular level nodes of the tank companies $C_1 \ldots C_4$ have no terminal nodes attached to them, so they do not need to run manager software. Thus, in each tank company ($C_1 \ldots C_4$), there is one manager and 23 agents on vehicular level. In addition to that, there are 48 agents on the terminal level. In C_5, there are 17 managers and 17 agents on vehicular level, and 34 agents on the terminal level. In C_6, the number of both managers and agent on vehicular level is 39, and there are 78 agents on the terminal level. Overall, there are a total of 304 agents on the terminal level, 60 managers and 152 agents on the vehicular level, three managers and five agents on the transferable level, and one manager on the core level. Hence, there are a total of 64 managers and 461 agents in the system.

During the preconfiguration phase, agents on all levels register themselves to the manager above them in the hierarchy. For that, 461 *Register Agent* messages are needed. To enable horizontal communication within a hierarchy level, the agent of each company HQ sends another registration to the manager of every other company HQ, and on the transferable level, the agents nodes $T_1 \ldots T_3$ register themselves to the managers of each other (additional 17 registrations). Thus, the total number of *Register Agent* messages that are needed is 478.

TABLE 3: AMP Agent ADM EDD extension for hierarchical management.

Name	OID	Description	AMP data type	Size in bytes	Primary usage
Uptime	[1].50	Uptime of the node running the agent	TS	4 (or less)	Reports that are sent upwards in the hierarchy
Battery left	[1].51	Remaining battery life (%) of the device running the agent. Value "0" means unknown	UINT	4	Reports from *terminal* nodes to *vehicular* nodes
Num neighs	[1].52	Number of neighbours (unique nodes) this nodes has been communicating with	UINT	4	In horizontal reports sent on *vehicular* level
Num agents	[1].53	Number of agents registered to (the manager run on) this node	UINT	4	In reports on *vehicular* level
Agent statuses	[1].54	List of (id, timestamp) pairs that tell the time when each of the agents that is registered to this node was seen last time	TBL(UINT, TS)	$7 + N \times 9$, where N is the number of agents	In reports on *vehicular* and *transferable* level
Bundles sent	[1].55	Bundles sent since last reboot	UINT	4	In reports on *transferable* and *core* level
Bytes sent	[1].56	Bytes sent since last reboot	UINT	4	In reports on *transferable* and *core* level
Bundles received	[1].57	Bundles received since last reboot	UINT	4	In reports on *transferable* and *core* level
Bytes received	[1].58	Bytes received since last reboot	UINT	4	In reports on *transferable* and *core* level
Messages in queue	[1].59	Number of messages in the queue waiting for delivery	UINT	4	In reports on *transferable* and *core* level
Disk space total	[1].60	Total disk space (in bytes) on the device running the agent	UVAST	8	In reports on *transferable* and *core* level
Disk space free	[1].61	Free disk space (in bytes) available on the device running the agent	UVAST	8	In reports on *transferable* and *core* level
Stats fusion	[1].62	Table that contains a row for each other agent (identified by id) that is on the same hierarchy level and which basic statistics ([1.52], [1.53]) are available	TBL(UINT, UINT, UINT)	$9 + N \times 13$, where N is the number of agents	In reports that are sent from *vehicular* nodes to *transferable* nodes
Messaging details fusion	[1].63	Table that contains a row for each other agent (identified by id) that is on the same hierarchy level and for which messaging details, disk space usage, and information about the registered agents (i.e., [1.55], [1.56], [1.57], [1.58], [1.59], [1.60], [1.61] are available	TBL(UINT, UINT, UINT, UINT, UINT, UINT, UVAST, UVAST)	$19 + N \times 41$, where N is the number of agents	In reports that are sent from *transferable* nodes to *core* nodes
Full agent details fusion	[1].64	Table that contains a row for each agent (identified by id) registered to this node and contains all the information that the agent sent from itself to this node (i.e., [1.50], [1.55], [1.56], [1.57], [1.58], [1.59], [1.60], [1.61], [1.54], [1.63])	TBL(UINT, UINT, UINT, UINT, UINT, UINT, UVAST, UVAST, TBL(UINT, TS), TBL(UINT, UINT, UINT, UINT, UINT, UINT, UVAST, UVAST))	$25 + \sum_{n=1}^{N}(71 + J_n \times 9 + K_n \times 41)$ where N is the number of agents registered to the core node, J_n is number agents registered to the nth agent of the core node, and K_n is the number of neighbouring agents (i.e., on the same hierarchy level) of the nth agent of the core node.	In horizontal reports sent on *core* level

Next, the report templates are defined. Each manager sends to the agent below it in the hierarchy the template of the report it wants to subscribe. The template definition is sent as a *Perform Control* message that consists of a *AddRptTpl* control. For the monitoring task of the Anglova scenario, 304 templates of *Terminal status report*, 104 templates of *Intervehicular report*, 60 templates of *Vehicular status report*, 6 templates of *Intertransferable report*, and 4

TABLE 4: AMP Agent Hierarchical Management Data (HMD) Report Templates.

Name	OID	Description	Primary usage	Definition	Size of *RptTpl control* (bytes)	Size of *Report entry* (bytes)
Terminal status report	[3].50	Battery life and uptime of the terminal node	Upward in the hierarchy from terminal nodes to vehicular nodes	[1].50, [1].51	19	8
Intervehicular report	[3].51	Simple statistical data about the vehicular node (number of agents registered to the manager run on the node, and total number of neighbours of the node)	To share data horizontally between vehicular nodes	[1].52, [1].53	19	8
Vehicular status report	[3].52	Basic information about the vehicular node and the nodes below it in the hierarchy (uptime, status of each agent registered to this node, fusion of statistics received from neighbouring vehicular nodes)	Upward in the hierarchy from vehicular nodes to transferable nodes	[1].50, [1].54, [1].62	24	$20 + N \times 9 + M \times 13$, where N is the number of agents registered to the node, and M is the number of agents from which a *Intervehicular report* has been subscribed
Intertransferable report	[3].53	Detailed data about the transferable node (messaging statistics, disk space usage, information about the agents registered to the node)	To share data horizontally between transferable nodes	[1].55, [1].56, [1].57, [1].58, [1].59, [1].60, [1].61, [1].54	49	$43 + N \times 9$, where N is the number of agents registered to the node
Transferable status report	[3].54	Detailed information about the transferable node and the nodes below it in the hierarchy	Upward in the hierarchy from transferable nodes to core nodes	[1].50, [1].55, [1].56, [1].57, [1].58, [1].59, [1].60, [1].61, [1].54, [1].63	59	$66 + N \times 9 + M \times 41$, where N is the number of agents registered to the node, and M is the number of agents from which a *Intertransferable report* has been subscribed
Intercore report	[3].55	All relevant information about the core node and detailed summary about the nodes below it in the hierarchy	To share data horizontally between core nodes	[1].55, [1].56, [1].57, [1].58, [1].59, [1].60, [1].61, [1].64	49	$61 + \sum_{n=1}^{N} 71 + J_n \times 9 + K_n \times 41$ where N is the number of agents registered to the core node sending the report, J_n is the number of agents registered to the nth agent of the core node, and K_n is the number of agents from which the nth agent of the core node has subscribed an *Intertransferable report*

Note. The sizes of the *RptTpl control* and the resulting report entry do not contain the overhead of the AMP messages carrying the payload, i.e., the header data of *Perform Control* and *Data report* messages, respectively.

templates of *Transferable status report* are needed. After the template definition, the managers subscribe to the defined reports by sending to the agents a *Perform Control* message with a *AddTimeRule* control. The rule makes the agents run a *GenerateRpts* control once in every ten minutes throughout the operation, and as a consequence to produce and deliver a *Data Report* to the manager. Summary of all management messages sent by the monitoring service of the Anglova scenario is shown in Table 5.

6.6. Results and Comparison. In this subsection, the results and performance of the monitoring service of the Anglova scenario are examined. Table 5 shows the number of different management messages sent between the actors, the sizes of the messages, and the number of bytes generated by the management messaging. We can see that the total amount of AMP management messaging is 176837 bytes. 53220 bytes (30.1%) of this is generated in preconfiguration phase and can be sent before the deployment of the troops. The remaining 123617 bytes (69.9%) is sent during the operation. The amount and the type of messaging in different node categories are shown in Figure 11.

On the terminal and transferable levels, around 35.3 and 33.7 kilobytes of data (19.9% and 19.0% of all data) is transferred, respectively. On the terminal level 89.7% and on

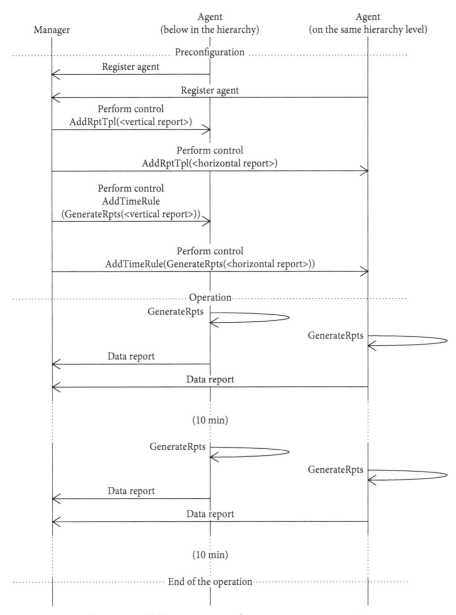

FIGURE 10: AMP messages sent by our management service.

the transferable level 79.0% of the data consist of data reports sent during the operation, and the rest of the data are registration and definitions sent during the preconfiguration phase of the operation. On the core level, only 552 bytes of data is transferred, which is natural, because there is only one core node and no horizontal data exchange takes place on the core level. Thus, all 552 bytes of data consists of report template definitions and additions of time rules sent to transferable nodes.

Interestingly, on the vehicular level, over 107 kilobytes of data is sent, which is 60.7% of all the management traffic sent during the operation. This high amount of data sent by the vehicular nodes is caused by the organization structure. There are 152 vehicular nodes that manage 304 terminal nodes below them in the hierarchy. Even though the details are kept to a minimum and the messages are relatively small in size, the aggregated amount of data is high due to the large number of nodes on the vehicular level. Also, proportionally

large amount (39.1%) of preconfiguration data is needed. On the terminal level, the reports that are sent upwards in the hierarchy are smaller, there is no horizontal data exchange, and the nodes never act as managers, which keeps the amount of preconfiguration data significantly smaller.

Despite that the majority of data transferred were sent by the vehicular nodes, the amount of data sent by a single node was clearly smallest on the terminal level and increased almost linearly between the node categories. On the terminal level, each node sent on average 116 bytes of data during the operation. On the vehicular and transferable levels, the amount of data sent by a node was on average 706 and 6731 bytes, respectively (in case of core nodes the comparison is not relevant due to the absence of horizontal traffic).

To examine the performance improvement gained from the hierarchical solution, also a nonhierarchical implementation of the network management service of the Anglova

TABLE 5: Hierarchical DTN-level management messaging of the Anglova scenario.

Description	End points	Message (OID)	Total number of messages	Message size (bytes)	Bytes total
Registration	Agent ⟷ manager	*Register Agent*	478	12	5736
Addition of report templates using *Perform Control* messages and *AddRptTpl* control	Vehicular level manager ⟷ terminal level agent	Template for *Terminal status report* ([3].50)	304	39	11856
	Manager of company HQ of C_n ⟷ agent of company HQ of C_n, where $n \in \{1,2,3,4\}$	Template for *Intervehicular report* ([3].51)	92	39	3588
	Manager of company HQ of C_n ⟷ agent of company HQ of C_m, where $n, m \in \{1,2,3,4\}, n \neq m$	Template for *Intervehicular report* ([3].51)	12	39	468
	Transferable level manager ⟷ agent of company HQ of $C_1 \ldots C_4$/Vehicular level agent of $C_5 \ldots C_6$	Template for *Vehicular status report* ([3].52)	60	44	2640
	Manager of transferable node T_n ⟷ agent of transferable node T_m, where $n, m \in \{1,2,3\}, n \neq m$	Template for *Intertransferable report* ([3].53)	6	69	414
	Core level manager ⟷ transferable level agent of $T_2 .. T_5$	Template for *Transferable status report* ([3].54)	4	79	316
Addition of time-based rules using *Perform Control* messages, and *AddTimeRule* and *GenerateRpts* controls	Vehicular level manager ⟷ terminal level agent	TRL for *Terminal status report* ([3].50) delivery	304	59	17936
	Manager of a company HQ of C_n ⟷ agent of a company HQ of C_n, where $n \in \{1, 2, 3, 4\}$	TRL for *Intervehicular report* ([3].51) delivery	92	59	5428
	Manager of a company HQ of C_n ⟷ agent of a company HQ of C_m, where $n, m \in \{1, 2, 3, 4\}, n \neq m$	TRL for *Intervehicular report* ([3].51) delivery	12	59	708
	Transferable level manager ⟷ agent of company HQ of $C_1 \ldots C_4$/Vehicular level agent of $C_5 \ldots C_6$	TRL for *Vehicular status report* ([3].52) delivery	60	59	3540
	Manager of transferable node T_n ⟷ agent of transferable node T_m, where $n, m \in \{1, 2, 3\}, n \neq m$	TRL for *Intertransferable report* ([3].53]) delivery	6	59	354
	Core level manager ⟷ transferable level agent of $T_2 \ldots T_5$	TRL for *Transferable status report* ([3].54) delivery	4	59	236
Delivery of reports defined in TRLs as *Data Report* messages	Agent of a terminal node ⟷ manager of a company HQ of $C_1 \ldots C_4$/Manager of a vehicular node of $C_5 \ldots C_6$	*Terminal status report* ([3].50)	$304 \times (1/10$ min$)\times$ 130 min = 3952	8	31616
	Agent of a vehicular node of a platoon of C_n ⟷ manager of a company HQ of C_n, where $n \in \{1, 2, 3, 4\}$	*Intervehicular report* ([3].51)	$92 \times (1/10$ min$) \times$ 130 min = 1196	8	9568
	Agent of a company HQ of C_n ⟷ manager of a company HQ of C_m, where $n, m \in \{1, 2, 3, 4\}, n \neq m$	*Intervehicular report* ([3].51)	$12 \times (1/10$ min$) \times$ 130 min = 156	8	1248
	Agent of a company HQ of $C_1 \ldots C_4$ ⟷ manager of a transferable node	*Vehicular status report* ([3].52)	$4 \times (1/10$ min$) \times$ 130 min = 52	518	26936
	Agent of a vehicular node of $C_5 \ldots C_6$ ⟷ manager of a transferable node	*Vehicular status report* ([3].52)	$56 \times (1/10$ min$) \times$ 130 min = 728	38	27664
	Agent of the transferable node T_1 ⟷ manager of the transferable node T_2/T_3	*Intertransferable report* ([3].53)	$2 \times (1/10$ min$) \times$ 130 min = 26	304	7904
	Agent of the transferable node T_2 ⟷ manager of the transferable node T_1/T_3	*Intertransferable report* ([3].53)	$2 \times (1/10$ min$) \times$ 130 min = 26	322	8372
	Agent of the transferable node T_3 ⟷ manager of the transferable node T_1/T_2	*Intertransferable report* ([3].53)	$2 \times (1/10$ min$) \times$ 130 min = 26	43	1118
	Agent of the transferable node T_2 ⟷ manager of the core node	*Transferable status report* ([3].54)	$1 \times (1/10$ min$) \times$ 130 min = 13	427	5551
	Agent of the transferable node T_3 ⟷ manager of the core node	*Transferable status report* ([3].54)	$1 \times (1/10$ min$) \times$ 130 min = 13	148	1924
	Agent of the transferable node T_4/T_5 ⟷ manager of the core node	*Transferable status report* ([3].54)	$2 \times (1/10$ min$) \times$ 130 min = 26	66	1716
Total					176837

Note. The given message size is the size of the type-specific AMP message including all its headers and payload.

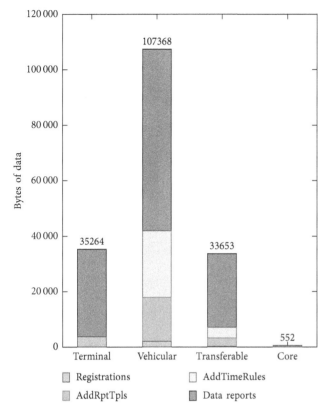

FIGURE 11: DTN management data sent by nodes in different categories.

scenario was made. For that, the same monitoring service was implemented in a nonhierarchical manner using the same technology (AMA and AMP) as in the implementation of the hierarchical service, which makes the results directly comparable with each other.

Regardless of the flat management hierarchy, the nodes still belong to the organization hierarchy, and the need to monitor them remains the same. In the flat management hierarchy, all the status reports are sent directly between the agent and the manager that needs the information, i.e., the subscriber who is the recipient of the status reports is no longer the next node above in the hierarchy. Thus, there is also no horizontal data exchange for the hierarchy-based summary reports of the nodes below in the hierarchy. The agents register themselves to all the managers that need to be aware of their statuses. To allow messaging that is needed to fulfill the required outcomes that were defined in Section 6.3, all the nodes need to send a registration to the CHQ. Further, the vehicular nodes of $C_1 \ldots C_4$ need to register themselves to the HQs of the companies $C_1 \ldots C_4$ and to the transferable nodes $T_1 \ldots T_3$. The vehicular nodes of C_5 and C_6 need to register themselves to $T_1 \ldots T_3$. The terminal nodes of $C_1 \ldots C_4$ need to send a registration to the HQs of the companies $C_1 \ldots C_4$ and to the transferable nodes $T_1 \ldots T_3$. The terminal nodes of C_5 and C_6 need to register themselves to the vehicular node that is monitoring them (in the same company) and also to the transferable nodes $T_1 \ldots T_3$. The resulting 3089 registration messages make the managers in different positions of the organization hierarchy aware of the

agents they need to monitor in order to get the information required by the monitoring service.

The report templates and the resulting reports used by the nonhierarchical service are similar to *Terminal status report* (OID [3].50), *Vehicular status report* (OID [3].52), and *Transferable status report* (OID [3].54) of Table 5 except that no summary of the nodes below in the hierarchy (OIDs [1].62 and [1].63) is added to the reports. For identification purposes, OIDs [3].60, [3].62, and [3].64 were assigned to these nonhierarchical status reports, respectively. The management data that are sent by the nonhierarchical monitoring service of the Anglova scenario are shown in Table 6.

In the nonhierarchical management service, a total of 1,854,972 bytes of management data is transferred between the nodes. 339,965 bytes (18.3%) of that data is sent in the preconfiguration phase and 1,515,007 bytes (81.7%) during the operation. 243,136 bytes (13.1%) of the data is sent by the terminal nodes, 1,269,248 bytes (68.4%) by the vehicular nodes, 297,235 bytes (16.0%) by the transferable nodes, and 45,353 bytes (2.4%) by the core node. Similarly, as in the hierarchical solution, most of the data are sent on the vehicular level. However, in the hierarchical solution, the terminal nodes send 4.8% more data than transferable nodes whereas in the nonhierarchical solution the transferable nodes send 22.3% more data. Further, the core node sends more report templates and subscriptions in the nonhierarchical solution. Figure 12 shows the amount of data sent by both solutions.

The results show that the amount of data sent in the nonhierarchical management service is approximately 10.5 times (1049%) as much as that of the hierarchical management solution. The increased amount of data sent is a direct consequence of the absence of the hierarchical methods. In order to provide the status of the network to the nodes that need it on the different levels of the organization, the statuses are sent multiple times (point-to-point) instead of utilizing the hierarchy-based summary reports. Also, the nonhierarchical model requires more preconfiguration data to enable the messaging between the nodes. Even though there is proportionally less preconfiguration data transferred, the absolute amount of that data is approximately 6.4 times larger in the nonhierarchical service compared to the hierarchical solution. However, as mentioned above, in the nonhierarchical solution, the data definitions and reports do not contain the complex structures required by the hierarchy-based summary messages. In that sense, the hierarchical methods increase the complexity of system but help cut down the amount of data sent between the nodes significantly.

7. Summary and Conclusions

In this paper, we studied network management of organizations that are hierarchically structured and operate in DTN or DTN-like environments. In many of these of organizations, the topology of the network follows, or is based on, the hierarchical structure of the organization. Examples of such organizations include, e.g., the military and different emergency agencies.

TABLE 6: DTN-level management messaging of the Anglova scenario when the management service is implemented in a nonhierarchical manner.

Description	End points	Message (OID)	Total number of messages	Message size (bytes)	Bytes total
Registration	Agent $\leftrightarrow$ manager	*Register Agent*	3089	12	37068
Addition of report templates using *Perform Control* messages and *AddRptTpl* control	Manager of company HQ of C_n $\leftrightarrow$ agent of a terminal node of C_n, where $n \in \{1, 2, 3, 4\}$	Template for *Terminal status report* ([3].60)	768	39	29952
	Vehicular level manager of $C_5 \ldots C_6$ $\leftrightarrow$ agent of a terminal node of $C_5 \ldots C_6$	Template for *Terminal status report* ([3].60)	112	39	4368
	Manager of $T_1 \ldots T_3$ $\leftrightarrow$ agent of a terminal node of $C_1 \ldots C_6$	Template for *Terminal status report* ([3].60)	912	39	35568
	Core level manager (CHQ) $\leftrightarrow$ terminal level agent	Template for *Terminal status report* ([3].60)	304	39	11856
	Manager of company HQ of C_n $\leftrightarrow$ agent of a vehicular level node of a platoon of $C_1 \ldots C_4$/agent of company HQ of C_m, where $n, m \in \{1, 2, 3, 4\}$, $n \neq m$	Template for *Vehicular status report* ([3].62)	380	39	14820
	Manager of $T_1 \ldots T_3$ $\leftrightarrow$ agent of a vehicular node of $C_1 \ldots C_6$	Template for *Vehicular status report* ([3].62)	456	39	17784
	Core level manager (CHQ) $\leftrightarrow$ vehicular level agent	Template for *Vehicular status report* ([3].62)	152	39	5928
	Core level manager $\leftrightarrow$ transferable level agent of $T_1 \ldots T_5$	Template for *Transferable status report* ([3].64)	5	74	370
Addition of time-based rules using *Perform Control* messages, and *AddTimeRule* and *GenerateRpts* controls	Manager of company HQ of C_n $\leftrightarrow$ agent of a terminal node of C_n, where $n \in \{1, 2, 3, 4\}$	TRL for *Terminal status report* ([3].60) delivery	768	59	45312
	Vehicular level manager of $C_5 \ldots C_6$ $\leftrightarrow$ agent of a terminal node of $C_5 \ldots C_6$	TRL for *Terminal status report* ([3].60) delivery	112	59	6608
	Manager of $T_1 \ldots T_3$ $\leftrightarrow$ agent of a terminal node of $C_1 \ldots C_6$	TRL for *Terminal status report* ([3].60) delivery	912	59	53808
	Core level manager (CHQ) $\leftrightarrow$ terminal level agent	TRL for *Terminal status report* ([3].60) delivery	304	59	17936
	Manager of company HQ of C_n $\leftrightarrow$ agent of a vehicular level node of a platoon of $C_1 \ldots C_4$/agent of company HQ of C_m, where $n, m \in \{1, 2, 3, 4\}$, $n \neq m$	TRL for *Vehicular status report* ([3].62) delivery	380	59	22420
	Manager of $T_1 \ldots T_3$ $\leftrightarrow$ agent of a vehicular node of $C_1 \ldots C_6$	TRL for *Vehicular status report* ([3].62) delivery	456	59	26904
	Core level manager (CHQ) $\leftrightarrow$ vehicular level agent	TRL for *Vehicular status report* ([3].62) delivery	152	59	8968
	Core level manager $\leftrightarrow$ transferable level agent of $T_1 \ldots T_5$	TRL for *Transferable status report* ([3].64) delivery	5	59	295

TABLE 6: Continued.

Description	End points	Message (OID)	Total number of messages	Message size (bytes)	Bytes total
	Agent of a terminal node of C_n $\leftrightarrow$ manager of company HQ of C_n, where $n \in \{1, 2, 3, 4\}$	*Terminal status report* ([3].60)	$768 \times (1/10 \text{ min}) \times$ 130 min = 9984	8	79872
	Agent of a terminal node of $C_5 \ldots C_6$ $\leftrightarrow$ vehicular level manager of $C_5 \ldots C_6$	*Terminal status report* ([3].60)	$112 \times (1/10 \text{ min}) \times$ 130 min = 1456	8	11648
	Agent of a terminal node of $C_1 \ldots C_6$ $\leftrightarrow$ manager of $T_1 \ldots T_3$	*Terminal status report* ([3].60)	$912 \times (1/10 \text{ min}) \times$ 130 min = 11856	8	94848
	Terminal level agent $\leftrightarrow$ core level manager (CHQ)	*Terminal status report* ([3].60)	$304 \times (1/10 \text{ min}) \times$ 130 min = 3952	8	31616
	Agent of a vehicular level node of a platoon of $C_1 \ldots C_4$ $\leftrightarrow$ manager of company HQ of C_n, where $n \in \{1, 2, 3, 4\}$	*Vehicular status report* ([3].62)	$368 \times (1/10 \text{ min}) \times$ 130 min = 4784	11	52624
Delivery of reports defined in TRLs as *Data Report* messages	Agent of company HQ of C_n $\leftrightarrow$ manager of company HQ of C_m, where $n, m \in \{1, 2, 3, 4\}, n \neq m$	*Vehicular status report* ([3].62)	$12 \times (1/10 \text{ min}) \times$ 130 min = 156	2594	404664
	Agent of a vehicular level node of a platoon of $C_1 \ldots C_4$ $\leftrightarrow$ manager of $T_1 \ldots T_3$/Core level manager (CHQ)	*Vehicular status report* ([3].62)	$368 \times (1/10 \text{ min}) \times$ 130 min = 4784	11	52624
	Agent of company HQ of $C_1 \ldots C_4$ $\leftrightarrow$ manager of $T_1 \ldots T_3$/Core level manager (CHQ)	*Vehicular status report* ([3].62)	$16 \times (1/10 \text{ min}) \times$ 130 min = 208	2594	539552
	Agent of a vehicular level node of $C_5 \ldots C_6$ $\leftrightarrow$ manager of $T_1 \ldots T_3$/Core level manager (CHQ)	*Vehicular status report* ([3].62)	$224 \times (1/10 \text{ min}) \times$ 130 min = 2912	29	84448
	Transferable level agent of $T_1 \ldots T_3$ $\leftrightarrow$ core level manager (CHQ)	*Transferable status report* ([3].64)	$3 \times (1/10 \text{ min}) \times$ 130 min = 39	4151	161889
	Agent of the transferable node T_4/T_5 $\leftrightarrow$ core level manager (CHQ)	*Transferable status report* ([3].64)	$2 \times (1/10 \text{ min}) \times$ 130 min = 26	47	1222
Total					1854972

Note. The given message size is the size of the type-specific AMP message including all its headers and payload.

In the paper, we described the gradual change in management centralization and network quality from the top to the bottom of the hierarchy. We introduced a node categorization of *core*, *transferable*, *vehicular*, and *terminal* nodes and showed the relation between the node categories and the organization hierarchy. We described how the organization and position of a single node within it affect the role and the responsibilities of the node. Further, we identified three fields of, namely, *contextual*, *technical*, and *role-based*, requirements and responsibilities for each node and defined *management responsibility stack* that describes how the parts of a layered system are interconnected in terms of the responsibilities related to network management. We also described how the hierarchical structure of the organization and the network affect the messaging and configurability of the nodes of a system.

To tie the theory to practice, we defined and implemented a monitoring service for the Anglova scenario. The Anglova scenario is a fictitious military scenario that has been developed by military experts to match a realistic military operation. In the Anglova scenario, a battalion performs a military operation in hilly terrain covered by forests. The battalion consists of four tank companies, a command and artillery company and a support and supply company, which all together contain 157 vehicles. For the operation, detailed movement patterns and radio connectivity between the vehicles are given. We defined and

implemented the monitoring service of the Anglova scenario using existing IETF AMA and AMP definitions.

Based on the given information about the companies and the organization structure, the movement patterns of the nodes, and the connectivity between the nodes, we identified the nodes that belong to each of the node categories. The management service was designed so that the Coalition HQ, that is a part of the core network, follows the overall status of the battalion performing the operation. The transferable nodes below the Coalition HQ in the hierarchy belong to the command and artillery company, and monitor the vehicular nodes connected to them. The vehicular nodes further monitor the terminal nodes. Thus, the management centralization decreases in the organization along with the hierarchy level, and the management traffic goes through the four categories of nodes. The terminal nodes deliver status data to nearby vehicles. The vehicles of the platoons of the tank companies connect to the company HQ that belongs to the same node category but is above them in the hierarchy. The company HQs and the vehicular nodes of the command and artillery company and the support and supply company connect to the transferable nodes of the command and artillery company. From the transferable nodes, there is a further connection to the core node of the Coalition HQ. Transferable and vehicular nodes also exchange data horizontally in the hierarchy to produce summaries to nodes above them in the organization.

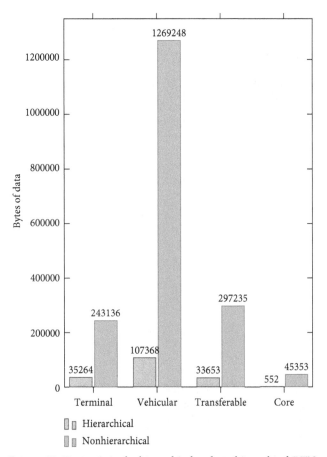

FIGURE 12: Data sent in the hierarchical and nonhierarchical DTN management service implementations of the Anglova scenario.

In the management service, each node has contextual, technical, and role-based requirements and responsibilities. The contextual requirements and responsibilities are system-wide and set by the environment and context for which the service is designed for and the way the service is used and the objectives of that usage. The management service of the Anglova scenario must function in the overlay network formed on top of the available connections between the vehicles of the battalion moving in the terrain of the scenario. Further, the management service must fulfill the required outcomes defined in Section 6.3. Each individual node must meet the technical requirements and responsibilities set by the devices and the radio hardware of the node and AMP and AMA which were used in the service implementation. The role-based requirements and responsibilities reflect the differences in the responsibilities between the nodes on the same hierarchical level. For example, in the scenario, transferable nodes $T_2 \ldots T_3$ communicate with the CHQ, whereas transferable node T_1 only relays traffic to them and has no direct connection to the CHQ. Similarly, on the vehicular level, the HQs of tank companies $C_1 \ldots C_4$ communicate with transferable nodes T_1 and T_2. However, due to their differing role in the hierarchy, the rest of the vehicular nodes of the tank companies have no connections to the nodes of the transferable level.

To adapt to the demands of hierarchical organization, the network management messaging of the Anglova scenario

follows the messaging categories defined in Table 2 in Section 5. For that, an extension to EDD of the Agent ADM was made by defining data types needed in the management of a device that is part of a hierarchically structured organization operating in DTN environment. Based on the extension, custom report types for horizontal and vertical communication on each hierarchy level were defined. Finally, the messaging between the managers and the agents was configured to happen so that each actor of the system was able to meet its requirements both vertically and horizontally in the hierarchy as illustrated in Figure 3 in Section 4.

The results show that in the hierarchical management service of the Anglova scenario, a total of 177 kilobytes of data was sent. Approximately, 30.1% of the data consisted of preconfiguration data needed by the management service, and the remaining 69.9% were data reports sent during the operation. To see the performance of our hierarchical solution, a nonhierarchical AMA/AMP-based implementation of the same management service was made. In the nonhierarchical solution, 1855 kilobytes of data was sent and 18.3% of that data was preconfiguration data. The results show that the hierarchical methods require proportionally more preconfiguration and in that way increase the complexity of the system. However, compared to nonhierarchical management, they improve the performance of network management significantly: in case of the Anglova scenario, 90.5% less data was sent when the hierarchical methods were used.

The latency and the delivery rate of the messages are fundamental and widely known problems in DTN systems. In the context of network management service, they cause additional uncertainty and make it difficult to distinguish delayed message delivery caused by natural disconnections from possible network failures. The monitoring service of the Anglova scenario uses the delivery rate of 10 minutes. However, no timeliness or successful delivery of the messages can be guaranteed. As future research, the DTN management solutions should find a way to solve, or mitigate, the impact of the problem. However, currently no such solution exists and also our hierarchical management methods omit the issue.

As the details and message size increase in each node category from the bottom to the top of the hierarchy, the authors expected that the amount of data sent would be shaped accordingly as well. However, it turned out that in the hierarchical monitoring service of the Anglova scenario, the majority of the data were transferred by the vehicular nodes. Further, it turned out that the amount of data sent on the bottom of the hierarchy on the terminal level were about the same as on the transferable level. This seems to be a result of the hierarchical structure of the organization. In a hierarchical military organization, such as the one of the Anglova scenario, there are a large number of vehicular nodes that manage even larger number of terminal nodes below them in the hierarchy. Even though the messages sent between the nodes are relatively small in size and scarce in granularity, the aggregated amount of total data sent in the node categories is relatively high. Further, the large number of nodes and the small message size result in large proportional amount of data definitions in the pre-configuration phase on the vehicular level.

It would be interesting to see if this kind of traffic shape is specific to the Anglova scenario only, to all military operations, or to all hierarchical organizations in general. However, based on a single scenario, strong conclusions on the traffic shape cannot be drawn. Yet, when observing the topic further in the future, the results shown in this paper can be used as a reference point.

Acknowledgments

The authors would like to thank Aleksi Marttinen from Aalto University for his help with the link budget calculation and radio parameter estimation for the analysis of the Anglova Scenario in Section 6.2.

References

[1] K. Scott, T. Refaei, N. Trivedi, J. Trinh, and J. P. Macker, "Robust communications for disconnected, intermittent, low-bandwidth (DIL) environments," in *Proceedings of Military Communications Conference (MILCOM)*, pp. 1009–1014, Baltimore, MD, USA, November 2011.

[2] K. Fall, "A delay-tolerant network architecture for challenged internets," in *Proceedings of Conference on Applications, Technologies, Architectures, and Protocols for Computer Communications (SIGCOMM '03)*, pp. 27–34, ACM, Karlsruhe, Germany, August 2003.

[3] A. McMahon and S. Farrell, "Delay- and disruption-tolerant networking," *IEEE Internet Computing*, vol. 13, no. 6, pp. 82–87, 2009.

[4] V. Cerf, S. Burleigh, A. Hooke et al., "Delay-tolerant networking architecture," RFC 4838, 2007.

[5] K. Fall and S. Farrell, "DTN: an architectural retrospective," *IEEE Journal on Selected Areas in Communications*, vol. 26, no. 5, pp. 828–836, 2008.

[6] K. Scott and S. Burleigh, "Bundle protocol specification," RFC 5050, 2007.

[7] R. Presuhn, "Version 2 of the protocol operations for the simple network management protocol (SNMP)," RFC 3416, 2002.

[8] E. Birrane and H. Kruse, "Delay-tolerant network management: the definition and exchange of infrastructure information in high delay environments," in *Proceedings of Infotech@Aerospace*, American Institute of Aeronautics and Astronautics, St. Louis, MO, USA, March 2011.

[9] L. Z. Granville, D. M. Da Rosa, A. Panisson, C. Melchiors, M. J. B. Almeida, and L. M. R. Tarouco, "Managing computer networks using peer-to-peer technologies," *IEEE Communications Magazine*, vol. 43, no. 10, pp. 62–68, 2005.

[10] J. C. Nobre, C. Melchiors, C. C. Marquezan, L. M. R. Tarouco, and L. Z. Granville, "A survey on the use of P2P technology for network management," *Journal of Network and Systems Management*, vol. 26, no. 1, pp. 189–221, 2018.

[11] J. C. Nobre, P. A. P. R. Duarte, L. Z. Granville, and L. M. R. Tarouco, "Delay-tolerant management using self-∗ properties and P2P technology," in *Proceedings of IFIP/IEEE International Symposium on Integrated Network Management (IM 2013)*, pp. 728–731, Ghent, Belgium, May 2013.

[12] J. C. Nobre, P. A. P. R. Duarte, L. Z. Granville, L. M. R. Tarouco, and F. J. Bertinatto, "On using P2P technology to enable opportunistic management in DTNs through statistical estimation," in *Proceedings of IEEE International Conference on Communications (ICC)*, pp. 3124–3129, Sydney, Australia, June 2014.

[13] C. Peoples, G. Parr, B. Scotney, and A. Moore, "Context-aware policy-based framework for self-management in delay-tolerant networks: a case study for deep space exploration," *IEEE Communications Magazine*, vol. 48, no. 7, pp. 102–109, 2010.

[14] J. Pierce-Mayer and O. Peinado, "DTN-O-Tron: a system for the user-guided semi-autonomous generation and distribution of CGR contact plans," in *Proceedings of IEEE International Conference on Wireless for Space and Extreme Environments (WiSEE)*, pp. 1–4, Aachen Germany, December 2015.

[15] J. Pierce-Mayer and O. Peinado, "DTN network management," in *Proceedings of 14th International Conference on Space Operations*, Deajeon, Korea, May 2016.

[16] S. Burleigh, "Contact graph routing," Internet-Draft, Version 1, July 2010, https://tools.ietf.org/html/draft-burleigh-dtnrg-cgr-01.

[17] G. Araniti, N. Bezirgiannidis, E. Birrane et al., "Contact graph routing in DTN space networks: overview, enhancements and performance," *IEEE Communications Magazine*, vol. 53, no. 3, pp. 38–46, 2015.

[18] J. Mayer and E. Birrane, "Asynchronous management protocol," Draft Version 3, Internet-Draft, June 2016.

[19] A. Papalambrou, A. G. Voyiatzis, D. N. Serpanos, and P. Soufrilas, "Monitoring of a DTN2 network," in *Proceedings of Baltic Congress on Future Internet and Communications*, pp. 116–119, Riga, Latvia, February 2011.

[20] J. L. Torgerson, "Network monitor and control of disruption-tolerant networks," in *Proceedings of 13th International Conference on Space Operations (SpaceOps)*, Pasadena, CA, USA, May 2014.

[21] S. Kumar, A. Mishra, and G. C. Robert, "Configuration management for DTNs," in *Proceedings of IEEE Globecom Workshops*, pp. 589–594, Singapore, December 2010.

[22] R. Enns, M. Bjorklund, A. Bierman, and J. Schönwälder, "Network configuration protocol (NETCONF)," RFC 6241, 2011.

[23] B. F. Ferreira, J. N. Isento, J. A. Dias, J. J .P. C. Rodrigues, and L. Zhou, "An SNMP-based solution for vehicular delay-tolerant network management," in *Proceedings of IEEE Global Communications Conference (GLOBECOM)*, pp. 250–255, Anaheim, CA, USA, Dec 2012.

[24] B. F. Ferreira, J. J. P. C. Rodrigues, J. A. Dias, and J. N. Isento, "Man4VDTN–a network management solution for Vehicular Delay-Tolerant Networks," *Computer Communications*, vol. 39, pp. 3–10, 2014.

[25] V. N. G. J. Soares, F. Farahmand, and J. J. P. C. Rodrigues, "A layered architecture for vehicular delay-tolerant networks," in *Proceedings of IEEE Symposium on Computers and Communications (ISCC)*, pp. 122–127, Sousse, Tunisia, July 2009.

[26] J. A. F. F. Dias, J. J. P. C. Rodrigues, J. F. de Paz, and J. M. Corchado, "MoM–a real time monitoring and management tool to improve the performance of vehicular delay tolerant networks," in *Proceedings of Eighth International Conference on Ubiquitous and Future Networks (ICUFN)*, pp. 1071–1076, Vienna, Austria, July 2016.

[27] E. M. Salvador, D. F. Macedo, J. M. Nogueira, V. D. D. Almeida, and L. Z. Granville, "Hierarchy-based monitoring of vehicular delay-tolerant networks," in *Proceedings of 13th IEEE Annual Consumer Communications Networking Conference (CCNC)*, pp. 447–452, Las Vegas, NV, USA, January 2016.

[28] E. M. Salvador, D. F. Macedo, and J. M. S. Nogueira, "HEMAN: hierarchical management for vehicular delay-tolerant networks," *Journal of Network and Systems Management*, vol. 23, no. 3, pp. 663–685, 2017.

[29] G. L. Campbell, "An SNMP gateway for delay/disruption tolerant network management," McClure School of Information and Telecommunication Systems Technical, a Project Report adviced by Hans Kruse, August 2010. http://www.its.ohiou.edu/kruse/publications/Campbell_SNMP_Gateway.pdf.

[30] H. Kruse, S. Ostermann, G. Clark, and G. Campbell, "DING protocol - a protocol for network management," February 2010. https://tools.ietf.org/html/draft-irtf-dtnrg-ding-network-management-02.

[31] W. Ivancic, "Delay/disruption tolerant networking-network management requirements," Internet-Draft, version 00, 2009. https://tools.ietf.org/html/draft-ivancic-dtnrg-network-management-reqs-00.

[32] E. Birrane, "Asynchronous management architecture," Draft Version 3. Internet-Draft, June 2016.

[33] E. Birrane, "Asynchronous management protocol agent application data model," Draft Version 02. Internet-Draft, June 2016.

[34] E. Birrane, M. Sinkiat, and S. Jacobs, "AMP manager SQL interface," Internet-Draft, September 2015.

[35] J. O. Kephart and D. M. Chess, "The vision of autonomic computing," *Computer*, vol. 36, no. 1, pp. 41–50, 2003.

[36] N. Samaan and A. Karmouch, "Towards autonomic network management: an analysis of current and future research directions," *IEEE Communications Surveys & Tutorials*, vol. 11, no. 3, pp. 22–36, 2009.

[37] N. Suri, A. Hansson, J. Nilsson et al., "A realistic military scenario and emulation environment for experimenting with tactical communications and heterogeneous networks," in *Proceedings of IEEE International Conference on Military Communications and Information Systems (ICMCIS 2016)*, pp. 1–8, Brussels, Belgium, May 2016.

[38] United States Army, *United States Army Field Manual 17-15*, Headquarters, Department of the Army, County, VA, USA, 1996.

[39] W. Eddy and E. Davies, "Using self-delimiting numeric values in protocols," RFC 6256 (Informational), 2011.

6

Creating Values out of Internet of Things: An Industrial Perspective

Partha Pratim Ray

Department of Computer Applications, Sikkim University, 6th Mile, Gangtok, Sikkim 737102, India

Correspondence should be addressed to Partha Pratim Ray; ppray@cus.ac.in

Academic Editor: Yasuhisa Omura

Internet of Things based cloud is envisaged to extract values other than the specified purpose for which it is to be utilized. It is hereby apprehended that different genre of values, rather business values, could efficiently be assimilated from the Internet of Things cloud platforms. It is also investigated to identify numerous domains of applications that are currently being associated with the similar cloud platforms. A case study on various types of value generation methods has been performed. A novel Internet of Things cloud stack is proposed to disseminate and aggregate the business values. Few research challenges are observed that shall need appropriate indulgence to generate more business values out of Internet of Things based cloud. This paper also seeks few research and industry related problems that need to be resolved. It further recommends several key parameters to the enterprise and government policymakers that should immediately be dealt with for long-term success.

1. Introduction

Recently, a large portion of the IT based industries is getting into a new buzz word "IoT cloud," that is, Internet of Things enabled cloud. Various forms of cloud deployment models such as public, community, private, and hybrid can be seen around the day-to-day livelihood. According to a recent report, Internet of Things (IoT) is being popularized as a business concept among the leading IT market players of the world that counts the giants like Intel, Microsoft, CISCO, Google, IBM, Samsung, Apple, Oracle, ARM, Accenture, Amazon, and so forth [1]. Similarly, global consumers are eventually developing their affinity towards full-time connectivity to the internet based commodities such as smart phones, PDAs, and tablets. In this context, new businesses policies are being intrigued by the overwhelming efficiency, business process implication, and revenue generation opportunities from the available IoT cloud solutions [2]. IDC has also estimated the market growth of IoT and enabled cloud services to reach up to $7.1 trillion by 2020.

Before going into the details, the definition of IoT and associated terms need to be understood. IoT may be defined as "a global infrastructure for the information society enabling advanced services by interconnecting (physical and virtual) things based on, existing and evolving, interoperable information and communication technologies" [3].

The definition of "cloud" is presented as prescribed by the NIST (National Institute of Standards and Technology) in its special publication of 7 pages (800–1457) in September 2011. According to it, "cloud computing is a model for enabling ubiquitous, convenient, on-demand network access to a shared pool of configurable computing resources (e.g., networks, servers, storage, applications, and services) that can be rapidly provisioned and released with minimal management effort or service provider interaction."

Henceforth, the novel definition of IoT cloud may be framed as "a model designed to facilitate the information society, enabling advanced services by interconnecting (physical and virtual) things based on, existing and evolving, interoperable information and communication technologies through ennoblement of ubiquitous, convenient, on-demand network access to a shared pool of configurable computing resources (e.g., networks, servers, storage, applications, and services) that can be rapidly provisioned and released with minimal management effort or service provider interaction that leverage the need and heterogeneous connectivity issues of the user centric things in well defined fashion."

Although IoT and cloud assisted technologies and service providers are constantly emerging into the IT market, due lack of overall knowledge about mechanism of extracting special business values from the IoT cloud platforms restricts researchers, developers, and business managers to choose a set of IoT cloud services when they are in phase with development of any product or solution utilizing IoT enabled technologies.

The goal of this paper is to provide an abstract concept towards the developers and business managers to efficiently utilize IoT cloud platforms to earn values, especially business ones. Here, value creation mechanism has been repeatedly depicted for better understanding of what it is meant for. "Value" is envisaged as performance that has been assigned to particular thing/object.

Main contributions of this paper are as follows:

(i) To identify the areas where IoT cloud service providers can generate business values in global market.

(ii) To provide a case study to make reader understand what else can be achieved from a designated "thing."

(iii) To propose an IoT cloud stack to augment the needs of more value generation from the attached devices/things with the system so as to enhance the capability of the envisaged business setup.

(iv) To point out industry based challenges to motivate the researchers to continue on the paths prescribed in this article.

(v) To recommend few new approaches so that IoT based industrial perspectives may be changed.

This article is framed as follows. Section 2 presents related works. Section 3 illustrates the various IoT cloud platforms available in current market and their association with business value creation. Section 4 describes the technologies behind the IoT cloud. A similar framework has been proposed in this section. Section 5 points out Industrial IoT based challenges to be taken care of by the corporate sector and scientific community. Section 6 presents various recommendations to solve these challenges in industrial perspectives. It is followed by Section 7 which concludes the paper.

2. Related Works

This section provides various tasks related to IoT and enabled cloud services where business "values" [4] are created in multiforms. Further, a linkage is been opted to establish a seamless flow for readers comprehension with previous section.

The field of applications of IoT cloud is diverse. The most promising area of application includes industry 4.0 [5] or the smart industry, where the production systems and production sites are built to be intelligent, connected, and autonomous in nature. In smart home or living area,

intelligent refrigerators, security cameras, intelligent lights, doors, and even kitchen utensils are earning huge attention, while smart energy meters, water meters, and gas meters are helping in optimized usage of the consumable resources. Similarly, smart city and vehicles are counting the bus timing, identifying less traffic routes, and monitoring the status of parking space, while smart health care systems are measuring vital signs of individual 24 × 7, helping in taking preventive measures before the actual disease may prune itself into the body, and connecting health to user, medical facilities, and caregivers [6–9].

In defence [10, 11], drones and high flight balloons do surveillance over the suspect region over the earth, while in smart agriculture area, dairy farming, bee keeping, cattle monitoring, and vine yard monitoring are getting popular; further information regarding resident or remote environmental parameters are no longer difficult to be accessed. Sports area is also being assimilated with IoT cloud so as to set up a connected ecosystem [12, 13]. Model driven tree reference model [14] and generalized domain model architecture [15] are proposed to cater the architectural value creation process in IoT. Strong need for integration of cloud and IoT is mentioned in [16] where an agent-oriented and cloud assisted paradigm is envisaged based on a novel reference architecture. After analyzing various depicted papers, a generic architecture is presented in [17] where an IoT supported cloud based smart device is evaluated to perform data monitoring, gathering, and processing. A brief survey of the state of the art in sensing services over cloud-centric IoT and recent challenges are mentioned aiming at defining the taxonomy of the stated surveyed schemes in [18]. *CloudIoT* platform [19] is proposed while highlighting the complementarity and the need for the integration of cloud and IoT together. Based on the results obtained from survey of the measurement for the wine growing season during 2014, an M2M (Machine-to-Machine) remote telemetry station in cooperation with a big data processing platform and several sensors is implemented to demonstrate the use of IoT cloud systems and big data processing in order to implement disease prediction and alerting application for viticulture [20]. Wang and Ranjan [21] describe various notions (i.e., datacenter cloud computing infrastructure service stack, data management service across datacenters, Data Intensive Workflow Computing (DIWC), benchmark, application kernels, standards, recommendations, etc.) to visualize how distributed IoT data could be processed in the clouds. An IoT based Software Defined Radio (SDR) enabled cloud computing paradigm is implemented to provide a unified view on accessing, configuring, and operating of the IoT cloud systems while implying dynamic and on-demand service frameworks [22]. Reference [23] proposes the U-GovOps, a novel framework for dynamic, on-demand governance of elastic IoT cloud systems under uncertainty while introducing a declarative policy language to simplify the development of uncertainty, and elasticity-aware governance strategies. Seven different principles of engineering IoT cloud systems are prescribed so as to comprehend and provide knowledge about how IoT cloud systems could provide a coherent software layer for continuous deployment, provisioning, and execution of applications for various domains [24]. An IoT cloud framework is designed to harmonize cloud-scale IoT services defining intention of user or device to enable communication between connected devices in cloud-scale IoT services [25]. Reference [26] discusses the prospective evolution of IoT clouds towards federated ecosystems, where IoT cloud systems cooperate to offer more flexible services by proposing a 3-layered federated IoT architecture. A framework is proposed for scalable and real-time provisioning of IoT cloud based services in smart cities. These two features have been achieved by employing a novel hierarchical model and populating them in a tree structure containing references to services and their real-time data [27]. Agent based IoT cloud computing is also provisioned to support the development of decentralized, dynamic, and cooperating open IoT cloud systems incorporating multiple IoT agents [28]. While talking about "values," temperature and humidity sensors are used to measure the thermal comfort for indoor occupants using IoT cloud as its backbone [29].

3. IoT Cloud Platforms and Business Value Creation

This section illustrates how IoT is being utilized in different sectors of industries. Further, a hypothetical case study is performed involving electric bulb, waste bin, and tractor to show how these "things" can give more business values other than their original and ordinary functional values.

Though IoT clouds vary in many factors, such as real-time data capture, data visualization, cloud type, data analytics, device configuration, API protocols, cost, and big data, the main purpose of IoT cloud is to facilitate intelligent integration and accessibility of the things/devices and associated surrounding ecosystem thus bridging the gap in the physical-digital divide.

The following list includes several existing IoT cloud service providers that enable end-to-end IoT based analytics, storage, and real-time processing support to the customers and business farms: Xively, ThingSpeak, Plotly, Exosite, GroveStreams, Temboo, ThingWorx, Carriots, Nimbits, KAA, IBM IoT, Oracle Open IoT, Microsoft Research Lab of Things, SensorCloud, Ayla's IoT Cloud Fabric, Arrayent Connect TM, Aer Cloud, thethings, io, SeeControl IoT, and Jasper Control Center.

The opportunities for the IoT cloud providers are of multifold. Figure 1 illustrates various areas where corporate investments are currently being sought for. It starts with leveraging a common platform for consumer-electronics and appliances design sector, while heterogeneous Machine-to-Machine (M2M) communication platform is cumulating the digital telephony among the devices, ubiquitous transportation systems are being implemented at various smart cities, smart health care facilitation gives the fully connected ambience to the patients, and environment monitoring is deliberately getting huge attention. Similarly, defence, security, and military forces seem to be keen on getting full exploration with IoT cloud using NFC (Near Field Communication) and innovative nanotechnology solutions at the war site. Smart agriculture systems are being popularized among the global

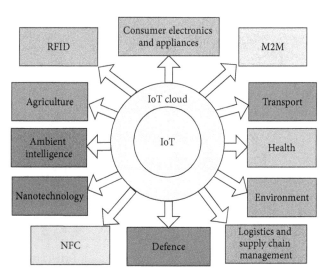

FIGURE 1: IoT cloud based investments.

farmers that use the intelligence of IoT cloud platform to result in a beginning of a new era of precision cum optimized agriculture for better yield. Ambient intelligence is another area where IoT cloud is momentarily getting itself.

The original business value of IoT cloud lies on its actual process of dissemination with things/devices to the extraction of information for some specific purposes. Value creation primarily depends on the IoT cloud stack which will be discussed in next section. Figure 2 presents the logical schema of such value creation. It illustrates that IoT cloud based solutions typically combine physical things/devices with information technology in the form of available hardware and software. IoT stack plays the crucial role in resolving these issues. IoT cloud stack is placed on top of IoT stack which results in thing-based functionalities either physical or local influence. Intelligent and assisted IoT cloud services empower user/customer/corporate farms to solicit in decision making, revenue generation, and inductive cum incumbent processes.

For the sake of understanding, let us take the activities of bulb shown in Figure 2. Normally the physical task of a bulb is to enlighten its periphery. However, when the bulb is attached to an integrated form of motion detector sensor through an IoT cloud, it shall be able to detect movement in its range. By this way, the light bulb may act as smart intrusion detection system. Further, the information of detection of any movement may be sent to the owner in form of e-mail, messages, or social status updates.

Similarly, a bin (garbage collector) is primarily used for storage of excess elements of household or office. This thing-based function may be enhanced with help of IoT cloud technology so that it can autonomously measure and monitor its current load in terms of weight, thus detecting its levels of stocks. It may further notify the municipal or community service providers to replenish its contents into the dust trays while activating GPS facilities by providing plan for automatic optimized traffic route through the busy roads of the city. Normally a tractor is meant for towing mechanical devices for

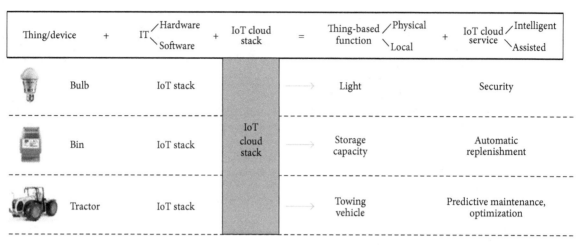

Thing/device	+	IT $\diagup$ Hardware $\diagdown$ Software	+	IoT cloud stack	=	Thing-based $\diagup$ Physical function $\diagdown$ Local	+	IoT cloud $\diagup$ Intelligent service $\diagdown$ Assisted
Bulb		IoT stack			$\longrightarrow$	Light		Security
Bin		IoT stack		IoT cloud stack	$\longrightarrow$	Storage capacity		Automatic replenishment
Tractor		IoT stack			$\longrightarrow$	Towing vehicle		Predictive maintenance, optimization

FIGURE 2: IoT cloud based value generation (based on [4]).

farming. However this physical thing-based function when attached to IoT cloud may allow the farmer to know about its predictive nature of maintenance and optimized driving sessions [30].

Not only is the value of things/devices limited to the connected behavior of IoT as presented, but also it may be uplifted to a higher abstraction level of superseded flow of business where a cumulative IoT ecosystem would enhance the basic functionality into a larger context. For instance, a set of IoT cloud served bulbs may create intelligent lighting system, which could include active and passive Infrared (IR) movement detector and heat sensor to extend the overall equipment efficiency of the lighting system. If it goes beyond the ordinary lighting system, it may be turned into a product system that could be attached with standards and upcoming telecommunication technologies, for example, 2G, 3G, LTE (4G); besides Bluetooth Low Energy (BLE) 4.0, IEEE 802.11 b/g/n-Wi-Fi, even Zigbee antennas could be plugged-in so that the energy consumption and accidental incidents be easily monitored, analyzed, and apprehended.

Data analytics in IoT cloud may improve the system's throughput in optimized manner. This may incur real value in the lighting system that may replenish the necessity of stochastic behavior by strengthening the base of IoT cloud and provide vibration to other sectors of business.

4. Technologies behind IoT Cloud Stack

This section describes IoT cloud stack architecture in detail to inculcate the business value generation process from IoT cloud platforms.

It is evident that the proper functioning of business-value-incorporated connected device is comprised of a stringent layered stack of relevant technologies as shown in Figure 3. The figure illustrates the principal activities of IoT cloud in a stack form on top of the IoT (which includes things, network connectivity, and middleware and is also supported by security issues while extending the interface of business computing) which lays the foundation for the prescribed system.

The IoT cloud stack is subdivided into four portions such as infrastructure, business applications, business services, and business processes.

In infrastructure module, networking components such as switches, servers, storage devices, routers, virtualization techniques, operating system, and other elements are included, while middleware and unstructured contents are placed over the distributed database.

Next higher level of abstraction is business applications layer that provides the APP based services. Modular (Java based composite/process app), packaged (CRM, ERP, HCM, etc.), and dedicated business support apps (BI, BPM, BAM, etc.) do run over here.

In IaaS layer, software attributed computing, definition, and networking attributes control the resources (hardware/software) for optimization, orchestration, and abstraction.

Cloud operating environment is created on the next higher layer, that is, PaaS, where various APIs are collaborated with the specific business related tasks; the result is obtained from SaaS layer, where collaborative marketplace is numerated by e-commerce and external business ecosystems.

In business services layer, web portal, product catalogue, inventory management, billing, product shipping, and so forth, core components are present.

In business process layer, mainly transaction related operations are performed. Order management, cash handling, transaction, and procurement monitoring tasks get processed. This topmost layer of IoT cloud stack holds interface with business users and customer providing sheer experience without exploring the underlying architecture of IoT based business protocols.

The aforementioned IoT cloud platform is capable of producing value out of connected objects in a modular fashion. Relevant corporate ancillaries act on the discussed IoT platform.

To the author's best knowledge, there is no standard IoT cloud stack available till date; hence a multitude of versions are being opted by the users and business farms.

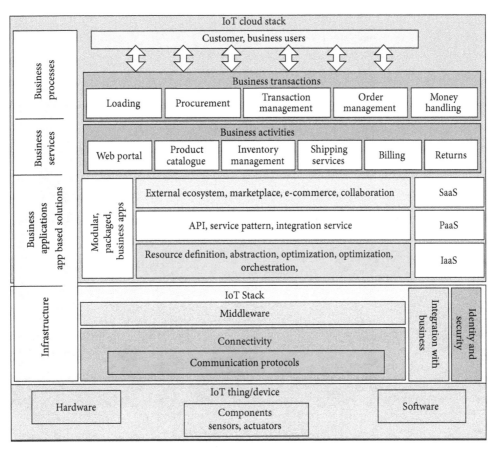

FIGURE 3: IoT cloud stack based on IoT stack.

Each platform varies from the other in terms of protocol inclusion and value generation methodologies.

5. Challenges Related to Industrial Internet of Things

Though Industrial Internet of Things (Industrial IoT) has great promising opportunities, many risk factors could hinder its future growth. Not surprisingly, security and interoperability are the two biggest hurdles. Lack of clearly defined Return on Investment (RoI), technology immaturity, legacy equipment, and so forth are among the other significant barriers. Several other issues and challenges are shown in Figure 4. As more physical things come online, vulnerabilities for cyberattacks do also prioritize. Cyberattack may be seen as very or extremely high risk factor associated with Industrial IoT. Privacy breach of personal data is another high risk factor. For example, when both types of risks are justified then one can consider such negative impacts as attacking a power plant to deny electricity to its customers which shall cause loss of public trust and interest resulting in any Industrial Internet-enabled system to be compromised. A recent report published by WTF has estimated around 3 trillion dollars in potential economic loss which may occur from cybersecurity issues by 2020. This evidently incurs the business investments to take countermeasures against it. According to Gartner, more than 20% of the existing enterprises will invest in

security measures in business initiatives incorporating IoT devices by 2017 [23]. Resulting potential disruption occurring into the existing business models may constitute several related risks for incumbent business players. The gross shifting from products to service oriented outcomes will not only disrupt internal corporate operations but eventually impact the mechanism of how they go to the global market.

Due to the openness in the access and control points among the current digital marketplace, this shall compel the companies to face tough competition from a larger set of key players which may include pure digital players based on innovative business models and the traditional digital platforms who are present from the very inception of computer. This shall levy an opportunity for the companies to have the flexibility to partner with other organizations across the industrial ecosystem. Obviously, such collaboration will harness an imperative impact on the companies which want to meet the ever growing customer expectations around the service or product delivery results. For example, it will be difficult to measure how one enterprise can master the entire digital value chain for which it has developed the product dissemination system. From the societal point of view, it shall be important to consider the potential job displacement ratio that will surely occur in some industrial sectors due to IoT based increased automation. This process is very similar to the communications switchboard job holders who were rapidly replaced by the software based technology solutions.

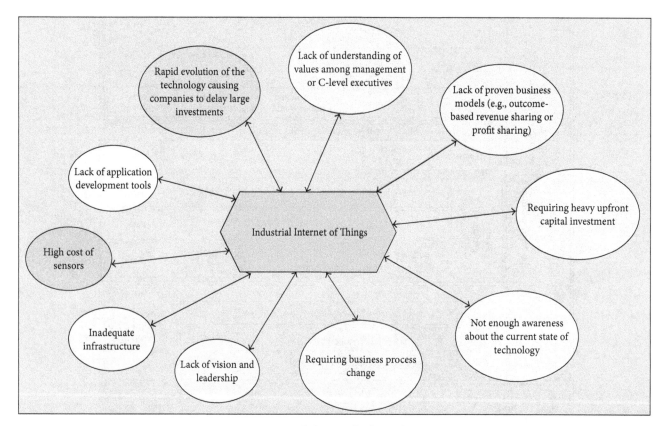

FIGURE 4: Risk factors of Industrial IoT.

With more intelligent machines becoming widespread, more human jobs will be displaced. For instance, if we consider the current pace of technology improvement, maid robots may replace human home maids in the next 20 years. However, we have to anticipate that many new and different types of jobs will be created in due action. Human having uniqueness, such as critical thinking, creativity, and collaboration, shall be employed in future. It is high time that industry and government leaders should understand the fact that improved technology is constantly upgrading the quality bar for the low-skilled jobs. This necessitates strong and urgent need to tackle current issues related to skill-less labor in the IoT based IT market. New action plans are urgently needed to reassess the attention on the current structure of education, adapting with the current propaganda of educational systems, and find innovative approaches to prepare new generations for the upcoming IoT based digital workplace.

Moreover the below-mentioned technological challenges need to be revised and reassessed:

(A) *Strategic Level.* Here, new and innovative dimensions need to be sought to make better and efficient implementation of IoT cloud stack into the business. Corporate houses should rethink the fundamental questions such as how to cover up the business around the newly developed technologies, how to frame the skeleton of the business rules, and how to adapt the incremental benefits from the stack, so that production be enhanced with less effort.

(B) *Operational Level.* Initial product development stage may now be redesigned for sake of leveraging space to new segments of improvisations including IoT. Questions such as how to degenerate the initiation of product development in view of smart IoT connected devices, how to integrate the followups with the existing business model, how to negotiate the sales procedure, and how to market the deliverables in advanced variations should be addressed.

(C) *Capacity Building.* When talking about social involvedness, IoT cloud stack shall revolutionize the human life in more ways than one. New knowledge and skills sets in nearly every field (statistics, engineering, and medicine) should be set in such a way that skilled man power be generated; citizen participation is another factor that should be grown among the people of society towards the hands on experience of IoT; moreover, quality of livelihood needs to be rebuilt while implying efficient urban-civic operations by a guaranteed framework of high yielding economic, societal, and environmental values for future generations.

(D) *Technological Level.* This area should be better highlighted to make IoT cloud based business process profit yielding by incorporating novel theories, structures, and applications, especially in the subject like computer science and mathematics.

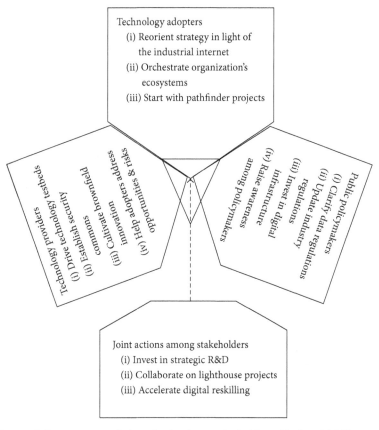

FIGURE 5: Key recommendations for the three stake holders of Industrial IoT sector.

(i) *Big Data*. High volume, high velocity, high variety, high veracity, and high value (5V) conglomerate into a new term called big data problem. Exponential increase of usage patterns of mobile and sensor enabled devices have developed a space where enormous amount of heterogeneous data get accumulated or trafficked through the network every instance of the clock. New methodologies, algorithms, and databases are to be framed to formulate the access and manipulation problems in current scenario.

(ii) *ICP*. Format identification, data capture, and data processing fields need to be revisited so the IoT enabled connected environments may be facilitated by extracting valuable information from it.

(iii) *Security*. Privacy, security, and trust issues are no longer a local notion but transborder measure of distributed data exchange and processing. Each device and each people's notion should be maintained to safeguard the proclamations of IoT cloud stack.

6. Recommendations for Industrial Internet of Things

As of now, we have discussed the Industrial IoT being already used for delivering actual benefits including improved business operational efficiency, flexibility in work experience, and monitorable and measurable business outcomes. At the same time, we have also pointed out a number of risk factors that might possibly slow down the pace of Industrial IoT development while increasing the various risks of adoption including security, data use policies, interoperability, upgraded education system, and skill gaps. This section provides necessary recommendations made that the business farms and government stakeholders need to take prompt actions so as to regain underlying opportunities, overcome key challenges, and accelerate the growth of Industrial IoT in digital domain. Figure 5 describes the Industrial IoT related interactions between three stakeholders in form of mandates to be asked by them to obtain the correct answer.

6.1. For Technology Adopters

(i) *Orientation of the Business Strategy*. Few questions need to be asked by the technology adopters to themselves for further progression in Industrial IoT such as the following:

Where is the present situation of the industry among the four-phase Industrial IoT evolution model? (See Figure 5.)

When is the probable next inflection point on business graph?

Business adopters should try to develop multitude of scenarios regarding various possible alternative features and map out the earlier mentioned strategy based on the company's current profile and requirement.

They should identify the exact structure of process as well as organization so as to achieve long-term success by asking how asset utilization can set up the company for future success.

How can we transit between each of the four phases?

What are the probable implications that got originated from existing assets and buyer-seller behavior?

(ii) *Define the Organization's Ecosystems.* One option is that multiple providers are required to collaborate for delivery of complex outcome while sharing costly investments. Few more questions need to be asked such as the following:

Having multiple product lines, which ecosystem(s) should the farm lead?

Where should the company play a supporting role?

What type of business partners will the company need to merge so as to boost overall capabilities to deliver the expected outcomes?

Will the present partners be the right ones for the future?

What activities shall the business perform to be a collaborative partner?

Who should the company partner with to reach higher phases?

How do we reduce risk?

How do we look across industry boundaries to seek emerging opportunities, so that it can find the potential partners that may help in regaining the scenario?

(iii) *Driving Issues of the Business.* Company should momentarily imply various issues such as cycle-time reductions, business process improvements, and cost savings to drive near-term measurable benefits. Few questions may be asked to seek the answers such as the following:

How can we balance the implementations of low-cost pilot projects?

Which business model implication is suitable for adaptation?

What kind of outcome-based services can it opt for?

What are the crucial requirements for conducting such pilot project?

How can support from governments at early stage be obtained?

6.2. For Technology Providers

(i) *Interoperability.* Technology providers should seek some questions to ascertain the solutions of the aforementioned problems such as the following:

How can real-world testbeds be developed to concatenate and support new use cases and product?

How can voice be directed in shaping futuristic Industrial IoT products and services?

What are the current trends?

What is the possible timing around probable market disruptions?

How can we bootstrap connected industry ecosystems and platforms?

(ii) *Share through a Global Commons.* Few questions need to get answered for sharing practice in a secure common means such as the following:

How do the safety and security practices vary across the ecosystem?

How do we step forward towards a common security framework?

How do we identify parameters for cybersecurity products?

How do we design a global security commons?

How can the commons help collective security awareness?

How can a unified industry voice be ensured?

(iii) *Cultivate the Innovation.* Technology providers need to know few facts by asking questions such as the following:

How and what new devices can be added to improve integrity of the existing machinery?

What components (hardware or software) of the system need to be revised?

What type of value added services can be provided?

What kind of new outcome-based opportunities may be opened?

(iv) *Market Opportunities and Risks.* The Industrial IoT is still in nascent stage. So, companies should leverage the knowledge by asking the following questions to develop a clear view before they start running on it:

What amount of benefits has been devised so far?

What are the potential barriers that need to be overcome at the earliest?

What is the knowledge earned from past issues?

How can we leverage the most effective ways to adopt experiences?

6.3. For Public Policymakers. Government and public figures shall pave new ways to cultivate Industrial IoT processing in timely manner. Few concepts are given as follows.

(i) *Define Data Policies.* Policies are a stake to realize the promising potential of Industrial IoT while drafting vivid strategies over data. Related questions to be sought are as follows:

Who will own the data generated by the Industrial Internet-enabled devices?

What type of sized information can be used?

How do we handle the data originated and used in different jurisdiction?

How do we segregate Industrial Internet data from that of consumer Internet?

How should government collaborate with each other around the globe?

What steps need to be taken to harmonize compliance requirements in data among the companies?

(ii) *Industry Regulations.* Industrial regulations are very much crucial for any government to control monitor over it. Few solutions should be sought out such as the following:

How should industries make benefit out of the Industrial IoT?

How can more flexibility among the company regulations be provided to help them invent?

How would the government use the utility to tap with industry for the sake of new power of transparency?

How can we leverage better customer services among the industries?

Which sector of industries should be regulated to avail security, efficiency, and services to public?

How would insurance regulations be implied over the growth of industries?

(iii) *Investment.* Infrastructure lays the foundation of success especially in the ubiquitous, broadband, and connectivity based sectors. Developed countries may invest in emerging digitized markets where it will have a unique opportunity by incorporating the Industrial Internet infrastructure. Besides investing in basic infrastructures such as roads, factories, and high rise buildings, state-of-the-art embedded sensors may be implanted on the real segments of life. Smart city is an area which may enable more efficient use of natural resources be it human or natural and provide better public safety and services. Industries along with the government shall seek prioritizing the infrastructure investments to provide long-term strategic benefits to incumbent the wealthy economic growth.

(iv) *Awareness.* As of now, a large portion of policymakers are not informed about how Industrial IoT might impact on citizens' livelihood, industries workplace, and governments. Similarly, they still do not know what government can perish to enhance the market and economic growth. Hence, it seems like an urgent need to bring the policymakers up to speed on the recent growth of technologies in Industrial IoT and its societal implications and impact on the government services.

6.4. Joint Actions among Stakeholders

(i) *Invest in Research and Development.* The futuristic approach and invasion of Industrial Internet of Things will engage numerous stakeholder efforts in various research fields (e.g., security, reliability, and interoperability). It shall also deliver huge societal benefits (e.g., smart city) to the citizen. However, security is such an issue that industry and government can only solve by getting together. At the same time, addressing these challenges shall need the involvement from academia, government, and industry. Few questions to be answered are as follows:

How can the stakeholders support technology transfer from within?

How can we fund this research among the academics?

(ii) *Reskilling Working Generation.* The emergence and growth of Industrial IoT will seek the talent gap among the industry workers. Analytical talent pool (including data scientists) is the demand of present time, though most of the current education approaches are equipped with the challenge. Industries and academia must come together to ask basic questions such as the following:

How do we define and implement new educational and training approaches?

How do we reskill the young generation in the classroom and online?

7. Conclusion

Value is an important parameter of any business/marketing system. It tells about the functional capabilities of the system. Until recently, value generation from a specific task was concentrated into a certain portion of prescribed rate. The advent of IoT has made this path clear while integrating cloud platforms to itself. Things are now easily integrated to perform targeted job easily. In this paper, IoT cloud is proposed to extract more values (multiple functionalities) from a particular thing. This indeed paves the revenue generation process in business activities more beneficial for the organization. A case study is performed to demonstrate the value generation mechanism from the things associated with IoT cloud. Research challenges are discussed to motivate the scientific community to come forward in this regard. Challenges towards successful implementation of Industrial Internet are also investigated. Recommendations are made for technology adaptors, providers, and public policymakers. Suggestions are provided for the joint actions among stakeholders to aggregate the collaborative notions among themselves. This paper truly paves the insightful investigation to create value out of the Industrial Internet of Things.

Competing Interests

The author declares that he has no competing interests.

References

[1] IoT Analytics, http://iot-analytics.com/20-internet-of-things-companies/.

[2] IDC, The internet of things moves beyond the buzz: worldwide market forecast to exceed $7 trillion by 2020, IDC says [press release], http://www.marketwatch.com/story/the-internet-of-moves-beyond-the-buzz-worldwide-market-forecast-to-exceed-7-trillion-by-2020-idc-says-2014-06-03.

[3] ITU-IoT definition, http://www.itu.int/ITU-T/newslog/New+ITU+Standards+Define+The+Internet+Of+Things+And+

[4] F. Wortmann and K. Fluchter, "Internet of things: technology and value added," *Business & Information Systems Engineering*, vol. 57, no. 3, pp. 221–224, 2015.

[5] H. Lasi, P. Fettke, T. Feld, and M. Hoffmann, "Industry 4.0," *Business & Information Systems Engineering*, vol. 6, no. 4, pp. 239–242, 2014.

[6] P. P. Ray, "Home Health Hub Internet of Things (H³IoT): an architectural framework for monitoring health of elderly people," in *Proceedings of the IEEE International Conference on Science Engineering and Management Research (ICSEMR '14)*, pp. 1–3, Chennai, India, November 2014.

[7] P. P. Ray, "Internet of Things for Sports (IoTSport): an architectural framework for sports and recreational activity," in *Proceedings of the IEEE International Conference on Electrical, Electronics, Signals, Communication and Optimization (EESCO '15)*, pp. 1–4, Visakhapatnam, India, January 2015.

[8] S. Sebastian and P. P. Ray, "Development of IoT invasive architecture for complying with health of home," in *Proceedings of the International Conference on Computing and Communication Systems (I3CS '15)*, pp. 79–83, Shillong, India, April 2015.

[9] P. P. Ray, "Internet of things based physical activity monitoring (PAMIoT): an architectural framework to monitor human physical activity," in *Proceedings of the IEEE National Conference on Electrical, Electronics, and Computer Engineering (CALCON '14)*, pp. 32–34, IEEE, Kolkata, India, 2014.

[10] P. P. Ray, "Towards an internet of things based architectural framework for defence," in *Proceedings of the IEEE International Conference on Control, Instrumentation, Communication and Computational Technologie (ICCICCT '15)*, pp. 411–416, December 2015.

[11] P. P. Ray, "Generic Internet of Things architecture for smart sports," in *Proceedings of the IEEE International Conference on Control, Instrumentation, Communication and Computational Technologies (ICCICCT '15)*, pp. 405–410, December 2015.

[12] P. P. Ray, "Internet of things based physical activity monitoring (PAMIoT): an architectural framework to monitor human physical activity," in *Proceedings of the CALCON*, pp. 32–34, Kolkata, India, November 2014.

[13] P. Majumder and P. P. Ray, "Hatch-Sens: a theoretical bio-inspired model to monitor the hatching of plankton culture in the vicinity of wireless sensor network," *International Journal of Computer Science and Information Technologies*, vol. 3, no. 4, pp. 4764–4769, 2012.

[14] P. P. Ray, A. Sharma, and R. Rai, "MDTRM: abstraction to model driven tree reference model of internet of things," in *Proceedings of the National Conference on Applied Electronics (NCAE '13)*, pp. 61–64, Adamas Institute of Technology (AIT), West Bengal, India, 2013.

[15] R. Rai, C. Lepcha, P. P. Ray, and P. Chettri, "GDMA: generalized domain model architecture of internet of things," in *Proceedings of the National Conference on Applied Electronics (NCAE '13)*, pp. 65–68, AIT Kolkata, October 2013.

[16] S. M. Babu, A. J. Lakshmi, and B. T. Rao, "A study on cloud based internet of things: CloudIoT," in *Proceedings of the Global Conference on Communication Technologies (GCCT '15)*, pp. 60–65, Thuckalay, India, April 2015.

[17] V. C. Emeakaroha, N. Cafferkey, P. Healy, and J. P. Morrison, "A cloud-based iot data gathering and processing platform," in *Proceedings of the 3rd International Conference on Future Internet of Things and Cloud (FiCloud '15)*, pp. 50–57, IEEE, Rome, Italy, August 2015.

[18] B. Kantarci and H. T. Mouftah, "Sensing services in cloud-centric internet of things: a survey, taxonomy and challenges," in *Proceedings of the IEEE International Conference on Communication Workshop (ICCW '15)*, pp. 1865–1870, London, UK, June 2015.

[19] A. Botta, W. De Donato, V. Persico, and A. Pescapé, "On the integration of cloud computing and internet of things," in *Proceedings of the 2nd International Conference on Future Internet of Things and Cloud (FiCloud '14)*, pp. 23–30, IEEE, Barcelona, Spain, August 2014.

[20] G. Suciu, A. Vulpe, O. Fratu, and V. Suciu, "M2M remote telemetry and cloud IoT big data processing in viticulture," in *Proceedings of the 11th Intercenational Wireless Communications and Mobile Computing Conferen (IWCMC '15)*, pp. 1117–1121, IEEE, Dubrovnik, Croatia, August 2015.

[21] L. Wang and R. Ranjan, "Processing distributed internet of things data in clouds," *IEEE Cloud Computing*, vol. 2, no. 1, pp. 76–80, 2015.

[22] S. Nastic, S. Sehic, D.-H. Le, H.-L. Truong, and S. Dustdar, "Provisioning software-defined IoT cloud systems," in *Proceedings of the 2nd International Conference on Future Internet of Things and Cloud (FiCloud '14)*, pp. 288–295, August 2014.

[23] S. Nastic, G. Copil, H. Truong, and S. Dustdar, "Governing elastic IoT cloud systems under uncertainty," in *Proceedings of the IEEE 7th International Conference on Cloud Computing Technology and Science*, pp. 131–138, Vancouver, Canada, 2015.

[24] H. Truong and S. Dustdar, "Principles for engineering IoT cloud systems," *IEEE Cloud Computing*, vol. 2, no. 2, pp. 68–76, 2015.

[25] S. W. Kum, J. Moon, T. Lim, and J. I. Park, "A novel design of IoT cloud delegate framework to harmonize cloud-scale IoT services," in *Proceedings of the IEEE International Conference on Consumer Electronics (ICCE '15)*, pp. 247–248, Las Vegas, Nev, USA, January 2015.

[26] A. Celesti, M. Fazio, M. Giacobbe, A. Puliafito, and M. Villari, "Characterizing cloud federation in IoT," in *Proceedings of the 30th International Conference on Advanced Information Networking and Applications Workshops*, pp. 93–98, 2016.

[27] A. Taherkordi and F. Eliassen, "Scalable modeling of cloud-based IoT services for smart cities," in *Proceedings of the 1st IEEE International Workshop on Context-Aware Smart Cities and Intelligent Transport Systems*, Sydney, Australia, March 2016.

[28] G. Fortino, A. Guerrieri, W. Russo, and C. Savaglio, "Integration of agent-based and cloud computing for the smart objects-oriented IoT," in *Proceedings of the 18th IEEE International Conference on Computer Supported Cooperative Work in Design (CSCWD '14)*, pp. 493–498, IEEE, Hsinchu, Taiwan, May 2014.

[29] P. P. Ray, "Internet of things cloud enabled MISSENARD index measurement for indoor occupants," *Measurement*, vol. 92, pp. 157–165, 2016.

[30] E. Fleisch, What is the internet of things—an economic perspective, Auto-ID labs white paper, 2014, http://cocoa.ethz.ch/downloads/2014/06/None_AUTOIDLABS-WP-BIZAPP-53.pdf.

7

Human Depth Sensors-Based Activity Recognition using Spatiotemporal Features and Hidden Markov Model for Smart Environments

Ahmad Jalal,[1] Shaharyar Kamal,[2] and Daijin Kim[1]

[1]*Pohang University of Science and Technology (POSTECH), Pohang, Republic of Korea*
[2]*KyungHee University, Suwon, Republic of Korea*

Correspondence should be addressed to Ahmad Jalal; ahmadjalal@postech.ac.kr

Academic Editor: Liangtian Wan

Nowadays, advancements in depth imaging technologies have made human activity recognition (HAR) reliable without attaching optical markers or any other motion sensors to human body parts. This study presents a depth imaging-based HAR system to monitor and recognize human activities. In this work, we proposed spatiotemporal features approach to detect, track, and recognize human silhouettes using a sequence of RGB-D images. Under our proposed HAR framework, the required procedure includes detection of human depth silhouettes from the raw depth image sequence, removing background noise, and tracking of human silhouettes using frame differentiation constraints of human motion information. These depth silhouettes extract the spatiotemporal features based on depth sequential history, motion identification, optical flow, and joints information. Then, these features are processed by principal component analysis for dimension reduction and better feature representation. Finally, these optimal features are trained and they recognized activity using hidden Markov model. During experimental results, we demonstrate our proposed approach on three challenging depth videos datasets including IM-DailyDepthActivity, MSRAction3D, and MSRDailyActivity3D. All experimental results show the superiority of the proposed approach over the state-of-the-art methods.

1. Introduction

Human tracking and activity recognition are defined as recognizing different activities by considering activity feature extraction and pattern recognition techniques based on specific input data from innovative sensors (i.e., motion sensors and video cameras) [1–5]. In recent years, advancement of these sensors has boosted the production of novel techniques for pervasive human tracking, observing human motion, detecting uncertain events [6–8], silhouette tracking, and emotion recognition in the real-world environments [9–11]. In these domains, the term which is most commonly used to cover all these topics is technically termed as human tracking and activity recognition [12–14]. In the motion sensors-based activity recognition, activity recognition is based on classifying sensory data using one or more sensor devices. In [15], Casale et al. proposed a complete review about the state-of-the-art activity classification methods using data

from one or more accelerometers. In this work, classification approaches are based on RFs features which classify five daily routine activities from bluetooth accelerometer placed at breast of the human body, using a 319-dimensional feature vector. In [16], fast FFT and decision tree classifier algorithm are proposed to detect physical activity using biaxial accelerometers attached on different parts of the human body. However, these motion sensors-based approaches are not feasible methods for recognition due to uncomfort of the users to wear electronic sensors in their daily life. Also, combining multiple sensors for improvement in recognition performance causes high computation load. Thus, video-based human tracking and activity recognition is proposed where the depth features are extracted from a RGB-D video camera.

Depth silhouettes have made proactive contributions and are the most famous representation for human tracking and activity recognition from which useful human shape features

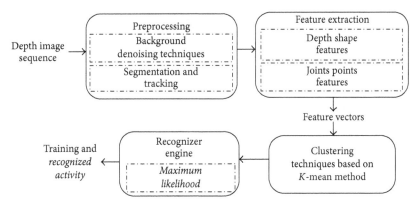

FIGURE 1: System architecture of the proposed human activity recognition system.

are extracted. These depth silhouettes explore research issues and are used as practical applications including life-care systems, surveillance system, security system, face verification, patient monitoring systems, and human gait recognition systems. In [17], several algorithms are developed for feature extraction from the silhouette data of the tracked human subject using depth images as the pixel source. These parameters include ratio of height to weight of the tracked human subject. Also, motion characteristics and distance parameters are used as features for the activity recognition. In [14], a novel life logging translation and scaling invariant features approach is designed where 2D maps are computed through Radon transform which are further processed as 1D feature profiles through R transform. These features are further reduced by PCA and symbolized by Linde, Buzo, and Gray (LBG) clustering technique to train and recognize different activities. In [18], a discriminative representation method is proposed as structure-motion kinematics features including the structure similarity and head-floor distance based on skeleton joint points information. However, these effective trajectory projection based kinematic schemes are learnt by a SVM classifier to recognize activities using the depth maps. In [19], an activity recognition system is designed to provide continuous monitoring and recording of daily life activities. The system includes depth silhouettes as an input to produce skeleton model and its body points information. This information is used as features and is computed using a set of magnitude and direction angle features which are further used for training and testing via hidden Markov models (HMMs). These state-of-the-art methods [14, 17–19] proved more efficiency for recognition accuracy using depth silhouette. However, it is still difficult to find best features from limited information such as joint points information especially during occlusions. It shows bad impact over recognition accuracy. Therefore, we needed to develop methodology which provides combined effects of full-body silhouettes and joints information to improve activity recognition performance.

In this paper, we proposed a novel method to recognize activities using sequence of depth images. During preprocessing steps, we extracted human depth silhouettes using background/floor removal techniques and tracked human

silhouettes by considering rectangular box having body shape measurements (i.e., height and width) to adjust the box's size. During spatiotemporal features extraction technique, a set of multifused features are considered as depth sequential history, motion identification, optical flow, joints angle, and joints location features. These features are further computed by principal component analysis (PCA) for global information and reduce dimensions. Then, these features are applied over K-mean for clustering and fed into a four-state left-to-right HMM for training/testing human activities. The proposed system is compared against the state-of-the-art approaches thus achieving best recognition rate over three challenging depth videos datasets as IM-DailyDepthActivity, MSRAction3D, and MSRDailyActivity3D datasets.

The rest of the sections of this paper are structured as follows. Section 2 describes the system architecture overview of the proposed system where depth maps preprocessing, feature extraction techniques, and training/testing human activities using HMM are explained. In Section 3, we explain experimental results by considering proposed and state-of-the-art methods. Finally, Section 4 presents the conclusion.

2. Proposed System Methodology

2.1. System Overview. The proposed activity recognition system consists of sequence of depth images captured by RGB-D video sensor, background removal, and human tracking from the time-sequential activity video images. Then, feature representation based on spatiotemporal features, clustering via K-mean, and training/recognition using recognizer engine are processed. Figure 1 explains the overall steps of proposed human activity recognition system.

2.2. Depth Images Preprocessing. During vision-based image preprocessing, we captured video data (i.e., digital and RGB-D) that retrieve both binary and depth human silhouettes from each activity. In case of binary silhouette, we received color images from digital camera which are further converted into binary images. In case of using depth silhouettes, we obtained the depth images from the depth cameras (i.e., PrimeSense, Bumblebee, and Zcam) to extract 320 × 240

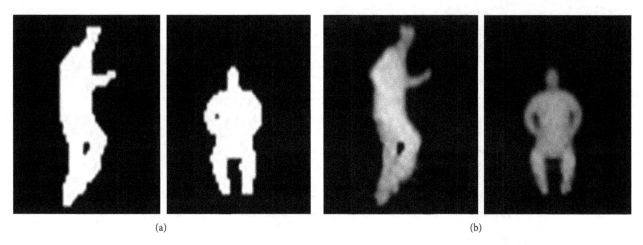

FIGURE 2: Images comparison as (a) binary silhouettes and (b) depth silhouettes of exercise and sit-down activities.

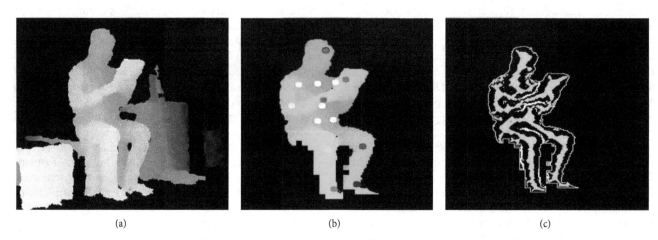

FIGURE 3: Depth images preprocessing as (a) raw depth images having noisy background, (b) labelled human silhouette, and (c) ridge body information.

depth levels per pixel [20, 34, 35]. These cameras deal with both RGB images and depth raw data.

For comparative study, it is examined that, in case of binary images, we can only obtain minimum information (i.e., black or white), while significant pixels values are dropped especially hands movement in front of chest or both legs crossing each other. However, in case of depth silhouettes, we received maximum information in the form of intensity values and additional body parts information (i.e., joint points), controlled during self-occlusion (see Figure 2).

Therefore, to deal with depth images, we remove noisy effects from background by simply ignoring ground line (i.e., y parameters) which acts as lowest value (i.e., equal to zero) corresponding to a given pair of x- and z-axis for floor removal. Next, we partitioned all objects in the frame using variation of intensity values in between consecutive frames. Then, we differentiate the depth values of corresponding neighboring pixels within a specific threshold and extract depth human silhouettes using depth center values of each object from the scenes. Finally, we apply human tracking by considering temporal continuity constraints (see Figure 3) between consecutive frames [21, 27], while human silhouettes

are enclosed within the rectangular bounding box having specific values (i.e., height and width) based on face recognition and motion detection [36–38].

2.3. Spatiotemporal Features Extraction.

For spatiotemporal features extraction, we composed features as depth history silhouettes, standard deviation, motion variation among images, and optical flow for depth shape features, while joints angle and joints location features are derived from joints points features. Combination of these features explores more spatial and temporal depth-based properties which are useful for activity classification and recognition. All features are explained below.

Depth Sequential History. Depth sequential history feature method is used to observe pixel intensity information in overall sequence of each activity (see Figure 4). It contains temporal values, position, and movement velocities. Therefore depth sequential history is defined as

$$H = \frac{1}{T} \sum_{t=t_i}^{t_f} I_t, \tag{1}$$

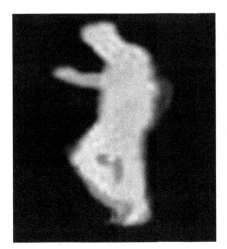  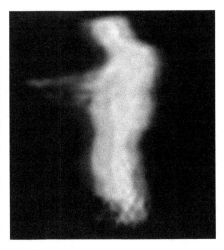

FIGURE 4: Depth sequential history features applied over exercise, kicking, and cleaning activities.

where t_f and t_i are the initial and final images I of an activity and T is the duration of activity period.

Different Intensity Values Features. Standard deviation is computed as the sum of all the differences of the image pairs P with respect to the time series (see Figure 5). It provides quite disperse output and hidden values (i.e., especially z coordinates) having large range of intensities values

$$SD(x, y, z) = \sqrt{\frac{\sum_{t=t_s}^{t_L} S_t^2}{P} - \left(\frac{1}{P}\sum_{t=t_i}^{t_L} S_t\right)^2}. \quad (2)$$

Depth Motion Identification. Motion identification feature mechanism is used to handle intra-/intermotion variation and temporal displacement (see Figure 6) among consecutive frames of each activity.

$$MV(x, y, z) = \frac{SD(x, y, z)}{H}. \quad (3)$$

Motion-Based Optical Flow Features. In order to make use of the additional motion information from depth sequence, we applied optical flow technique based on the Lucas Kanade method. Basically, it calculates the motion intensity and directional angular values between two images. Figure 7 shows some samples of optical flows calculated from two depth silhouettes images.

Joints Angle Features. Due to similar or complex postures of different activities, it is not sufficient to just deal with silhouettes features; therefore, we developed skeleton model having 15 joints' points information (see Figure 8).

However, joints angle features measure the directional movements of the ith joints points between consecutive frames [39, 40] t and $t - 1$ as

$$\vartheta_{\cos} = \cos^{-1}\left(\frac{J_i^t * J_i^{t-1}}{|J_i^t| |J_i^{t-1}|}\right), \quad (4)$$

where J_i indicates all three coordinate axes (x, y, z) of the body joints with respect to consecutive frames [41–43].

Joints Location Features. Joints location features measure the distance between the torso joint point J_C and all other fourteen joints' points J_o in each frame t of sequential activity as

$$F_{\text{Loca}}(t) = \sqrt{(J_C^x - J_o^x) + (J_C^y - J_o^y) + (J_C^z - J_o^z)}. \quad (5)$$

Finally, we obtained the feature vector size of joints angle and joints location features as 1×15 and 1×14 dimensions. Figures 9(a) and 9(b) shows the 1D plots of both joints angle and joints location features for exercise, kicking, and cleaning activities.

2.4. Feature Reduction. Since spatiotemporal feature extraction using depth shape features consists of larger number of features dimension, thus PCA is introduced to extract global information [44, 45] from all activities data and approximate the higher features dimension data [46] into lower dimensional features. In this work, 750 principal components of the spatiotemporal features are chosen from the whole PC feature space and the size of feature vector becomes 1×750.

2.5. Symbolization, Training, and Recognition. Each feature vector of individual activity is symbolized based on K-mean clustering algorithm. However, a HMM consists of finite states where each state is involved in transition probability and symbol observation probability [47, 48]. During HMM, the underlying hidden process is observable by another set of stochastic processes that provides observation symbols. In case of training each activity, initially, HMM is trained having a size of codebook of 512. During HAR, trained HMMs of each activity are used to choose maximum likelihood of desired activity [49–52]. However, sequence of trained data is generated and maintained by buffer strategy [31, 53]. Figure 10 describes the transition and emission probabilities of cleaning HMM after training.

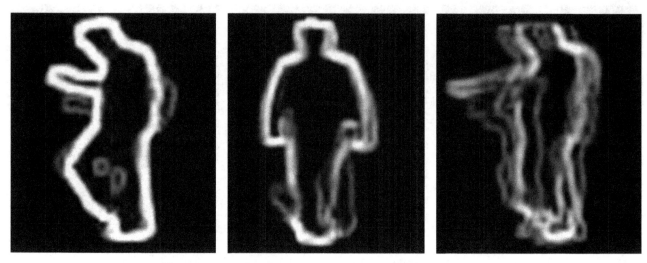

FIGURE 5: Different intensity values features applied over exercise, kicking, and cleaning activities.

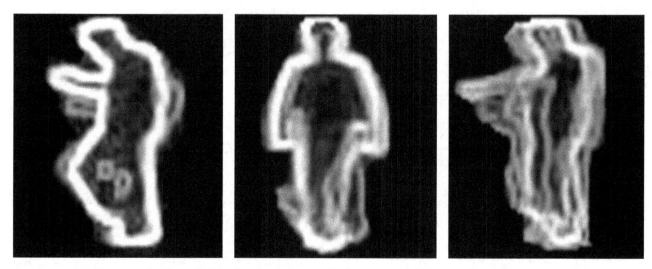

FIGURE 6: Depth motion identification features applied over exercise, kicking, and cleaning activities.

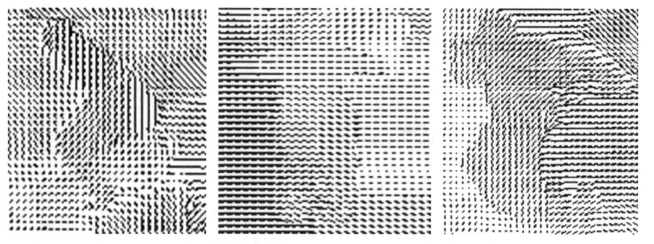

FIGURE 7: Examples of depth silhouettes images using motion-based optical flow.

  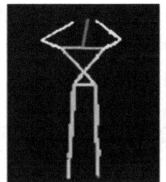 

FIGURE 8: Samples of human skeleton model for different activities.

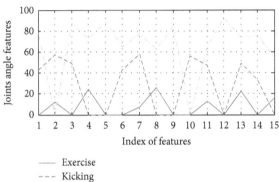 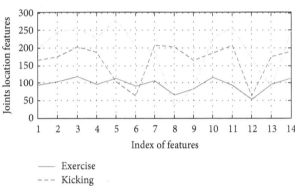

(a)   (b)

FIGURE 9: 1D plots of (a) joints angle and (b) joint locations features for exercise, kicking, and cleaning activities.

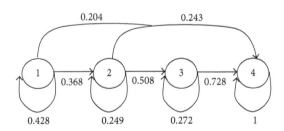

FIGURE 10: Transition and emission probabilities distribution of cleaning activity of trained HMM based on left-to-right HMM approach.

3. Experimental Results and Descriptions

3.1. Experimental Settings. The proposed method is evaluated on three challenging depth videos datasets. First is our own annotated depth dataset known as IM-DailyDepthActivity [54]. It includes fifteen types of activities as *sitting down, both hands waving, bending, standing up, eating, phone conversation, boxing, clapping, right hand waving, exercise, cleaning, kicking, throwing, taking an object, and reading an article.* During experimental evaluation, we used 375 videos sequences for training and 30 unsegmented videos for testing. All videos are collected in indoor environments (i.e., labs,

classroom, and halls) performed by 15 different subjects. Figure 11 shows some depth activities images used in IM-DailyDepthActivity dataset.

Second is public depth database as MSRAction3D dataset and third is MSRDailyActivity3D dataset. In the following sections, we explain and compare our method with other state-of-the-art methods using all three depth datasets.

3.2. Comparison of Recognition Rate of Proposed and State-of-the-Art Methods Using IM-DailyDepthActivity. We compare our spatiotemporal features method with the state-of-the-art methods including body joints, eigenjoints, depth motion maps, and super normal vector features using depth images. It is cleared in Table 1 that the spatiotemporal features achieved highest recognition rate as 63.7% over the state-of-the-art methods.

3.3. Recognition Results of Public Dataset (MSRAction3D). The MSRAction3D dataset is a public dataset captured by a Kinect camera based on game consoles phenomenon. It includes twenty actions as *high arm wave, horizontal arm wave, hammer, hand catch, forward punch, high throw, drawing X, drawing tick, drawing circle, hand clap, two-hand wave, side boxing, bending, forward kicking, side kicking, jogging, tennis swing, tennis serve, golf swing, and pickup and*

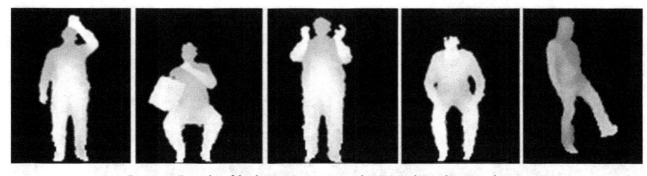

FIGURE 11: Examples of depth activities images used in IM-DailyDepthActivity dataset.

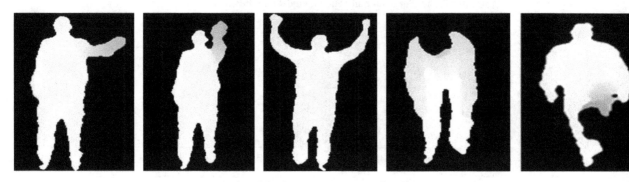

FIGURE 12: Examples of depth actions images used in MSRAction3D dataset.

TABLE 1: Comparison of recognition accuracy using IM-DailyDepthActivity.

Method	Recognition accuracy
Recognized body parts features [19]	28.4
Eigenjoints [20]	40.3
Super normal vector [1]	51.6
Depth silhouettes context features [21]	57.69
Proposed method	*63.7*

TABLE 2: Recognition results of proposed HAR system.

Actions	Accuracy
High arm wave	**93.7**
Horizontal arm wave	**90.4**
Hammer	**89.2**
Hand catch	**95.5**
Forward punch	**91.1**
High throw	**89.7**
Drawing X	**93.4**
Drawing tick	**97.1**
Drawing circle	**92.3**
Hand clap	**89.7**
Two-hand wave	**94.5**
Side boxing	**92.4**
Bending	**86.8**
Forward kicking	**91.3**
Side kicking	**98.6**
Jogging	**96.7**
Tennis swing	**87.1**
Tennis serve	**86.9**
Golf swing	**97.8**
Pickup and throw	**94.3**
Mean recognition accuracy = 92.4	

throw. The overall dataset consists of 567 (i.e., 20 actions × 10 subjects × 2 or 3 trails) depth map sequences. Also, this dataset is quite complex due to similar postures of different actions. Examples of different actions used in this dataset are shown in Figure 12.

To perform experimentation over MSRAction3D, we evaluated all 20 actions and examined their recognition accuracy performance based on LOSO (leave-one-subject-out) cross-subject training/testing mechanism. Table 2 shows the recognition accuracy of this dataset.

While some other researchers used MSRAction3D [22–26, 28] dataset by dividing it into action set 1, action set 2, and action set 3 as mentioned in [22], we compare the recognition performance of spatiotemporal method with other state-of-the-art methods in Table 3. All methods are implemented by us using similar instructions provided by their respective papers.

3.4. Recognition Results of Public Dataset (MSRDailyActivity3D). The MSRDailyActivity3D dataset is a depth activity dataset collected by a Kinect device based on living room daily routine. It includes sixteen activities as *stand up, sit*

FIGURE 13: Some depth images used in MSRDailyActivity3D dataset.

TABLE 3: Comparison of recognition accuracy of proposed method and state-of-the-art methods using MSRAction3D dataset.

Method	Recognition accuracy
Bag of 3D points [22]	74.7
Shape and motion features [23]	82.1
Eigenjoints [20]	82.3
Spatiotemporal motion variation [24]	84.6
STOP features [25]	84.8
Joints plus body features [26]	85.6
Actionlet ensemble [11]	88.2
Cuboid similar features [27]	89.3
Spatial and temporal part-sets [28]	90.2
Pose-based features [29]	91.5
Proposed method	*92.4*

TABLE 4: Recognition results of proposed HAR system.

Activities	Accuracy
Drink	**95.4**
Eat	**87.8**
Read book	**96.3**
Call phone	**89.1**
Write	**96.7**
Use laptop	**90.5**
Use cleaner	**100**
Cheer up	**88.5**
Sit still	**94.6**
Toss paper	**94.2**
Play game	**86.3**
Lay down	**98.7**
Walk	**95.3**
Play guitar	**88.2**
Stand up	**96.5**
Sit down	**93.6**
Mean recognition accuracy = 93.2	

down, walk, drink, write on a paper, eat, read book, call on cell phone, use laptop, use vacuum cleaner, cheer up, sit still, toss paper, play game, lie down on sofa, and play guitar. This dataset includes 320 (i.e., 16 activities × 10 subjects × 2 trails) depth videos activities mostly operated in a room. These activities also involved human-object interactions. Some of the examples of the MSRDailyActivity3D dataset are shown in Figure 13.

Table 4 shows the accuracy performance of 16 different human activities that is obtained from the proposed spatiotemporal features method over the specific dataset.

Finally, we reported the comparison of recognition accuracy over the MSRDailyActivity3D dataset where the proposed method shows superior recognition rate over state-of-the-art methods in Table 5.

4. Conclusions

In this paper, we proposed spatiotemporal features based on depth images derived from Kinect camera for human activity recognition. The features include depth sequential history to represent the spatial-temporal information of human silhouettes in each activity, motion identification to calculate the change among motion in between consecutive frames, and optical flow to represent in the form of partial image to get optimum depth information. During

TABLE 5: Comparison of recognition accuracy of using MSRDaily-Activity3D dataset.

Method	Recognition accuracy
Only joints position features [11]	68.0
Moving pose [6]	73.8
Motion features [30]	79.1
Hybrid features [31]	85.3
Actionlet ensemble [11]	85.7
Super normal vector [1]	86.2
Volumetric spatial features [32]	89.7
Spatiotemporal features learning [33]	90.4
Proposed method	*93.2*

experimental results, these features are applied over proposed IM-DailyDepthActivity, MSRAction3D, and MSRDailyActivity3D datasets, respectively. Our proposed activity recognition system shows superior recognition accuracy performance as 63.7% over the state-of-the-art methods using our depth annotated dataset. In case of public datasets, our method achieved accuracy performance as 92.4% and 93.2%, respectively. Our future work needs to explore more enhanced feature techniques for complex activities and multiple person interactions.

Competing Interests

The authors declare that there are no competing interests regarding the publication of this paper.

Acknowledgments

The research was supported by the Implementation of Technologies for Identification, Behavior, and Location of Human Based on Sensor Network Fusion Program through the Ministry of Trade, Industry and Energy (Grant no. 10041629). This work was supported by Institute for Information & communications Technology Promotion (IITP) grant funded by the Korea government (MSIP) (B0101-16-0552, Development of Predictive Visual Intelligence Technology).

References

[1] X. Yang and Y. Tian, "Super normal vector for activity recognition using depth sequences," in *Proceedings of the 27th IEEE Conference on Computer Vision and Pattern Recognition (CVPR '14)*, pp. 804–811, IEEE, Columbus, Ohio, USA, June 2014.

[2] A. Jalal, J. Kim, and T. Kim, "Human activity recognition using the labeled depth body parts information of depth silhouettes," in *Proceedings of the 6th International Symposium on Sustainable Healthy Buildings*, pp. 1–8, 2012.

[3] G. Okeyo, L. Chen, and H. Wang, "An agent-mediated ontology-based approach for composite activity recognition in smart homes," *Journal of Universal Computer Science*, vol. 19, no. 17, pp. 2577–2597, 2013.

[4] A. Jalal, S. Lee, J. Kim, and T. Kim, "Human activity recognition via the features of labeled depth body parts," in *Proceedings of the International Conference on Smart Homes and Health Telematics*, pp. 246–249, June 2012.

[5] A. Jalal, J. Kim, and T. Kim, "Development of a life logging system via depth imaging-based human activity recognition for smart homes," in *Proceedings of the 8th International Symposium on Sustainable Healthy Buildings*, pp. 91–95, Seoul, Republic of Korea, September 2012.

[6] M. Zanfir, M. Leordeanu, and C. Sminchisescu, "The moving pose: an efficient 3D kinematics descriptor for low-latency action recognition and detection," in *Proceedings of the 14th IEEE International Conference on Computer Vision (ICCV '13)*, pp. 2752–2759, Sydney, Australia, December 2013.

[7] A. Jalal and Y. Kim, "Dense depth maps-based human pose tracking and recognition in dynamic scenes using ridge data," in *Proceedings of the 11th IEEE International Conference on Advanced Video and Signal Based Surveillance (AVSS '14)*, pp. 119–124, IEEE, Seoul, Republic of Korea, August 2014.

[8] F. Xu and K. Fujimura, "Human detection using depth and gray images," in *Proceedings of the IEEE Conference on Advanced Video and Signal Based Surveillance (AVSS '03)*, pp. 115–121, IEEE, Colorado Springs, Colo, USA, July 2003.

[9] A. Jalal and IjazUddin, "Security architecture for third generation (3G) using GMHS cellular network," in *Proceedings of the 3rd International Conference on Emerging Technologies (ICET '07)*, pp. 74–79, IEEE, Islamabad, Pakistan, November 2007.

[10] A. Farooq, A. Jalal, and S. Kamal, "Dense RGB-D map-based human tracking and activity recognition using skin joints features and self-organizing map," *KSII Transactions on Internet and Information Systems*, vol. 9, no. 5, pp. 1856–1869, 2015.

[11] J. Wang, Z. Liu, Y. Wu, and J. Yuan, "Mining actionlet ensemble for action recognition with depth cameras," in *Proceedings of the IEEE Conference on Computer Vision and Pattern Recognition (CVPR '12)*, pp. 1290–1297, Providence, RI, USA, June 2012.

[12] A. Jalal, M. Z. Uddin, J. T. Kim, and T.-S. Kim, "Recognition of human home activities via depth silhouettes and R transformation for smart homes," *Indoor and Built Environment*, vol. 21, no. 1, pp. 184–190, 2012.

[13] A. Jalal, Y. Kim, and D. Kim, "Ridge body parts features for human pose estimation and recognition from RGB-D video data," in *Proceedings of the IEEE International Conference on Computing, Communication and Networking Technologies (ICCCNT '14)*, pp. 1–6, IEEE, Hefei, China, July 2014.

[14] A. Jalal, Z. Uddin, and T.-S. Kim, "Depth video-based human activity recognition system using translation and scaling invariant features for life logging at smart home," *IEEE Transactions on Consumer Electronics*, vol. 58, no. 3, pp. 863–871, 2012.

[15] P. Casale, O. Pujol, and P. Radeva, "Human activity recognition from accelerometer data using a wearable device," in *Proceedings of the 5th International Conference on Pattern Recognition and Image Analysis (IbPRIA '11)*, pp. 289–269, Las Palmas de Gran Canaria, Spain, June 2011.

[16] L. Bao and S. Intille, "Activity recognition from user-annotated acceleration data," in *Proceedings of the International Conference on Pervasive Computing*, pp. 1–17, April 2004.

[17] S. Kamal and A. Jalal, "A hybrid feature extraction approach for human detection, tracking and activity recognition using depth sensors," *Arabian Journal for Science and Engineering*, vol. 41, no. 3, pp. 1043–1051, 2016.

[18] C. Zhang and Y. Tian, "RGB-D camera-based daily living activity recognition," *Journal of Computer Vision and Image Processing*, vol. 2, no. 4, pp. 1–7, 2012.

[19] A. Jalal, N. Sarif, J. T. Kim, and T.-S. Kim, "Human activity recognition via recognized body parts of human depth silhouettes for residents monitoring services at smart home," *Indoor and Built Environment*, vol. 22, no. 1, pp. 271–279, 2013.

[20] X. Yang and Y. L. Tian, "EigenJoints-based action recognition using Naïve-Bayes-Nearest-Neighbor," in *Proceedings of the IEEE Computer Society Conference on Computer Vision and Pattern Recognition Workshops (CVPRW '12)*, pp. 14–19, Providence, RI, USA, June 2012.

[21] A. Jalal, S. Kamal, and D. Kim, "Individual detection-tracking-recognition using depth activity images," in *Proceedings of the 12th International Conference on Ubiquitous Robots and Ambient Intelligence (URAI '15)*, pp. 450–455, Goyang, Republic of Korea, October 2015.

[22] W. Li, Z. Zhang, and Z. Liu, "Action recognition based on a bag of 3D points," in *Proceedings of the IEEE Computer Society Conference on Computer Vision and Pattern Recognition Workshops (CVPRW '10)*, pp. 9–14, IEEE, San Francisco, Calif, USA, June 2010.

[23] A. Jalal, S. Kamal, and D. Kim, "Shape and motion features approach for activity tracking and recognition from kinect video camera," in *Proceedings of the 29th IEEE International*

Conference on Advanced Information Networking and Applications Workshops (WAINA '15), pp. 445–450, IEEE, Gwangiu, South Korea, March 2015.

[24] A. Jalal, S. Kamal, A. Farooq, and D. Kim, "A spatiotemporal motion variation features extraction approach for human tracking and pose-based action recognition," in *Proceedings of the International Conference on Informatics, Electronics and Vision (ICIEV '15)*, pp. 1–6, Fukuoka, Japan, June 2015.

[25] A. Vieira, E. Nascimentio, G. Oliveira, Z. Liu, and M. Campos, "STOP: space-time occupancy patterns for 3d action recognition from depth map sequences," in *Proceedings of the 17th Iberoamerican Congress on Pattern Recognition*, pp. 252–259, Buenos Aires, Argentina, September 2012.

[26] A. Jalal, Y. Kim, S. Kamal, A. Farooq, and D. Kim, "Human daily activity recognition with joints plus body features representation using Kinect sensor," in *Proceedings of the International Conference on Informatics, Electronics and Vision (ICIEV '15)*, pp. 1–6, IEEE, Fukuoka, Japan, June 2015.

[27] L. Xia and J. K. Aggarwal, "Spatio-temporal depth cuboid similarity feature for activity recognition using depth camera," in *Proceedings of the 26th IEEE Conference on Computer Vision and Pattern Recognition (CVPR '13)*, pp. 2834–2841, IEEE, Portland, Ore, USA, June 2013.

[28] C. Wang, Y. Wang, and A. L. Yuille, "An approach to pose-based action recognition," in *Proceedings of the 26th IEEE Conference on Computer Vision and Pattern Recognition (CVPR '13)*, pp. 915–922, Portland, Ore, USA, June 2013.

[29] A. Eweiwi, M. S. Cheema, C. Bauckhage, and J. Gall, "Efficient pose-based action recognition ," in *Computer Vision—ACCV 2014: 12th Asian Conference on Computer Vision, Singapore, Singapore, November 1–5, 2014, Revised Selected Papers, Part V*, vol. 9007 of *Lecture Notes in Computer Science*, pp. 428–443, Springer, Berlin, Germany, 2015.

[30] A. Jalal, S. Kamal, and D. Kim, "A depth video sensor-based life-logging human activity recognition system for elderly care in smart indoor environments," *Sensors*, vol. 14, no. 7, pp. 11735–11759, 2014.

[31] A. Jalal and S. Kim, "Algorithmic implementation and efficiency maintenance of real-time environment using low-bitrate wireless communication," in *Proceedings of the IEEE International Workshop on Software Technologies for Future Embedded and Ubiquitous Systems*, pp. 1–6, April 2006.

[32] S.-S. Cho, A.-R. Lee, H.-I. Suk, J.-S. Park, and S.-W. Lee, "Volumetric spatial feature representation for view-invariant human action recognition using a depth camera," *Optical Engineering*, vol. 54, no. 3, Article ID 033102, 8 pages, 2015.

[33] L. Liu and L. Shao, "Learning discriminative representations from RGB-D video data," in *Proceedings of the 23rd International Joint Conference on Artificial Intelligence (IJCAI '13)*, pp. 1493–1500, Beijing, China, August 2013.

[34] S. Kamal, A. Jalal, and D. Kim, "Depth images-based human detection, tracking and activity recognition using spatiotemporal features and modified HMM," *Journal of Electrical Engineering and Technology*, vol. 11, no. 3, pp. 1921–1926, 2016.

[35] A. Jalal, Z. Uddin, J. Kim, and T. Kim, "Daily human activity recognition using depth silhouettes and R transformation for smart home," in *Proceedings of the 9th International Conference on Toward Useful Services for Elderly and People with Disabilities: Smart Homes and Health Telematics (ICOST '11)*, pp. 25–32, Montreal, Canada, June 2011.

[36] A. Jalal and S. Kim, "Advanced performance achievement using multi-algorithmic approach of video transcoder for low bit rate wireless communication," *ICGST Journal on Graphics, Vision and Image Processing*, vol. 5, no. 9, pp. 27–32, 2005.

[37] A. Jalal and S. Kim, "Global security using human face understanding under vision ubiquitous architecture system," *World Academy of Science, Engineering, and Technology*, vol. 13, pp. 7–11, 2006.

[38] M. Turk and A. Pentland, "Face recognition using eigenfaces," in *Proceedings of the International Conference on Computer Vision and Pattern Recognition*, pp. 586–591, Maui, Hawaii, USA, June 1991.

[39] A. Jalal and Y. A. Rasheed, "Collaboration achievement along with performance maintenance in video streaming," in *Proceedings of the IEEE Conference on Interactive Computer Aided Learning*, pp. 1–8, Villach, Austria, 2007.

[40] A. Jalal and M. A. Zeb, "Security and QoS optimization for distributed real time environment," in *Proceedings of the 7th IEEE International Conference on Computer and Information Technology (CIT '07)*, pp. 369–374, Aizuwakamatsu, Japan, October 2007.

[41] L. Chen, P. Zhu, and G. Zhu, "Moving objects detection based on background subtraction combined with consecutive frames subtraction," in *Proceedings of the International Conference on Future Information Technology and Management Engineering (FITME '10)*, pp. 545–548, IEEE, Changzhou, China, October 2010.

[42] A. Jalal and S. Kim, "The mechanism of edge detection using the block matching criteria for the motion estimation," in *Proceedings of the Conference on Human Computer Interaction (HCI '05)*, pp. 484–489, January 2005.

[43] A. Jalal, S. Kim, and B. J. Yun, "Assembled algorithm in the real-time H.263 codec for advanced performance," in *Proceedings of the 7th International Workshop on Enterprise Networking and Computing in Healthcare Industry (HEALTHCOM '05)*, pp. 295–298, IEEE, Busan, South Korea, June 2005.

[44] Y.-H. Taguchi and A. Okamoto, "Principal component analysis for bacterial proteomic analysis," in *Proceedings of the IEEE International Conference on Bioinformatics and Biomedicine Workshops (BIBMW '11)*, pp. 961–963, IEEE, Atlanta, Ga, USA, November 2011.

[45] A. Jalal and S. Kim, "A complexity removal in the floating point and rate control phenomenon," in *Proceedings of the Conference on Korea Multimedia Society*, vol. 8, pp. 48–51, January 2005.

[46] A. Jalal and A. Shahzad, "Multiple facial feature detection using vertex-modeling structure," in *Proceedings of the International Conference on Interactive Computer Aided Learning*, pp. 1–7, September 2007.

[47] P. M. Baggenstoss, "A modified Baum-Welch algorithm for hidden Markov models with multiple observation spaces," *IEEE Transactions on Speech and Audio Processing*, vol. 9, no. 4, pp. 411–416, 2001.

[48] A. Jalal, Y. Kim, Y. Kim, S. Kamal, and D. Kim, "Robust human activity recognition from depth video using spatiotemporal multi-fused features," *Pattern Recognition*, vol. 61, pp. 295–308, 2017.

[49] A. Jalal, S. Kamal, and D. Kim, "Depth map-based human activity tracking and recognition using body joints features and Self-Organized Map," in *Proceedings of the 5th International Conference on Computing, Communication and Networking Technologies (ICCCNT '14)*, pp. 1–6, IEEE, Hefei, China, July 2014.

[50] A. Jalal and S. Kamal, "Real-time life logging via a depth silhouette-based human activity recognition system for smart

home services," in *Proceedings of the 11th IEEE International Conference on Advanced Video and Signal-Based Surveillance (AVSS '14)*, pp. 74–80, Seoul, South Korea, August 2014.

[51] S.-S. Jarng, "HMM voice recognition algorithm coding," in *Proceedings of the International Conference on Information Science and Applications (ICISA '11)*, pp. 1–7, IEEE, Jeju, South Korea, April 2011.

[52] A. Jalal and M. Zeb, "Security enhancement for e-learning portal," *International Journal of Computer Science and Network Security*, vol. 8, no. 3, pp. 41–45, 2008.

[53] A. Jalal, S. Kamal, and D. Kim, "Depth silhouettes context: a new robust feature for human tracking and activity recognition based on embedded HMMs," in *Proceedings of the 12th International Conference on Ubiquitous Robots and Ambient Intelligence (URAI '15)*, pp. 294–299, Goyang, South Korea, October 2015.

[54] A. Jalal, "IM-DailyDepthActivity dataset," 2016, http://imlab.postech.ac.kr/databases.htm.

8

AMCCR: Adaptive Multi-QoS Cross-Layer Cooperative Routing in Ad Hoc Networks

Mahadev A. Gawas,[1] **Lucy J. Gudino,**[1] **and K. R. Anupama**[2]

[1]*Department of Computer Science and Information System, BITS-Pilani K K Birla, Goa Campus, Goa, India*
[2]*Department of Elecrical, Electronics and Instrumentation Engineering, BITS-Pilani K K Birla, Goa Campus, Goa, India*

Correspondence should be addressed to Mahadev A. Gawas; mahadev@goa.bits-pilani.ac.in

Academic Editor: Liansheng Tan

The cooperative communication technique in an ad hoc network exploits the spatial diversity gains inherent in multiuser systems and mitigates the multipath fading. This technique is necessary but perhaps not sufficient to meet the QoS demands in ad hoc network. This is due to the fact that routing protocol at the network layer is more responsible for the successful packet delivery and QoS support. In this paper, we propose an adaptive multi-QoS cross-layer cooperative routing (AMCCR) protocol that enhances the performance through the cooperation of physical, MAC, and network layers. We first formulate an approach to analyze the channel state variations for effective communication schemes at the physical layer. Secondly, we dynamically select the transmission mode to employ cooperative MAC scheme by exploiting spatial diversity. Thereafter, the network layer chooses an optimized route from source to destination through the selected best relay candidates based on multiple QoS metrics. The paper is further extended to support dual-hop half-duplex communication via selected relay by coding technique. The proposed protocol is validated by extensive simulations and compared with CD-MAC and CODE protocols. The results clearly show that the proposed cooperative cross-layer design approach significantly improves the average delay, throughput, and network lifetime of the system.

1. Introduction

The wireless ad hoc network has gained immense popularity due to the ubiquity of portable mobile devices and the convenience of infrastructure-less communication. Today the significant advances in wireless communication have brought a revolution in the area of mobile communication. With the increasing time-sensitive multimedia traffic on the Internet, there is a demand to set QoS features to meet the rigorous performance demands [1, 2]. The QoS is defined as a set of constraints such as end-to-end delay, throughput, packet loss, and energy which need to be satisfied by the network.

In wireless communications, errors in data transmissions occur due to the unreliability of wireless channel caused by the node's mobility, energy exhaustion, and channel fading. This consequently leads to retransmission when erroneous data frames are detected, which further results in an increase in delay and decrease in the packet delivery ratio of the network. Thus, achieving multiobjective QoS in ad hoc network

is challenging. These circumstances motivate the innovation of a new technology, known as cooperative communication (CC) [3, 4].

Recently, cooperative communication has received considerable interest of research fraternity in wireless networks. The idea of cooperative communications has been mainly concentrated on the physical layer with the advances in the techniques such as modulation and coding to allow nodes to cooperate in their transmissions to improve the overall performance of the wireless networks [5]. The cooperative communication at the physical layer comprises decision-making in selecting cooperative relaying schemes like store and forward, amplify-and-forward [6], and decode-and-forward [7], choosing power for signal transmission, and selecting scheme for relay selection.

The innovation of cooperative communication is not restricted to the physical layer only. To subjugate the constant node mobility, it would be ideal to expose the physical layer information for the cooperation to different higher protocol layers. In the recent time, the cooperative MAC scheme in ad hoc wireless networks has also attracted much attention [8]. These schemes use handshaking techniques to reserve the channel and avoid the collision problems. These schemes use cross-layer design between the physical and MAC layers for relay selection with the criteria related to rate adaptation and power control. Due to random nature of the wireless channel, MAC layer should know when to initiate the cooperative transmission. Thus, the cooperative MAC should utilize the assistance from a relay node to forward the data using better link adaptation techniques and higher data rates to enhance the network throughput.

Usage of cooperative communication together with rate adaptation techniques can enable the nodes to adapt their data rates to match the channel conditions and node mobility. Combining both these techniques can provide a substantial throughput improvement in direct and conventional multi-hop network.

In this paper, we establish cooperation between physical, MAC, and network layers. We propose an effective distributed cross-layer cooperative routing algorithm for mobile nodes by using multi-QoS cooperative metrics that use the potential cooperation gain to find the optimal route. The cross-layer coordination between the MAC and network layers is used to select an optimal next hop, while the cross-layer coordination between the MAC and physical layers is used to select the best relay.

The main objectives of the proposed algorithm are as follows:

(1) An energy-aware, end-to-end delay efficient route discovery scheme is proposed among the network nodes in order to increase the network lifetime.

(2) Using the channel state information at the physical layer, the proposed algorithm determines whether cooperation on the link is necessary or not.

(3) In case the cooperation on the link is necessary, multi-QoS metric is used to determine the potential relay nodes for a cooperative transmission over each link. The cooperative mode activation is implemented in the MAC layer.

(4) We exploit the cross-layer approach to the routing layer for relay selections and resource allocations that reflect the potential cooperation gain to find the optimal paths. The best relay node selection strategy is executed in distributed manner.

(5) The proposed algorithm is analyzed with single relay participation for cooperative scheme and further extended for supporting network coding scheme.

(6) The best relay selection is enabled with collision avoidance mechanism.

The rest of the paper is organized as follows. Section 2 discusses the related work. In Section 3, we describe the physical model and assumptions. Section 4 describes our adaptive cooperative cross-layer architecture. In Section 5, we propose our cooperative network coding technique. The NAV is analyzed in Section 6. Performance evaluation and conclusions are presented in Sections 7 and 8, respectively.

2. Related Work

In the recent time, the cooperative MAC schemes in ad hoc wireless networks have attracted much attention. These schemes use handshaking techniques to reserve the channel and avoid the collision problems. These schemes uses cross-layer design between the physical and MAC layers for relay selection with the criteria related to rate adaptation and power control.

Sai Shankar et al. proposed a protocol called CMAC [9] with minor modifications to the standard IEEE 802.11 Distributed Coordination Function (DCF). When the source node sends the data packets and if destination node receives them with errors or fails to receive them, the source node selects a cooperative relay node to forward the lost data packet. Although CMAC provides the reliability of data transmission and throughput enhancement, it assumes that the link between any nodes is ideal and error-free. The relay-enabled DCF (rDCF) [10] and cooperative MAC (Coop-MAC) [11] were proposed to exploit the multirate capability and counter the throughput bottleneck caused by the low data rate links. The CoopMAC and rDCF protocols choose to send packets at a high data rate using relay node in a two-hop manner instead of a low data rate with direct transmission and improve the network performance. In rDCF, the best relay node is selected by the receiver, based on the piggybacked information in the control frame. Meanwhile, in CoopMAC, the relay node itself decides whether to cooperate or not, based on its local information maintained in the cooperative table. Both protocols are not suitable for multihop ad hoc networks and do not have any provision to deal with hidden node and exposed node. In UtdMAC [12], data packets are transmitted through the relay whenever a direct transmission fails due to fading. But, in UtdMAC, it is assumed that the relay is selected a priori and will be ready to transmit in a cooperative method whenever necessary. Thus, this protocol does not have to deal with much of the relay selection overhead and management. The cooperative diversity MAC (CD-MAC), proposed by [13], is based on the DCF mode. In CD-MAC, nodes use Distributed Space-Time Coding (DSTC). In CD-MAC, the transmission of multiple copies of a data stream is distributed among the cooperating nodes, which act as a virtual antenna array. The cooperating nodes encode the data by using orthogonal codes and simultaneously transmit it to the destination. The packet scheduling technique CD-MAC is similar to that of ARQ scheme, where cooperation is triggered when a direct transmission of a control packet fails. A source node sends an RTS packet to the destination node. If the destination replies with a CTS before the timeout period expires, then CD-MAC does not initiate cooperation; else, it activates the cooperation in the next phase. The source node intimates the need for cooperation to relay nodes through repeated RTS (C-RTS) packet. The destination node replies to a C-RTS with C-CTS simultaneously to relay and source node. During cooperation using DSTC, source node first sends a packet to the relay in the first phase and then both the source and relay simultaneously transmit the coded packet to the destination node. In CD-MAC, each node maintains an estimate of neighbor nodes link quality through periodic broadcast of Hello packets. However, due to repeated transmission of control packets, the nodes suffer in terms of end-to-end latency. CD-MAC does not handle the issue effectively in case the relay node is unavailable. Also, the energy consumption is not addressed properly; hence, due to repeated control packet transmissions, the latency gets increased; this further results in higher energy consumption for CD-MAC.

In the traditional layering network protocol architecture, the strict boundary between the layers ensures the easy deploying of network, but the encapsulation of the layers prevents sharing of certain vital information between layers. Traditional routing protocol optimizes each of the three layers, namely, physical, MAC, and network layers, independently, which may contribute to suboptimal network designs [14]. The traditional ad hoc routing protocols are designed for point-to-point communication, which do not take advantage of the cooperative diversity technique [6, 15].

Recently, there has been an increased interest in protocols for mobile ad hoc networks to exploit the significant interactions between various layers of the protocol stack for performance enhancements [16]. The research at the physical layer and MAC layer can be combined with higher layers, in particular the routing layer, to realize a fully cooperative network [17]. However, the problem of combining routing with cooperative diversity has received very little attention.

In some of the proposed researches towards cooperative routing, the primary objective of the routing is focused on energy efficiency [18], reduced collisions [19], enhanced throughput [20], outage probability [21], and so forth. Most of these cooperative routing algorithms are designed with the specific demand of requirements on single QoS parameter for a particular application. Hence, it is difficult to make comprehensive cooperative routing satisfying the needs of all applications. Further, significant effort has not been done in QoS provisioning for cooperative routing in wireless networks, especially in the context of achieving multiobjective QoS services, namely, end-to-end delay, reliability, throughput, and network lifetime. The existing cooperation techniques mentioned above do not consider cross-layer coordination between physical layer, MAC layer, and network layer.

3. System Model

Consider the mobile wireless ad hoc network comprising nodes $V_i, V_{i+1}, \ldots, V_n$. These nodes transmit a signal to neighbor nodes directly or may employ one relay node among the neighborhood. We consider the IEEE 802.11g PHY layer, which uses different modulation techniques to support multiple data rates of 6, 9, 12, 18, 24, 36, 48, and 54 Mbps [10]. All the control packets and headers, namely, RTS, CTS, PHY, and MAC headers, are transmitted at a fixed rate of 1 Mb/s.

In our experiments, we consider only one relay node selection in each hop in order to control complexity and the interference from simultaneous transmissions. Let R_i represent the relay node in the ith hop; thus the set of N relays is denoted by $R_i, R_{i+1}, \ldots, R_n$. The system considers slow Rayleigh fading channel model. Each node is equipped with single antenna, imposed with half-duplex constraint

with the impracticality of concurrent radio transmission and reception.

Let $h_{V_i,V_{i+1}}$, h_{V_i,R_i}, and $h_{R_i,V_{i+1}}$ represent the channel gain from the node V_i to the next hop V_{i+1}, from node V_i to relay R_i, and from relay R_i to node V_{i+1}, respectively. Statistically, they are modeled as independent and identically distributed (i.i.d) circularly symmetric complex Gaussian random variable with zero mean and equal variance: $\sigma^2_{V_i,V_{i+1}}$, $\sigma^2_{V_i,R_i}$, and $\sigma^2_{R_i,V_{i+1}}$, respectively. The noises $\eta_{V_i,V_{i+1}}$ and $\eta_{R_i,V_{i+1}}$ are modeled as zero mean complex Gaussian random variables with variance N_0.

We model the cooperation approach in two phases. In phase 1, the source node V_i broadcasts its information to the next hop V_{i+1}, which is overheard by neighbor R_i nodes. The signal received at the next hop and the neighbor relay are represented as $y_{V_i,V_{i+1}}$ and y_{V_i,R_i}, respectively.

$$y_{V_i,V_{i+1}} = \sqrt{P1}h_{V_i,V_{i+1}}x + \eta_{V_i,V_{i+1}}$$
$$y_{V_i,R_i} = \sqrt{P1}h_{V_i,R_i}x + \eta_{V_i,R_i}, \tag{1}$$

where $P1$ is the power transmitted at the node V_i and x represents the transmitted information symbol. In phase 2, the neighbor node R_i processes the received signal by amplify-and-forward (AF) or decode-and-forward (DF) techniques depending on the following specified criteria:

(1) For adaptive cooperation with amplify-and-forward (AF) technique, in phase 2, under the AF technique implementation, the selected relay terminal simply amplifies the received signal and forwards it to the next hop with transmission power $P2$. As stated in [6], under AF technique, the achievable rate between V_i and V_{i+1} with R_i is given as

$$C_{AF} = W \cdot I_{AF}(V_i, V_{i+1}, R_i), \tag{2}$$

where W represents the bandwidth of channels at node V_i and relay R_i and the average mutual information $I_{AF}(V_i, V_{i+1}, R_i)$ between the input and the outputs achieved by i.i.d complex Gaussian inputs is given by

$$I_{AF}(V_i, V_{i+1}, R_i)$$
$$= \log_2\left(1 + SNR_{V_i,V_{i+1}} + \frac{SNR_{V_i,R_i} \cdot SNR_{R_i,V_{i+1}}}{SNR_{V_i,R_i} + SNR_{R_i,V_{i+1}} + 1}\right)$$
$$SNR_{V_i,V_{i+1}} = \frac{P1}{\sigma^2_{V_i,V_{i+1}}}\left|h_{V_i,V_{i+1}}\right|^2$$
$$SNR_{V_i,R_i} = \frac{P1}{\sigma^2_{V_i,R_i}}\left|h_{V_i,R_i}\right|^2$$
$$SNR_{R_i,V_{i+1}} = \frac{P2}{\sigma^2_{R_i,V_{i+1}}}\left|h_{R_i,V_{i+1}}\right|^2. \tag{3}$$

The signal received at the next hop is represented as

$$y_{R_i,V_{i+1}} = \frac{\sqrt{P1P2}}{\sqrt{P1\left|h_{V_i,R_i}\right|^2 + N_0}}h_{R_i,V_{i+1}}h_{V_i,R_i}x + \eta'_{R_i,V_{i+1}}, \tag{4}$$

where

$$\eta'_{R_i,V_{i+1}} = \frac{\sqrt{P2}}{\sqrt{P1\left|h_{V_i,R_i}\right|^2 + N_0}} h_{R_i,V_{i+1}} \eta_{V_i,R_i} + \eta_{R_i,V_{i+1}}. \quad (5)$$

η_{V_i,R_i} and $\eta_{R_i,V_{i+1}}$ are assumed to be independent. Thus, $\eta'_{R_i,V_{i+1}}$ is modeled as a zero mean complex Gaussian random variable with a variance

$$\left(\frac{P2\left|h_{R_i,V_{i+1}}\right|^2}{P1\left|h_{V_i,R_i}\right|^2 + N_0} + 1\right) N_0. \quad (6)$$

The next hop node, on receiving the signal from the relay and previous hop node, detects the symbols transmitted with the knowledge of the channel gains $h_{V_i,V_{i+1}}$ and $h_{R_i,V_{i+1}}$, respectively. The next hop node implements a Maximum Ratio Combiner (MRC) technique [22] to decode the signals received from the previous hop node and the relay node. The MRC output at the next hop is given as

$$y = a_1 y_{V_i,V_{i+1}} + a_2 y_{R_i,V_{i+1}}, \quad (7)$$

where a_1 and a_2 are given as

$$a_1 = \frac{\sqrt{P1} h^*_{V_i,V_{i+1}}}{N_0},$$

$$a_2 = \frac{\sqrt{\left(P1P2/\left(P1\left|h_{V_i,R_i}\right|^2 + N_0\right)\right)} h^*_{V_i,R_i} h^*_{R_i,V_{i+1}}}{\left(P2\left|h_{R_i,V_{i+1}}\right|^2 / \left(P1\left|h_{V_i,R_i}\right|^2 + N_0\right) + 1\right) N_0}, \quad (8)$$

where h^* is the conjugated channel gain corresponding to the received symbol. Assuming that the average energy of transmitted symbol x in (1) is 1, the SNR of MRC output is represented as

$$\gamma = \gamma_1 + \gamma_2, \quad (9)$$

where γ_1 and γ_2 are given as

$$\gamma_1 = \frac{P1\left|h_{V_i,V_{i+1}}\right|^2}{N_0},$$

$$\gamma_2 = \frac{1}{N_0} \frac{P1P2\left|h_{V_i,R_i}\right|^2 \left|h_{R_i,V_{i+1}}\right|^2}{P1\left|h_{V_i,R_i}\right|^2 + P2\left|h_{R_i,V_{i+1}}\right|^2 + N_0}. \quad (10)$$

(2) For adaptive cooperation with decode-and-forward (DF) technique, in phase 2, to implement the technique, if the selected relay terminal is able to decode the symbols of the received information from the forwarding node V_i correctly, then it retransmits the information with power $P2$ to the next hop. We assume that if the SNR received at the relay is greater

than the threshold, then the symbol will be correctly decoded. As stated in [6], under DF technique, the achievable rate C_{DF} between V_i and V_{i+1} via R_i is given as

$$C_{DF} = W \cdot I_{DF}\left(V_i, R_i, V_{i+1}\right), \quad (11)$$

where average mutual information $I_{AF}(V_i, R_i, V_{i+1})$ between the input and the outputs, achieved by i.i.d complex Gaussian inputs, is given by

$$\begin{aligned} I_{DF}\left(V_i, R_i, V_{i+1}\right) = \min \Big\{ &\log_2\left(1 + \text{SNR}_{V_i,R_i}\right), \\ &\log_2\left(1 + \text{SNR}_{V_i,V_{i+1}} + \text{SNR}_{R_i,V_{i+1}}\right) \Big\}. \end{aligned} \quad (12)$$

The signal received at the next hop node is given as

$$y_{r,d} = \sqrt{P2} h_{R_i,V_{i+1}} x + \eta_{R_i,V_{i+1}}. \quad (13)$$

The channel gains $h_{V_i,V_{i+1}}$, $h_{R_i,V_{i+1}}$, and h_{V_i,R_i} are assumed to be known at the receiver but not at the transmitter and are assumed to be independent of each other. The next hop V_{i+1}, on receiving the signal from the relay and previous forwarding node, detects the symbols transmitted with the knowledge of the channel gains $h_{V_i,V_{i+1}}$ and $h_{R_i,V_{i+1}}$, respectively. The next hop implements a MRC. The MRC maximizes the SNR at the receiver so that the bit error rate is minimized. The combined signal at the next hop is represented as

$$y = a_1 y_{V_i,V_{i+1}} + a_2 y_{R_i,V_{i+1}}, \quad (14)$$

where a_1 and a_2 are computed to maximize the SNR of MRC output at the next hop node and are represented as

$$a_1 = \frac{\sqrt{P1} h_{V_i,V_{i+1}}}{N_0},$$

$$a_2 = \frac{\sqrt{P2} h_{R_i,V_{i+1}}}{N_0}. \quad (15)$$

Assuming that the average energy of transmitted symbol x in (1) is 1, the SNR of MRC output is represented as

$$\gamma = \frac{P1\left|h_{V_i,V_{i+1}}\right|^2 + P2\left|h_{R_i,V_{i+1}}\right|^2}{N_0}. \quad (16)$$

4. AMCCR Cross-Layer Architecture

In this section, we propose AMCCR cross-layer scheme, which uses an energy-efficient QoS routing to meet the requirements of the application. We also propose using the adaptive MAC to identify the relay nodes satisfying certain QoS metrics to cooperate the data transmission with the intermediate hops in the path discovered in routing phase.

4.1. Energy-Aware QoS Routing. The QoS routing is an essential component of a AMCCR architecture. The QoS factor aims at improving the quality of service in the wireless communication. The wireless ad hoc networks are power-constrained as the nodes have limited battery energy. Therefore, the energy of the node is a crucial QoS factor in the design of the routing algorithm [23]. We propose an energy-efficient routing scheme for the wireless ad hoc networks in order to increase the network lifetime while forwarding the packets through energy-constrained nodes. The energy efficiency can be measured by the time for which the network can maintain a desired performance level, called network lifetime. The minimum energy routing is different from the routing to maximize the network lifetime, as sometimes minimum energy routing invites more flows in an area, and the nodes in the route are exhausted very early. Thus, the entire network cannot perform due to failure of these nodes. Hence, it is vital to route the packets in a network by balancing the lifetime of all the nodes, so that desired network performance can be achieved for a long time. Hence, energy efficiency is not only measured by the power consumption but more generally it can be measured by the duration of time over which the network can maintain a certain performance level.

In the proposed QoS routing scheme, we use AODV [15] as a routing algorithm with minimal modifications. When a source node has data to send to the destination node, it floods with the route request packet, RREQ, to its neighbors. The ⟨source-address, broadcast-id⟩ pair is used to identify the RREQ uniquely to control the overhead created by flooding and reducing the transmission of repeated information. In the proposed routing scheme, the source incorporates a minimum required node energy threshold value E_{thresh} and minimum residual energy of the node E_{residual}. The hop count and reserved field in RREQ frame are replaced with E_{thresh}, and E_{residual}, respectively. Thus, no additional overhead for modifications is needed in the RREQ frame structure. The E_{residual} field is initialized to zero by the source.

On receiving the RREQ, node checks if its residual energy is higher than the E_{thresh} value specified in the frame. If true, then it updates E_{residual} field of RREQ with its own E_{residual} value and rebroadcasts the RREQ to its neighbors. An intermediate node can collect multiple RREQ copies for the predetermined time duration $\text{RREQ}_{\text{wait}}$, which is assumed as 20 ms. The intermediate node retains the RREQ with highest E_{residual} value and processes further. The destination node replies to source using the path with the highest E_{residual} value. Thus, the scheme ensures that the path discovered does not consist of energy acute nodes.

4.2. Cooperative MAC. To optimize the performance, we exploit the MAC cooperation, while selecting the route from source to destination. Once the route from the source V_i to the destination V_j is discovered, any two adjacent nodes can select a relay node for cooperation to meet certain QoS requirements. Consider the example shown in Figure 1, where path is discovered between V_i and the destination V_j. Any two adjacent nodes like V_i and V_{i+1} in the path can select and utilize the relay node R_i, which is in the interference range

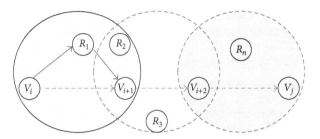

FIGURE 1: Multihop cooperative routing path.

of both these nodes for cooperative transmission as shown in Figure 1.

For each hop on the routing path, determining the need of relay node R_i between two adjacent nodes and selecting the optimal one from them are challenging. To address this problem, we propose an adaptive cooperative MAC. The primary focus of cooperative setup in the MAC layer is to meticulously allocate the resources and to engage cooperative nodes in setting up the cooperative environment.

The nodes willing to communicate over the 802.11 network use four-way handshake procedure to eliminate the hidden terminal issue. The communication between nodes is initiated by exchanging RTS/CTS packets. We assume that the link is symmetric. The node V_i transmits the RTS along with the payload of length L. The receiving node V_{i+1}, based on SNR of received RTS signal, computes the bit error rate (BER) and selects the appropriate data rate $\text{DR}_{V_i\text{-}V_{i+1}}$ for transmission from the node V_i. The broadcast nature of the wireless channel allows neighboring nodes of the sender V_i to overhear the RTS and determine the appropriate data rate $\text{DR}_{V_i\text{-}R_i}$ between the transmitter and themselves based on the estimated SNR and BER. The receiving node V_{i+1} transmits CTS incorporating $\text{DR}_{V_i\text{-}V_{i+1}}$ to node V_i. The neighboring node, to qualify as relay node, checks channel allocation for any ongoing communication in the interference region through network allocation vectors (NAV) to alleviate hidden terminal problems. If NAV is not set, it decodes the CTS transmitted from the node V_{i+1} and selects the appropriate data rate $\text{DR}_{R_i\text{-}V_{i+1}}$, based on receiving signal SNR value.

4.3. Best Relay Selection Criteria. To participate in cooperative communication between transmitter V_i and receiver node V_{i+1} as relay node, neighbor node goes through certain QoS metric. The selection of good-quality relay nodes is essential to achieve the objectives such as energy efficiency and high throughput, which enhances the system's performance. In the existing schemes, the relay selection mechanism mostly incurs extra overhead for complicated interactions among the neighbor links. Thus, it is essential to analyze the impact of complicated interactions among the neighbor links on cooperative diversity performance and minimize it to the lowest possible. In MANETs, there might be several neighbor nodes willing to join the transmitting node in cooperation communication and selecting the optimal one from them is challenging. If every neighbor node starts transmitting the request to the source, it will lead to wastage of bandwidth and energy of the nodes, which may further incur additional delay. So, to deal with such cases, we primarily focus on certain effective criteria for relay selection described as follows:

(1) Distributed relay selection: in some of the schemes such as centralized relay selection technique [24], the relay selection is done in a passive listening mode with centralized control. In this technique, all the neighbor relay's channel state information (CSI) is accumulated and compared, which induces complexity and delay. The scheme proposed in [11] requires periodic broadcast of readiness message by each neighbor node to its one-hop neighbors, irrespective of whether the cooperative mode is needed or not

(2) Adaptive relay selection: in fixed relaying scheme, data transmission always happens via relay node even when the destination node can directly receive and decode the data packets transmitted from the source. Hence, time slot used by the relay to forward the data packets is a waste of resources and takes double the time to transmit packets compared to the direct transmission. To counter these problems, adaptive relay selection would be more recommendable

(3) Optimal number of relays: to improve the network performance, many researchers [24] proposed using multiple relay nodes with the intent of increasing the diversity gain. However, the multiple relay nodes participating in cooperative communication create a larger interference area and cause additional coordination overhead, thus affecting the overall throughput. The authors in [25] proved that single relay node achieves the same diversity gain as that of multiple relay nodes

In this paper, distributed adaptive relay selection method is proposed. In the proposed scheme, selection of best relay node is carried out when the direct transmission from the transmitting node V_i to receiving node V_{i+1} in a multihop network fails due to fading or the relay path transmission time is better than the direct path. In such a scenario, the neighboring node with a potential to be a relay node participates in relay node selection process and uses local information collected by it. The neighbor nodes will have to satisfy certain QoS metric checks to qualify as the best relay node among the other competing neighboring nodes. If the direct transmission path between transmitting node and receiving node satisfies the QoS requirements, the relay nodes will not participate in the communication and the protocol will be reduced to simple DCF. The neighbor nodes undergo the following QoS metric test to qualify as relay node. The various QoS metric tests a neighbor node has to pass to qualify as a relay node to support cooperative MAC mechanism are as follows:

(1) For transmission time, the first QoS metric is the transmission time. The neighbor node, on hearing the RTS and CTS between transmitting node V_i and receiving node V_{i+1}, estimates the data rate from the SNR of receiving signals. Then, it estimates the cooperative transmission time that would incur between

the node V_i and node V_{i+1}, if it participates as a relay node. The cooperative transmission time T_{coop} and the direct transmission time T_{direct} are computed as

$$T_{\text{coop}} = \frac{L}{\text{DR}_{V_i\text{-}R_i}} + \frac{L}{\text{DR}_{R_i\text{-}V_{i+1}}} + T_{\text{RE}} + 2 * T_{\text{SIFS}}$$

$$T_{\text{direct}} = \frac{L}{\text{DR}_{V_i\text{-}V_{i+1}}}, \qquad (17)$$

where L is the packet length, T_{RE} is the transmission time for RE frame which is sent by the candidate relay node to V_i and V_{i+1} to notify its willingness to participate in the cooperative communication, and T_{SIFS} is the short interframe space (SIFS) interval.

If the neighbor node prefers to be a relay node, the total transmission time via relay node, that is, T_{coop}, should be less than the direct transmission time T_{direct}.

(2) For channel contention metric, it focuses on the channel contention. In MANETs, due to constant topological change, nodes may cluster at certain area and there could be high inflow and outflow of data within that region, leading to high interference. Therefore, the average channel contention time of the node may increase, thereby degrading the throughput of the network. In the proposed protocol, a node having a packet to forward will run a contention counter $T_{\text{cc}}(t)$ from the start of channel contention till it wins the channel access. The average contention time for a node $T_{\text{cc-avg}}(t)$ is computed using exponential weighted moving average over time Δt and is given by

$$T_{\text{cc-avg}}(t) = \alpha T_{\text{cc}}(t) + (1 - \alpha) T_{\text{cc-avg}}(t - 1), \qquad (18)$$

where α is a constant smoothing factor between 0 and 1.

If the neighbor node prefers to be a relay node, $T_{\text{cc-avg}}(t)$ should be less than $T_{\text{cc-thresh}}$, specified acceptable time duration.

(3) For energy utilization factor, the third metric, energy efficiency is undoubtedly one of the apt metrics for quality evaluation. The network lifetime is defined as the time from the deployment of the nodes to the instant the first node dies. So, to maximize the network lifetime, data has to be routed such that energy expenditure is fairly among the nodes in proportion to their energy reserved. The energy levels of all the nodes in the network have to be balanced and the nodes death due to frequent communication should be minimized to extend the network lifetime. In the proposed algorithm, the energy required by the neighbor node during cooperative communication is computed as

$$E_{\text{cooperative}} = \frac{P_{\text{receiver}}}{\text{DR}_{V_i\text{-}R_i}} + \frac{P_{\text{transmitter}}}{\text{DR}_{R_i\text{-}V_{i+1}}}, \qquad (19)$$

Frame control	Duration	Source address (V_i)	Relay address (R_i)	Next hop address (V_{i+1})	Sequence control	Data rate $(DR_{V_i\text{-}R_i})$	Data rate $(DR_{R_i\text{-}V_{i+1}})$	$L_{vi\text{-}v_{i+1}}$	$L_{v_{i+1}\text{-}v_i}$	Priority bit	FCS
2 bytes	2 bytes	6 bytes	6 bytes	6 bytes	2 bytes	1 byte	1 byte	2 bytes	2 bytes	1 byte	2 bytes

FIGURE 2: RE frame format.

where P_{receiver} is the power required to receive the data packet from the source and $P_{\text{transmitter}}$ is the power required to transmit the data packet to the destination.

Each neighbor node also stores its residual energy, E_{residual}. The proposed AMCCR protocol uses a novel way of interpreting energy using a metric called the energy utilization factor to select a relay node that not only is energy-efficient but also assists in improving the network lifetime. The energy utilization metric ε value is given as

$$\varepsilon = \frac{E_{\text{cooperative}}}{E_{\text{residual}}}. \tag{20}$$

Energy utilization metric ε is a better parameter compared to $E_{\text{cooperative}}$ or E_{residual} metric. For example, consider the two neighbor nodes N_1 and N_2 satisfying the above two QoS metric tests. Let us assume that N_1 and N_2 have the residual energy of 30 J and 50 J, respectively. Many of the routing protocols select the next hop based on residual energy or the minimum power needed to transmit. Let us assume that if N_1 or N_2 is selected as the relay node for cooperation, the energy required for transmission would be 10 J and 25 J, respectively. So, according to maximum residual energy selection criteria, N_2 is selected and after cooperative transmission the residual energy of N_1 and N_2 would be 30 J and 25 J, respectively.

According to the proposed energy utilization selection metric, the value of ε for N_1 and N_2 will be $\varepsilon(N_1) = 10/30$ and $\varepsilon(N_2) = 25/50$, respectively. The node with minimum ε will be selected, that is, node N_1. Thus, after cooperative transmission, the residual energy of N_1 and N_2 would be 20 and 50, respectively. Even though the ε factor does not guarantee total energy consumption minimization, it maximizes the minimum value of E_{residual} and maintains energy levels of the nodes in the network in a balanced state. Therefore, this factor extends the node survival time and improves the network lifetime.

In the network, there may be several nodes that have qualified all the three QoS metric tests and are candidate nodes for best relay node selection. So, to optimally select the best relay node, each node computes the network utilization weight based on the individual QoS metric weight. Each node

TABLE 1: Priority for 802.11 data rate pair $(V_i\text{-}R_i, R_i\text{-}V_{i+1})$.

Priority	Data rate pair $(V_i\text{-}R_i, R_i\text{-}V_{i+1})$
1	54-54, 54-48, 54-36, 54-24, 54-18
2	48-48, 48-36, 48-24, 48-54, 48-18, 36-36, 36-24, 36-54, 36-48, 36-18
3	24-24, 24-54, 24-48, 24-36, 24-18, 18-54, 18-48, 18-36, 18-24, 18-18
4	54-12, 54-9, 48-12, 48-9,
5	36-12, 36-9, 24-9
6	24-12, 18-12, 18-9,
7	12-54, 12-48, 12-36, 12-24, 12-18, 12-12, 12-9
8	9-54, 9-48, 9-36, 9-24, 9-18, 9-12, 9-9

computes its weight W_{relay} at regular interval of time and is given by

$$W_{\text{relay}} = \delta_1 * \frac{T_{\text{coop}}}{T_{\text{coop-max}}} + \delta_2 * \frac{T_{\text{cc-avg}}}{T_{\text{cc-max}}} + \delta_3 * \varepsilon, \tag{21}$$

where $\sum_{i=1}^{3} \delta_i = 1$, $T_{\text{coop-max}}$ is the maximum acceptable cooperative transmission time, and $T_{\text{cc-max}}$ is the maximum acceptable channel contention time.

It can be seen from the above equation that the metrics are normalized by their maximum values with some multiplicative factor δ.

4.3.1. Relay Eligible Frame. In the proposed scheme, the control format is extended to include source address, next hop address, relay address, data rates between source relay, relay next hop, packet length from source to next hop, and packet length from next hop to source, and priority. This new control format is known as relay eligible frame (RE) which is as shown in Figure 2.

On completion of RTS and CTS exchange, the node satisfying the condition to be a relay node sends the RE frame. On receiving the RE frame from a neighbor node, node V_i selects the appropriate MAC scheme. If RE frame is not received within timeout, the node V_i adopts direct transmission. The retransmission attempt is denied if RE frames collide or the relay backoff counter is reduced to zero. The sender node V_i will transmit the data at rate DR_{s-d} after a SIFS.

Each node maintains a priority table that consists of a pair of data rate between transmitter-relay and relay-receiver paths as shown in Table 1. The relay node on self-accessing sets the priority field in RE frame that matches with the corresponding data rate pair as per Table 1 and forwards the RE frame to the transmitting node and the next hop.

TABLE 2: Comparison of various relay selection schemes.

Protocol	Cooperation decision	Centralization	Selection overhead	Network coding functionality	Number of QoS metrics
CD-MAC	Transmitter	Centralized	Preselect, historical information	No	Single
rDCF	Receiver	Distributed	Preselect, historical information	No	Single
CODE	Transmitter	Centralized	Periodic broadcast	Partial	Single
CoopMAC	Transmitter	Centralized	Passive monitoring	No	Single
UtdMAC	Relay	Centralized	Preselect	No	Single
AMCCR	Relay	Distributed	RTS-CTS contention	Yes	Multiple

Table 2 shows comparison of some of the existing schemes and proposed scheme for relay selection. From Table 2, we can infer the novelty of relay selection in our proposed AMCCR protocol, which employs distributed relay selection based on multi-QoS metrics, initiated by the relay based on local information.

4.3.2. Relay Selection Overhead. Due to the mobility of nodes, multiple relay nodes may be available satisfying the QoS metric. This may lead to collisions of RE frames. Such frequent collisions may reduce the cooperation opportunity and degrade system's performance. Thus, it is a challenging task to select the best relay efficiently with lower collision rate. So we need to make a trade-off between relay selection period and collision probability. In order to avoid the collision of RE frame from multiple nodes qualified to be a relay, each qualifying neighbor node waits for an additional λ time after SIFS time. We divide the λ time slot into multiple τ slots of length σ. σ and τ are computed as

$$\sigma = 2 * P_{\text{delay}} + T_{\text{switch}}$$
$$\tau = \left\lfloor \frac{\lambda}{\sigma} \right\rfloor, \tag{22}$$

where P_{delay} is a channel propagation delay and T_{switch} is transceiver switching time.

We further divide the time slots τ into ϕ to map W_{relay} value, which is given as

$$\phi = \frac{W_{\text{relay}_{\text{max}}} - W_{\text{relay}_{\text{min}}}}{\tau}. \tag{23}$$

Each source node starts its ϕ counter from zero, and when it reaches its W_{relay} value, it sends RE frame in that time slot.

4.3.3. Relay Reassignment. Every relay node maintains a table containing the information about the ongoing neighbors transmissions. This restrains the neighbor nodes from unnecessarily participating in ongoing cooperative transmission. Due to nodes mobility, fading, or not satisfying the relay qualifying criteria, the selected best relay node may no longer be eligible to participate in the cooperative transmission. The existing cooperative protocols mentioned in literature do not address the issue in case a selected relay goes offline or is unavailable. In such cases, we propose a mechanism to automatically reelect the new relay node. The neighbor nodes on not hearing the RE frame from the current relay node will spontaneously initiate the transmission of RE frame in the

next RE time slot. So, whichever neighbor node is successful in forwarding the RE frame without collision replaces the previous relay node as the current best relay node. The efficient relay selection scheme proposed in AMCCR has the following characteristics:

(1) Relay selection is time-efficient.

(2) Collision probability of relay selection is minimized.

(3) Relay selection dynamically adapts to time-varying channel condition and nodes mobility.

(4) Relay selection is done in a distributed manner.

(5) There is no hidden node problem.

4.4. Adaptive Cooperative MAC Schemes in AMCCR. In AMCCR protocol, the data transmission can be in one of the four categories:

(1) Direct transmission

(2) Sender-relay-receiver

(3) Cooperative transmission scheme using DF technique

(4) Cooperative transmission scheme using AF technique

These MAC schemes are adaptively selected based on priority field of RE frame. The cross-layer adaptive data transmission is briefly explained in Algorithm 1. To facilitate the proper selection of transmission scheme, CTS packet is modified to accommodate a flag known as FLAG_P.

4.4.1. Direct Transmission. Based on the received signal quality transmitted from node V_i, the receiving node V_{i+1} sets its FLAG_P field while replying with CTS. If the direct transmission is sufficient, that is, SNR of received signal is greater than $\text{SNR}_{\text{thresh}}$, then FLAG_P is set to 0. The neighbor node, while decoding the CTS, will notice the FLAG_P field and refrain from interfering in the ongoing communication if it is set to 0. Figure 3(a) demonstrates the scheme.

4.4.2. Sender-Relay-Receiver Transmission. If FLAG_P is set to 1 and the priority field of RE frame contains the value between 1 and 3, then AMCCR protocol prefers simple sender-relay-receiver transmission scheme. Priority 1–3 indicates a high data rate estimated between the link V_i-R_i and R_i-V_{i+1} and, hence, the probability of data received at relay node or the receiver node with error is very minimal. Since

```
(1)  if RE frame not received within timeout then
(2)      Transmission mode = direct transmission
(3)  end if
(4)  if RE frame received then
(5)      Check the Priority field in RE frame
(6)      if 1 ≤ Priority ≤ 3 then
(7)          Transmission mode = sender-relay-receiver transmission
(8)      if 4 ≤ Priority ≤ 6 then
(9)          Transmission mode = DF cooperative transmission
(10)     else if Priority > 6 then
(11)         Transmission mode = AF cooperative transmission
(12)     end if
(13)   end if
(14) end if
```

ALGORITHM 1: Adaptive cooperative MAC data transmission.

the transmission rate from sender node to relay node is too high, receiver node does not overhear it due to reduced range and hence minimizes the interference.

4.4.3. DF Cooperative Transmission. When priority field of RE frame contains the value between 4 and 6, the data rate estimate from source to relay node is higher compared to that from relay node to destination node. When the relay is located closer to the source terminal, channel quality between node V_i and relay R_i is better than that between relay R_i and node V_{i+1}. When relay R_i moves away from the source, the BER increases and the relay node may send erroneous bits to the destination. Under this situation, DF technique is always better than AF technique and guarantees a performance diversity of the second order [26]. Therefore, when FLAG_P is set to 1 and the priority field of RE frame contains the value between 4 and 6, AMCCR protocol prefers DF cooperative transmission. DF technique is always better than AF technique and guarantees a performance diversity of the second order. Figure 3(b) demonstrates the scheme.

4.4.4. AF Cooperative Transmission. If FLAG_P is set to 1 and the priority field of RE frame contains the value greater than 6, the AMCCR protocol prefers the AF cooperative transmission. Priority greater than 6 indicates low data rate estimate between V_i and R_i and high data rate estimate between R_i and V_{i+1}. Performance in terms of BER is good when the relay node is closer to the destination node. As the relay node moves away from the destination, signal strength drops due to high data rate. Hence, cooperative scheme with AF is preferred to guarantee a performance diversity of order two as compared to DF scheme.

On receiving the RE frame with priority bit, the node V_{i+1} prepares for receiving data packets from relay node. The node V_i waits for SIFS time and sends data at the data rate $DR_{V_i \text{-} R_i}$ to relay node. On receiving the data packet, relay node waits for another SIFS time and forwards the packet to destination node D at the data rate $DR_{R_i \text{-} V_{i+1}}$. On receiving the data correctly, node V_{i+1} replies with an ACK packet to node V_i after SIFS.

If node V_i does not receive the RE frame within Timeout$_{\text{RE}}$, it prefers direct communication. Figure 3(c) explains the scheme.

4.5. Cooperative Routing. In MANETs, cooperation at the MAC layer can be exploited at the network layer to enhance the system's performance. Unlike the traditional routing protocol, we exploit the MAC cooperation, while selecting the route from source to destination. Thus, cooperative routing is activated whenever the opportunity of cooperation gain exists. Consider a simple network topology given in Figure 1. Let us assume that the proposed routing scheme discovers the route from node V_i to node V_j via nodes V_{i+1} and V_{i+2} during initial route discovery phase. During the control packet exchange between V_i and V_{i+1}, if R_i qualifies to be the best relay node to support cooperative transmission, then nodes V_i and V_{i+1} will update their route table with the additional entry for the relay node. Thus, the route layer will have access to cooperative link metrics of relay between two adjacent nodes. The route layer fully exploits this information while choosing the best next hop from the route table. The possible route from node V_i to V_j can be V_i-R_i-V_{i+1}-V_{i+2}-V_j. Hence, the cross-layer mechanism utilizes cooperative diversity that helps in improving the network performance.

5. Network Coding through Cooperative Communication

In a dual-hop half-duplex relay network, the throughput performance is reduced to half as it cannot transmit or receive simultaneously. To counter this fallback, we implement the network coding scheme in cooperative mode to support efficient communication. Network coding [27] is the technique that forwards the data received from multiple nodes by combining the input data packets into one or more output data packets. This results in a reduced number of packet transmissions, reducing the delay and enhancing the network performance. This technique is widely being accepted and can be exploited in the cooperative communication. Consider an example as shown in Figure 4, where nodes V_i and

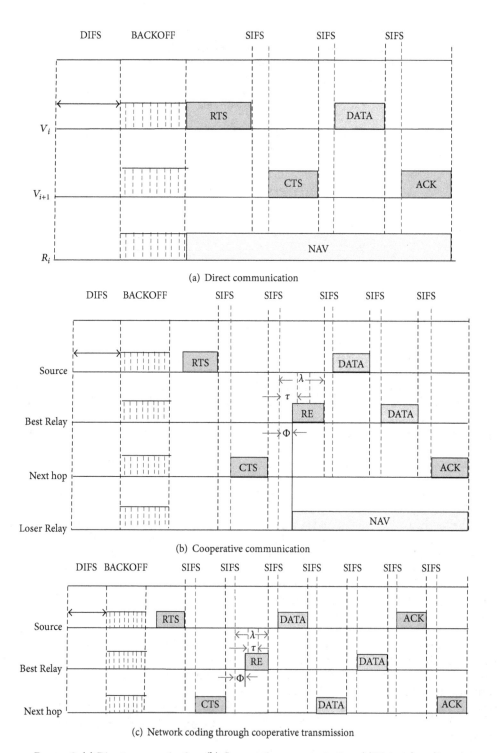

FIGURE 3: (a) Direct communication. (b) Cooperative communication. (c) Network coding.

V_{i+1} want to exchange the data packets for communication through the selected relay node R_i. Network coding technique works in half-duplex mode which is divided into three phases, where the channel is time-multiplexed. Figure 3(c) demonstrates the exchange of control packets in cooperative coding technique. In phase 1, node V_i forwards the data packet $L_{V_i\text{-}V_{i+1}}$ to relay R_i. In phase 2, node V_{i+1} forwards the data packet $L_{V_{i+1}\text{-}V_i}$ to relay R_i. Finally, in phase 3, relay

node R_i broadcasts $L_{V_i\text{-}V_{i+1}}$ XOR $L_{V_{i+1}\text{-}V_i}$ to nodes V_i and V_{i+1}. The nodes V_i and V_{i+1} recover the received data packets destined to themselves. Therefore, by implementing network coding scheme, single-channel contention is needed. At the end of phase 3, ACK packets are exchanged between nodes V_i and V_{i+1}, and transmission completes. In case of ACK packet getting lost, retransmission of packet is initiated. The length of packets from source to destination $L_{V_i\text{-}V_{i+1}}$ and from

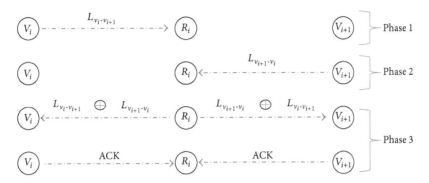

FIGURE 4: Network coding scheme.

destination to the source $L_{V_{i+1}-V_i}$ is computed through the duration values in RTS and CTS, respectively. The condition for relay node to participate in cooperative network coding technique is revised as

$$\frac{L_{V_i-V_{i+1}}}{DR_{V_i-R_i}} + \frac{L_{V_{i+1}-V_i}}{DR_{R_i-V_{i+1}}} + \frac{\max\left(L_{V_i-V_{i+1}}, L_{V_{i+1}-V_i}\right)}{\min\left(DR_{V_i-R_i}, DR_{R_i-V_{i+1}}\right)}$$
$$+ T_{RE}$$
$$< \frac{L_{V_i-V_{i+1}}}{DR_{V_i-V_{i+1}}} + \frac{L_{V_{i+1}-V_i}}{DR_{V_i-V_{i+1}}} + T_{RTS} + T_{CTS} + T_{SIFS}$$
$$+ T_{DIFS} + T_{backoff}. \tag{24}$$

Figure 5 demonstrates the flow chart of detailed functionality of proposed AMCCR protocol.

6. NAV Adaptation

The IEEE 802.11 wireless network uses a virtual carrier sensing mechanism that uses network allocation vector (NAV). NAV helps to limit the nodes access to wireless medium which in turn avoids multiple interferences and conserves energy. The transmitting node specifies the transmission time required for the frames like RTS, CTS, and DATA, during which the channel will be busy. All nodes listening to channel on the network set their NAV for which they defer their transmission. The NAV is calculated based on the transmission data rate. In cooperative communication, since the data rate varies based on relay node location and channel condition, setting NAV for RTS and CTS accurately is not feasible until the relay node information is available to the source and the destination node. Thus, setting the effective NAV is vital. Updating the NAV of control packets in proposed AMCCR protocol is described as follows:

(1) Whenever a node V_i has data to forward, it senses the channel to check if it is idle for a DCF interframe space (DIFS) time. Upon completing the required backoff timer, it sends RTS and reserves the channel for RTS_{NAV} time. At this instance, since V_i has no idea about the cooperation or network coding, it uses basic data rate to compute channel reservation based on direct communication.

$$RTS_{NAV} = 4 * T_{SIFS} + T_{CTS} + \frac{L_{V_i-V_{i+1}}}{DR_{V_i-V_{i+1}}} + T_{ACK}, \tag{25}$$

where L is the length of the data packet and $DR_{V_i-V_{i+1}}$ is the data rate from node V_i to node V_{i+1}.

(2) The node V_{i+1} on receiving RTS replies with CTS after a SIFS time and reserves the channel for NAV duration CTS_{NAV}.

$$CTS_{NAV} = 3 * T_{SIFS} + \frac{L_{V_i-V_{i+1}}}{DR_{V_i-V_{i+1}}} + T_{ACK}. \tag{26}$$

(3) When the neighboring node receives the RTS and CTS frame, it checks if it is eligible to be a relay node as per best relay selection algorithm. If it qualifies to be a relay node, it sends a RE frame to node V_i and node V_{i+1} after a SIFS time and reserves the channel for NAV duration of RE_{NAV}. If CTS includes the information for dual-hop half-duplex communication from V_{i+1}, the relay node prepares to forward the data using network coding scheme. Else, the protocol uses cooperative scheme.

For cooperative scheme,

$$RE_{NAV} = 2 * T_{SIFS} + \frac{L_{V_i-V_{i+1}}}{DR_{V_i-Ri}} + \frac{L_{V_i-V_{i+1}}}{DR_{Ri-V_{i+1}}}. \tag{27}$$

For network coding scheme,

$$RE_{NAV} = 3 * T_{SIFS} + \frac{L_{V_i-V_{i+1}}}{DR_{V_i-Ri}} + \frac{L_{V_{i+1}-V_i}}{DR_{Ri-V_{i+1}}}$$
$$+ \frac{\max\left(L_{V_i-V_{i+1}}, L_{V_{i+1}-V_i}\right)}{\min\left(DR_{V_i-Ri}, DR_{Ri-V_{i+1}}\right)}. \tag{28}$$

(4) If node V_i and node V_{i+1} receive RE frame within timeout, they send the data through either cooperative technique or network coding. Else, node V_i sends the data packet through a direct transmission to node V_{i+1}.

$$RE_{timeout} = T_{SIFS} + T_{RE}. \tag{29}$$

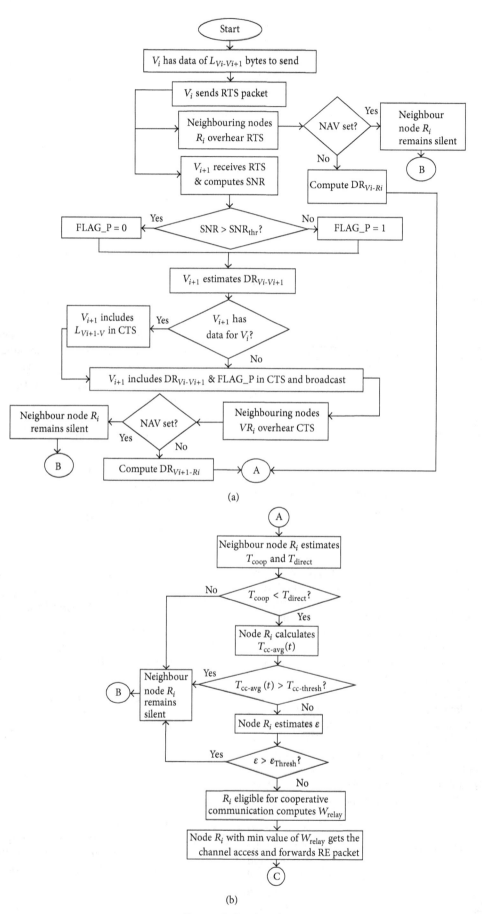

(a)

(b)

FIGURE 5: Continued.

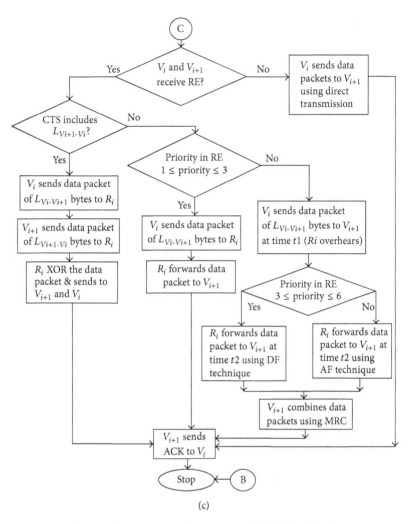

(c)

FIGURE 5: Flow chart of the proposed AMCCR protocol.

For cooperative scheme,

$$DATA_{V_i\text{-}Ri} = 2 * T_{SIFS} + \frac{L_{V_i\text{-}V_{i+1}}}{DR_{Ri\text{-}V_{i+1}}} + T_{ACK}. \tag{30}$$

$$DATA_{R_i\text{-}V_{i+1}} = T_{SIFS} + T_{ACK}$$

For network coding scheme,

$$DATA_{V_i\text{-}Ri} = 4 * T_{SIFS} + \frac{L_{ds}}{DR_{Ri\text{-}V_{i+1}}} + 2 * T_{ACK}$$

$$+ \frac{\max\left(L_{V_i\text{-}V_{i+1}}, L_{V_{i+1}\text{-}V_i}\right)}{\min\left(DR_{V_i\text{-}Ri}, DR_{Ri\text{-}V_{i+1}}\right)}$$

$$DATA_{V_{i+1}\text{-}Ri} = 3 * T_{SIFS} + 2 * T_{ACK} \tag{31}$$

$$+ \frac{\max\left(L_{V_i\text{-}V_{i+1}}, L_{V_{i+1}\text{-}V_i}\right)}{\min\left(DR_{V_i\text{-}Ri}, DR_{Ri\text{-}V_{i+1}}\right)}$$

$$DATA_{NC} = 2 * T_{SIFS} + 2 * T_{ACK}.$$

(5) On successful reception of data, receiver node V_{i+1} sends ACK packet back to transmitter node V_i. If V_i receives ACK within $ACK_{timeout}$, the data transmission is successful. Else, the transmitter node V_i resumes the backoff process to contend for the channel.

For cooperative scheme,

$$ACK_{timeout} = 2 * T_{SIFS} + \frac{L_{V_i\text{-}V_{i+1}}}{DR_{V_i\text{-}Ri}} + \frac{L_{V_i\text{-}V_{i+1}}}{DR_{Ri\text{-}V_{i+1}}} \tag{32}$$

$$+ T_{ACK}.$$

For network coding scheme,

$$ACK_{timeout} = 2 * T_{SIFS} + \frac{L_{V_i\text{-}Ri}}{DR_{V_i\text{-}Ri}} + \frac{L_{Ri\text{-}V_{i+1}}}{DR_{Ri\text{-}V_{i+1}}} + 2 \tag{33}$$

$$* T_{ACK}.$$

(6) The nodes that receive only RTS from S but not the CTS set their NAV until the end of ACK.

TABLE 3: Simulation parameters in the MAC layer.

Parameters	Value
MAC header	272 bits
PHY header	192 bits
Rate for MAC/PHY header	1 Mbps
RTS	352 bits
CTS	304 bits
ACK	304 bits
Slot time	$20\,\mu s$
SIFS	$10\,\mu s$
DIFS	$50\,\mu s$
$CW_{\min}/CW_{\max}$	32/1024

7. Experimental Setup

In this section, we analyze the performance of the proposed AMCCR by using the NS2 simulator [28]. We evaluate the performance of AMCCR by comparing the results with CD-MAC for cooperative mode and CODE for network coding. The AMCCR is evaluated for MANETs based on IEEE 802.11g. In our simulation, we consider a network over an area of 1000 * 100 meters. The experiment is simulated for 900 sec time duration, and the results are averaged after 20 executions. Each execution uses a seed value ranging from 1 to 9 for randomness in node placement and steady results. The random movement of mobile nodes is modeled using the random way-point modeling with a speed set to 5 m/s. The environment noise is modeled as Gaussian random variables: level ranging from −83 dBm to indicate harsh communication environment to −92 dBm to indicate a good communication environment for 802.11g with a standard deviation of 1 dBm. The source generates Constant Bit Rate (CBR) traffic packets at a rate of 5 packets/s with size of 512 bytes. The source-destination pairs are randomly selected. The initial energy of all nodes is set to 60 J and E_{thresh} is assumed to be 5 J. The channels between each pair of nodes are set as independent Rayleigh fading channels. The transmission rate of the data packet is computed as the average SNR value of the received signal at the receiver. The channel in the physical layer utilizes the multirate transmission defined in IEEE 802.11g. The simulation parameters assumed at the MAC layer are mentioned in Table 3.

7.1. Performance Evaluation. In this section, we evaluate the performance of the AMCCR protocol in different scenarios, firstly using the cooperative mode and secondly using network coding technique with varying environment noise level. For cooperative mode, AMCCR is compared with CD-MAC and noncooperative scheme 802.11 DCF.

7.1.1. Evaluation Metrics. Evaluation metrics are listed as follows:

(1) Average end-to-end delay: it is computed as the average delay experienced by packet from source to destination which is successfully delivered. The delay time comprises transmission delay, propagation delay,

node processing delay, and queuing delay at each intermediate node

(2) Throughput: it is the ratio of the total amount of data that reaches a receiver from a sender to the time it takes the receiver to get the last packet. It is expressed in bits per second

(3) Network lifetime: the network lifetime of a node depends on the energy consumption in its own transmissions as well as data transmission from neighbor nodes. Thus, we compute the network lifetime with respect to energy consumed per unit time. Thus the network lifetime depends on the energy consumption during both phases. Thus we compute the network lifetime with respect to energy consumed per unit time. Thus the lifetime of any node L_V is computed as $L_V = E_{\text{initial}}/E_{\text{consumed}}$, where E_{consumed} is energy consumed per unit time. The total network lifetime is computed as $\text{NL} = \min_{V \in N}(L_V)$, where N is total nodes in the network.

7.1.2. Cooperative Mode with Varying Number of Traffic Flows. In this simulation, we vary the network load, that is, by varying the number of concurrent TCP traffic flows from 4 to 20, with two different noise levels at a rate of 4 packets/s. The number of nodes is assumed to be 50, randomly distributed. The source and destination nodes are randomly selected for a TCP connection pair.

Figure 6(a) shows the throughput performance proposed AMCCR, CD-MAC, and noncooperative 802.11 DCF protocols. All the protocols perform similarly in the initial stage. But as the traffic load increases with deteriorating environment, CD-MAC and noncooperative 802.11 DCF protocols' performance degrades. Also, as the network overhead increases, it leads to increase in packet collisions. Interestingly, the AMCCR offers excellent performance and better throughput improvement due to optimal relay node selection from the lesser congested area with minimal overhead, providing the highest data rate for packet transmission and influencing the network throughput.

In Figure 6(b), we observe the end-to-end delay performance of the AMCCR in comparison with CD-MAC and noncooperative 802.11 DCF protocols. As the traffic flow increases, overall average delay increases for all the three protocols. But AMCCR significantly performs better. This is because of the adaptive cooperative approach in AMCCR that uses higher dynamic data rate adaptation that decreases the average transmission time and allows more packets to be transmitted faster via the relay node, reducing the overall transmission time duration. Also, in AMCCR, if a packet is lost due to the collision, relay node forwards the backup copy of data packets, reducing the retransmissions.

Figure 6(c) compares the network lifetime as a function of increasing traffic load. The lifetime of the network gradually decreases with the increasing traffic load. The reason for the decline in the lifetime is the extra energy consumption by the node and therefore it is exhausted early. As AMCCR efficiently chooses nodes with optimal residual energy, lifetime

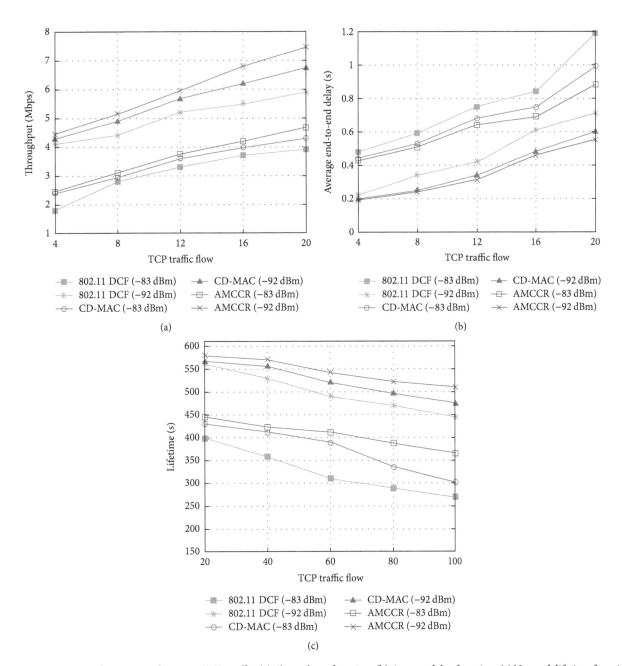

FIGURE 6: AMCCR performance with varying TCP traffic. (a) Throughput function. (b) Average delay function. (c) Network lifetime function.

slowly declines and hence network is sustained for a longer time as compared to other two protocols.

7.1.3. Cooperative Mode with Varying Node Density. In this simulation, we vary the network density by varying the network size from 20 nodes to 100 nodes at two different noise levels with 10 TCP traffic flows between randomly selected connection pairs.

Figure 7(a) shows the throughput performance of the proposed AMCCR, CD-MAC, and noncooperative 802.11 DCF protocols. The throughput performance curve of AMCCR is better compared to other protocols and performs consistently better. This is because the proposed protocol

dynamically adapts to channel conditions. Also, as the network density increases, more relay nodes are available to support adaptive cooperative routing benefits for utilizing higher data rates.

Figure 7(b) shows the performance of average end-to-end delay of three protocols. As the environment deteriorates with the increase in node density, the packet delay curve of CD-MAC and noncooperative 802.11 DCF protocols has an upsurge. In AMCCR, because of its judicious selection of transmission mode and relay node, it optimizes the reliability and delay on hop-by-hop basis. The AMCCR exploits higher data rates offered by relay nodes to transmit packets, reducing the end-to-end delay.

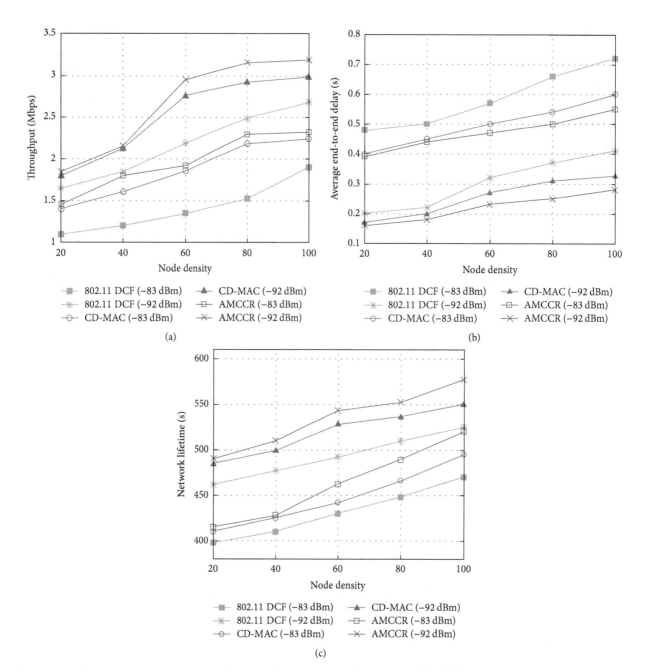

FIGURE 7: AMCCR performance with varying node density. (a) Throughput function. (b) Average delay function. (c) Network lifetime function.

Figure 7(c) shows the network lifetime performance. We can observe that as the node density increases, the network lifetime curve in the graph increases. The network lifetime of the proposed AMCCR performs comparatively better than the other protocols at noise level of −92 dBm. The AMCCR has the longest lifetime as it optimally selects the nodes with sufficient energy level. The other protocols underperform as network lifetime is shorter.

7.1.4. Network Coding with Varying Number of Traffic Flows. In this simulation, we vary the network load, that is, by varying the number of UDP-based concurrent VOIP traffics at two different noise levels. The voice traffic is encoded into

a VoIP flow with ITU-T G.711 [29], with average source bit rate of 64 kbps and the packet size of 160 bytes. The number of nodes is assumed to be 50. We assume the number of flows from 4 to 20, with the source and destination nodes randomly selected for a UDP connection pair. We compare the AMCCR protocol with a cooperative communication scheme called CODE and 802.11 DCF under the network coding scheme. In CODE, network coding is partially utilized. The relay node is randomly selected and not optimally by broadcasting the messages repeatedly.

From Figure 8(a), we can analyze the throughput performance of AMCCR in comparison with two other protocols. The proposed AMCCR even under the worst environment

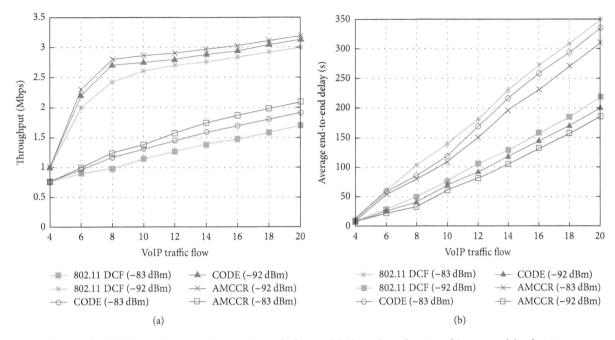

FIGURE 8: AMCCR performance with varying node density. (a) Throughput function. (b) Average delay function.

conditions shows 12–15% improved throughput compared to CODE. The performance of 802.11 DCF is the worst as it works in a noncooperative method.

Figure 8(b) shows the delay performance curve for all three protocols against the UDP VOIP traffic. The delay increases with the increase in traffic and deteriorating environment. The AMCCR outperforms CODE with 10–12% reduction in delay, as it optimally selects the best relay for cooperative coding. The adaptive decisions on transmission mode and relay selections at each hop in AMCCR provide the reliability and make it more robust to link failures, thus enhancing the delay performance.

8. Conclusions

The paper proposes a novel adaptive cooperative protocol, AMCCR for MANETs. In AMCCR, we developed a cross-layer algorithm for energy-efficient routing in MANETs using cooperative diversity. In AMCCR, routing scheme exploits the adaptive cooperative MAC scheme for reliable data transfer. AMCCR provides a distributed relay selection scheme using multi-QoS metric to choose the best relay that can help to receive data packets and transmit to the next hop using a cross-layer scheme. It is observed that, in order to design an energy-efficient network for reliable data transfer and to maximize the network lifetime, joint cooperation between several layers is needed, that is, link quality in the physical layer, relay selection in the MAC layer, and routing in the network layer. The extensive simulation conducted shows that, in cooperative mode, AMCCR significantly shows better performance in terms of throughput, delay, and network lifetime compared to CD-MAC and 802.11 DCF even under the harsh environment. The proposed AMCCR also outperforms the CODE protocol as it exploits both cooperation and coding together to enhance system's performance.

References

[1] W. A. Jabbar, M. Ismail, and R. Nordin, "On the performance of The current MANET routing protocols for VoIP, HTTP," *Journal of Computer Networks and Communications*, vol. 2014, Article ID 154983, 16 pages, 2014.

[2] K. R. Anupama, L. J. Gudino, and M. A. Gawas, "Cross layer adaptive congestion control for best-effort traffic of IEEE 802.11e in mobile ad hoc networks," in *Proceedings of the 10th International Symposium on Communication Systems, Networks and Digital Signal Processing, CSNDSP 2016*, cze, July 2016.

[3] M. A. Gawas, L. J. Gudino, and K. R. Anupama, "Cross layered adaptive cooperative routing mode in mobile ad hoc networks," in *Proceedings of the 22nd Asia-Pacific Conference on Communications, APCC 2016*, pp. 462–469, idn, August 2016.

[4] A. Scaglione, D. L. Goeckel, and J. N. Laneman, "Cooperative communications in mobile ad hoc networks," *IEEE Signal Processing Magazine*, vol. 23, no. 5, pp. 18–29, 2006.

[5] A. M. Akhtar, M. R. Nakhai, and A. H. Aghvami, "On the use of cooperative physical layer network coding for energy efficient routing," *IEEE Transactions on Communications*, vol. 61, no. 4, pp. 1498–1509, 2013.

[6] J. N. Laneman, D. N. Tse, and G. . Wornell, "Cooperative diversity in wireless networks: efficient protocols and outage behavior," *Institute of Electrical and Electronics Engineers. Transactions on Information Theory*, vol. 50, no. 12, pp. 3062–3080, 2004.

[7] T. Wang, A. Cano, and G. B. Giannakis, "Efficient demodulation in cooperative schemes using decode-and-forward relays," in *Proceedings of the 39th Asilomar Conference on Signals, Systems and Computers*, pp. 1051–1055, 2005.

[8] P. Ju, W. Song, and D. Zhou, "Survey on cooperative medium access control protocols," *IET Communications*, vol. 7, no. 9, pp. 893–902, 2013.

[9] N. Sai Shankar, C.-T. Chou, and M. Ghosh, "Cooperative communication MAC (CMAC) - A new MAC protocol for next

generation wireless LANs," in *Proceedings of the 2005 International Conference on Wireless Networks, Communications and Mobile Computing*, pp. 1–6, usa, June 2005.

[10] H. Zhu and G. Cao, "rDCF: a relay-enabled medium access control protocol for wireless ad hoc networks," *IEEE Transactions on Mobile Computing*, vol. 5, no. 9, pp. 1201–1214, 2006.

[11] P. Liu, Z. Tao, S. Narayanan, T. Korakis, and S. S. Panwar, "CoopMAC: a cooperative MAC for wireless LANs," *IEEE Journal on Selected Areas in Communications*, vol. 25, no. 2, pp. 340–354, 2007.

[12] N. Agarwal, D. ChanneGowda, L. N. Kannan, M. Tacca, and A. Fumagalli, "IEEE 802.11b cooperative protocols: a performance study," in *Proceedings of the 6th International IFIP-TC6 Conference on Ad Hoc and Sensor Networks, Wireless Networks, Next Generation Internet (NETWORKING '07)*, pp. 415–426, Springer.

[13] S. Moh and C. Yu, "A cooperative diversity-based robust MAC protocol in wireless ad hoc networks," *IEEE Transactions on Parallel and Distributed Systems*, vol. 23, no. 3, pp. 353–363, 2012.

[14] F. Mansourkiaie and M. H. Ahmed, "Cooperative routing in wireless networks: a comprehensive survey," *IEEE Communications Surveys and Tutorials*, vol. 17, no. 2, pp. 604–626, 2015.

[15] C. E. Perkins and E. M. Royer, "Ad-hoc on-demand distance vector routing," in *Proceedings of the 2nd IEEE Workshop on Mobile Computing Systems and Applications (WMCSA '99)*, pp. 90–100, New Orleans, La, USA, February 1999.

[16] V. Srivastava and M. Motani, "Cross-layer design: a survey and the road ahead," *IEEE Communications Magazine*, vol. 43, no. 12, pp. 112–119, 2005.

[17] J. A. Stine, "Cross-layer design of MANETs: the only Option," in *Proceedings of the Military Communications Conference 2006, MILCOM 2006*, October 2006.

[18] M. Dehghan, M. Ghaderi, and D. Goeckel, "Minimum-energy cooperative routing in wireless networks with channel variations," *IEEE Transactions on Wireless Communications*, vol. 10, no. 11, pp. 3813–3823, 2011.

[19] F. Mansourkiaie, M. H. Ahmed, and Y. Gadallah, "Minimizing the probability of collision in wireless sensor networks using cooperative diversity and optimal power allocation," in *Proceedings of the 2013 9th International Wireless Communications and Mobile Computing Conference, IWCMC 2013*, pp. 120–124, July 2013.

[20] L. Wang and K. Liu, "An throughput-optimized cooperative routing protocol in ad hoc network," in *Proceedings of the 2009 3rd IEEE International Symposium on Microwave, Antenna, Propagation and EMC Technologies for Wireless Communications, MAPE 2009*, pp. 1255–1258, October 2009.

[21] M. Mohammadi, H. A. Suraweera, and X. Zhou, "Outage probability of wireless ad hoc networks with cooperative relaying," in *Proceedings of the 2012 IEEE Global Communications Conference, GLOBECOM 2012*, pp. 4410–4416, December 2012.

[22] V. K. Sakarellos, D. Skraparlis, A. D. Panagopoulos, and J. D. Kanellopoulos, "Cooperative diversity performance of selection relaying over correlated shadowing," *Physical Communication*, vol. 4, no. 3, pp. 182–189, 2011.

[23] T. Kunz and R. Alhalimi, "Energy-efficient proactive routing in MANET: energy metrics accuracy," *Ad Hoc Networks*, vol. 8, no. 7, pp. 755–766, 2010.

[24] B. Guo, Q. Guan, F. R. Yu, S. Jiang, and V. C. M. Leung, "Energy-efficient topology control with selective diversity in cooperative wireless ad hoc networks: a game-theoretic approach," *IEEE Trans. Wireless Communications*, vol. 13, no. 11, pp. 6484–6495, 2014.

[25] X. Liang, I. Balasingham, and V. C. M. Leung, "Cooperative communications with relay selection for QoS provisioning in wireless sensor networks," in *Proceedings of the 2009 IEEE Global Telecommunications Conference, GLOBECOM 2009*, usa, December 2009.

[26] J. Boyer, D. D. Falconer, and H. Yanikomeroglu, "Multihop diversity in wireless relaying channels," *IEEE Transactions on Communications*, vol. 52, no. 10, pp. 1820–1830, 2004.

[27] S. R. Li, R. W. Yeung, and N. Cai, "Linear network coding," *Institute of Electrical and Electronics Engineers. Transactions on Information Theory*, vol. 49, no. 2, pp. 371–381, 2003.

[28] The Network Simulator NS-2, http://www.isi.edu/nsnam/ns/.

[29] Y. Hiwasaki and H. Ohmuro, "ITU-T G.711.1: extending G.711 to higher-quality wideband speech," *IEEE Communications Magazine*, vol. 47, no. 10, pp. 110–116, 2009.

9

SDN-Enabled Communication Network Framework for Energy Internet

Zhaoming Lu,[1,2] Chunlei Sun,[1,2] Jinqian Cheng,[1,2] Yang Li,[3] Yong Li,[4] and Xiangming Wen[1,2]

[1]*School of Information and Communication Engineering, Beijing University of Posts and Telecommunications, Beijing 100876, China*
[2]*Beijing Laboratory of Advanced Information Networks, Beijing 100876, China*
[3]*China Electric Power Research Institute, Beijing 100192, China*
[4]*Department of Electronic Engineering, Tsinghua University, Beijing 100084, China*

Correspondence should be addressed to Zhaoming Lu; lzy_0372@163.com

Academic Editor: Sabrina Gaito

To support distributed energy generators and improve energy utilization, energy Internet has attracted global research focus. In China, energy Internet has been proposed as an important issue of government and institutes. However, managing a large amount of distributed generators requires smart, low-latency, reliable, and safe networking infrastructure, which cannot be supported by traditional networks in power grids. In order to design and construct smart and flexible energy Internet, we proposed a software defined network framework with both microgrid cluster level and global grid level designed by a hierarchical manner, which will bring flexibility, efficiency, and reliability for power grid networks. Finally, we evaluate and verify the performance of this framework in terms of latency, reliability, and security by both theoretical analysis and real-world experiments.

1. Introduction

"Smart grid" applies communication and networking technologies into the power grid to allow for more efficient generation, transmission, distribution, and usage of energy [1], which lead to a sustainable energy generation and consumption. With the increasingly serious situation of energy shortage and environment pollution, DG (distributed generator) has been adopted by more and more countries as renewable and green energy resources. However, compared with the development of distributed renewable energy generations and long distance power transmission technologies like Ultrahigh Voltage (UHV), a series of advanced information technologies, such as smart metering and control, data fusion and mining, smart scheduling, and optimization, are also critical for power grid. Besides, the traditional unidirectional power grid turns into bidirectional power grid with the introduction of DGs. Hence, energy Internet brings an exciting prospect of the future energy utilization containing all phases of novel energy generation, storage, transmission, and distribution [2].

Technically, energy Internet brings three aspects of innovation for power grids. Firstly, more distributed renewable energy terminals, such as wind power and solar power, can be allowed to access the energy Internet through ubiquitous networks. They will considerably improve the proportion of renewable energy usage and reduce greenhouse gas emissions. Secondly, smart grid technologies, such as microgrid technologies, can just support effective energy utilization in local scope, while energy Internet brings about more effective energy utilization in both of small and large scopes by smart communication networks. Thirdly, energy Internet is able to protect the power grid from cascading failure. Cascading failure (also known as blackout) is notoriously known as one of the most devastating forces, which usually results in disastrous damage to modern societies. Independence and isolation are two main reasons for cascading failure. And energy Internet could resist the cascading failure in power grid by extensive interconnecting, which will improve the stability of power systems.

Therefore, energy Internet has attracted increasing attention of government and institutions, such as the US

Department of Energy [3], the German Federal Government [4], and the Japan Digital Grid Group [5]. In 2013, Chinese government and the State Grid Corporation of China (SGCC) started the global energy Internet project [6], by which they expected to build a strong smart grid with the support of "Internet+." The energy Internet can adapt to a series of requirements of distributed energy generations and transport renewable energy to all kinds of users flexibly, reliably, and safely. Due to the rigorous requirements of flexibility, latency, reliability, and safety for energy Internet, a lot of work is required to be done in the information and communication system, such as low-latency data interaction, virtual operation, and safe information transmission. Actually, Information and Communication Technologies (ICT) are essentially important components of the underlying infrastructures in energy Internet and play a key role in monitoring, metering, scheduling, and so forth [7–9]. However, as the traditional networks cannot be deployed and managed in an efficient and flexible way, the rigorous and diverse communication requirements of energy Internet have greatly exceeded the capabilities of traditional communication frameworks, and novel communication network framework is urgently required to be designed. Hence, considering that different countries take different strategies in energy Internet and the deployments of power grids also display various characteristics, we just focus on the communication network framework design of energy Internet in China in this paper.

The main contributions of this paper are summarized as follows. Firstly, we proposed an SDN-enabled hierarchical communication network architecture, which satisfies the requirements for information interaction in energy Internet. Besides, the network frameworks of microgrid cluster level and global grid level are designed, respectively. Secondly, performances such as latency, reliability, and security of the proposed communication network framework are analyzed and some available approaches are enumerated, which can contribute to ensuring these performances. Thirdly, one testbed for revealing the feasibility of SDN-enabled networks is constructed and related experimental results are displayed to demonstrate the performance of our proposed framework.

The rest of this paper is arranged as follows. Requirements and related work for communication networks are summarized in Section 2. SDN-enabled hierarchical communication network framework is depicted in Section 3. Application cases of the proposed SDN-enabled communication network framework in the background of Virtual Power Plants (VPPs) and energy e-commerce are described in Section 4. Performance is evaluated by theoretical analysis and experiments, respectively, in Sections 5 and 6. Finally, Section 7 concludes this work.

2. Requirements and Related Works for Communication Networks

Smart grid has been studied for several years in China, and a series of achievements have been obtained for assurance of energy supply. To allow more distributed generators and increase energy efficiency, the current energy system needs to be improved with the aim of evolving to energy Internet.

2.1. State-of-the-Art Development of Energy Internet. In 2009, the State Grid Corporation of China (SGCC) declared that they would start up the strong and smart grid plan in China and they would focus on four working areas, including strong grid, extensive interconnection, high intelligence, and open interaction. In 2010, "the 12th Five-Year Plan" launched by SGCC affirmed achievements on the upgrades of wildly interconnected power grid and transmission system, for example, pharos measurement units (PMUs), online security and stability, large-scale wind turbines, and solar photovoltaics monitoring. However, in the early 2010s, the power market in China was almost in the state of monopoly. To ensure the safety of power systems, power plants were deployed in a centralized way and the power transaction was almost operated in the planned model in which the electricity price was fixed without any adjustments neither in peak hours nor in trough hours. Limitation of the traditional communication network architecture leads to the passive consumption of power energy and low efficiency of energy utilization. However, there was no obvious change occurring in these years for this in spite of the implementation of peak-valley price in minority urban cities. Hence, there is still lots of work to do for energy Internet.

With the further development of the market economy, a series of sweeping reforms are coming in China, which will result in the further openness of energy market, and will allow more distributed energy generators to access power grids. In order to build energy Internet in China, the government encourages distributed power generation and liberalized electricity transaction, which is regarded as the milestone of the energy Internet development in China.

2.2. Requirements of Communication Network. According to the current situation of energy system, Figure 1 illustrates the future vision and system framework of energy Internet in China.

Users are the terminal nodes of energy Internet. Microgrids are small self-management areas in local distribution grids, which can contribute to the utilization of renewable energy resources and improve the energy efficiency by reducing transmission loss. And the bulk power system is mainly composed of power generation systems, Ultrahigh Voltage backbone grids, responsible for the long distance power transmission to relieve the unbalance between power consumption and resource location in different regions, power distribution networks, end-users, and so forth. To guarantee the safety and stability of power grid, energy flows and information flows will be deeply integrated with each other under the support of ICT.

Though ICT has been already involved in traditional power grid to strengthen the intelligence of the power system, the communication capabilities in traditional power grid were very weak, especially in China. Compared with traditional power grid, energy Internet is characterized by the access of massive distributed DGs, highly intelligent control, highly effective energy utilization, flexible energy trading online, and series of novel business scenarios. As DGs have features like small capacity, high quantity, and fluctuant and uneven distribution, the reliable low-latency managements of

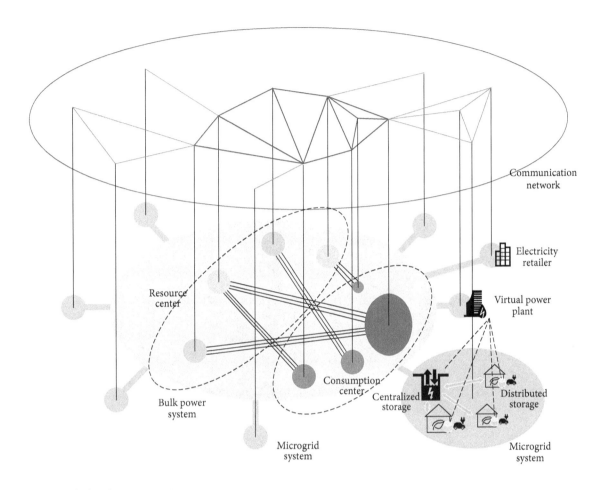

=== Ultrahigh Voltage transmission

FIGURE 1: Framework and vision of energy Internet in China.

fluctuant generators and dynamic consumption of DGs by communication networks are indispensable. Meanwhile, in the distributed and customer-based energy Internet, increasing information of energy production, energy transaction, and control also requires advanced and interconnected communication network. Therefore, to implement open and liberalized energy market and accept various kinds of DGs, open, flexible, and reliable communication network framework is required.

2.3. Related Work of Communication Network Framework. Massive DGs will generate large amounts of metering, monitoring, and control data, which brings specific requirements of communication networks. IP-based networks have been considered as the infrastructure of communication networks of energy Internet [6]. However, most current researches on energy Internet have just focused on the single issues in energy Internet, such as the SOFIA (Service-Oriented Information Centric Networking), which just focuses on service-oriented application information transmission [7], and ICN (Information Centric Networking), which just emphasizes machine-to-machine data delivery [12]. The grid communication system is divided into several parts in [13], including energy management system, distribution management

system, and WAMS (Wide Area Measurement System), and network issues corresponding to these different parts are usually discussed separately. Hence, rare work investigates the communication network framework with a global view so as to design an open, flexible, and reliable communication network. Furthermore, the existing work of communication network framework does not comply with the specific features of power grid in China. Therefore, it is necessary to design a kind of communication network framework to meet the requirements of energy Internet and to support the construction and development of energy Internet in China.

Fortunately, in recent years, Software Defined Networking (SDN) has attracted much attention. It proposes a flexible, effective, and reliable network framework that abstracts the control plan from the packet forwarding hardware (data plane) to an external software controller [14, 15]. Therefore, SDN is perceived to have tremendous potential for utilization in the communication network of the energy Internet.

3. SDN-Enabled Hierarchical Communication Network Framework

As is shown in Figure 2, energy Internet is expected to involve a large number of distributed renewable energy generators

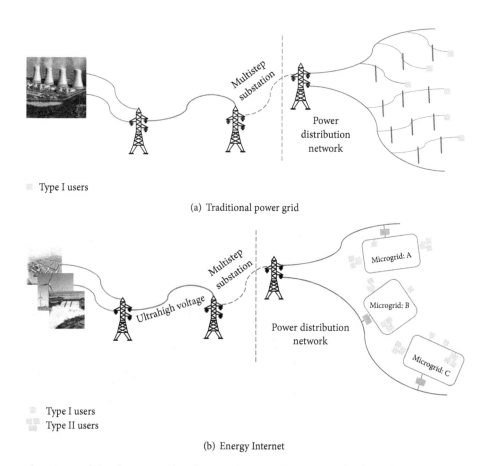

(a) Traditional power grid

(b) Energy Internet

FIGURE 2: Differences between traditional power grid and energy Internet. *Type I users (traditional users) represent those that just equal common loads, while Type II users (distributed energy users) denote those that possess abilities of power generation and storage besides consumption).*

and improve the efficiency of energy utilization with the combination of self-consumption of power in small scope and power transmission in long distance.

As the basic cell of energy Internet, microgrid is a stable and independent microsystem responsible for small scope power consumption. Type I users could directly obtain power energy from Type II users in the same microgrid, if there is any redundant energy produced or stored by them. This small scope self-consumption model can not only improve the utilization efficiency of renewable energy, but also decrease the power transmission loss and cost. When this energy transaction occurs, massive state information, such as load state, generation state, and storage state of users, should be collected in real-time by the microgrid energy controller to strictly guarantee the real-time balance of power supply and demand. Hence, highly frequent interaction of information between communication terminals is typical of microgrid level. Meanwhile, the adjustment of energy supply-demand among adjacent microgrids will take place when it is beyond the self-balance abilities of only one microgrid. When this cross-domain transaction occurs, amounts of information among different microgrids will be generated.

In addition, long distance transmission by UHV (Ultrahigh Voltage) would also be needed in order to realize large scope balance of energy supply and demand, such as the

West-East Electricity Transmission Project in China, which is significant for the optimization of energy allocation among different regions. In this case, it is important to insure the reliable transmission of scheduling information, control information, and monitoring information as well as service operation and management in wide area.

In order to enhance the efficiency of communication system, communication genre and information frequency should be concerned specially. Therefore, we propose an SDN-enabled hierarchical framework of communication network, which can be implemented by the following two parts.

3.1. Microgrid Cluster Level Communication Network Framework. As is shown in Figure 3, several adjacent microgrids can constitute a local microgrid cluster. In each microgrid, there are several switches managed by a centralized local domain controller. The local domain Forwarding Information Base (FIB), containing all routing information inside the microgrid, can be established by the local domain controller. By forwarding this FIB message in local domain, the major communication requirements caused by small scope energy self-consumption can be met, which occupies the majority of energy and communication businesses in microgrid. Moreover, one or more switches in each microgrid are selected

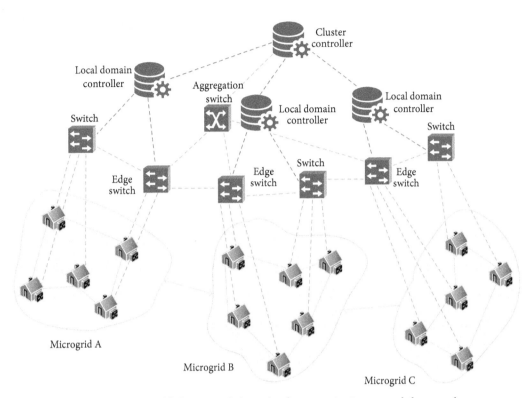

FIGURE 3: SDN-enabled microgrid cluster level communication network framework.

as edge switches to connect with those in other domains or the aggregation switch controlled by a centralized cluster controller. This cluster controller also manages those local domain controllers within its domain. Thus communication among different microgrids can be realized under the control of cluster controllers. In this cluster level framework, it has been adequately considered that the more frequent message interaction within local domains always occurs compared with that among multidomains, which is a typical feature of energy Internet communication and is usually caused by the energy self-consumption within local domains. This framework can tremendously contribute to the improvement of communication efficiency.

3.2. Global Grid Level Communication Network Framework.

As is shown in Figure 4, the global control domain can be constructed by the large-scale interconnection of cluster controllers, which take charge of the aggregation switches and local domain controllers within their domain. The consistent global view of the whole network can be established by the cooperation of these distributed global controllers, or called cluster controllers. Based on this, the wide area measurement and scheduling can be achieved.

In brief, this hierarchical communication network framework, from local domain to global domain, is in accordance with the hierarchical energy network framework, from local energy self-consumption to wide area energy scheduling. Different level controllers are responsible for different network functions and this hierarchical framework would make communication networks of energy Internet more reliable.

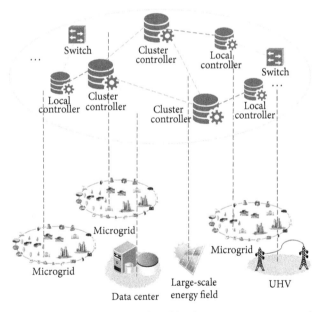

FIGURE 4: SDN-enabled global grid level communication network framework.

3.3. Characteristics of Proposed Framework.

As is shown in Figure 5, SDN-enabled communication network framework can be divided into four tiers, that is, data plane, control plane, orchestration tier, and application tier. Different tiers are responsible for different functions of the network. By decoupling data plane and control plane on the basis of SDN,

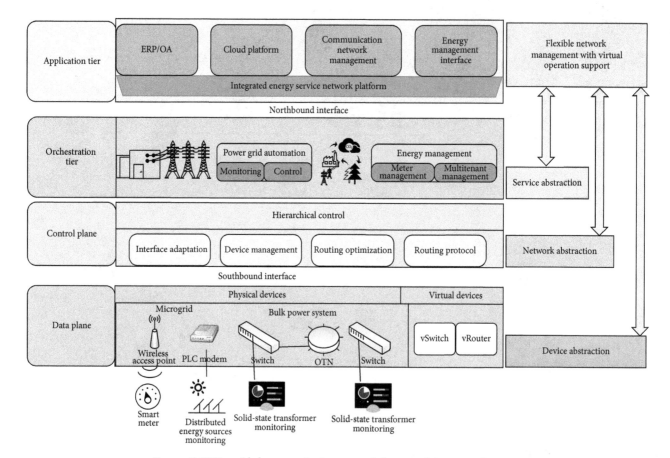

FIGURE 5: SDN-enabled communication network framework in energy Internet.

three characteristics of the aforementioned SDN-enabled network framework can be summarized as follows.

Flexibility. SDN allows network administrators to configure network functions flexibly by software. This is done by decoupling control plane from the data plane. Hence, through the north interface of SDN controller, flexible coordination of energy management and communication network management could be achieved. In addition, since the controller has a global view of the whole network topology, it can find the optimal forwarding path and control traffic flow according to different strategies, such as low-latency driven or security driven ones.

Efficiency. Owning to the highly frequent information interaction always occurring inside microgrid, most of message forwarding tasks can be accomplished according to the flow table distributed by the local domain controller. Only if it fails to provide necessary routing information will the message be delivered to the cluster controller. Compared with other SDN-enabled communication network frameworks, such as the flat controller model in [16], the proposed hierarchical framework can reduce communication delay and lessen the burden of cluster controllers effectively.

Reliability. Global control domain consisted of a series of distributed cluster controllers which can survive from the danger of single point failure. In addition, benefiting from the

global view, when one or more communication links break down, infrastructure sharing from other links will take place under the control of the controller to achieve fast recovery, by which the reliability of communication network can be exactly strengthened.

4. Application Cases of SDN-Enabled Communication Network in Energy Internet

With the influence of the "Internet," energy Internet is also expected to be qualified for more complex and flexible businesses, which cannot be realized without the support of prominent communication network. Two most typical cases will be shown as follows, which can also provide credible evidence that SDN-enabled communication network is required in energy Internet.

4.1. Virtual Power Plants (VPPs). At present, power industry is undergoing a period of marketization at home and abroad. For instance, Chinese government has enacted the correlated policies to promote the marketization of power distribution businesses. It can break the monopoly of SGCC and CSG (China Southern Power Grid) in power transmission and distribution, which will create opportunities for the springing up of new power operators. However, those newborn operators have no enough abilities or no permission to build

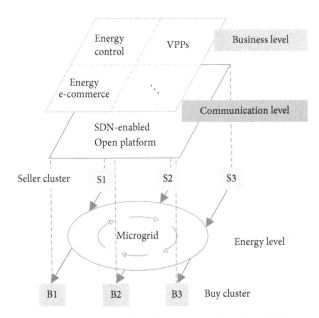

FIGURE 6: Multiple and flexible businesses based on SDN.

their own power grid infrastructure. Under this background, the VPP will become an effective approach to relieving their insufficiency of infrastructure.

The south protocol and north protocol can enable more flexible and dynamic configures of network resources. By the north interfaces of SDN-enabled framework, VPPs can logically abstract and integrate distributed utility resources in different microgrids, such as DGs, storage devices, and controllable loads, in order to realize the self-governed management and optimization towards local resources [17] without affecting each other. It can enable different virtual operators to share the same infrastructure but implement their own operations and businesses independently.

4.2. Energy E-Commerce. The primary prospection of energy Internet is to realize energy sharing, which means loads can get supplies from those near DGs with rich power [13]. For instance, when there is a pair of users having made agreement on energy trading via a third-party platform, the seller will send its power to the third-party platform in terms of the preceding agreement. Then the buyer can obtain the same amount of electricity from the third-party platform as depicted in Figure 6. This third-party platform driven energy e-commerce is regarded as another prospective scenario under the background of the marketization of power industry. Compared with traditional network, the programmability and openness of SDN can make it easier to achieve the management of network resources and the deployment of new businesses.

In order to illustrate how this SDN-enabled hierarchical architecture can successfully support these open businesses more clearly, we will give a case of intradomain or interdomain energy trading and then briefly analyze the deployment of flow rules and the orchestration of hierarchical controllers in this subsection. As is shown, Figure 7(a) displays the complete network architecture, while Figure 7(b) displays the

logical links of data plane in global topology maintained by cluster controllers. And we note that in order to make the diagram more legible there are some unimportant links that have been omitted, such as links between the local controller and the common switch, as the deployment of flow rules and the orchestration of hierarchical controllers in SDN are not our main concern. Here, we will just give a simple analysis. Actually, there are some related excellent studies that have already been done, such as [18–22].

Firstly, as for the local topology, the local controller can periodically construct a LLDP (Link Layer Discovery Protocol) packet for each switch port. If there is any new link between two different switch ports found, a packet-in message will be triggered. Then the local controller receives this message and infers that there is a link existing between the two involved switches and makes a record. In this process, edge switches and interdomain links can also be found. In addition, local controller can take advantage of Dijkstra-based routing algorithms, or other algorithms, to calculate shortest paths [23] and generate the local FIB. As for global topology, to reduce the difficulties of calculating global paths, the size of global topology is required to be limited. Thus instead of providing all details of the local topology in each local domain, the global view only contains edge switches, aggregation switches, interdomain links, and logical intradomain links, as is shown in Figure 7(b). Up to now, there are several multidomain routing algorithms in SDN that have been well researched, including the calculation of logical intradomain routes, such as [24, 25]. Given the limited space, we will not give more details about these. We note that each local controller just maintains the detailed routing information within its local scope and cannot obtain the views of other microgrids, while all cluster controllers have consistent global logic views. And all what switches should do is to forward messages to the next hop switch or the default switch according to the flow table distributed by controllers. If there is no rule matched, it will ask local controller for route messages.

Secondly, in the real process of message forwarding, when frequent intramicrogrid energy trading occurs, which is the most common event in energy e-commerce, massive local information exchange requirements will be produced at the same time. And all switches are OpenFlow switches and can forward messages according to the flow table sent by the local controller with high speed. If there is a new flow arriving, the source switch will send a packet-in message to the local controller to require a new flow entry. In this process, rare interdomain information will be produced and nearly no access requests to cluster controllers will occur, while when energy trading among several adjacent microgrids in the same microgrid cluster occurs, large amounts of interdomain information exchange requirements will be generated. Once the source local controller infers that the message is an interdomain one and no local rules matched, it will send requests to the cluster controller. And the cluster controller then determines a global path and sends a reply to each local controller whose domain is passed through by the determined path. Each reply contains the information of each domain's ingress and egress switches or ports. Next, local

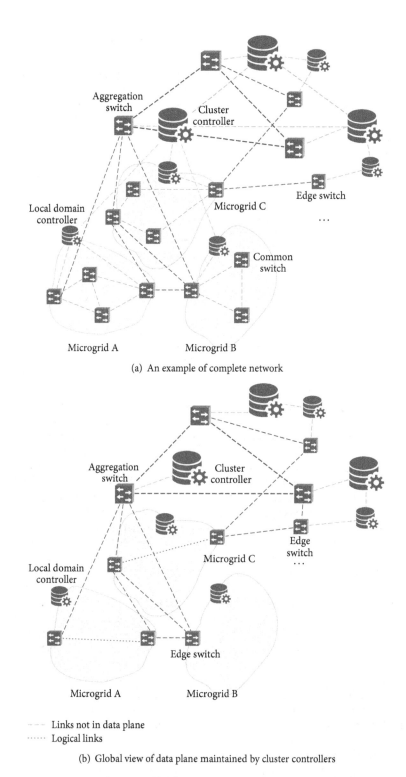

(a) An example of complete network

--- Links not in data plane
······ Logical links

(b) Global view of data plane maintained by cluster controllers

FIGURE 7: A case of SDN-enabled hierarchical architecture in energy e-commerce.

controller receives the route reply and expands this logical link to its corresponding physical path and installs rules along the involved switches within its scope. Furthermore, when large scope energy transmission occurs, such as interprovince power transmissions based on UHV, which just have 13 lines in China up to now, more than one cluster controller and corresponding aggregation switches will be involved. Because all cluster controllers have consistent global views, the global path can be calculated by the nearest cluster controller instead of asking routing information from all cluster controllers whose domain is passed through. In this process, aggregation switches controlled by cluster controllers directly will take part in the message forwarding among these far-distance microgrids to reduce end-to-end delay. Once there is an

TABLE 1: Communication latency requirements for electric substation automation [10].

Information types	Internal substation	External substation
Protecting information	4 ms	8–12 ms
Monitoring and control information	16 ms	1 s
Operations and maintenance information	1 s	10 s
Text strings	2 s	10 s
Processed data files	10 s	30 s
Program files	1 min	10 min
Image files	10 s	1 min
Audio and video data streams	1 s	1 s

aggregation switch coming, the cluster controller will be asked to deploy table rules in corresponding aggregation switched, besides local controllers. By the above deployment of flow rules and orchestration of hierarchical controllers, SDN-enabled hierarchical architecture can adapt to energy Internet perfectly.

In summary, the openness and flexibility of SDN will make it behave better than traditional IP-based network in these complex business scenarios. The hierarchical framework brings higher efficiency and preferable global performance. These are the original motivations for our research on SDN-enabled communication network in energy Internet.

5. Performance Analysis of SDN-Enabled Communication Network Framework

According to the above analysis, obviously SDN-enabled network will play prominent roles in energy Internet on account of its openness and flexibility. Meanwhile it is necessary to do sufficient investigations on the performance of SDN-enabled network, including availability (low-latency) and reliability.

5.1. Availability. The performance of communication network can be influenced by several factors of bandwidth, latency, channel quality, and so forth. Compared to the Internet, latency issues of communication network play more important roles in the protection and control of power system, especially for the crucial nodes, such as substations, energy control centers, and other vital devices. As is shown in Table 1, IEEE has classified the information types of power systems into several categories. To ensure the security of power systems, private networks, such as TDM + SDH, traditionally transmit higher priority businesses. Although latency issues are not the inherent characteristics of IP-based network, there is the tendency to be all-IP for the communication network in energy Internet owing to its characteristics of businesses, flexibility, and inexpensive cost [26]. Fortunately, SDN-enabled communication network framework could reduce the latency of network to make it competent for power systems. Table 2 depicts the latency of an SDN-enabled network with 1 GB/s bandwidth and 200 km long links in the case of transmitting 1250-byte data [11]. From

the comparison of Tables 1 and 2, it is obvious to find that SDN-enabled networks could meet the latency requirements for either internal substation or external substation of power systems with reasonable strategies.

There are two reasons contributing to the reduction of queue and cache latency. Firstly, compared with traditional IP-based networks, SDN-enabled networks greatly improve the speed of flow forwarding on account of the separation of control plane and data plane, which could considerably reduce processing latency. Secondly, with the global view, it is easier for the controller to deploy optimal strategies for congestion control and load balancing, which could greatly reduce the unpredictable latency produced by traffic burst and hence improve the stability and controllability of network latency. All these could be utilized to reduce the latency of communication network.

However, when forwarding new packets in an SDN-enabled network, the interactions between switches and controllers would produce extra latency. Especially when massive mice flows occur, frequent requesting to controllers will increase the round-trip time. Fortunately, the hierarchical framework proposed in this paper can greatly ease the burdens of global controllers. Recent work [18] shows that the hierarchical controller mode could lead to more than 90% events being processed locally, which makes the workload of global controllers go down to nearly 1/300 of that in normal OpenFlow networks, and the round-trip time is reduced.

In addition, there are plenty of strategies investigated to reduce the latency of SDN-enabled networks further, such as CheetahFlow [27], DIFANE [28], DevoFlow [29], and FlowShadow [30]. Mice flows account for a large portion of the total number of flows usually corresponding to the most important information in power grid, such as protection and control information. CheetahFlow is a forecasting scheme which can install flow entries to the switches proactively on the basis of historical communication records to reduce setup latency. This scheme is expert in reducing extra latency in SDN via forwarding most of the flows in terms of the advanced rules in data plane without asking for the decision of the controllers. When a mess of mice flows occur, the controller would be frequently invoked and the network performance would be apparently impaired. It applies SVM (Support Vector Machine) to identify frequent communication pairs with high accuracy. Then the forwarding rules with the shortest paths between frequent pairs will be installed in advance, which is of great significance in power systems due to the existence of numerous frequent and significant pairs, such as energy controllers and transformers.

5.2. Reliability. Reliability is another challenge of IP-based networks, which is important for power systems. Fortunately, with the development of SDN, various flow optimization and congestion control technologies have been proposed and many simulations of latency for SDN have also been done [31]. As depicted above, the distributed global controllers are conductive to avoid single point failures, and SDN-enabled fast recovery from failures also makes great contribution in avoiding congestion and packet loss.

TABLE 2: Network latency in SDN-enabled communication network [11].

Operation type	Propagation latency/us	Processing latency/us	Queuing latency/us	Sending latency/us	Minimum total latency/ms
The simple transmission with single flow table	1000	10	$[0, \infty)$	10	1.02
The complex transmission with multiclass flow table	1000	500	$[0, \infty)$	10	1.51

In general, the recovery process in communication network could be divided into two steps: the failure detection and network recovery. Firstly, credible failure detection is the basis of the whole recovery process. Multiple efficient protocols and schemes on failure detection have been established, such as BFD (Bidirectional Forwarding Detection) [32] and OpenFlow Fast Failover Group Table [33]. The BFD protocol is successfully used in providing fast and low-cost failure detection for higher-plane control protocols, with a speed of millisecond level. The OpenFlow Fast Failover Group Table, supported in OpenFlow switches and independent of the controllers, could be configured to monitor the state of ports and interfaces, as well as switch forwarding actions accordingly.

Secondly, network recovery is usually complex and time-consuming in both traditional IP-based network and SDN-enabled networks. Plenty of work, contributing to the reduction of recovery latency, has been done up to now. Meanwhile multiple SDN-enabled fast recovery schemes have shown great potential. For instance, when failures are detected, the recovery process proposed in [33] could be divided into two steps: the switch-initiated recovery based on preconfigured backup path pairs to guarantee end-to-end connectivity and the controller-initiated recovery based on new optimal paths calculated by controllers. This fast failover scheme realizes the fastest recovery time of 3.3 ms through combining preconfigured backup paths and fast link failure detection in SDN, which shows an enormous improvement compared to present average recovery time varying from 28.2 to 48 ms.

6. Testbed and Experimental Results

The performance of flexibility brought by SDN is obvious; thus we verify the latency and reliability in this section. In our proposed hierarchical communication network framework, the global grid level communication network is composed of several microgrid cluster level communication networks. As the microgrid is the basic unit of energy Internet, in this section, we consider a single microgrid scenario where information terminals of energy devices communicate with each other through three OpenFlow switches managed by one controller. If the latency and reliability of the communication network are ensured, the performance of communication network in energy Internet could be ensured evidently. Therefore, a testbed based on communication network of microgrid is built and experimental results are presented.

6.1. Testbed Implementation. A typical microgrid is implemented, which contains AC and DC loads, renewable energy resources, and energy storage devices. Meanwhile, based on the physical energy infrastructure, a SDN-enabled communication network which consists of a SDN domain controller, several OpenFlow switches, and a large number of information terminals is also established as shown in Figure 8. In this testbed, SDN controller *Floodlight*, which could provide a Web GUI for network operator, is implemented on a server which has physical links with switches. The information terminals of energy devices communicate with each other by sending ICMP packets. Three x86 PC modules installed with 64-bit Ubuntu 12.04.3, 3.8.0-25-generic Linux Kernel and *OpenvSwitch* 2.3.0 are used as SDN switches. Each switch is equipped with 2-core 1.8 GHz Intel Celeron 1037U CPU, 2 G RAM, and 6 Intel PCI-E 1000 M network interface cards. To easily configure network parameters, all devices are set in the same network segment 192.168.1.x. When switches and information terminals get connected with controller, the state of network will be displayed on Web GUI.

6.2. Experimental Results

(1) Latency. First of all, the mode of *OpenvSwitch* is set to standalone, which means, without a controller, the switch could forward packets in a traditional way. Thus, as illustrated in Figure 9(a), the average RTT between two information terminals is measured and calculated, respectively, in proposed SDN-enabled framework and traditional communication network framework. If the SDN controller is shut down, the proposed SDN-enabled network framework will turn into traditional network framework. With the proposed framework, it is obvious that packets always have a lower latency less than 1 ms except for the first one. The reason is that the switch does not know how to forward packets by optimal routing path for the first time, until the controller discovers the links among switches and sends flow tables to the switches along the routing path, which introduces extra latency in this discovery and delivery process. Our results also coincide with the measurements in [27, 29]. Meanwhile, the latency of packets with the traditional network framework is a little bit higher than that with the proposed network framework. It is because each switch acts as a regular MAC-learning switch when the controller cannot be contacted. In addition, compared with traditional network framework, the delay jitter of SDN-enabled network framework is lower.

(2) Reliability. Reliability of communication networks plays a significant role in ensuring the stability of energy Internet. The SDN-enabled network has an inherent advantage in enhancing communication network reliability as infrastructure sharing could be easily implemented by the SDN

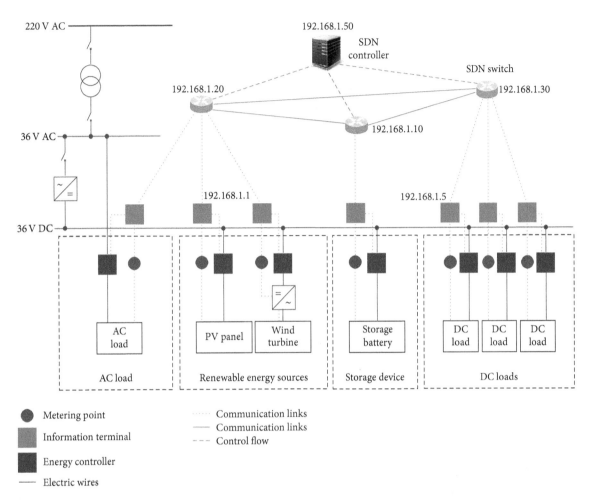

FIGURE 8: Implementation of testbed for communication network of microgrid.

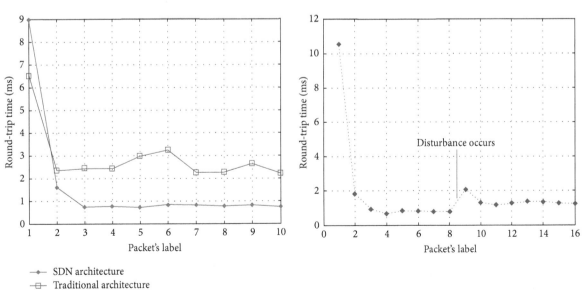

(a) Round-trip time of two frameworks

(b) Round-trip time when disturbance occurs

FIGURE 9: Round-trip time of SDN-enabled network.

controller. When disturbance occurs in a communication link, the packets transmitted via this path will be forwarded by switches according to the flow table delivered from the controller. As depicted in Figure 9(b), when the link between switch 2 (with IP address 192.168.1.20) and switch 3 (with IP address 192.168.1.30) is disturbed, the communication link will recover fast and the RTT increases slightly with packets forwarded by switch 1 (with IP address 192.168.1.10). Such fast recovery mechanism is significant for the reliability of communication network in energy Internet, especially for the transmission of energy control and monitor information.

7. Conclusion and Future Work

In this paper, we have summarized the state-of-the-art development for energy Internet in China and analyzed the requirements such as flexibility, latency, and reliability for communication networks in energy Internet. Then related work of communication network frameworks in energy Internet is discussed. Furthermore, a novel SDN-enabled hierarchical communication network framework for energy Internet is proposed. At last, performances such as latency and reliability of this novel communication network framework are verified by theoretical analyses and experiments. Actually, this proposed network framework could be applied in not only the power grid of China, but also other countries with hierarchical grid.

In our future work, specific methods and strategies related to security issues in this SDN-based framework will be investigated to support the development of energy Internet. Besides the latency and reliability analyzed above, security is also significant for communication networks in energy Internet. With the vast DG's access, the authentication and data protection for users and equipment become more vital and complex than before. Meanwhile, the security problems in SDN have already attracted widespread attention. SDN-enabled security schemes characterized by openness and intercommunity could make more advantageous performances compared with traditional physical isolation schemes. The centralization of control plane makes it possible to guarantee the global consistent security. The controller can also provide more fine-grained security control via configuring global security approaches from the network view. Hence, the SDN-enabled security schemes would be an effective approach for data protection in energy Internet.

References

[1] N. Golmie, A. Scaglione, L. Lampe, and E. Yeh, "Guest editorial - Smart grid communications," *IEEE Journal on Selected Areas in Communications*, vol. 30, no. 6, pp. 1025-1026, 2012.

[2] A. Q. Huang and J. Baliga, "FREEDM System: Role of power electronics and power semiconductors in developing an energy internet," in *Proceedings of the 21st International Symposium on Power Semiconductor Devices and IC's*, pp. 9–12, IEEE, Barcelona, Spain, June 2009.

[3] Smart Grid System Report, United States Department of Energy, Washington DC, August 2014.

[4] Federation of German Industries (BDI), *Internet of Energy: ICT for Energy Markets of the Future*, vol. 29, Berlin, Germany, December 2008.

[5] J. Boyd, "An internet-inspired electricity grid," *IEEE Spectrum*, vol. 50, no. 1, pp. 12–14, 2013.

[6] Z. Liu, *Global Energy Internet*, China Electric Power Press, Beijing, China, February 2015.

[7] K. Katsaros, W. Chai, N. Wang, G. Pavlou, H. Bontius, and M. Paolone, "Information-centric networking for machine-to-machine data delivery: A case study in smart grid applications," *IEEE Network*, vol. 28, no. 3, pp. 58–64, 2014.

[8] C. A. Macana, N. Quijano, and E. Mojica-Nava, "A survey on cyber physical energy systems and their applications on smart grids," in *Proceedings of the 2011 IEEE PES Conference on Innovative Smart Grid Technologies Latin America, ISGT LA 2011*, col, October 2011.

[9] N. Bui, A. P. Castellani, P. Casari, and M. Zorzi, "The internet of energy: a web-enabled smart grid system," *IEEE Network*, vol. 26, no. 4, pp. 39–45, 2012.

[10] 2004.

[11] Y. Lyu, "Chuanhe Huang, Yonghong Jia, , Simulation of switchs processing delay in software defined network," *Journal of Computer Network and Applications*, vol. 34, no. 9, pp. 2472–2475, 2014.

[12] Q. Wu, Z. Li, J. Zhou et al., "SOFIA: Toward service-oriented information centric networking," *IEEE Network*, vol. 28, no. 3, pp. 12–18, 2014.

[13] J.-W. Cao, Y.-X. Wan, and G.-Y. Tu, "Information system architecture for smart grids," *Chinese Journal of Computers*, vol. 36, no. 1, pp. 143–167, 2013.

[14] Z. Jianchao, S. Boon-Chong, L. Tek-Tjing, and F. Chuan Heng, "Opportunities for software-defined networking in smart grid," in *Proceedings of the 9th International Conference on Information, Communications and Signal Processing, ICICS 2013*, twn, December 2013.

[15] J. Rubio-Loyola, A. Galis, A. Astorga et al., "Scalable service deployment on software-defined networks," *IEEE Communications Magazine*, vol. 49, no. 12, pp. 84–93, 2011.

[16] W. Xia, Y. Wen, C. H. Foh, D. Niyato, and H. Xie, "A survey on software-defined networking," *IEEE Communications Surveys & Tutorials*, vol. 17, no. 1, pp. 27–51, 2015.

[17] Z. Wei, S. Yu, G. Sun, Y. Sun, Y. Yuan, and D. Wang, "The Concept and Development of Virtual Power Plants," *Automation of Electric Power Systems*, vol. 37, no. 13, pp. 1–3, 2013.

[18] S. Hassas Yeganeh and Y. Ganjali, "Kandoo: a framework for efficient and scalable offloading of control applications," in *Proceedings of the Proceeding of the 1st ACM International Workshop on Hot Topics in Software Defined Networks (HotSDN '12)*, pp. 19–24, New York, NY, USA, August 2012.

[19] R. Vilalta, A. Mayoral, J. Baranda et al., "Hierarchical SDN orchestration of wireless and optical networks with E2E provisioning and recovery for future 5G networks," in *Proceedings of the Optical Fiber Communications Conference and Exhibition, OFC*, pp. 1–3, IEEE, USA, March 2016.

[20] J. S. Choi and X. Li, "Hierarchical distributed topology discovery protocol for multi-domain SDN networks," *IEEE Communications Letters*, vol. 21, no. 4, pp. 773–776, 2017.

[21] J.-J. Huang, Y.-Y. Chen, C. Chen, and Y. H. Chu, "Weighted routing in hierarchical multi-domain SDN controllers," in *Proceedings of the 17th Asia-Pacific Network Operations and Management Symposium, APNOMS 2015*, pp. 356–359, kor, August

2015.

[22] Y. Liu, A. Hecker, R. Guerzoni, Z. Despotovic, and S. Beker, "On optimal hierarchical SDN," in *Proceedings of the IEEE International Conference on Communications, ICC 2015*, pp. 5374–5379, gbr, June 2015.

[23] C. Li, *The Design of Realization of Routing Algorithm in SDN*, Beijing University of Posts and Telecommunications, Beijing, China, 2016.

[24] A. Tootoonchian and Y. Ganjali, "HyperFlow: A distributed control plane for OpenFlow," in *Proceedings of the Internet Network Management Conference*, Research on Enterprise Networking, April 2010.

[25] T. Koponen, M. Casado, N. Gude et al., "Onix: a distributed control platform for large-scale production networks," in *Proceedings of the Operating Systems Design and Implementation*, pp. 351–364, The ACM, Vancouver, BC, Canada, 2010.

[26] W. Wang, Y. Xu, and M. Khanna, "A survey on the communication architectures in smart grid," *Computer Networks*, vol. 55, no. 15, pp. 3604–3629, 2011.

[27] Z. Su, T. Wang, Y. Xia, and M. Hamdi, "CheetahFlow: Towards low latency software-defined network," in *Proceedings of the 2014 1st IEEE International Conference on Communications, ICC 2014*, pp. 3076–3081, aus, June 2014.

[28] M. Yu, J. Rexford, M. J. Freedman, and J. Wang, "Scalable flow-based networking with DIFANE," in *Proceedings of the 7th International Conference on Autonomic Computing, SIGCOMM 2010*, pp. 351–362, ind, September 2010.

[29] A. R. Curtis, J. C. Mogul, J. Tourrilhes, P. Yalagandula, P. Sharma, and S. Banerjee, "DevoFlow: Scaling flow management for high-performance networks," in *Proceedings of the ACM SIGCOMM*, pp. 254–265, New York, NY, USA, August 2011.

[30] Y. Wang, D. Tai, T. Zhang et al., "Flowshadow: A fast path for uninterrupted packet processing in SDN switches," in *Proceedings of the 11th ACM/IEEE Symposium on Architectures for Networking and Communications Systems, ANCS 2015*, pp. 205-206, usa, May 2015.

[31] P. T. Congdon, P. Mohapatra, M. Farrens, and V. Akella, "Simultaneously reducing latency and power consumption in openflow switches," *IEEE/ACM Transactions on Networking*, vol. 22, no. 3, pp. 1007–1020, 2014.

[32] D. Katz and D. Ward, "Bidirectional Forwarding Detection (BFD)," (Proposed Standard) RFC5880, Internet Engineering Task Force, 2010.

[33] N. L. M. Van Adrichem, B. J. Van Asten, and F. A. Kuipers, "Fast recovery in software-defined networks," in *Proceedings of the 3rd European Workshop on Software-Defined Networks, EWSDN 2014*, pp. 61–66, hun, September 2014.

10

Assessing Contact Graph Routing Performance and Reliability in Distributed Satellite Constellations

J. A. Fraire,[1,2] P. Madoery,[2] S. Burleigh,[3] M. Feldmann,[4] J. Finochietto,[2] A. Charif,[1] N. Zergainoh,[1] and R. Velazco[1]

[1]Université Grenoble-Alpes, INPG, TIMA Laboratoires, Grenoble, France
[2]Universidad Nacional de Córdoba-CONICET, Laboratorios LCD, Córdoba, Argentina
[3]Jet Propulsion Laboratory, California Institute of Technology, Pasadena, CA, USA
[4]Faculty of Computer Science, Technische Universität Dresden, Dresden, Germany

Correspondence should be addressed to J. A. Fraire; juanfraire@gmail.com

Academic Editor: Sandra Céspedes

Existing Internet protocols assume persistent end-to-end connectivity, which cannot be guaranteed in disruptive and high-latency space environments. To operate over these challenging networks, a store-carry-and-forward communication architecture called Delay/Disruption Tolerant Networking (DTN) has been proposed. This work provides the first examination of the performance and robustness of Contact Graph Routing (CGR) algorithm, the state-of-the-art routing scheme for space-based DTNs. To this end, after a thorough description of CGR, two appealing satellite constellations are proposed and evaluated by means of simulations. Indeed, the DtnSim simulator is introduced as another relevant contribution of this work. Results enabled the authors to identify existing CGR weaknesses and enhancement opportunities.

1. Introduction

The autonomous transmission of information resources and services through Internet has changed the lifestyle on Earth. Moreover, the potential benefits of extending Internet into space have been analyzed by the community [1–4]. Nonetheless, the consideration of Internet for space missions has been limited due to fundamental environmental differences. In particular, in a space flight mission, the highly varying communication ranges, the effect of planet rotation, and on-board power restrictions compels communication systems to face several disruptive situations nonexistent on Internet systems. Furthermore, the propagation delay of signals on Deep Space environments is generally in the order of minutes or even hours. These delay and disruption conditions contraindicate traditional Internet protocol operations as they are largely based on instant flow of information among sending and receiver nodes.

As a result, Delay/Disruption Tolerant Networks (DTNs) have recently been considered as an alternative to extending Internet boundaries into space [5]. In particular, recent studies have considered their applicability in Low-Earth Orbit (LEO) satellite constellations [6–11]. To overcome link disruptions, DTN nodes temporarily *store* and *carry* in-transit data until a suitable next-hop link becomes available [12]. To overcome delays, end-to-end feedback messages are no longer assumed continuous nor instantaneous. This distinctive characteristic allows DTN to operate in environments where communications can be challenged by latency, bandwidth, data integrity, and stability issues [13].

During the last decade, the DTN Bundle protocol, along with different adaptation layers, has been proposed [14–19], several routing strategies were studied [20–30], and diverse software stacks were publicly released [31–35]. Furthermore, some of the latter approaches were successfully validated both on LEO [36] and Deep Space missions [37] driven by the UK Space Agency and NASA, respectively. Also, DTN has been in pilot studies in the International Space Station (ISS) since 2009 [38] and has been operational on ISS since May of 2016. Presently, the Internet research community [39] along with several space organizations [40, 41] has joined the industry in the standardization of DTN protocols [42].

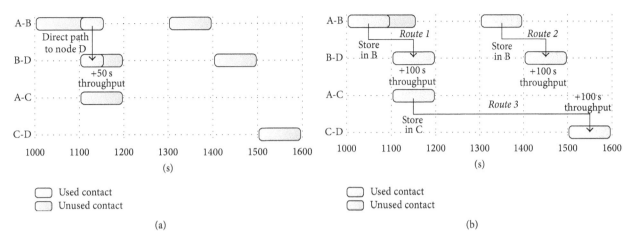

FIGURE 1: DTN topology example. Effective throughput with (a) Internet protocols and (b) DTN store-and-forward.

In spite of the recent advances in the area, the analysis of the fault-tolerance of existing DTN solutions remains an open research topic. Studying reliability of DTN is mandatory before seriously considering its applicability in the harsh space environment where radiation effects, vibrations, collisions, and outgassing, among others, pose significant challenges for man-made spacecraft. In [43], the reliability of opportunistic DTNs was studied, but their results do not apply to the space domain where communications are deterministic. More recently, authors have presented preliminary results on a reliability assessment of DTN for space applications [44]. However, the provided simulation analysis was based on simplistic satellite networks without a comprehensive analysis on the behavior of the underlying routing algorithm.

In this work, we tackle the weaknesses of [44] by providing an extensive fault injection analysis based on two appealing and realistic case studies of delay-tolerant satellite constellations previously presented in [10]. An initial performance comparison of these topologies is one of the contributions of this work. For the reliability analysis, the state-of-the-art version of Contact Graph Routing (CGR) algorithm was considered [30]. However, to the best of the authors' knowledge, there is a lack of an in-depth description of the latest CGR algorithm which is only available as part of an open-source DTN implementation [32]. This results in a fuzzy interpretation of the algorithm which is specifically an issue because several further approaches claim to leverage CGR as a basis (such as [45, 46]). Consequently, providing an accurate and thorough description of how CGR is currently implemented is another contribution of this paper. The CGR algorithm was implemented in DtnSim, a new simulator specifically designed to evaluate space DTNs. DtnSim is also introduced in this article for the first time and is expected to be available via open-source licensing. Results obtained from DtnSim are the final contribution of this article: an assessment of the fault-tolerance capability of the CGR algorithm in DTN constellations. This work can thus be considered an improved, extended, and archival quality version of [44].

The present paper is structured as follows. In Section 2 an overview of DTN, a detailed description of the CGR algorithm, and an appealing failure model are provided. Two realistic satellite constellation scenarios are described and analyzed by means of a new simulation framework in Section 3. In Section 4 open research aspects are summarized and discussed before concluding in Section 5.

2. DTN Overview and System Model

A simple disrupted network of 4 nodes is illustrated in Figure 1, where node A sends data to node D. Similar examples can be found in [47, 48] describing the behavior of satellite constellations with sporadic connectivity as well as Deep Space networks. The time-evolving topology is represented by a timeline of 1600 seconds, where different communication opportunities (also known as *contacts*) exist among nodes A, B, C, and D. Formally, a contact is defined in [47] as an interval during which it is expected that data will be transmitted by one DTN node to another. For example, node A has two direct contacts with B (A-B) from 1000 s to 1150 s and from 1300 s to 1400 s. However, the effective utilization of these communication episodes depends on the implemented protocols.

Figure 1(a) shows the expected performance of Internet protocols which require a persistent connectivity with the final destination (also known as end-to-end path). Due to the disruptive nature of the network, node A is only able to directly reach nodes D through B from 1100 s to 1150 s (cyan-colored contacts), which allows for an effective throughput of 50 s multiplied by the node's data-rate. Other contacts will remain unutilized by Internet protocols (yellow-colored contacts). By exploiting a local storage within each node, DTN is able to make a better utilization of the communication resources as shown in Figure 1(b). For example, in order to better use the B to D contact at 1100 s, node A can transmit in advance the data to node B starting from 1000 s. Furthermore, two other delay-tolerant paths can be considered to node D, one via node C at 1100 s and another via node B at 1300 s. Thus, the effective throughput of DTN in this example is of 300 s (600% higher than traditional Internet protocols). For a more general overview, Table 1 compares different aspects between Internet and DTN Protocols.

TABLE 1: IP and DTN protocols comparison.

	Internet protocols	DTN protocols
Connectivity	Continuous end-to-end transaction.	Sporadic or none end-to-end transaction and high link latency.
Storage	Small buffers to mitigate link congestion.	Large memories to overcome link disruption.
Underlying protocols	Ethernet, WiFi, fiber optic, and so forth.	Internet protocols, ethernet, WiFi, fiber optic, and so forth.
Applications	Internet, mobile networks without disruptions, and wireless sensor networks.	Deep Space systems, satellite networks, underwater networks, and mobile networks with disruptions.

TABLE 2: Contact plan example.

Contact #	From	To	Ini	End	Rate
1	A	B	1000	1150	1000
2	B	A	1000	1150	1000
3	B	D	1100	1200	1000
4	D	B	1100	1200	1000
5	A	C	1100	1200	1000
6	C	A	1100	1200	1000
7	A	B	1300	1400	1000
8	B	A	1300	1400	1000
9	B	D	1400	1500	1000
10	D	B	1400	1500	1000
11	C	D	1500	1600	1000
12	D	C	1500	1600	1000

In spite of the data delivery improvement, different challenges and optimization opportunities exist in DTN. For example, the first contact of nodes A to B in Figure 1(b) is not fully utilized. This is because node A was able to make a good "guess" on node B's connectivity and its residual capacity with final destination D. However, it can be quite difficult to accurately make such estimations without a stable and permanent connection with neighbor nodes. Without this local knowledge assumed by node A, more data could have been transmitted provoking congestion at node B. Congestion is, indeed, a popular and open research topic in DTN [49–51]. In general, and in contrast with Internet protocols, nodes' reliance on a realistic local understanding of the current connectivity in the network is not always feasible and depends on the type of DTN they run on.

As a result, existing routing and forwarding schemes for DTN have sought to acquire the most complete and precise network state information. In *opportunistic* DTNs, no assumptions can be made as encounters between nodes occur unexpectedly [28]. For these networks, epidemic strategies based on message replication driven by different criteria have been applied [27, 29]. Nevertheless, in realistic situations, contacts are rarely totally random but obey nodes' movement with greater probability of meeting certain neighbors than others. Protocols such as [20, 25, 26] are popular solutions that propose to infer the encounter probability to improve data delivery metrics. On the other hand, connectivity in certain DTNs such as space networks can be precisely anticipated based on accurate mathematical models describing object trajectories in space. In the literature, these networks are known as *scheduled* or *deterministic* DTNs [12] and are the appropriate model to study satellite constellations.

In general, spacecraft trajectories and orientation can be accurately predicted by means of appropriate mathematical models [52]. Also, mission operations generally account for precise models of the communication systems both on-board and on-ground. As a result, the forthcoming spacecraft to spacecraft or spacecraft to ground contacts can be determined or even controlled in advance. This unique characteristic has made routing in scheduled DTN a distinct research area of increasing interest during the last decade.

First analysis on routing in scheduled DTNs dates back to 2003 where Xuan et al. proposed time-evolving graph to represent changes in network topologies to then study shortest, foremost, and fastest journey metrics [21]. Later, a specific routing framework was introduced in [22] to derive a space-time routing table comprising next hops for each time interval. Similar schemes were reported in [23]. However, these static route calculation approaches relied on a complete precalculation of routes on ground and a timely distribution to the network nodes. Due to the precalculation, these approaches lacked responsiveness to varying traffic conditions and topology changes resulting from dynamically added or removed contacts. An alternative approach addressing this shortcoming was later introduced under the name of *Contact Graph Routing* (CGR).

2.1. Contact Graph Routing. Instead of a centralized route calculation, CGR, proposed by S. Burleigh (NASA JPL), follows a distributed approach: the next hop is determined by each DTN node on the path by recomputing the best route to destination, as soon as a bundle (i.e., bundle protocol data unit) is received. This routing procedure assumes that a global *contact plan*, comprising all forthcoming contacts, is timely distributed in advance in order to enable each node to have an accurate understanding of the network [47]. Table 2 shows the contact plan for the sample network from Figure 1. Routes can thus be calculated by each node on demand, based on extensive topological knowledge of the network combined with the assumed traffic status. This workflow is illustrated in Figure 2 where a contact plan is initially determined by means of orbital propagators and communication models, then distributed to the network, and finally used by the DTN nodes to calculate efficient routes to the required destinations. Indeed, by combining the contact plan with local information such as outbound queue backlog and excluded neighbors (e.g., unresponsive neighbors), CGR is able to dynamically respond to changes in network topology and traffic demands. An early version of CGR was flight-validated in Deep Space

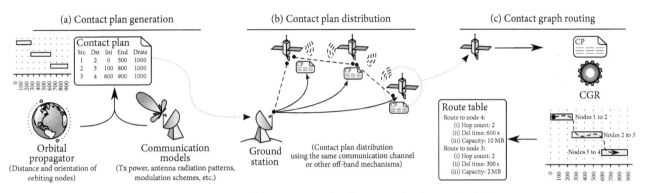

FIGURE 2: Contact plan generation, distribution, and utilization by CGR.

by NASA in 2008 [37] and CGR has been one of the most studied routing solutions for space networking since then.

CGR was initially documented in 2009 and later updated in 2010 as an experimental IETF Internet Draft [53]. By the end of the same year, Segui et al. [54] proposed earliest-arrival-time as a convenient monotonically decreasing optimization metric that avoids routing loops and enables the use of standard Dijkstra's algorithm for path selection [55]. This enhancement was then introduced in the official version of CGR, included in the Interplanetary Overlay Network (ION) DTN Stack developed by the Jet Propulsion Laboratory [32]. In 2012, Birrane et al. proposed source routing to reduce CGR computations in intermediate nodes at the expense of packet header overhead [56]. Later, in 2014, authors studied the implementation of temporal route lists as a mean to minimize CGR executions [57]. In the same year, Bezirgiannidis et al. [58] suggested to monitor transmission queues within CGR as they increase the earliest transmission opportunity (CGR-ETO). On the same paper, a complementary *overbooking management* innovation enables proactive reforwarding of bundles whose place in the outbound queue was taken by subsequent higher priority traffic. Both ETO and overbooking management are now included in the official CGR version. Regarding congestion management, further extensions were proposed as well [49–51]. Most recently, in 2016, Burleigh et al. introduced an opportunistic extension as a means of enlarging CGR applicability from deterministic space networks to opportunistic terrestrial networks [48]. The latter is not a trivial contribution since it could, if successful, pave the way towards implementing space DTN advances on ground-based networks. At the time of this writing, CGR procedure is being formally standardized as part of the Schedule-Aware Bundle Routing (SABR) procedure in a CCSDS Blue Book [47]. All these modifications have been implemented in ION software. As a result, this software becomes an important point of reference for the latest routing and forwarding mechanisms for space DTNs. The current version 3.5.0 of ION was released in September 2016 and is available as free software [33].

Even though the latest version of the CGR algorithm is implemented as part of the ION 3.5.0 open-source code (in fact, the CGR algorithm implemented in ION 3.5.0 includes a few parameters and procedures related to opportunistic CGR (O-CGR) [48]; O-CGR is an experimental CGR extension

that also considers discovered contacts in addition to those in the contact plan; since in this work all contacts are scheduled, the probabilistic calculations are not discussed nor described in this section), there is no detailed and formal description of the algorithm available yet (the CCSDS documentation is still under development [47]). As a result, in this section, an in-depth explanation of the CGR scheme is provided. For the sake of clarity, the discussed algorithms are structured following their implementation in ION; however, they can be translated to more compact and elegant expressions without *continue*, *break*, and *return* statements.

The CGR Forward routine depicted in Algorithm 1 is called at any network node every time a new bundle B is to be forwarded. Initially, the algorithm checks if the local view of the topology expressed in the contact plan Cp was modified or updated since the last call (Algorithm 1, lines (2) and (3)). If modified, a route list Rl structure, holding all valid routes to each known destination, is cleared in order to force an update of the route table. Indeed, the route list Rl is derived from the local contact plan Cp. It is interesting to note that, in contrast with Internet routes, DTN routes are expressed in function of time. Therefore, they are only valid for a given period of time and need to be revisited by CGR for every new bundle. Next, the procedure populates a proximate nodes list Pn comprising all possible nodes that, according to the route list Rl, have a valid path towards the destination (Algorithm 1, lines (6)). This step is executed by the *identifyProxNodes* routine which is detailed in Algorithm 2 and discussed below. An excluded nodes list En is used in this step to avoid the consideration of administratively forbidden neighbors (e.g., unresponsive nodes) or the previous bundle sender to minimize route loops (Algorithm 1, lines (4) and (5)).

Once populated, the Pn list can be used to forward the bundle to the appropriate neighbors. If the bundle is critical (a special type of bundle), the bundle is cloned and enqueued to all possible neighbors in the Pn list (Algorithm 1, lines (7) to (9)). If the bundle is of normal type, a single candidate node is chosen from the proximate nodes list Pn. Neighbors with best arrival times to the destination are the top priority, then those with least hop count (in CGR terminology, one contact is one hop), and finally those with a smaller node id (Algorithm 1, lines (11) to (23)). Then, if a suitable proximate node is found, the bundle B is inserted in the corresponding outbound queue before executing the overbooking management

---

input: bundle to forward B, contact plan Cp, route list Rl, excluded nodes En, proximate nodes Pn

output: bundle B enqueued in the corresponding queue

(1) $En \leftarrow \emptyset$;

(2) **if** *Cp changed since last Rl calculation* **then**

(3) $Rl \leftarrow \emptyset$;

(4) **if** *B forbids return to sender* **then**

(5) $En \leftarrow B$ sender node;

(6) $Pn \leftarrow$ `identifyProxNodes` (B, Cp, Rl, En);

(7) **if** *B is critical* **then**

(8)   enqueue a copy of B to each node in Pn;

(9)   **return**

(10) set *nextHop* to empty;

(11) **for** $pn \in Pn$ **do**

(12)   **if** *nextHop is empty* **then**

(13)   *nextHop = pn*

(14)   **else if** *pn.arrivalTime < nextHop.arrivalTime* **then**

(15)   *nextHop = pn*

(16)   **else if** *pn.arrivalTime > nextHop.arrivalTime* **then**

(17)   **continue**

(18)   **else if** *pn.hops < nextHop.hops* **then**

(19)   *nextHop = pn*

(20)   **else if** *pn.hops > nextHop.hops* **then**

(21)   **continue**

(22)   **else if** *pn.id < nextHop.id* **then**

(23)   *nextHop = pn*

(24) **if** *nextHop is not empty* **then**

(25)   enqueue B to *nextHop*;

(26)   `manageOverbook` $(B, nextHop)$

(27) **else**

(28)   enqueue B to limbo

(29) **return**

ALGORITHM 1: CGR.

procedure (the overbooking management procedure defined in [58] aims at reordering the local outbound queues when bundles with higher priorities replace less urgent bundles; since in this work we assume all bundles have the same priority, this procedure is not described) (Algorithm 1, lines (25) to (26)). However, if the CGR Forward fails to find a suitable neighbor, the bundle is stored in special memory space called *limbo* waiting for a higher level process to either erase it or retry a new forwarding later (e.g., after a contact plan update). As a result, after the CGR routine is completed, one or more bundles might be stored in the local memory waiting for the contact with the corresponding proximate node. As discussed later, if, for one reason or another (i.e., congestion or failure), the bundle is not transmitted during the expected contact, it will be removed from the queue and rerouted by this CGR routine.

The *identifyProxNodes* routine, depicted in Algorithm 2, explores existing routes in order to derive a proximate node list Pn. The Pn list is used by the main CGR routine and is formed by a set of nonrepeating neighbor nodes that are capable of reaching the bundle destination. If the route list Rl is empty (i.e., first time the routing routine is executed after a contact plan update), the load route list function is called in order to find all routes towards the destination of B (Algorithm 2, lines (1) and (2)). At this stage, Rl accounts

for all possible routes to the destination. Each of them needs to be evaluated in order to populate the proximate node list Pn. Initially, those routes that do not satisfy specific selection criteria are discarded (Algorithm 2, lines (3) to (14)). In particular, routes with the latest transmission time (*toTime*) in the past, an arrival time later than the bundle deadline, a capacity less than the bundle size, and a proximate node within the excluded nodes, or that require a local outbound queue that is depleted, are ignored. Remaining routes are then considered suitable, and the corresponding proximate node in the Pn list is either replaced by a better route (Algorithm 2, lines (15) to (24)) or directly added to the list (Algorithm 2, lines (26) and (27)). The replacement criteria is coherent with Algorithm 1: best arrival time is considered first and then route hop count. During this process, necessary route metrics such as arrival time and hop count of the best route are also stored in each proximate node data structure contained in Pn.

The routines in Algorithms 1 and 2 are executed on a per-bundle basis. The reason behind this is that the parameters of each bundle (destination, deadline, and size), the local outbound queue status, and the excluded nodes list need to be revised on every new forwarding in order to base the decision on an up-to-date version of the proximate nodes list Pn. In general, these routines are considered part of a *forwarding process* of CGR. On the other hand, the route list (Rl) will

```
     input: bundle to forward B, contact plan Cp, route list Rl, excluded nodes En,
     output: proximate nodes list Pn
 (1) if Rl is empty then
 (2)     Rl ← loadRouteList (B, Cp);
 (3) Pn ← ∅;
 (4) for route ∈ Rl do
 (5)     if route.toTime ≤ currentTime then
 (6)         continue (ignore past route)
 (7)     if route.arrivalTime ≥ B.deadline then
 (8)         continue (route arrives late)
 (9)     if route.capacity < B.bitLenght then
 (10)         continue (not enough capacity)
 (11)     if route.nextHop ∈ En then
 (12)         continue (next hop is excluded)
 (13)     if localQueue(route.nextHop) < B.bitLength then
 (14)         continue (outbound queue depleted)
 (15)     for pn ∈ Pn do
 (16)         if pn = route.nextHop then
 (17)             if pn.arrTime > route.arrTime then
 (18)                 replace pn with route.nextHop
 (19)             else if pn.arrTime < route.arrTime then
 (20)                 continue (previous route was better)
 (21)             else if pn.hops > route.hops then
 (22)                 replace pn with route.nextHop
 (23)             else if pn.hops < route.hops then
 (24)                 continue (previous route was better)
 (25)             break
 (26)     if route.nextHop ∉ Pn then
 (27)         pn ← route.nextHop;
 (28)         Pn ← pn;
 (29) return Pn
```

ALGORITHM 2: CGR: Identify proximate node list.

need to be updated whenever the local contact plan Cl is modified. The determination of the routes is considered part of a *routing* process of CGR and is described below.

In general, to find all possible routes from a source to a destination, CGR uses a *contact graph* expression of the contact plan. A contact graph is a conceptual directed acyclic graph whose vertices correspond to contacts while the edges represent episodes of data retention (i.e., storage) at a node [47]. Also, two notional vertices are added: the root vertex, which is a contact from the sender to itself, and a terminal vertex, which is a contact from the destination to itself. Even though the resulting contact graph structure may seem counterintuitive, it is a convenient static representation of a time-evolving topology that can be used to run traditional graph algorithms such as Dijkstra's searches. For example, Figure 3 illustrates the contact graph corresponding to the network shown in Figure 1. The three discussed routes with their corresponding metrics are also included in the illustration (note that another feasible path from A to D exists through contacts 1 and 9).

In order to find all possible routes in the contact plan, the load route list routine performs a series of Dijkstra's searches over a contact graph derived from the contact plan. The algorithm is listed in Algorithm 3 and is described as follows. A *work* area is reserved for each contact in the contact plan

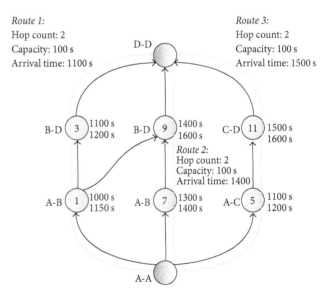

Route 1:
Hop count: 2
Capacity: 100 s
Arrival time: 1100 s

Route 3:
Hop count: 2
Capacity: 100 s
Arrival time: 1500 s

Route 2:
Hop count: 2
Capacity: 100 s
Arrival time: 1400

FIGURE 3: Contact graph example.

in order to run Dijkstra's searches. Initially, the algorithm clears all the required parameters in each working area of the contacts (Algorithm 3, lines (2) to (7)). Then, the routine

```
input: bundle to forward B, contact plan Cp
output: route list Rl
(1)  Rl[B.destination] ← ∅;
(2)  for contact ∈ Cp do
(3)      contact.work.arrivalTime ← inf;
(4)      contact.work.capacity ← 0;
(5)      contact.work.predecessor ← 0;
(6)      contact.work.visited ← false;
(7)      contact.work.suppressed ← false;
(8)  set anchorContact to empty;
(9)  while  1 do
(10)     route ← Dijkstra (B.dst, Cp, rootContact);
(11)     if route is empty then
(12)         break (no more routes in contact graph)
(13)     firstContact ← route.firstHop;
(14)     if anchorContact not empty then
(15)         if anchorContact ≠ firstContact then
(16)             for contact ∈ Cp do
(17)                 contact.work.arrivalTime ← inf;
(18)                 contact.work.predecessor ← 0;
(19)                 contact.work.visited ← false;
(20)                 if contact.source ≠ local node then
(21)                     contact.work.suppressed ← false;
(22)                 anchorContact.work.suppressed ← true;
(23)                 set anchorContact to empty;
(24)             continue (go to next Dijkstra's search)
(25)     Rl[B.destination] ← route;
(26)     if route.toTime = firstContact.endTime then
(27)         limitContact ← firstContact;
(28)     else
(29)         anchorContact ← firstContact;
(30)         for contact ∈ route.hops do
(31)             if contact.toTime = route.toTime then
(32)                 limitContact ← contact;
(33)                 break (limit contact found)
(34)     limitContact.work.suppressed ← true;
(35)     for contact ∈ Cp do
(36)         contact.work.arrivalTime ← inf;
(37)         contact.work.predecessor ← 0;
(38)         contact.work.visited ← false;
(39) return
```

ALGORITHM 3: CGR: Load route list.

loops to find different routes using Dijkstra's algorithm (Algorithm 3, line (10)). The metric driving the shortest path search is the arrival time, which must be calculated from the starting time and expected delay of each contact in the explored path. In order to guarantee that each Dijkstra execution provides a distinct route, the load route list process removes the *limiting contact* of the last route found from the following search. The limiting contact is defined as the earliest ending contact in the route path [47]. In general, the limiting contact often happens to be the first contact of the route (e.g., see contacts 1, 7, and 5 in Figure 3). Therefore, removing the limiting contact forces the shortest path search to provide the next best route towards the destination (Algorithm 3, line (13)). However, in some special cases, the transmitter node is behind a very long contact (e.g., an Internet contact). For these cases, an *anchoring* mechanism allows the algorithm to find several routes through longer contacts. The anchor search begins as soon as the algorithm detects that the first contact is not the limiting contact (Algorithm 3, lines (26) to (28)). In this stage, the anchor contact is stored and the limiting contact in the path is found and suppressed for further calculations (Algorithm 3, lines (29) to (34)). After clearing the working area (Algorithm 3, lines (35) to (38)), a new search is executed, now with the limiting contact detached from the contact graph. As soon as the first route without the anchor contact as the first contact is found, the anchored search ends suppressing the anchor contact and the normal search continues (Algorithm 3, lines (15) to (24)). The search ends when no more routes can be found in the contact graph.

Although a complex and extensive algorithm, CGR is considered to be among the most mature strategies towards forwarding and routing in space DTNs [30]. To the best of authors' knowledge, this section constitutes one of the most detailed overviews of the algorithm in the literature as of today. The correctness of such description is supported by the implementation of CGR in a simulator platform where the satellite network is submitted to faults as described below.

2.2. Fault Model. Over the last years, the semiconductor industry has been particularly concerned by the effects of radiation on integrated circuits and embedded systems in general [59]. The rationale behind this motivation lies not only in the use of these systems in radioactive environments but also in the increasing degree of integration of devices embedded in the same chip. Recent studies have shown that the smaller the feature sizes, the greater the sensitivity to radiation-induced errors [60]. As a consequence, modern embedded systems may be susceptible to low-energy particles including those observed within the Earth's atmosphere.

This effect is even more dramatic in space missions, which require systems that can operate reliably for long periods of time with little or no maintenance. This is the case in satellite constellations under study in this work. Among the possible errors, transient errors occur in the system temporarily and are usually caused by radiation interference, also known as *single event upsets* (SEUs). In particular, any circuit comprising memory elements (registers, flip-flops, internal memory, etc.) can at any moment undergo the modification of one or several bits of information due to ionizing particles. Other transient outages might be provoked by overheating, radio-frequency interference, or a processor reboot following a software exception. Traditionally, missions are designed to tolerate these failures by detecting the erroneous behavior and then recovering the system, typically by means of a full restart [59].

The random occurrence in time and space of such failure phenomenon, the probability of the error to happen, and the probability of effectively detecting an unwanted behavior, can be modeled by means of an exponential (Poisson) distribution [61]. The exponential model makes emphasis on the number of failures, the time interval over which they occur, and the environmental factors that may have affected the outcomes. As a result, it provides two feasible outputs at every moment: normal operation or failure. The model does not assume wear-out or depletion (as in batteries), implying that it only accounts for failures occurring at random intervals but with fixed long-term average frequency. Indeed, the outcome of this kind of failure model is also known as *memoryless* distribution [62]. The exponential distribution model is the most commonly adopted fault model, mainly due to its simplicity and effectiveness. It takes a single known average failure rate parameter and can be conveniently described by means of

$$F(t) = \int_0^t \lambda e^{-\lambda \tau} = 1 - e^{-\lambda \tau}. \tag{1}$$

In (1) λ is known as the *failure rate* and τ is the *time*. The failure rate reduces to the constant λ for any time: this proves that the exponential model is indeed memoryless. One

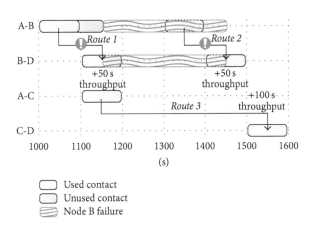

FIGURE 4: Failures in a DTN network.

of the input parameters for obtaining the modules outages is the Mean Time To Failure (MTTF), which is MTTF = $1/\lambda$. Moreover, while the time to failure is determined by the exponential model with the MTTF, the Mean Time To Repair (MTTR) defines the time to recover after the failure. Both the error detection and system recovery mechanism are presented as part of the MTTR interval. Accurately determining both MTTF and MTTR for a real spacecraft component was investigated in [63].

By means of the MTTF, MTTR, and the fault model, a fault injection system was designed to study the resulting traffic flow of a DTN based on CGR algorithm under failure conditions. In particular, MTTF and MTTR are used as parameters to randomly select fault position (i.e., node to fail), starting point, and end point in the DTN network. This phenomenon is illustrated by an example in Figure 4, where a failure in node B at 1150 s and a subsequent recovery at 1450 s forces making a partial usage of route 1 and forbids sending any data through route 2. In this particular example, 50% of route 1 data is kept stored in node B memory after the failure is found (i.e., a reliable storage is assumed in each node). Once recovered, the node finds it has bundles stored for a previous contact that need to be reforwarded. As per the description of Section 2.1, CGR will find that the ongoing direct contact with D (from 1400 s to 1500 s) is a valid path. However, all data that node A was supposed to forward to B via route 2 will need to be reforwarded to an alternative path. In CGR, this will happen after the contact ends with bundles in the outbound queue. As a result, the overall throughput of the DTN system as well as the delivery time of the data might be degraded by transient errors that block the calculated route path.

Although this example may be intuitively obvious, the complexity of the analysis drastically increases as more nodes, more contacts, more traffic flows, and more failures are injected in the network. Furthermore, the system degradation is expected to depend on the network topology and the derived contact plan. In consequence, the CGR algorithm and the exponential failure model were integrated into a single simulation framework designed to provide accurate measurements of the degradation of the metrics of DTNs in presence of transient failures.

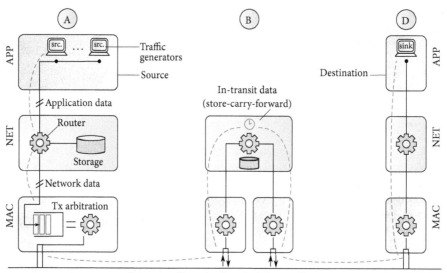

FIGURE 5: DTN node architecture in DtnSim.

3. Simulation Analysis

3.1. Simulation Platform. There exist several tools to evaluate DTNs. Among them, the ONE simulator [64] has been extensively used for DTN studies; however, the platform is specifically designed to model opportunistic DTNs (social networks, vehicular networks, etc.). On the other hand, emulation environments such as CORE [65] are available to directly test existing DTN implementations; but CORE has to be executed in real time, which hinders its application in extensive analysis. To tackle these limitations, a new simulator called DtnSim (DtnSim is still under development; however, the code will be made publicly available under an open-source license at https://bitbucket.org/lcd-unc-ar/dtnsim) was implemented in Omnet++ [66], a discrete event network simulator platform. Using an event driven framework allows DtnSim to efficiently simulate scenarios at accelerated speeds. This is crucial for space environments where analysis over orbital periods spanning several days or weeks of duration is required. Indeed, the architecture of DtnSim is specifically designed to evaluate scheduled DTNs such as satellite and Deep Space systems.

An indefinite number of DTN nodes can be spanned and configured by a single file in DtnSim. Each of these nodes are based on the layered architecture illustrated in Figure 5. This architecture is a simplification of the original DTN architecture [12] that has been adapted for DTN-based satellite systems in [10] and is comprised of an application (APP), network (NET), and Medium Access Control (MAC) layer. Physical layer effects such as bit error rate can be modeled within the MAC layer if required.

The APP layer is the element that generates and consumes user data. In general, in the case of Earth observation missions, a large amount of information is produced in onboard remote sensing instruments and is required to be delivered to a centralized node on Earth [10]. On the other hand, in communication or data relay systems, the data is generated or demanded by end users on ground and is generally sent via satellites to another node on ground (i.e., Internet gateway or mission control center). Typically, the traffic exchange in communication-oriented DTN systems is of the publish/subscribe type, instead of a client/server as traditionally seen on Internet. A publish/subscribe system allows nodes to autonomously generate and send data to those nodes which can potentially be interested without relying on instantaneous feedback messages, a key principle in DTN. As a result, in DtnSim, the APP layer allows generating either a large amount of punctual traffic or periodic amounts of data.

The NET layer is the element in charge of providing delay-tolerant multihop transmission (i.e., routes) and is probably the most mature module of DtnSim at the moment. In this layer, each DTN node includes a local storage unit (nonvolatile memory model) in order to store in transit bundles. Also, the CGR routing algorithm described in Section 2.1 was implemented as an exchangeable submodule of the network layer; thus, other algorithms can easily be supplied via a clearly defined interface. Independently from the routing submodule, the NET layer can take a contact plan as an input which defines the forthcoming contact opportunities among the nodes. The contact plan format is based on the format used in the ION software stack: a text file comprised of a list of contacts in the following form:

```
contact <start> <end> <source> <destination> <rate>
```

TABLE 3: Satellite parameters.

		Common parameters		
Orbit epoch		1 Jan 2017 10:00:00.000 UTCG		
Semimajor axis [km]		6878.14		
Eccentricity		0		
Arg. perigee [deg]		0		
EID Satellite 1, 5, 9, 13	32	36	40	44
EID Satellite 2, 6, 10, 14	33	37	41	45
EID Satellite 3, 7, 11, 15	34	38	42	46
EID Satellite 4, 8, 12, 16	35	39	43	47
	Walker formation			
	Plane A	Plane B	Plane C	Plane D
Inclination [deg]		50		
RAAN [deg]	0	90	180	270
True Anomaly Sat 1	0	22.626	45.245	67.619
True Anomaly Sat 2	90	112.626	135.245	157.619
True Anomaly Sat 3	180	202.626	225.245	247.619
True Anomaly Sat 4	270	292.626	315.245	337.619
	Along-track formation			
Inclination [deg]		97.03		
RAAN [deg]	0	0	0	0
True Anomaly Sat 1	0	20	40	60
True Anomaly Sat 2	5	25	45	65
True Anomaly Sat 3	10	30	50	70
True Anomaly Sat 4	15	35	55	75

The MAC layer of the DtnSim node is designed to provide a reliable wireless link and to multiplex the shared medium among nodes with wireless interfaces. Although each DtnSim node is based on a single APP and NET layer, several MAC modules can be attached to the NET module in order to mimic various transceivers on a single node. Thus, this layer sets the real bundle transmission rate which will depend on the transmitter/receiver module bit-rate as well as any possible medium arbitration mechanism (e.g., contention). An example analysis based on this layer has been presented in [10], where dynamic and static channel negotiations are compared. For the sake of simplicity, the MAC layer used for the present analysis transparently sends and receives bundles without further intervention. Thus, the same module is used to communicate nodes connected through Internet on ground.

Finally, DtnSim was extended with a fault-injector module based on the exponential model described in Section 2.2. In particular, the MTTF and MTTR are provisioned to each node so as to determine when the node is in a failure or normal operation state. When a node is in a failure state, the node is not able to send nor receive bundles by any of its MAC interfaces. However, if it has bundles stored in the local storage, they are not modified. Such a model mimics existing nonvolatile spacecraft data recorder systems typically on board of medium and high-end spacecraft. Nonetheless, the fault model can be easily extended to delete or corrupt stored data.

3.2. Simulation Scenarios. In order to assess CGR behavior under transient failures in realistic delay-tolerant satellite constellations, two appealing and realistic configurations are proposed and discussed below: a sun-synchronous along-track and a Walker-delta formation. Both constellations are based on 16 cross-linked LEO satellites (max. link range of 1000 Km at 500 km height), 25 ground target points, and 6 ground stations. The specific orbital parameters of the satellites are summarized in Table 3 while the ground stations and target locations are in Table 4 (the resulting contact plans used for the simulations as well as the STK [67] scenario of the Walker formation can be found in https://upcn.eu/icc2017.html). Systems Tool Kit (STK) [67] software was used to propagate these parameters for an analysis period of 24 hs. An intuitive illustration of the node's location on a world map is provided in Figure 6. The left side of the picture plots the ground tracks of the Walker formation while the along-track is on the right.

3.3. Simulation Results. In the along-track formation, all 16 satellites are equally spaced and follow a very similar orbital trajectory. In this analysis, each satellite is able to reach the next neighbor in the front and in the back along the trajectory. Among the many benefits of such formation, satellites do not require complex transfer maneuvers if launched from the same vector. Also, since satellites perceive similar gravitational perturbations, significant savings in propellant for formation-keeping can be made [68]. From a

Table 4: Ground station and ground target parameters.

Station	Lat [deg]	Lon [deg]	EID
Córdoba	−31.524	−64.463	1
A. Springs	−23.758	133.883	2
Leolut	39.908	116.42	3
Neustrelitz	53.329	13.07	4
Hartebeesthoek	−25.886	27.712	5
JPL (USA)	34.203	−118.173	6
Target	Lat [deg]	Lon [deg]	EID
Afghanistan	33.833	66.025	7
Argentina	−40.843	−68.090	8
Australia	−23.274	129.385	9
Bangladesh	23.730	90.306	10
Brazil	−10.813	−55.460	11
Chile	−53.132	−70.915	12
Congo	−0.842	15.230	13
Egypt	26.756	29.860	14
Iraq	33.045	43.775	15
Kazakhstan	44.161	79.766	16
Kenya	0.577	37.839	17
Mali	17.357	−3.527	18
Mongolia	46.836	103.067	19
Namibia	−22.150	17.177	20
Nepal	28.259	83.944	21
Nigeria	9.560	8.077	22
Papua NG	−6.889	146.214	23
Peru	−3.732	−73.240	24
Russia	50.339	127.553	25
Algeria	25.808	10.021	26
Sudan	16.085	30.087	27
Suriname	4.217	−55.889	28
Bolivia	−21.521	−64.738	29
Vietnam	16.940	106.816	30
Zambia	12.407	9.254	31

communications perspective, the topological stability of this formation also favors the simplicity of fixed antennas against complex gimbal mounts or electronically steered antennas for ISLs. Similar topologies have been used in previous satellite DTN studies [10].

On the other hand, a Walker constellation pattern is defined by 4 orbital planes each with 4 satellites. In comparison with along-track, this constellation provides wider coverage at the expense of reduced ISLs communication time. Indeed, as shown in Figure 6, contacts among satellites are only feasible when orbital planes cross. This setup is known to provide efficient communication opportunities [69] and can also be used for DTN studies.

To the best of the authors' knowledge, this is the first time these topologies have been compared within the DTN communication paradigm.

The chosen constellations are suitable for Earth observation missions [10], data-collection, or high-latency communication systems [11]. If used for Earth observation, the

ground target locations would represent points of interest from which on-board instrumentation can acquire optical or radar images, or other remote sensing data. If used for data-collection or high-latency communication systems, ground targets would stand for ground-based equipment relaying either science or local user data (a.k.a. cold spots). In both cases, data sent from ground targets would be addressed via orbiting satellites to a centralized Mission Operations and Control (MOC) reachable through Internet (i.e., any of the 6 ground stations). Indeed, a MOC could act as an Internet gateway to deliver traffic to otherwise inaccessible ground targets. As a result, the publish/subscribe traffic pattern analyzed in the simulation is bidirectional: from all ground targets to the MOC and in reverse. In particular, each ground target will generate a bundle of 125000 Bytes per hour to be delivered to the MOC. In turn, the MOC will send one bundle of equal characteristics to each ground target also every hour. In both cases, traffic generation will only occur during the first 10 hs of the 24 hs of simulation. Therefore,

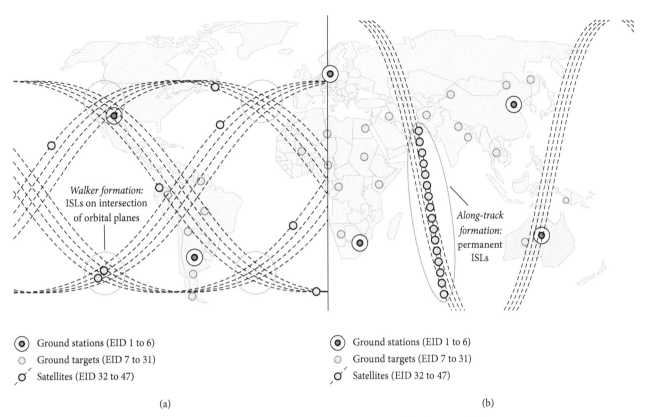

Walker formation:
ISLs on intersection
of orbital planes

Along-track
formation:
permanent
ISLs

⊙ Ground stations (EID 1 to 6)
○ Ground targets (EID 7 to 31)
○́ Satellites (EID 32 to 47)

⊙ Ground stations (EID 1 to 6)
○ Ground targets (EID 7 to 31)
○́ Satellites (EID 32 to 47)

(a)

(b)

FIGURE 6: Simulation case studies: (a) Walker formation and (b) along-track formation.

250 bundles will flow to the MOC and 250 to the ground targets in the return path. Also, the transmission data-rates for both intersatellite and Earth-to-satellite links were set to 100 Kbps, which can be obtained from a state-of-the-art CubeSat transponder (a CubeSat is a type of miniaturized satellite that is made up of multiples of $10 \times 10 \times 11.35$ cm cubic units [70]; CubeSats are gaining increased popularity as they leverage existing Commercial Off-The-Shelf (COTS) components providing a cost-efficient alternative to building distributed satellite constellations) [71].

Simulation results are plotted in Figure 7. The abscissa axis shows the variation in MTTF including an infinite (INF) value standing for a single simulation execution without the occurrence of failures. Indeed, measurements at this last point in the horizontal axis stand for a reference performance for each of the proposed constellations. For the rest of MTTF values (MTTF from 100 s up to 2200 s were considered with a step of 300 s), resulting metrics are averaged over 160 simulation runs and then averaged over bundles or nodes accordingly. On the other hand, the mean recovery time (MTTR) was set to 5 minutes mimicking a full system reboot. Failures were enabled only in orbiting satellites; ground stations and ground targets were not assumed to fail in this analysis.

The effective fail time curve on the left shows the accumulated amount of time that a given node in the network refrained from transmitting a bundle either because of a local or a remote (i.e., next-hop node) fault condition. In general, the along-track formation exhibits a higher effective

fail rate which is consistent with the higher connectivity of a permanently connected constellation. In other words, the probability of finding a failure during a contact is higher in the along-track than in the Walker system.

A not so intuitive result is shown in the total bundles received curve. This metric measures the quantity of bundles that arrived at the final destination (application layer). The Walker constellation is able to deliver the full traffic load of 500 bundles for MTTF of 700 s and higher. However, the along-track formation is unable to deliver such load even without any failures injected in the nodes (453 bundles reach the destination in this case). After a thorough analysis of the simulation traces, it was found that a pathological routing behavior impeded CGR to find all feasible routes leaving certain bundles without valid routes (i.e., in the limbo). These miscalculations are magnified as the failure rate increases. The issue found in CGR statement is related to the anchoring concept and is discussed in detail in Section 4.

The mean bundle delay curve is shown with the absolute mean delay value measured in minutes as well as relative to the metric observed without faults in the network (i.e., the delay for infinite MTTF). These results confirm that the Walker formation provides a better overall bundle delivery time. However, the along-track system results significantly more stable with the variation of the MTTF. In other words, the along-track formation is less sensitive (i.e., more robust) to faults than the Walker constellation. This effect is clearly observed in the relative expression of the mean bundle delay. It is interesting to note that given the delay-tolerant nature

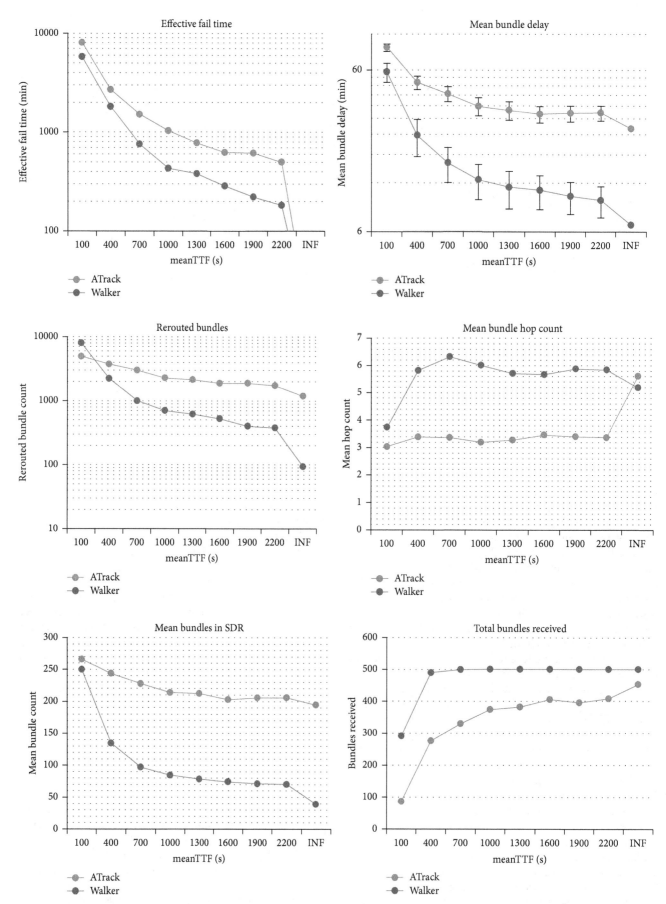

FIGURE 7: Continued.

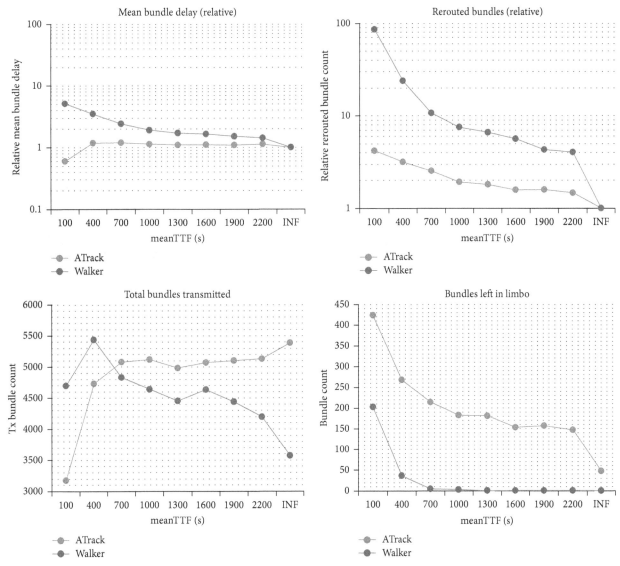

FIGURE 7: Simulation results.

of both systems, the fact that latency remains in the order of minutes is completely reasonable.

The rerouted bundles curves are also expressed in absolute and relative format. These results show the number of bundles that had to be routed while in transit because a contact ended with a nonempty outbound queue. As previously discussed, this happens when the capacity allocated by the first CGR execution did not match the real capacity in the system. Successive CGR executions are necessary either because of failures or congestion problems [49–51]. Indeed, the result without failures (infinite MTTF) shows the quantity of rerouting required due to congestion in both constellations. The relative curve thus evidences that rerouting in Walker constellation increases more dramatically than the along-track in the presence of failures. Such an increase can also be justified by the higher delivery rate of this formation. This metric then confirms that the along-track formation results more insensible towards higher fault rates.

The mean bundle hop count curve shows that the Walker constellation makes a more extensive usage of multihop paths. Such a feature is only observed in the along-track system in the absence of failures. For all other cases, the along-track constellation uses 3 hop paths (MOC to ground station, ground station to satellite, and satellite to ground target) meaning that several ISLs opportunities are underutilized in the presence of failures. Moreover, the along-track system evidences higher total transmitted bundles in most cases. This curve measures the total quantity of bundles transmitted by all nodes in the network (either for local or remote traffic). This metric can thus be directly correlated with energy usage in the node transmitter. In this case, the along-track not only uses lower hop counts but also evidences a higher energy usage due to bundle transmissions.

The last two plots on the right provide a metric on the storage used by the nodes. The upper curve depicts the overall spacecraft data recorder (SDR) memory used (outbound queue buffers occupancy) while the lower one shows the

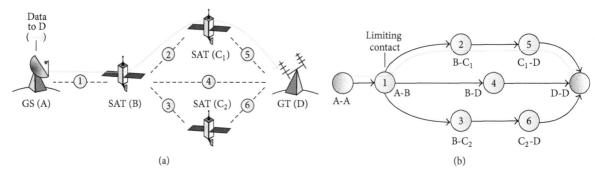

FIGURE 8: Routes overlooked by CGR.

quantity of bundles that remains in the limbo at the end of the simulations because of the absence of feasible routes. In general, a significant number of bundles remains in the limbo for the along-track formation. Also, the Walker constellation evidences a lower memory utilization. This is coherent with previous analysis and confirms the inability of CGR of finding all feasible routes in the along-track topology. Such a problem is not observed in the Walker system which also features a significantly lower storage utilization as shown in the bundles in SDR plot.

4. Discussion

In order to describe the CGR inability to find all feasible routes in the along-track constellation, a simplified along-track topology and its corresponding contact graph are presented in Figures 8(a) and 8(b), respectively. In contrast to the Walker formation, the along-track formation exhibits a remarkable link redundancy since a single point on Earth is able to simultaneously reach several orbiting nodes while each satellite has simultaneous access to the front and back neighbor. In this example, a ground station (GS A) can reach a satellite (SAT B) which in turn can reach the front and back satellites in the constellation (SAT C_1 and SAT C_2). Eventually, the three satellites will be able to reach a ground target (GT D) when the constellation passes over that ground area (notice that contacts 4, 5, and 6 might occur later in time requiring a temporal storage of data in the satellites).

Even though the existence of several paths towards D is desirable from a reliability perspective, it requires a routing algorithm that is able to discover and manage several parallel paths towards a given destination. However, the CGR specification discussed in Section 2.1 was found to overlook several valid paths in this kind of scenarios. In this example, the first Dijkstra search executed in node A will find a valid route towards D, let us say via contacts 1, 2, and 5 (cyan arrow). The limiting contact in this path is contact 1, which will end before the ISLs which are permanent in an along-track formation. As previously discussed in Algorithm 3, this contact will then be removed from the contact graph in order to begin the next search. But removing contact 1 will hinder the discovery of other two feasible paths via contacts 1 and 4, and contacts 1, 3, and 6. Therefore, node A will refrain from sending more bundles than those that can fit in the discovered route (as discussed in Algorithm 2, route residual capacity must be

enough to accommodate the forwarded bundle). The capacity in the remaining routes will remain underutilized favoring a partial delivery of bundles, increased delay, congestion, and an increased storage utilization as evidenced in Figure 7. It is worth noticing that this issue is not an implementation matter but part of the inner core of current CGR definition.

At the moment, the authors are investigating alternative DTN routing algorithms leveraging a contact graph. As part of these efforts, an alternative definition of the CGR algorithm is under development that can enhance current route discovery capabilities. A generalization of the anchoring concept might lead to a complete route discovery. Also, relying on K-Shortest Path (KSP) algorithms is also being considered [72]. Another future work involves the investigation of novel mechanisms that could exploit MTTF and MTTR parameters (generally known or estimated in advance) to support proactive fault-avoidance forwarding measurements. This research line might be based on similar approaches to the ones used in opportunistic CGR [48]. Finally, the presented analysis can be further extended by modeling high channel delays and more complex custody transfer protocols. In real networks, the lack of a custody acceptance is the means by which a DTN node can realize that a neighbor is unresponsive. Even though disregarded in presented simulations, timeout configurations of custody messaging and significant channel delays can play a significant role in a correct and timely reaction towards network faults.

5. Conclusion

In this work, an extensive analysis on the reliability of satellite-based Delay/Disruption Tolerant Networks (DTN) was presented. Two appealing and realistic Low-Earth Orbit constellations using state-of-the art routing algorithms were considered and compared by means of simulations. To this end, a unique overview of Contact Graph Routing (CGR) was provided and implemented in DtnSim, a novel space DTN simulator provided to the DTN community.

Results include the first evidence of the performance of Walker and along-track formations under different failure rates. As expected, the higher the failure rate, the more significant the performance degradation. The Walker formation proved to provide better delivery and resource utilization metrics, while the along-track was found more insensitive (i.e., robust) towards faults. Even though the intrinsic redundancy present in the along-track topology favors an improved fault-tolerance, analysis showed that current version of CGR was unable to make an optimal utilization of the communication resources. A proper identification of the algorithm weakness was presented and discussed based on the detailed overview of CGR.

The presented analysis becomes a solid starting point towards an improved CGR statement, which is currently under study by the authors. Also, future work includes the exploration of further CGR enhancements that could improve its robustness when implemented in fault-prone DTN systems.

Acknowledgments

Part of this research was carried out in the frame of the "Calcul Parallèle pour Applications Critiques en Temps et Sûreté" (CAPACITES) project. Part of this research was carried out at the Jet Propulsion Laboratory, California Institute of Technology, under a contract with the National Aeronautics and Space Administration. Government sponsorship is acknowledged.

References

[1] M. D'errico, *Distributed Space Missions for Earth System Monitoring*, vol. 31, Springer, New York, NY, USA, 2013.

[2] H. F. Rashvand, A. Abedi, J. M. Alcaraz-Calero, P. D. Mitchell, and S. C. Mukhopadhyay, "Wireless sensor systems for space and extreme environments: a review," *IEEE Sensors Journal*, vol. 14, no. 11, pp. 3955–3970, 2014.

[3] O. Brown and P. Eremenko, "The value proposition for fractionated space architectures," in *Proceedings of the AIAA-2006-7506*, AIAA Space, San Jose, Calif, USA, 2006.

[4] M. Mosleh, K. Dalili, and B. Heydari, "Optimal modularity for fractionated spacecraft: the case of system F6^a," *Procedia Computer Science*, vol. 28, pp. 164–170, 2014.

[5] S. Burleigh, A. Hooke, L. Torgerson et al., "Delay-tolerant networking: an approach to interplanetary internet," *IEEE Communications Magazine*, vol. 41, no. 6, pp. 128–136, 2003.

[6] C. Caini, H. Cruickshank, S. Farrell, and M. Marchese, "Delay- and disruption-tolerant networking (DTN): an alternative solution for future satellite networking applications," *Proceedings of the IEEE*, vol. 99, no. 11, pp. 1980–1997, 2011.

[7] C. Caini and R. Firrincieli, "DTN for LEO satellite communications," in *Proceedings of the International Conference on Personal Satellite Service*, pp. 186–198, Springer, Berlin, Germany, 2011.

[8] C. Caini and R. Firrincieli, "Application of contact graph routing to LEO satellite DTN communications," in *Proceedings of the IEEE International Conference on Communications, ICC*, pp. 3301–3305, IEEE, Ottawa, Canada, June 2012.

[9] P. G. Madoery, J. A. Fraire, and J. M. Finochietto, "Analysis of communication strategies for earth observation satellite constellations," *IEEE Latin America Transactions*, vol. 14, no. 6, pp. 2777–2782, 2016.

[10] J. A. Fraire, P. G. Madoery, J. M. Finochietto, P. A. Ferreyra, and R. Velazco, "Internetworking approaches towards along-track segmented satellite architectures," in *Proceedings of the International Conference on Wireless for Space and Extreme Environments, WiSEE*, pp. 123–128, IEEE, Aachen, Germany, September 2016.

[11] S. C. Burleigh and E. J. Birrane, "Toward a communications satellite network for humanitarian relief," in *Proceedings of the 1st International Conference on Wireless Technologies for Humanitarian Relief, ACWR*, pp. 219–224, ACM, Kerala, India, December 2011.

[12] V. Cerf, S. Burleigh, A. Hooke et al., "Delay-tolerant networking architecture," Internet Requests for Comments, RFC Editor 4838, 2007.

[13] K. Fall, "A delay-tolerant network architecture for challenged internets," in *Proceedings of the Conference on Applications, Technologies, Architectures, and Protocols for Computer Communications, SIGCOMM*, pp. 27–34, ACM, New York, NY, USA, August 2003.

[14] K. Scott and S. Burleigh, "Bundle protocol specification," Internet Requests for Comments, RFC Editor 5050, 2007.

[15] M. Demmer, J. Ott, and S. Perreault, "Delay-tolerant networking tcp convergence-layer protocol," Internet Requests for Comments, RFC Editor 7242, 2014.

[16] H. Kruse, S. Jero, and S. Ostermann, "Datagram convergence layers for the delay- and disruption-tolerant networking (DTN) bundle protocol and licklider transmission protocol (LTP)," Internet Requests for Comments, RFC Editor 7122, 2014.

[17] S. Burleigh, "Compressed bundle header encoding (CBHE)," Internet Requests for Comments, RFC Editor 6260, 2011.

[18] N. Bezirgiannidis, F. Tsapeli, S. Diamantopoulos, and V. Tsaoussidis, "Towards flexibility and accuracy in space DTN communications," in *Proceedings of the 8th ACM MobiCom Workshop on Challenged Networks, CHANTS*, pp. 43–48, New York, NY, USA, September 2013.

[19] M. A. Alfonzo, J. A. Fraire, E. Kocian, and N. Alvarez, "Development of a DTN bundle protocol convergence layer for spacewire," in *Proceedings of the 2nd IEEE Biennial Congress of Argentina, ARGENCON 2014*, pp. 770–775, IEEE, Bariloche, Argentina, June 2014.

[20] A. Lindgren, A. Doria, and O. Schelén, "Probabilistic routing in intermittently connected networks," *ACM SIGMOBILE Mobile Computing and Communications Review*, vol. 7, no. 3, pp. 19-20, 2003.

[21] B. B. Xuan, A. Ferreira, and A. Jarry, "Computing shortest, fastest, and foremost journeys in dynamic networks," *International Journal of Foundations of Computer Science*, vol. 14, no. 2, pp. 267–285, 2003.

[22] S. Merugu, M. Ammar, and E. Zegura, "Routing in space and time in networks with predictable mobility," Tech. Rep., Georgia Institute of Technology, 2004.

[23] M. Sheng, G. Xu, and X. Fang, "The routing of interplanetary internet," *China Communications*, vol. 3, no. 6, pp. 63–73, 2006.

[24] A. Lindgren, A. Doria, E. Davies, and S. Grasic, "Probabilistic routing protocol for intermittently connected networks," Internet Requests for Comments, RFC Editor 6693, 2012.

[25] J. Burgess, B. Gallagher, D. Jensen, and B. N. Levine, "MaxProp: routing for vehicle-based disruption-tolerant networks," in *Proceedings of the 25th IEEE International Conference on Computer Communications, INFOCOM*, pp. 1–11, IEEE, Barcelona, Spain, April 2006.

[26] T. Spyropoulos, K. Psounis, and C. S. Raghavendra, "Spray and wait: an efficient routing scheme for intermittently connected mobile networks," in *Proceedings of the ACM SIGCOMM Workshop on Delay-Tolerant Networking, WDTN*, pp. 252–259, ACM, Philadelphia, Pa, USA, August 2005.

[27] Z. Feng and K.-W. Chin, "A unified study of epidemic routing protocols and their enhancements," in *Proceedings of the 26th IEEE International Parallel and Distributed Processing Symposium Workshops & PhD Forum, IPDPSW*, pp. 1484–1493, IEEE, Shanghai, China, May 2012.

[28] S. Palazzo, A. T. Campbell, and M. Dias De Amorim, "Opportunistic and delay-tolerant networks," *EURASIP Journal on Wireless Communications and Networking*, vol. 2011, Article ID 164370, 2011.

[29] Y. Wu, S. Deng, and H. Huang, "Performance analysis of epidemic routing in DTNs with limited forwarding times and selfish nodes," *International Journal of Ad Hoc and Ubiquitous Computing*, vol. 13, no. 3-4, pp. 254–263, 2013.

[30] G. Araniti, N. Bezirgiannidis, E. Birrane et al., "Contact graph routing in DTN space networks: overview, enhancements and performance," *IEEE Communications Magazine*, vol. 53, no. 3, pp. 38–46, 2015.

[31] "DTN2: a DTN reference implementation," https://sourceforge.net/projects/dtn/.

[32] S. Burleigh, "Interplanetary overlay network an implementation of the DTN bundle protocol," in *Proceedings of the 4th Annual IEEE Consumer Communications and Networking Conference, CCNC*, pp. 222–226, IEEE, Las Vegas, Nev, USA, January 2007.

[33] "Interplanetary Overlay Network (ION) software home page," https://sourceforge.net/projects/ion-dtn/.

[34] S. Schildt, J. Morgenroth, W.-B. Pöttner, and L. Wolf, "Performance comparison of DTN Bundle Protocol implementations," in *Proceedings of the 6th ACM workshop on Challenged networks*, pp. 61–64, ACM, Las Vegas, Nev, USA, September 2011.

[35] M. Feldmann and F. Walter, "Micro pcn; a bundle protocol implementation for microcontrollers," in *Proceedings of the International Conference on Wireless Communications and Signal Processing, WCSP*, pp. 1–5, IEEE, Nanjing, China, October 2015.

[36] W. Ivancic, W. M. Eddy, D. Stewart et al., "Experience with delay-tolerant networking from orbit," in *Proceedings of the 4th Advanced Satellite Mobile Systems, ASMS*, pp. 173–178, IEEE, Bologna, Italy, August 2008.

[37] J. Wyatt, S. Burleigh, R. Jones, L. Torgerson, and S. Wissler, "Disruption tolerant networking flight validation experiment on NASA's EPOXI mission," in *Proceedings of the 1st International Conference on Advances in Satellite and Space Communications, SPACOMM*, pp. 187–196, IEEE, Colmar, France, July 2009.

[38] "NASA and ESA use experimental interplanetary internet to test robot from international space station," https://www.nasa.gov/home/hqnews/2012/nov/HQ_12-391_DTN.html.

[39] Internet Engineering Task Force (IETF), "Delay tolerant network research group (DTNRG)," http://www.dtnrg.org/wiki/Home.

[40] Internet Society (ISOC), "InterPlanetary Networking Special Interest Group (IPNSIG) Chapter," http://ipnsig.org.

[41] Consultative Committee for Space Data Systems (CCSDS), "Delay tolerant networking working group (SIS-DTN)," http://www.ccsds.org.

[42] Internet Engineering Task Force (IETF), "Delay tolerant networking working group (DTNWG)," https://datatracker.ietf.org/wg/dtnwg/charter/.

[43] M. Tanase and V. Cristea, "Quality of service in large scale mobile distributed systems based on opportunistic networks," in *Proceedings of the IEEE International Conference on Advanced Information Networking and Applications Workshops, WAINA*, pp. 849–854, IEEE, Singapore, March 2011.

[44] J. A. Fraire and P. A. Ferreyra, "Assessing DTN architecture reliability for distributed satellite constellations: preliminary results from a case study," in *Proceedings of the IEEE Biennial Congress of Argentina, ARGENCON*, pp. 564–569, IEEE, Bariloche, Argentina, June 2014.

[45] Y. Wu, Z. Yang, and Q. Zhang, "A Novel DTN routing algorithm in the geo-relaying satellite network," in *Proceedings of the 11th International Conference on Mobile Ad-Hoc and Sensor Networks, MSN*, pp. 264–269, IEEE, Shenzhen, China, December 2015.

[46] S. E. Alaoui and B. Ramamurthy, "Routing optimization for DTN-based space networks using a temporal graph model," in *Proceedings of the IEEE International Conference on Communications, ICC*, pp. 1–6, IEEE, Kuala Lumpur, Malaysia, May 2016.

[47] C. Secretariat and CCSDS, "Schedule-Aware Bundle Routing (SABR), White Book," ccsds 232.0-b-2ed, Recommendation for Space Data System Standards, 2016.

[48] S. Burleigh, C. Caini, J. J. Messina, and M. Rodolfi, "Toward a unified routing framework for delay-tolerant networking," in *Proceedings of the IEEE International Conference on Wireless for Space and Extreme Environments, WiSEE*, pp. 82–86, IEEE, Aachen, Germany, September 2016.

[49] E. J. Birrane, "Congestion modeling in graph-routed delay tolerant networks with predictive capacity consumption," in *Proceedings of the IEEE Global Communications Conference, GLOBECOM*, pp. 3016–3022, IEEE, Atlanta, Ga, USA, December 2013.

[50] H. Yan, Q. Zhang, and Y. Sun, "Local information-based congestion control scheme for space delay/disruption tolerant networks," *Wireless Networks*, vol. 21, no. 6, pp. 2087–2099, 2015.

[51] J. A. Fraire, P. Madoery, J. M. Finochietto, and E. J. Birrane, "Congestion modeling and management techniques for predictable disruption tolerant networks," in *Proceedings of the IEEE 40th Conference on Local Computer Networks, LCN*, pp. 544–551, IEEE, Clearwater Beach, Fla, USA, October 2015.

[52] J. Fraire, P. Ferreyra, and C. Marques, "Opencl-accelerated simplified general perturbations 4 algorithm," in *Proceedings of the 14th Argentine Symposium on Technology, AST*, vol. 2013.

[53] S. Burleigh, "Contact graph routing, IETF-Draft draft-burleigh-dtnrg-cgr-01," 2009.

[54] J. Segui, E. Jennings, and S. Burleigh, "Enhancing contact graph routing for delay tolerant space networking," in *Proceedings of the IEEE Global Telecommunications Conference, GLOBECOM*, pp. 1–6, IEEE, Kathmandu, Nepal, December 2011.

[55] E. W. Dijkstra, "A note on two problems in connexion with graphs," *Numerische Mathematik*, vol. 1, no. 1, pp. 269–271, 1959.

[56] E. Birrane, S. Burleigh, and N. Kasch, "Analysis of the contact graph routing algorithm: bounding interplanetary paths," *Acta Astronautica*, vol. 75, pp. 108–119, 2012.

[57] J. A. Fraire, P. Madoery, and J. M. Finochietto, "Leveraging routing performance and congestion avoidance in predictable delay tolerant networks," in *Proceedings of the International IEEE Conference on Wireless for Space and Extreme Environments, WiSEE*, pp. 1–7, IEEE, Noordwijk, Netherlands, October 2014.

[58] N. Bezirgiannidis, C. Caini, D. D. P. Montenero, M. Ruggieri, and V. Tsaoussidis, "Contact graph routing enhancements for delay tolerant space communications," in *Proceedings of the 7th Advanced Satellite Multimedia Systems Conference, ASMS and the 13th Signal Processing for Space Communications Workshop, SPSC*, pp. 17–23, IEEE, Livorno, Italy, September 2014.

[59] R. R. Velazco, P. Fouillat, and R. Reis, *Radiation Effects on Embedded Systems*, Springer, Secaucus, NJ, USA, 2007.

[60] E. Ibe, H. Taniguchi, Y. Yahagi, K.-I. Shimbo, and T. Toba, "Impact of scaling on neutron-induced soft error in SRAMs from a 250 nm to a 22 nm design rule," *IEEE Transactions on Electron Devices*, vol. 57, no. 7, pp. 1527–1538, 2010.

[61] P. A. Ferreyra, C. A. Marqués, R. T. Ferreyra, and J. P. Gaspar, "Failure map functions and accelerated mean time to failure tests: new approaches for improving the reliability estimation in systems Exposed to single event upsets," *IEEE Transactions on Nuclear Science*, vol. 52, no. 1, pp. 494–500, 2005.

[62] H. Hecht, *Systems Reliability and Failure Prevention*, Artech House Inc, Norwood, Mass, USA, 2004.

[63] P. A. Ferreyra, G. Viganotti, C. A. Marqués, R. Velazco, and R. T. Ferreyra, "Failure and coverage factors based Markoff models: a new approach for improving the dependability estimation in complex fault tolerant systems exposed to SEUs," *IEEE Transactions on Nuclear Science*, vol. 54, no. 4, pp. 912–919, 2007.

[64] A. Keranen, J. Andott, and T. Karkkainen, "The ONE simulator for DTN protocol evaluation," in *Proceedings of the 2nd International Conference on Simulation Tools and Techniques, Simutools*, pp. 1–10, ICST, Rome, Italy, March 2009.

[65] J. Ahrenholz, "Comparison of CORE network emulation platforms," in *Proceedings of the Military Communications Conference, MILCOM*, pp. 166–171, IEEE, San Jose, Calif, USA, November 2010.

[66] A. Varga, "Using the OMNeT++ discrete event simulation system," in *Proceedings of the European Simulation Multiconference, ESM*, Pargue, Czech, 2013.

[67] "AGI Systems Tool Kit (STK)," http://www.agi.com/STK.

[68] Z. Yoon, W. Frese, A. Bukmaier, and K. Brieß, "System design of an S-band network of distributed nanosatellites," *CEAS Space Journal*, vol. 6, no. 1, pp. 61–71, 2014.

[69] C. Wang, "Structural properties of a low Earth orbit satellite constellation—the Walker delta network," in *Proceedings of the Military Communications Conference, MILCOM*, vol. 3, pp. 968–972, IEEE, Boston, Mass, USA, October 1993.

[70] The CubeSat Program Cal Poly SLO, "CubeSat Design Specification rev. 13," 2014.

[71] "GomSpace NanoCom S100 Communication Module (NanoCom U482C)," http://gomspace.com/?p=products-u482c.

[72] J. Y. Yen, "Finding the *K* shortest loopless paths in a network," *Management Science*, vol. 17, no. 11, pp. 712–716, 1971.

11

Modeling Handover Signaling Messages in OpenFlow-Based Mobile Software-Defined Networks

Modhawi Alotaibi [ID],[1,2] **Ahmed Helmy** [ID],[1] **and Amiya Nayak** [ID][1]

[1]*School of Electrical Engineering and Computer Science, University of Ottawa, Ottawa, Canada*
[2]*College of Computer Science and Engineering, Taibah University, Medina, Saudi Arabia*

Correspondence should be addressed to Modhawi Alotaibi; malot075@uottawa.ca

Guest Editor: Ting Wang

The software-defined networking (SDN) paradigm has become essential in tackling several issues and challenges in conventional networking, especially in mobile/cellular networks. In order to realize the benefits brought by SDN to mobility management, we study the effects of SDN in conjunction with OpenFlow protocol on the handover procedure. However, in this new setting, the handover still suffers from delay due to the exchange of OpenFlow signaling messages. In this paper, we focus on SDN in mobile networks and quantify the delays of handover-related OpenFlow messages in order to identify the performance measures as well as the underlying challenges. For our analysis, we provide an analytical model, using which we modeled two handover-related OpenFlow messages in such networks. To the best of our knowledge, no previous work has modeled OpenFlow messages other than *Packet-in* messages. In this paper, in addition to the Packet-in message, we model *Port-status* messages. Following our analysis, we propose a novel solution to make handover more efficient and less interruptive. Furthermore, we study our solution in an LTE architecture and compare it to an existing solution. We show that, in normal traffic conditions, our solution can decrease the handover delay as much as 20%.

1. Introduction

Current computer networks are built out of an enormous number of forwarding devices and middleboxes scattered on large-scales. Each device has some logic and local intelligence to perform certain roles. This networks' architecture has reportedly been suffering from multiple issues that get exaggerated with the increase in traffic demands and with new applications and protocols requirements. For instance, inflexible adaptability to network changing conditions is a major challenge that burdens network managers; additionally, the high cost due to hardware commodity is another issue [1, 2]. Moreover, scaling and managing due to the need to configure networks' devices in a low-level manner are two unavoidable challenges. On a global scale, another challenge is "Internet ossification," which means the difficulty of Internet evolution in terms of physical infrastructure and protocol installation [3].

The software-defined networking (SDN) paradigm has been introduced to solve some of the issues mentioned above and offers solutions such as reducing upgrade costs and using network resources efficiently [2]. The paradigm divides the network architecture into two planes: control and data, which makes it possible to program and configure a controller as well as manage the network dynamically and globally [4]. In fact, SDN facilitates the management of large-scale congested networks such as datacenters and cloud infrastructures. For instance, on Aug 21, 2017, Cisco announced their plan to integrate their software-defined networking product, called Application Centric Infrastructure (ACI), into the top three major public cloud platforms in the market: Amazon Web Services, Microsoft Azure, and Google Cloud Platform [5]. This incentive shows the expected wide spread of SDN concept in the future.

The SDN concept has been integrated into both wired and wireless networks. Even though the SDN technology is introduced to solve some issues in the current wireless architecture, the nature of the wireless networks nowadays imposes critical challenges due to the rapid and extensive growth of mobile traffic [6]. Meeting the users' requirements and providing a high quality of service become necessary and more challenging [7]. One of the main concerns of mobility management is maintaining a user ongoing session continuity with relatively minimum interruption or, in other words, minimizing handover latency. Therefore, in our research, we study mobile/cellular networks, and we focus on the handover of hosts between different switches. Specifically, our focus is on minimizing handover latency by targeting one of its causes, the delay caused by exchanging control messages. The completion of a handover procedure requires the exchange of signaling messages between the control and data planes, especially in the case of hard handover, where the "breakage" in an ongoing session correlates to the exchange of management and reconfiguration messages [8]. Interestingly, Duan et al. [9] showed that an SDN-based solution is more suitable for "less sensitive" to latency applications. However, we know for a fact that the handover is sensitive to latency, and the primary goal here is to minimize handover latency. This fact motivated us to further analyze the main contributors to delay.

In cellular networks such as Long Term Evolution (LTE), the SDN concept has been incorporated into different parts, especially into the Evolved Packet Core (EPC). EPC is made of multiple components such as Mobility Management Entity (MME), Home Subscriber Server (HSS), Serving Gateway (S-GW), and Packet Data Network Gateway (P-GW). MME is a key module responsible for some mobility management tasks. Module HSS is considered a central database that has all the subscribers' information. S-GW and P-GW are gateways; S-GW forwards data between eNodeBs, while P-GW connects the end-user to external networks. In SDN-based LTE architecture, the deployment of the control plane can be centralized or distributed. As for the centralized approach, all EPC's components are virtualized and placed into a single controller. Alternatively, the distributed EPC controller architecture can be represented in different ways: either through implementing a distributed set of EPC controllers or by distributing the functionalities of an EPC controller. Thus, the mobility management can be centralized or distributed based on the choice of the control plane deployment.

According to the design of SDN, the communication between the control and data planes is going through what is referred to as a southbound interface. OpenFlow protocol is the most well-known and is also the industry-standard southbound protocol in SDN-based networks. It was proposed by McKeown et al. [2] and is now maintained by Open Networking Foundation (ONF). The OpenFlow protocol manages the interaction between the data and control planes through the use of particular messages. Analyzing those OpenFlow messages helps understanding and identifying latency issues.

In recent years, SDN has gained massive attention in both academia and the industry. This emerging technology has been studied extensively in the literature [3, 10–12].

However, most of the work related to SDN that we have come across was based solely on experiments and simulations. Recently, theoretical analysis has been gaining attention [13–15]. A mathematical model can provide researchers with insights into how an OpenFlow architecture performs according to certain given parameters under given circumstances, thus leading to propose efficient algorithms. Therefore, we provide an analytical model based on results from the queueing theory of an OpenFlow-based mobile network. We restrict our analysis of the handover delay to target the delay caused by exchanging handover-related OpenFlow messages. We are, therefore, interested in minimizing the delay caused by the exchange of signaling messages between the control and data planes. To the best of our knowledge, no other work has modeled OpenFlow messages in relation to the handover procedure completion. In fact, our analysis provides a novel mathematical modeling for such messages. Consequently, we discuss two different mobility management approaches and their impacts on handover delay. Our model and results are verified through simulations, and we place emphasis on LTE as an example of cellular networks and show results based on experimentation in Section 6.

In general, SDN is assumed to be adopted in the backhaul/transport portion rather than the operation of a mobile network. In this paper, we try to link different aspects including OpenFlow-based SDN, queueing theory, cellular networks, and mobility management approaches. By linking theses aspects, we step forward to realize issues in the handover procedure in SDN-based mobile networks in general and LTE in particular. Hence, we discuss and compare different solutions.

This paper is structured as follows. Section 2 explores some of the related work. Section 3 describes our network model, including assumptions and limitations. We then go through our analytical model in Section 4. After that, we present our proposal in detail in Section 5. We then discuss our simulation results in Section 6. We finally conclude the paper with Section 7.

2. Related Work

In this section, we go through some papers that studied SDN-based solutions. We divide the analysis here into two parts: reviewing the papers that provided analytical models based on the queueing theory and the papers that provided mobility management solutions for cellular networks such as LTE.

2.1. Modeling OpenFlow Messages. The authors of [7] studied the causes for overall latency in SDN-based mobile core networks. They linked latency to two major factors: transmission delay and processing delay. Transmission delay is described as the time taken for the data to be transmitted between the controller and the switches; placement algorithms can play an important role here. Processing delay describes the delay within the controller or a switch. Marqueza et al. observed that the number of hops influences the increase in processing latency but that the real cause is buffering handling. They argued that the load of the connection requests plays a more significant role than the number of hops that need to be configured for each request. Regarding the processing delay, the authors suggested two strategies:

(1) To optimize the handling procedures of exchange of signaling messages in the OpenFlow channels between the controllers and switches

(2) To define forwarding mechanisms, which reduce the number of switches involved in configurations, in the data plane

In light of their results, we got motivated to investigate the theoretical aspects of the processing delay, which led us to develop an analytical model based on the queueing theory.

The author in [16] explored the challenges and benefits of using the queueing theory to model SDN. He presented several challenges in modeling SDN systems, for instance, the latencies imposed by moving data between different caches, resource contention among threads, interruptions triggered by hardware or software processes, and the implementation design of queues. Another challenge involved is the modeling of the finite capacity of a system and limited buffer size. However, most of the related works, as the author mentioned, have omitted these two challenges and have considered them infinite.

The work in [17] by Jarschel et al. is one of the initial attempts to model the OpenFlow-based interaction between a switch and a controller. The authors provided a performance model based on the queueing theory of an OpenFlow system. They derived some performance parameters in order to introduce an analytical model. To do so, they set up an OpenFlow testbed. They considered a feedback-oriented queueing system model, which was divided into a forwarding queue system, i.e., a switch, and a feedback queue system, i.e., a controller. Their model for the switch was based on a M/M queue and a $M/M - S$ for the feedback queue, meaning the queue size was infinite at the switch as opposed to finite queue size at the controller. Their model has some limitations; for instance, it captured only the interaction between a single node and the controller.

As Duan et al. showed in [9], the average delay relies on the flow table state within switches. They defined the average packet delay as the result of two kinds of delay. One is a delay within the switch if it has to forward to the controller. The other is a delay after the handover decision has been made, as the two switches that are involved in the process have to contact the controller to accomplish the handover. In their work, the authors provided an analytical framework to quantify the total packet delay in an SDN-based network in a centralized controller setting. They studied the single-node model in which they did not capture the handover control messaging exchanged between a switch and the controller.

In [18], the single-node model, where they modeled the feedback interaction between a switch and the controller, is also considered. They used the Jackson network to model the data plane with modifications to fit the nature of the traffic

flow in an OpenFlow-based network. The controller is modeled as an external entity based on a M/M queue. They assumed the Poisson distribution for arrival rates at both the switch and the controller and had exponential service rate in both. Their performance measures were the average packets sojourn time and the distribution of time spent by the packet.

In addition to using the queueing theory for evaluating SDN deployment, the authors of [19] provided an analytical modeling based on network calculus theory. They evaluated the SDN controller and switch in terms of delay and queue length. They provided the upper bound of packet processing delay of switches and the upper bound of the controller queue length. However, they did not consider the feedback between the switch and controller. Additionally, there were no simulation data recorded to validate their mathematical model.

Most of the literature works reviewed have modeled the single-node case, meaning they have modeled the interaction between one switch in the data plane and one controller. A downside to the single-node modeling is that it is an unrealistic modeling for such architectures. They omit the possibility of incoming flows from multiple switches, meaning that their input to the switch is inaccurate. To the best of our knowledge, the work in [20] by Mahmood et al. is the first that considered the multiple-node case, where more than one switch exists in the data plane. They extended their work in [18] to model OpenFlow *Packet-in* messages in the multiple node case. The authors presented an analytical model to estimate the packets' sojourn time and the density of the packets that can be pumped into the network. They studied both infinite and finite buffer size scenarios. However, their modeling did not consider the propagation delay. Even though this delay might be small, it is essential to be considered while modeling multiple nodes, where the propagation times may differ as the multiple nodes get placed in different locations. Moreover, another study that took into account modeling several switches interacting with one controller is shown in [14]. Shang et al. studied the impact of *Packet-in* messages on the performance of OpenFlow switches and controller. Additionally, they modeled switches as M/H_2, where the service rate follows a two-phase hyperexponential distribution, whereas the controller is modeled as M/M. They also showed that the performance of the network drops rapidly as the probability of *Packet-in* messages increases. They provided an analytical model; however, no simulation data were recorded.

In all the mentioned studies, the proposed models consider only the case of exchanging one kind of message, *Packet-ins*. However, based on our research direction, we need to incorporate another type of message that is tightly coupled with handover procedures, i.e., *Port-status* messages. Additionally, we need to consider the multiple node case.

2.2. Mobility Management Solutions for LTE. Through analyzing existing LTE architecture, one can find several proposals focusing on SDN for changing the current cellular network. Nguyen et al. in [21] gave a general view of challenges faced by LTE architecture: it is expensive to modify and upgrade the current system, it lacks the support of new network services and applications, and it generates ineffective management of existing network resources. They also provided a new way to fix the current LTE system by using SDN. The authors provided a potential possibility for changing the current cellular network to SDN and virtualization-based architecture.

Chourasia and Sivalingam in [22] revealed a possible solution for using SDN to replace existing LTE architecture. In this architecture, they proposed the use of a centralized controller that has a global view of the whole network, which makes the resources management easier. Based on their simulation results, this solution has outperformed existing LTE architecture in terms of signaling cost and handover latency. On the contrary, the work in [23] showed that physically centralized SDN has disadvantages; it limits the distribution of handover decisions and has scalability issues.

In [24], the authors discussed the mobility management of future cellular networks. They argued that the mobility management function should be distributed in order to handle an increasing load of data and support scalability of the system. They showcased three approaches for distributing mobility management: a PMIPv6-based approach, a routing-based approach, and an SDN-based approach. The first approach is based on Proxy Mobile IPv6 protocol. The idea here is to distribute mobility access gateways (MAGs), which work close with the local mobility anchor (LMA). The second approach works in a distributed way by removing existing anchors in the system. When users move to new locations, nodes in the system need to calculate new routing tables information. The last approach is based on the SDN concept; the controller in this approach configures rules for switches, which are working as distributed mobility management gateways.

Valtulina et al. in [25] elaborated on an SDN architecture that provides distributed core functions as entities in the network and uses cloud-computing technology to process network data. This architecture provides traffic redirection during the handover and can keep user's data transfer seamless using OpenFlow protocol. Moreover, Braun and Menth in [26] described the operation of OpenFlow and different aspects of SDN-based architecture design. For the control plane, they discussed the controller distribution as well as methods of signaling management.

3. Network Model

The communication between a switch and the controller takes place through the OpenFlow channel where only certain types of messages are standardized [27]. It is a bi-directional channel so that both parties can initiate messages. In OpenFlow v.1.3.1, from a switch to the controller, a switch may initiate either asynchronous messages or symmetric messages. The asynchronous messages include *Packet-in*, *Port-status*, *Flow-Removed*, and *Error* messages. The symmetric messages include *Hello*, *Echo*, and *Experimenter*

messages. These messages provide means to the controller to implement all kinds of functions, such as forwarding, filtering, blocking, etc., by configuring forwarding devices' flow tables. Note that we use the words switch, node, and forwarding device, interchangeably referring to the data plane devices, throughout this paper.

Regarding a *Packet-in* message, when a packet arrives at a switch, we have two cases. First, the packet has a flow entry that matches the packet's header, so it is forwarded based on matching fields. Second, the packet has no entry; then a *Packet-in* message is sent to the controller to obtain knowledge. The controller decides on the best forwarding path and updates relevant switches with new flow entries to be installed in their flow tables. Regarding a *Port-status* message, when a mobile node (MN) is disconnected from a switch, a *Port-status* message is initiated by that switch and sent to the controller. Similarly, when an MN is connected to a new switch, another *Port-status* message is initiated by the new switch and sent to the controller. Upon receiving a *Port-status* message, the controller updates some or all of the nodes with up-to-date entries about that MN.

To serve the purpose of our network, i.e., a mobile network, the two main messages that would frequently be sent by a switch are *Packet-in* and *Port-status*. However, the exchange of the rest of the messages is relatively small as they are either initiated upon the start up of the network or for testing purposes. Therefore, we considered analyzing the behavior of *Packet-in* and *Port-status* messages combined in our system.

We consider a network where hosts are connected to n OpenFlow switches. All of the OpenFlow switches are controlled by a centralized controller, C, which resides in a relatively remote location and has a global view. Our network is a typical OpenFlow-based network, where *Packet-in* messages are considered a cornerstone of its implementation.

In our network, any host can belong to one of two groups at time t. A group of hosts is connected to a switch, s_i, without attempting to handover while the other group is switching from one switch, s_i, to another, s_j. We refer to the hosts of the second group as mobile nodes (MNs). An MN handover requires two connection requests to the controller, one from its old switch and the other from its new switch, *off-port* and *on-port*, respectively. The movement of the MN from one location to another requires a clear configuration of all or multiple switches (i.e., sending out *Flow-mod* messages by C). Figure 1 gives a visual illustration of the exchange of messages between the switches and controller triggered by the mobility of a node.

In this section, we aim at quantifying the handover delay incurred due to the propagation of control messages between switches and controller as well as for processing and queueing those messages at the switches and controller.

3.1. Assumptions. We assume that every *off-port* message corresponds to an *on-port* message. Intuitively, the number of *off-port* messages equals the number of *on-port* messages; therefore, we can say that both kinds of control messages can

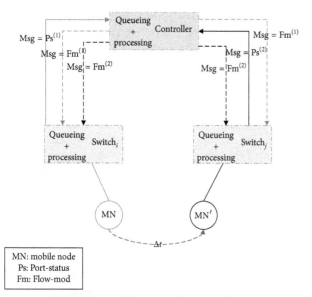

FIGURE 1: The exchange of messages between the switches and controller upon mobility.

be represented as *Port-status* message. We also assume that the controller has infinite buffer size, which means no packets are dropped. It is debatable whether or not this assumption can be adopted because, usually, controllers are equipped with huge resources that are virtually infinite but actually limited. However, for simplicity, we assume infinite queue size at the controller. We additionally assume infinite switches' queues in line with previous works [9, 13, 17, 28], as studying the impact of limited buffers and dropping packets rates are out of the scope of our analysis.

Regarding the handover calls distribution, the authors of [29, 30] have shown that they can be modeled as Poisson. Convinced by their validated results, we assumed that the occurrences of *Port-status* events follow the Poisson distribution. To put it another way, we argue that since the arrival rate of *Port-status* events are human-initiated, the interarrival and service times are independent and exponentially distributed and features the memoryless property. Additionally, in our modeling, we assumed that the service rates of all nodes were load-independent.

3.2. Model Description.

In this section, we start with modeling the *Port-status* messages; then we expand our model to include other types of messages that are essential in SDN-based networks, *Packet-in* message.

3.2.1. Modeling Port-Status Message.

Regarding handover, we consider analyzing the hard handover, i.e., break-before-make approach. Our analysis focuses on the process that follows a handover decision. When an MN is disconnected from one switch, say s_i, it gets attached to another switch, say s_j, where $i, j \in \{1, 2, \ldots, n\}$. This process triggers two asynchronous *Port-status* messages to update the controller of MN's movement. On the controller side, its network map has to be in an up-to-date state. Accordingly, the controller

initiates *Flow-mod* messages to all or some of the switches changing the flow entries of that MN.

A *Port-status* message generated by a switch can be either *off-port* or *on-port* message. Let us intuitively assume that the number of *off-port* messages in our network equals the number of *on-port* messages. Both types of *Port-status* messages are treated the same, but, of course, the controller can distinguish between them; therefore, we refer to both kinds of messages as one, *Port-status*.

In part, every *Port-status* message triggers three other messages: *Flow-mod* messages by C, another *Port-status* message by the new switch, and a second *Flow-mod* message by C upon receiving the new switch's message.

Based on the principles of modeling using the queueing theory, there are a set of parameters that need to be identified, including the arrival rate of requests, service time, the capacity of the system, the size of the source, and the service disciplines [31]. Taking into consideration our assumptions and using Kendall's notations [32] for queueing systems, the switches and the controller are modeled as M/M systems, where we assume that the queues are infinite and the service discipline is FIFO. We considered having an open queueing network where events can enter the system from outside and can also depart the network from any node. We additionally assumed a Markovian system, where a system's state is defined by the number of events (i.e., jobs) at nodes. If k_i is considered as the number of jobs at node i, then the state of the network is defined as $(k_1, k_2, \ldots, k_n)$. Note that throughout this paper, we use the words jobs and events interchangeably to refer to the buffered elements that need to be processed in a queue.

Now, let us assume that the arrival rate of *Port-status* messages initiated by a node i is λ_{ih}. Then, the flow of *Port-status* events captured by any node i is modeled as

$$\gamma_{ih} = \lambda_{ih}. \tag{1}$$

Note that a port can change from *on* to *off*, or a new port gets attached. Either way, the two events are treated alike.

Accordingly, Γ_{ih} is the total net arrival rate of port changes from the whole network to node i (Figure 2) and is given as follows:

$$\Gamma_{ih} = \gamma_{ih} + \sum_{j=1, j\neq i}^{n} \left(\lambda_{jh} \times v_j^i\right), \tag{2}$$

where $v_j^i \in \{0, 1\}$ is an indicator applied to model the effect of the *Port-status* message after being handled by the controller. If i's flow table has to be configured based on j's *Port-status* message, then $v_j^i = 1$; otherwise, $v_j^i = 0$. Note that some or all nodes may be configured by the controller upon receiving a *Port-status* message. Regarding the controller, Γ_{ch} is the total net arrival rate of *Port-status* messages at C and is given as follows:

$$\Gamma_{ch} = \sum_{i=1}^{n} \lambda_{ih}. \tag{3}$$

So far, our modeling includes only *Port-status* messages, meaning that we consider a single-class queueing network.

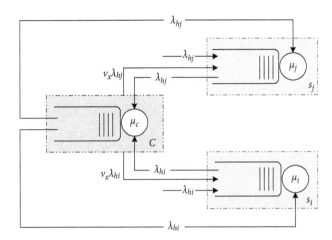

FIGURE 2: A queueing model of *Port-status* messages.

However, our model is extended in the following section and includes another type of message, *Packet-in*.

3.2.2. Multiclass Open Network Modeling.

When we model a network of queues where all the jobs are of the same type with regard to their service times and routing probabilities, then this is called a *single-class network*. If the network model, however, is extended to include multiple job classes, then it is called a *multiclass network*. In this extended model, different types of traffic can be combined in an open or closed setting [33]. In our case, so far, we have considered modeling the *Port-status* messages in a network, which is unrealistic. In any SDN-based network, *Packet-in* messages are essential. As has been shown by [27], other types of messages are exchanged between the data plane and the control plane for different purposes. However, in a mobile network, the most common two messages are *Packet-in* and *Port-status*. These two messages are treated differently, as illustrated in the flow chart in Figure 3. Therefore, our network is modeled as a *multiclass network*, where we restrict our analysis to the two types of messages.

To our queueing network that contains two job classes, we need to define the following symbols:

(i) R is the number of job classes, where in our network $R = 2$.

(ii) k_{ir} is the number of jobs of class r at node i, let $r = h$ if the intended class is *Port-status*, and $r = p$ if the class is *Packet-in*. Similarly, k_{cr} is the number of jobs of class r at the controller.

(iii) K is the number of jobs in different classes.

(iv) S_i is the state of node i, where $S_i = (k_{ih}, k_{ip})$. Similarly, S_c represents the state of C.

(v) S is the overall state of the network with multiple jobs where the state probability is represented by $\pi(S_1, S_2, \ldots, S_n)$. Note that the sum of the probabilities of all states should be one since we assume stability in the system.

(vi) μ_{ir} is the service rate of node i for the job class r. In our network, we have μ_{ip}, which represents the

service rate at a switch for *Packet-in* messages, while μ_{ih} is the service rate for *Port-status* messages. In our model, we assume $\mu_{ip} = \mu_{ih}$. Similarly, μ_{cr} is used to represent the service rates for the two messages at C.

(vii) λ_{ir} is the arrival rate of job class r at node i, so λ_{ir} is either λ_{ip} or λ_{ih}.

(viii) Γ_{ir} and Γ_{cr} represent the traffic of class r at node i and C, respectively, and they are both functions of λ_{ir} and λ_{ip}.

So far, we have defined the parameters of modeling the *Port-status* message in the previous section. Now, we define *Packet-in* message parameters in addition to the aforementioned parameters. Let the arrival rate of packets, in general, to a node i be λ_{ip}. Then, the probability of a *Packet-in* message to be sent to the controller from node i is q_i^{nf}, which means there is no flow entry regarding that packet. On the contrary, in case a switch matches an entry for incoming packets, our modeling should include the traffic between nodes. Therefore, the probability between any two nodes i and j is p_{ij}. At any node i, the flow of input packets can be modeled as

$$\gamma_{ip} = \lambda_{ip} + \sum_{j=1, j \neq i}^{n} p_{ij} \gamma_{jp}. \tag{4}$$

Then, the total net arrival rate of packets, excluding *Port-status* messages, is given as

$$\Gamma_{ip} = \gamma_{ip} + q_i^{nf} \lambda_{ip} + \sum_{j=1, j \neq i}^{n} \left(q_j^{nf} \times u_j^i \right) \lambda_{jp}, \tag{5}$$

where $u_j^i \in \{0, 1\}$ is an indicator of whether a flow has to be routed between i and j or not, as used in [20]. Using this indicator, the updates the controller sends to all or a subset of the nodes upon receiving *Packet-in* are included. Accordingly, the arrival rate of *Packet-in* messages to the controller is given as

$$\Gamma_{cp} = \sum_{i=1}^{n} q_i^{nf} \lambda_{ip}. \tag{6}$$

3.3. Limitations.

Here, we list the limitations of our model. Firstly, we modeled the controller and switches as a single queue and not per interface. Also, we did not consider the case of dropped packets at either the controller or switches due to overload, which goes in line with our assumptions that we have infinite queue sizes.

OpenFlow protocol has different message types to be exchanged between a switch and the controller, and in our model, we only focused on two types of messages that are the most frequent messages in the networks we studied, i.e., *Port-status* and *Packet-in* messages. Moreover, we assumed TCP traffic only, meaning only the header of the first packet of each new flow is sent to the controller, in contrast to UDP traffic, where the incoming packets of a new flow are relayed to the controller until the associated flow entry is installed.

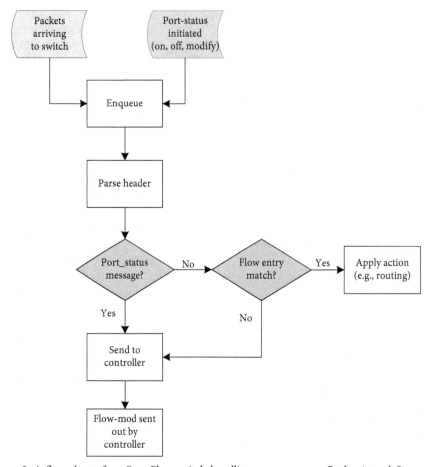

FIGURE 3: A flow chart of an OpenFlow switch handling two messages, *Packet-in* and *Port-status*.

4. Performance Measures

In this section, based on our model, the goal is to quantify the handover delay that occurs as a result of exchanging OpenFlow-related messages. It is imperative to distinguish between three main delays: waiting time, sojourn time, and total delay. The waiting time is the time an event spends in a queue at node i with respect to class r. However, the sojourn time, T_{ir}, is the time an event spends at node i, including the time it is being serviced. Regarding our main metric, the total time, D_{tot}, is the time an MN experiences before completing the handover procedure as it will be discussed in further detail in this section.

Let W_i^c be the time of interaction between node i and C upon a *Port-status* event, triggered by s_i. Then, W_i^c can be defined as

$$W_i^c = T_{ih} + T_{i(\text{prop})}^c + \max\left\{T_{x(\text{prop})}^c\right\} + T_{ch}. \tag{7}$$

Note that $T_{i(\text{prop})}^c$ is the time for propagating a *Port-status* message from s_i to C, given that the T_{prop} between the controller and all switches are assumed to have the same link parameters. In OpenFlow design, the controller reacts to a *Port-status* message by sending out a *Flow-mod* message to all or a subset of switches in parallel. In other words, C sends reactive *Flow-mod* message(s) to switches in parallel, which may take roughly the propagation time required to reach the

furthest switch; hence, we define the maximum propagation time as

$$\max\left\{T_{x(\text{prop})}^c\right\} \text{ where } x \in \{1, 2, \ldots, n\} \text{ and } x \neq i. \tag{8}$$

Then, the expected value of W_i^c can be further written as

$$E[W_i^c] = E[T_{ih}] + T_{i(\text{prop})}^c + \max\left\{T_{x(\text{prop})}^c\right\} + E[T_{ch}]. \tag{9}$$

Based on the above explanation of how the controller handles *Port-status* messages, we infer that to complete the handover procedure of an MN, the total delay experienced by that MN is

$$D_{\text{tot}} = W_i^c + W_j^c, \tag{10}$$

where W_i^c represents the time of an *off-port* message handled by an old switch s_i, and W_j^c represents the time of an *on-port* message handled by a new switch s_j. This yields to

$$D_{\text{tot}} = E[T_{ih}] + T_{\text{prop}} + E[T_{jh}] + E[T_{ch}] + E[T_{ch}^{(2)}], \tag{11}$$

where

$$T_{\text{prop}} = T_{i(\text{prop})}^c + \max\left\{T_{x(\text{prop})}^c\right\} + T_{j(\text{prop})}^c + \max\left\{T_{y(\text{prop})}^c\right\}$$

$$\text{and } x \neq i, y \neq j.$$

$$\tag{12}$$

Note that $T_{\text{ch}}^{(2)}$ represents the sojourn time of an *on-port* message at the controller. We distinguish the two times because they are independent.

To find the mean response time of a *Port-status* event, we use the Mean Value Analysis (MVA) solution. MVA has been introduced as an iterative technique to obtain an exact solution for some performance measures including sojourn times in separable queueing networks. However, the MVA's original version was proposed for closed networks only. In 1981, Zahorjan and Wong in [15] presented the MVA solutions for open and mixed networks. Note that we are in line with their assumptions, which are the existence of a FIFO queueing discipline and a single server. In this section, we use their findings to compute our performance measures of interest. The MVA for open queueing networks depends on two theorems, Little's theorem [34] and the arrival instant theorem [35]. Therefore, we consider the Poisson Arrivals See Time Averages (PASTA) property of Poisson arrivals, which indicates that in a network in statistical equilibrium, the time averages equal the arrival averages [36]; hence, the sojourn time can be formulated as

$$E[T_{ih}] = \frac{1}{\mu_i}\left(1 + \left(E[K_{ip}] + E[K_{ih}]\right)\right). \quad (13)$$

As proven by [15], for any two classes, in our case h and p, the following relation is satisfied:

$$E[K_{ih}] = \frac{\rho_{ih}}{\rho_{ip}}E[K_{ip}], \quad (14)$$

where ρ_{ih} and ρ_{ip} are the utilization of node i with respect to *Port-status* and *Packet-in* messages, respectively. As we mentioned in our model description, the utilization is load-independent.

With the help of Little's theory, $E[K] = \lambda.E[T]$, and by substituting it in the previous equations, we get

$$E[K_{ih}] = \frac{\rho_{ih}}{1 - \left(\rho_{ip} + \rho_{ih}\right)}. \quad (15)$$

Similarly, the previous equation is applied to find the controller's response time regarding *Port-status* messages.

So far, based on our assumption, and the findings and theories of previous works, we formulated the expected response time of a handover procedure in an OpenFlow-based network. However, there is a constraint that needs to be satisfied for our model to work. The utilization of queues has to be less than unity. Let ρ_i and ρ_c represent the total utilization of switch i and controller C, respectively; then, $\rho_i < 1$ and $\rho_c < 1$, given the following:

$$\rho_i = \rho_{ih} + \rho_{ip}. \quad (16)$$

Similarly, ρ_c is defined.

5. Proposed Approach

As authors in [9] showed, an SDN-based solution is more suitable for "less-sensitive" to latency applications. However, mobility management applications are latency-sensitive. In fact, there are two salient factors that contribute to increased latency, transmission delay, and processing delay [7]. Therefore, we need to configure an SDN-based solution that minimizes handover latency in terms of transmission and processing delays.

5.1. Main Idea. In our approach, we aim at targeting the two aforementioned contributors. Firstly, we need to minimize processing latency, and to do so, we propose offloading handover handling to dedicated entities that are separate from our controller and switches. We call these entities Mobility Handling Entity (MHE). Secondly, we aim at minimizing transmission latency by placing the MHE physically closer to switches. Essentially, by offloading the burden of handling *Port-status* messages to entities other than the controller, we efficiently minimize latency. In short, the role of each element in our solution is as follows:

(i) Controller: it maintains the information of all devices in the network, MHEs, OpenFlow switches, etc. Mainly, it has the global view.

(ii) Mobility Handling Entity (MHE): MHEs are placed physically close to switches and handle handover procedures asynchronously with the controller.

(iii) OpenFlow switch: switches focus on keeping data flowing from the source to the target. They are managed by the controller through the OpenFlow protocol. They exchange commands with the controller to perform several tasks, such as updating the flow table, triggering *Port-status* messages, and other stats-related messages.

In our solution, the functionality of handling handover is installed on MHEs to allow them to work asynchronously with the controller. In this case, the controller has to maintain specific information about MHEs in the network. Each MHE is associated with a table of four columns, MHE_ID, MHE_IP, Status, and Update_Time. MHE_ID and MHE_IP are used to locate a specific MHE. The Status is used to indicate whether that MHE is "active" or "inactive." Lastly, the Update_Time marks the time an MHE gets updated by the controller. As for the switches, we assume that they exchange handover-related messages with MHEs through OpenFlow channels. Therefore, in our approach, MHEs are considered SDN-controllers with limited functionality and a specific task.

5.2. Proposed EPC Controller Architecture. In this section, we apply the proposed solution to a cellular network where mobile nodes are connected to eNodeBs, assuming that every eNodeB is connected to an OpenFlow switch. All OpenFlow switches are controlled by a centralized controller that resides in a relatively remote location and, so, has a global view; thus, it governs the handover procedure. Additionally, we consider a hard handover, which is in practice in LTE systems. Our preliminary work on this setting has been published in [37].

As previously stated, the handover signaling latency can be reduced by minimizing the processing and transmission delays of managing entities [7]. Therefore, we presented our proposed solution in the LTE setting, where we assigned entities that have to be responsible for handover messages. Thus, we distributed the functionality of the EPC controller. Our proposed EPC controller architecture enables multiple functional entities to work in conjunction with the controller, which operate as MME and other handover-related functions (Figure 4). With proper routing information from the controller, these entities can work asynchronously to handle handover in the network. Using these functional entities, we can potentially reduce the workload of the controller and make the handover process more efficient and the system more scalable.

Different from the centralized EPC controller architecture proposed by [22], our proposed EPC controller architecture divides the traditional controller into a basic controller and multiple MHEs. Hence, the control plane functionality is not exclusive to the controller. MHEs serve functions such as MME, S-GW, and P-GW combined. They are placed physically close to eNodeBs and perform handover procedures asynchronously with the controller. The protocol of our proposed solution is illustrated in Figure 5(b) as opposed to the protocol proposed by [22] in Figure 5(a).

6. Numerical Results and Analysis

In this section, we divide our analysis into four directions. Firstly, we verify and validate our analytical model by comparing its results to a conducted simulation experiment output. Secondly, we evaluate and analyze our proposed solution in more detail. Thirdly, we summarize our results published in [37]. Lastly, we discuss some implementation issues in SDN-based LTE systems that need to be addressed.

6.1. Verifying Analytical Model. An experiment was conducted to compare the simulation results to our analytical model results. We have developed a discrete event simulator using Matlab, and our simulation parameters are listed in Table 1. For the value of q^{nf}, Jarschel et al. in [17] showed that in a production network, the probability of *Packet-in* messages is 4%. We also borrowed some of the measurements in [17], such as the service rates of controller and switches. The size of OpenFlow messages are mentioned in [27]. We needed the sizes to determine the transmission and total delays based on our assumptions of the link type and speed, as listed below.

For the arrival rates of *Port-status* and *Packet-in*, we used the aforementioned values and substituted them in the following equations.

$$\rho_c = \frac{\Gamma_{cp} + \Gamma_{ch}}{\mu_c}, \quad (17)$$

$$\rho_i = \frac{\Gamma_{ip} + \Gamma_{ih}}{\mu_i}. \quad (18)$$

By equating Equations (17) and (18) at load ≈ 1, we got values of λ_{ip} and λ_{ih}. Note that λ_{ih} has to be much smaller than λ_{ip} in practice.

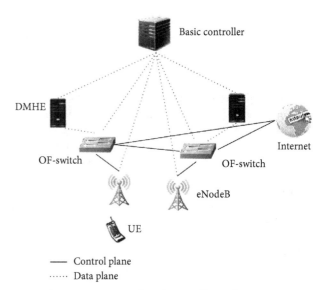

FIGURE 4: Proposed EPC controller architecture.

Our comparison of the simulation results and the analytical computations shows similar trends that start and end almost the same, as depicted in Figure 6. Additionally, they both show a rapid increase in delay around load = 0.7, which is expected. However, the divergence that occurs around load = 0.3 can be contributed to the simulation running time and/or hardware specifications.

After gaining confidence in our simulation setup, we carry out our analysis in the following section.

6.2. Evaluating Proposed Approach. To show the difference that an MHE causes, we simulated the response time *Port-status* messages experience in two approaches: a network of queues excluding MHE and a network of queues including MHE. Note that our network of queues consists of one switch, one controller, and an offloading entity in the second topology. Initially, we compared the two topologies when both MHE and *C* have the same processing time, which is considered the worst-case scenario regarding MHE's service rate. As depicted in Figure 7, the response time drops tremendously in the case where MHE handles the *Port-status* messages.

MHEs are entities assigned by the network designer to handle *Port-status* messages separately from the controller for the sole purpose of decreasing the time that a handover procedure may take. Those entities can be designed to be separate queues in the controller or can be separate physical devices that can be placed anywhere in between the controller and the switches. Additionally, they can be given different service rates to indicate different capabilities. Therefore, we break down our analysis in the following part into the impact of different service rates and the impact of physical placement.

6.2.1. Impact of Different Service Rates. MHEs' design is determined by the network operator. In this part, we try to give different options and analyze their impacts.

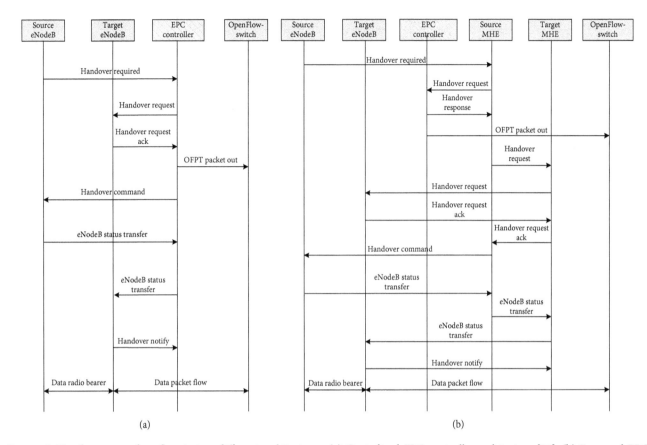

FIGURE 5: Handover procedure flow in two different architectures. (a) Centralized EPC controller architecture [22]. (b) Proposed EPC controller architecture.

TABLE 1: Simulation parameters.

Parameter	Value
Probability to send *Packet-in* to controller q^{nf}	0.04 (4%)
Average service time of the controller	= 240 μs
Average service time of a switch	= L9.8 μs
Size of *Packet-in* message	128 B
Size of *Port-status* message	128 B
Size of *Flow-mod* message	128 B
Distance between switches and controller	1–5 kms
Links between switches and controller	Optical
Link speed	1 Gbps

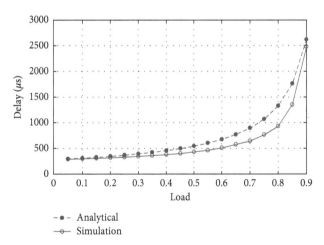

FIGURE 6: The simulation and analytical model results.

As a matter of fact, the service rate plays an important role in queues' processing times. As we are adding MHEs, we have the freedom to choose the service rate. However, we will compare three service time values, 9.8 μs, 240 μs, and 125 μs. We deliberately chose those three values. We wanted to see the impact of having an MHE with a service time as fast as that of the switch (i.e., 9.8 μs). Then, we studied the impact of having a service time as slow as that of the controller (i.e., 240 μs). Lastly, we suggested a service time value that is in between the two aforementioned values (i.e., 125 μs). Intuitively, the impact is quite obvious, as depicted in Figure 8. Based on the purpose and resources that are available, the network designer has to determine a suitable service rate.

6.2.2. Impact of Physical Placement. In networking systems, delivery time can be broken down into transmission time and propagation delay. The transmission delay represents the time from the beginning until the end of a message transmission, so it is correlated with the packet size and the bit rate of the medium. The propagation delay is the time the first bit takes to travel from a source to a destination, and therefore, it depends on the physical medium as well as the distance separating the correspondents. In our analysis, we

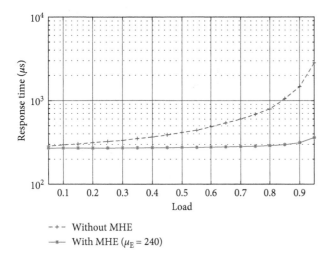

FIGURE 7: Comparing *Port-status* response time of a model with MHE to a model without MHE.

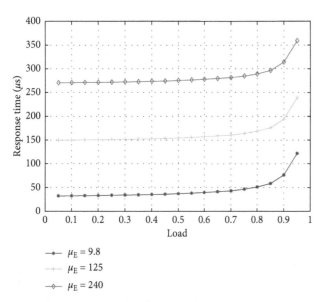

FIGURE 8: Response time of MHE with different service rates.

assumed 1 Gbps optical links over 1 to 5 km distance. We found that in this setting, the difference between 1 km and 5 km is a matter of microseconds. Therefore, we argue that the location of MHEs in our setup does not have much impact on the total delay, so the entities can be placed in convenient locations whether within the controller unit or physically separate in a particular place. However, using different link parameters may have an apparent impact on transmission latency.

6.3. Preliminary Results.

We conducted a comparative analysis between the centralized EPC controller [22] and our proposed EPC controller architectures [37]. This was undertaken with the widely used discrete event simulator NS3 [38]. In our experiment, we utilized the available cellular network modules and OpenFlow to simulate LTE functions in SDN architecture. By analyzing the handover latency and

average throughput per user, we aimed at showing the performance of these two different architectures under certain circumstances.

6.3.1. Handover Latency. The handover latency measures the time that elapses from the time the source eNodeB sends the handover request to the controller or to another handover-handling entity until it receives the handover notification from target eNodeB. In order to achieve an overall comparison of the two architectures in terms of the handover latency, we generated UDP packets for each link from one end to the other with different occupancy percentages of background traffic to simulate a real-life environment. We took three scenarios into consideration: the idle network as 30% of background traffic, the standard network as 50%, and the busy network as 70%. In each simulation, we made mobile nodes handover from source eNodeB to target eNodeB and generated the sum of the latency of all MNs. As shown in Figure 9, for both architectures, the handover latency increased along with the growing background traffic from 30% to 70%, whereas the proposed EPC controller architecture continuously outperformed the centralized EPC controller architecture with smaller handover latency under the same background traffic. In standard traffic conditions, our architecture experienced 20% less handover latency than the centralized architecture. However, in busy networks (i.e., 70%), the performance of both architectures degraded in terms of handover latency. Regardless, these results indicate that our proposed EPC controller architecture has better performance when dealing with handover under the same circumstances.

6.3.2. Average Throughput per User. The average throughput is a critically important metric that measures the system usability and scalability. It can be calculated using the following formula:

$$V_T = \frac{B}{(T \cdot n)}, \tag{19}$$

where V_T is the average throughput per user, B represents the total bytes successfully delivered, while T represents the time that elapses during the reception of the data, and n represents the number of users in the system. We set 20% of the users to perform handover while simulating a real-life environment. Each MN sent 5 packets per second to a remote host, and the size of each packet was 38 bytes. After recording the data, Equation (19) is applied to calculate the average throughput per user. As shown in Figure 10, for the same number of users in each system, we can see that our proposed EPC controller architecture had greater value on throughput over centralized EPC controller architecture. With a growing number of users, the average throughput for proposed EPC controller architecture decreased as it did for the centralized EPC controller architecture. Nonetheless, our proposed EPC still outperformed the centralized EPC under each user category. These results indicate that the proposed EPC controller architecture can provide better data service for each user under the same conditions.

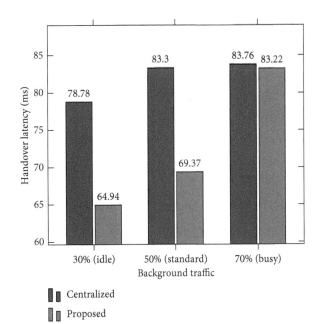

FIGURE 9: Handover latency under different traffic conditions.

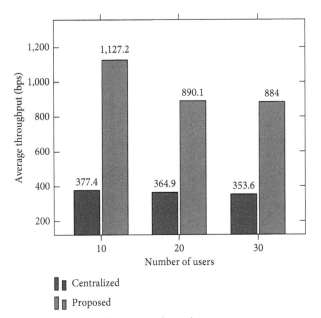

FIGURE 10: Average throughput per user.

In part, the proposed functionality-distributed EPC controller architecture sacrifices the general view held by the MHEs and may potentially increase the operational cost. However, it has distinct advantages in the areas of handover latency and carries a higher average throughput per user when compared to the centralized EPC controller architecture. As a result, this is a better option for service providers who prefer low handover latency and a high average throughput per user of the system.

6.4. Implementation Issues. According to the specifications of OpenFlow v.1.3.1, a switch initiates a *Port-status* message

if a port was added, a port was removed, or an attribute of a port has changed. In our case, the switches have to send *Port-status* messages upon the connection/disconnection of mobile nodes. Note that, in our system, MNs are connected to eNodeBs and not directly connected to the OpenFlow switches. Therefore, the current deployment of SDN-based LTE systems should be modified to enable direct linking between MNs' mobility and the switches. To overcome this challenge, one option, which we assumed in our simulation, is to embed the OpenFlow switches in the eNodeBs to make the OpenFlow switch's interfaces connected directly to MNs. Another option is to make adaptations and modifications to the OpenFlow protocol. For this option, the modification should allow interpreting connection/disconnection alerts from eNodeBs into *Port-status* messages in the switches.

7. Conclusion

It is important to model the OpenFlow controller to switch interaction in terms of the two kinds of messages that are commonly used in mobile networks. Indeed, this modeling helps us better understand the underlying causes of handover delay and then helps us propose effective methods to minimize it. In this model, we have modeled two OpenFlow messages: *Packet-in* and *Port-status* in a multiclass open network. We have modeled each message independently since they are two different traffic and need to be treated differently by the controller. Our aim has been to quantify the handover delay incurred due to queueing, processing, and propagating handover control messaging between switches and the controller. Then, we have proposed off-loading the mission of handling *Port-status* messages to separate entities in order to overcome some of the short-comings of the SDN paradigm. Our solution has been validated and evaluated in simulation and applied to an LTE system. We have performed a comparative analysis of a centralized EPC controller architecture and our proposed functionality-distributed EPC controller architecture in the LTE setting. We then have studied two main metrics, handover latency and average throughput per user. Simulations have shown that the proposed EPC controller architecture has better performance in both metrics as compared to the centralized approach, under the same network conditions. Therefore, we argue that the distributed mobility management approach can benefit the handover handling.

In effect, OpenFlow-based SDN and mobile networks as well as distributed mobility management approaches have been extensively discussed in the past but so far not materialized into actual 3GPP networks. SDN is assumed to be applied for the backhaul services rather than directly involved in the operation of a mobile network. In this paper, we have tried to fill in that gap and propose a solution that increases handover efficiency, especially in highly dynamic networks.

For future work, we will tackle some of the limitations mentioned in our queueing model and attempt to improve the proposed solution. Moreover, we plan to extend our work to study other forms of distributing mobility management such as the multicontroller scenario.

References

[1] ONF Solution, *Openflow-Enabled Mobile and Wireless Networks*, white paper, 2013.

[2] N. McKeown, T. Anderson, H. Balakrishnan et al., "Open-Flow," *ACM SIGCOMM Computer Communication Review*, vol. 38, no. 2, pp. 69–74, 2008.

[3] B. A. A. Nunes, M. Mendonca, X.-N. Nguyen, K. Obraczka, and T. Turletti, "A survey of software-defined networking: past, present, and future of programmable networks," *IEEE Communications Surveys & Tutorials*, vol. 16, no. 3, pp. 1617–1634, 2014.

[4] Open Networking Foundation, https://www.opennetworking.org/sdn-resources/openflow.

[5] Cisco Blogs, https://blogs.cisco.com/news/aci-anywhere.

[6] Cisco visual networking index: Global mobile data traffic forecast update, 2016–2021, White Paper, 2017.

[7] C. Marquezan, X. An, Z. Despotovic, R. Khalili, and A. Hecker, "Identifying latency factors in sdn-based mobile core networks," in *Proceedings of Symposium on Computers and Communication*, pp. 484–491, Messina, Italy, June 2016.

[8] K. Tantayakul, R. Dhaou, and B. Paillassa, "Impact of sdn on mobility management," in *Proceedings of 30th International Advanced Information Networking and Applications Conference*, pp. 260–265, Crans-Montana, Switzerland, March 2016.

[9] X. Duan, A. Akhtar, and X. Wang, "Software-defined networking-based resource management: data offloading with load balancing in 5g hetnet," *EURASIP Journal on Wireless Communications and Networking*, vol. 2015, no. 1, p. 181, 2015.

[10] H. Farhady, H. Lee, and A. Nakao, "Software-defined networking: a survey," *Computer Networks*, vol. 81, pp. 79–95, 2015.

[11] N. Feamster, J. Rexford, and E. Zegura, "The road to sdn: an intellectual history of programmable networks," *ACM SIGCOMM Computer Communication Review*, vol. 44, no. 2, pp. 87–98, 2014.

[12] D. Kreutz, F. Ramos, P. Verissimo, C. Rothenberg et al., "Software-defined networking: a comprehensive survey," *Proceedings of the IEEE*, vol. 103, no. 1, pp. 14–76, 2015.

[13] B. Xiong, K. Yang, J. Zhao, W. Li, and K. Li, "Performance evaluation of openflow-based software-defined networks based on queueing model," *Computer Networks*, vol. 102, pp. 172–185, 2016.

[14] Z. Shang and K. Wolter, "Delay evaluation of openflow network based on queueing model," http://arxiv.org/abs/1608.06491, 2016.

[15] J. Zahorjan and E. Wong, "The solution of separable queueing network models using mean value analysis," in *Proceedings of ACM SIGMETRICS Performance Evaluation Review*, pp. 80–85, Las Vegas, NV, USA, September 1981.

[16] C. Thieme, "Challenges for modelling of software-based packet processing in commodity-hardware using queueing theory," *Network*, vol. 49, 2017.

[17] M. Jarschel, S. Oechsner, D. Schlosser et al., "Modeling and performance evaluation of an openflow architecture," in *Proceedings of The 23rd International Teletraffic Congress*, pp. 1–7, San Francisco, CA, USA, September 2011.

[18] K. Mahmood, A. Chilwan, O. Østerbø, and M. Jarschel, "On the modeling of openflow-based sdns: the single node case," http://arxiv.org/abs/1411.4733, 2014.

[19] S. Azodolmolky, R. Nejabati, M. Pazouki et al., "An analytical model for software defined networking: a network calculus-based approach," in *Proceedings of Global Communications Conference*, pp. 1397–1402, Atlanta, GA, USA, December 2013.

[20] K. Mahmood, A. Chilwan, O. Østerbø, and M. Jarchel, "Modelling of openflow-based software-defined networks: the multiple node case," *IET Networks*, vol. 4, no. 5, pp. 278–284, 2015.

[21] V. Nguyen, T. Do, and Y. Kim, "Sdn and virtualization-based lte mobile network architectures: a comprehensive survey," *Wireless Personal Communications*, vol. 86, no. 3, pp. 1401–1438, 2016.

[22] S. Chourasia and K. Sivalingam, "Sdn-based evolved packet core architecture for efficient user mobility support," in *Proceedings of first IEEE Network Softwarization Conference*, pp. 1–5, London, UK, 2015.

[23] S. Kukliński, Y. Li, and K. Dinh, "Handover management in sdn-based mobile networks," in *Proceedings of Global Communications Conference Workshops*, pp. 194–200, Austin, TX, USA, December 2014.

[24] F. Giust, L. Cominardi, and C. Bernardos, "Distributed mobility management for future 5g networks: overview and analysis of existing approaches," *IEEE Communications Magazine*, vol. 53, no. 1, pp. 142–149, 2015.

[25] L. Valtulina, M. Karimzadeh, G. Karagiannis, G. Heijenk, and A. Pras, "Performance evaluation of a sdn/openflow-based distributed mobility management (dmm) approach in virtualized lte systems," in *Proceedings of Global Communications Conference Workshops*, pp. 18–23, Austin, TX, USA, December 2014.

[26] W. Braun and M. Menth, "Software-defined networking using openflow: protocols, applications and architectural design choices," *Future Internet*, vol. 6, no. 2, pp. 302–336, 2014.

[27] Open Networking Foundation, "Openflow switch specification version 1.3.1," Tech. Rep., 2012.

[28] L. Yao, P. Hong, and W. Zhou, "Evaluating the controller capacity in software defined networking," in *Proceedings of 23rd International Computer Communication and Networks Conference*, pp. 1–6, Shanghai, China, August 2014.

[29] Y. Kirsal and O. Gemikonakli, "Performability modelling of handoff in wireless cellular networks with channel failures and recovery," in *Proceedings of 11th International Computer Modelling and Simulation Conference*, pp. 544–547, Melbourne, Australia, January 2009.

[30] E. Chlebus and W. Ludwin, "Is handoff traffic really poissonian?," in *Proceedings of Fourth International Universal Personal Communications Conference*, pp. 348–353, Tokyo, Japan, November 1995.

[31] J. Sztrik, *Basic Queueing Theory: Foundations of System Performance Modeling*, GlobeEdit, Riga, Latvia, European Union, 2016.

[32] D. Kendall, "Some problems in the theory of queues," *Journal of the Royal Statistical Society*, vol. 13, pp. 151–185, 1951.

[33] G. Bloch, S. Greiner, H. de Meer, and K. Trivedi, *Queuing networks and Markov chains: Modeling and performance evaluation with computer science applications*, John Wiley & Sons, 2006.

[34] J. Little, "A proof of the queueing formula: L=λw," *Operations Research*, vol. 9, no. 3, pp. 383–387, 1961.

[35] R. Muntz, *Poisson departure processes and queueing networks*, IBM Thomas J. Watson Research Center, 1972.

[36] R. Wolff, "Poisson arrivals see time averages," *Operations Research*, vol. 30, no. 2, pp. 223–231, 1982.

[37] M. Alotaibi and A. Nayak, "A distributed approach to improving epc controller performance," in *Proceedings of 86th Vehicular Technology Conference*, pp. 1–6, Toronto, Canada, September 2017.

[38] Ns-3 tutorial, 2013, https://www.nsnam.org/docs/release/3.17/tutorial/singlehtml/index.html.

12

Reliable and Energy Efficient Protocol for MANET Multicasting

Bander H. AlQarni and Ahmad S. AlMogren

Computer Science Department, College of Computer and Information Sciences, King Saud University,
P.O. Box 51178, Riyadh 11543, Saudi Arabia

Correspondence should be addressed to Bander H. AlQarni; alqarni.bander@gmail.com

Academic Editor: Tzonelih Hwang

A mobile *ad hoc* network (MANET) consists of a self-configured set of portable mobile nodes without any central infrastructure to regulate traffic in the network. These networks present problems such as lack of congestion control, reliability, and energy consumption. In this paper, we present a new model for MANET multicasting called Reliable and Energy Efficient Protocol Depending on Distance and Remaining Energy (REEDDRE). Our proposal is based on a tone system to provide more efficiency and better performance, and it combines solutions over the Medium Access Control (MAC) layer. The protocol consists of a new construction method for mobile nodes using a clustering approach that depends on distance and remaining energy to provide more stability and to reduce energy consumption. In addition, we propose an adjustment to the typical multicast flow by adding unicast links between clusters. We further present in our model a technique to provide more reliability based on a busy tone system (RMBTM) to reduce excessive control overhead caused by control packets in error recovery. We simulate our proposal using OPNET, and the results show enhancement in terms of reliability, packet delivery ratio (PDR), energy consumption, and throughput.

1. Introduction

Nowadays, most organizations and companies make their services available on the Internet so that they may be reached by many different users. In contrast, if multiple users ask for a service, it is better to use multicast transmission in order to save time and effort. By using the broadcast nature of wireless transmission, a multicast can be used to improve the efficiency of a network by sending a number of copies instead of sending one copy individually; this may reduce the communications cost of applications that use multicast instead of unicast.

A great number of current applications require a reliable multicast scheme, meaning that one sender must ensure data delivery to multiple receivers; this may sometimes be hard to do, especially in a wireless environment. Wireless environments may suffer from packet loss more frequently than wired environments, but such losses still happen in both environments. By using multicast transmission, we can reduce the consumption of links' bandwidth and reduce the time for using these links.

A mobile *ad hoc* network is a combination of moving mobile nodes that form a temporary network without support from any centralized admission or infrastructure such as access points or base stations. The term *ad hoc* is of Latin origin and means "for this purpose," which in this case signifies that the network exists for special circumstances and is dismantled easily (on-the-spot) [1].

In MANETs, all moving nodes coordinate among themselves to enable communication and to manage routing and resources; this is done in a distributed manner. This means that each node in the MANET must be more intelligent, so that it can operate as a sender for transmitting messages, can receive data from another master sender that received the original message, and can work as a router for forwarding packets to other nodes [2].

MANETs work in a highly dynamic and distributed nature, and nodes are mostly battery powered and have a limited power source; thus, energy consumption is a key issue in MANETs, sometimes causing failures in a node that can affect the whole network. If one node runs out of power, the probability of network separation will increase; therefore, to prolong the lifetime of the MANET, we need to consider energy efficient ways to reduce the consumption of network energy, such as announcing the remaining energy of a node, which will avoid depletion of energy and reduce the probability of network separation [1].

This paper is organized as follows. Section 2 discusses MANET multicasting issues and challenges. In Section 3, we build a tree-based clustering approach for construction of a network depending on distance and remaining energy (REEDDRE) to reduce energy consumption. In Section 4, we present a model called RMBTM for providing reliability in a MANET and we report its architecture and description. In Section 5, we list the simulation results. Finally, we present the conclusion in Section 6.

2. MANET Multicasting: Challenges and Issues

Issues and challenges presented by MANET multicasting include the following [2–10].

2.1. Resource Management. Mobile nodes in MANETs are limited in resources such as power and memory, so a multicast protocol minimizes the consumption of these resources and utilizes them in such a manner as to ensure competent handling of information with efficient resource consumption, such as by minimizing the use of state information packets.

2.2. Link Failure. Because of the random mobility of the nodes and the wireless nature of links, link stability is hard to preserve in mobile *ad hoc* networks.

2.3. Control Overhead. In multicast transmission, we need to keep track of the members involved in the multicast transmission; thus, we need control packets to be exchanged between them. Since only limited bandwidth is provided in MANETs, this may result in significant overhead requirements, so the design of MANET should take into consideration the need to keep the control packet size to a minimum.

2.4. Efficiency. In MANETs, errors and failure are more likely to happen than in ordinary networks due to their mobility and limited bandwidth. Therefore, in the multicast protocol design, efficiency is very important. Efficiency as used here is the ratio of received data to the total number of transmitted packets in the network.

2.5. Reliability. Reliability is the key issue in multicast transmissions in MANETs, and this can be difficult to deliver due to the differentiation in the members involved and the fact that any member can disconnect from the network at any time, in consideration of its environmental conditions.

2.6. Wireless Nature. The wireless nature of a MANET makes it vulnerable to the numerous types of attacks that are common to wireless links such as snooping, interference, and eavesdropping, which may also affect the network resources. Attackers can use these methods to prevent the normal

communication scenario among nodes or to capture valuable information.

2.7. No Defined Physical Boundary. Due to mobility, we cannot define exactly the boundaries of our network, and the nodes can join or leave the network because of radio coverage. The scalability of MANETs is changing, so the security mechanism must be able to handle large networks as well as smaller networks, which makes for a difficult task.

2.8. Absence of Centralized Management. Detection of possible attacks is difficult due to the absence of centralized management such as an access point or base station that can monitor the traffic in a MANET, especially if the network is deployed over a large scale, which may delay the trust between involved nodes.

2.9. Infrastructure. Mobile *ad hoc* networks are infrastructureless, and there is no central administration that can regulate the communication between involved nodes. This means that every node can communicate with other nodes, which makes it difficult to detect faults happening in the network, and because of the highly dynamic topology of MANET, frequent network separation and route changing can result in the loss of packets.

2.10. Limitation in Power. The nodes in mobile *ad hoc* networks are battery powered; this restriction may cause problems such as the loss of packets, or the nodes may work in a selfish manner, meaning that they do not forward messages received.

2.11. Trust. The lack of central administration and the highly dynamic topology of MANETs may result in a lack of trust between involved nodes due to the absence of verification and the fact that some nodes may participate in a transmission even if they are not part of the network, which may result in security breaches in the network or leaks of valued information.

2.12. Security. Attacks may happen in MANETs due to their wireless nature and the lack of centralized admission of mobile *ad hoc* networks, which make these networks vulnerable to attacks such as eavesdropping and wormhole or black hole attacks. As such, it is essential for the multicast protocol to ensure security.

2.13. Quality of Service. The applications that currently rely on MANETs vary greatly, and these include military applications. Quality of service is an important issue in such applications, but ensuring quality of service by multicast can be difficult for reasons including throughput, delay, and reliability. The design of a multicast protocol should take into consideration the need to provide these parameters.

3. Reliable and Energy Efficient Protocol Depending on Distance and Remaining Energy (REEDDRE)

We propose herein a hierarchical tree-based design with a specified type of predefined clustering approach for MANET multicasting. From the literature on routing protocols, we found that most routing protocols do not depend on power preservation of nodes, which is critical to provide the reliable multicast which is our goal. We propose a new reactive technique that depends on the distance and the remaining energy of nodes in the mobile *ad hoc* network, which we call the Reliable and Energy Efficient protocol Depending on Distance and Remaining Energy (REEDDRE).

The proposal comprises the following stages. In its first stage, we define the route request and route replay mechanism. In the second stage, we build a multicast tree with clustering approach from the master sender (MS), which is the node that sends the original message to the involved members, by dividing these nodes into three clusters according to two calculated thresholds of distance: cluster 1, the nodes nearest to the MS; cluster 2, the nodes at a medium distance according to threshold 1; and cluster 3, the farthest nodes from the MS according to threshold 2. In the third stage, we propose an efficient way of saving resources in all nodes in all clusters in our tree construction by calculating the remaining energy. In the final stage, we propose an adjustment to the flow of the multicast such that, according to our construction, each cluster will receive the message in a consecutive order.

3.1. Route Discovery in REEDDRE Protocol. In REEDDRE, routes are established based on on-demand techniques. Route discovery in our protocol and other reactive protocols is based on the request route (RREQ) packet and route reply (RREP) packet has been used for traditional AODV protocol. In our protocol, we propose a modification to this request-reply packet procedures. In our model, we apply tones to these request and reply packets that will be sent before the RREQ and RREP packets to make our model more efficient in terms of saving the network resources. Since our model is supporting using tones of short pluses, we will add predefined tones for the request and reply mechanism.

For RREQ, the relative tones are called route request tones (RRQT) and for RREP the relative tones are called route reply tone (RRPT). Using these tones will enable the system to avoid control overhead and collision of packets and can reduce the effect of black hole attacks happening in such reactive protocols. For establishing routes in our protocol, all route requests will be sent and from the node that has the original message, which is called the master sender (MS) and collected from other mobile nodes toward this node.

The MS in our protocol will send two route request tones (RRQT) having a predefined duration (i.e., 20 microseconds each) prior to the request packet in order to search for a destination. If the destination is reached, it will respond with two route reply tones (RRPT) also of a predefined duration (i.e., 25 microseconds each) prior to the reply packets. Request and reply packets will be sent only if the tones are received

successfully. This will introduce some kind of reliability and will prevent reply packets from colliding.

To utilize using tones for our protocol, the duration and the spacing between tones should be unified and predefined. Fortunately, there are many standards that offer spacing frames that have been offered in IEEE 802.11 WLAN that can offer collision avoidance mechanism. We will use them in our model but with minor modification to be adopted for MANET. In our model, we will use a standard frame space and a backoff algorithm with a distributed coordination function (DCF) using interframe space (DIFS) that contain short interframe space (SIFS) which will be mainly used in our model.

The procedures of route discovery in our model will be as follows: first for RREQ method, RREQ consists of two spaced RRQT sent before the RREQ packet and each RRQT is bounded by two SIFS. Second for RREP method, if the destination is reached and also the RRQT is received, it will reply with appropriate two spaced RRPT also bounded by two SIFS and then RREP packet as depicted in Figure 1. We shall use different durations for the route request tone and the route reply tone to distinguish between them and to avoid malfunctioning of the system.

The MS will save the routes to this destination as well as the intermediate nodes that make the route to this destination valid in the routing table. This process will be repeated if there is need to establish new routes. This will introduce some delay in the process but only successful received tones will make the destination respond with a packet and this will reduce the waste of the network by using short tones which involve short pulses and will not cost the network.

In MANET, the nodes are moving freely without any constraints to this mobility. In order to keep track of all mobile nodes, mobile nodes should send an updating message when they change their location broadcasted in the network. If the number of update messages is large, a new routing discovery procedure should be established to update the routing tables for the new locations and the intermediate nodes.

If no update message is received, we assume that all routes remain in the same position and other messages with different master senders should take the same discovered routes. This will reduce the overhead required in using route discovery techniques.

3.2. Distance Distribution and Clusters Construction. In our REEDDRE protocol, we build three hierarchical clusters between the MS and the receiving node, depending on distance. In our approach, we assume that all nodes are equipped with devices that calculate the position of involved nodes (e.g., GPS). The geographical locations of all nodes are thus measured periodically by a GPS device, and these nodes will broadcast their locations. Update messages will be sent only if the nodes move to another location to reduce the overhead delivered from these update messages.

From the information delivered by the GPS device, we can determine the two farthest nodes reached in the whole network. From there, we can define two distance thresholds to divide our network for clustering purposes. We divide our network into three levels according to the two distance

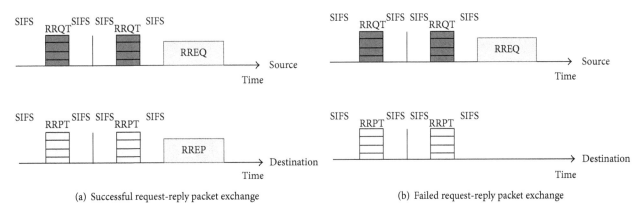

(a) Successful request-reply packet exchange

(b) Failed request-reply packet exchange

FIGURE 1: Route discovery in our REEDDRE.

thresholds calculated based on the transmission of a message from the MS to the two farthest nodes in the network.

We list the following formulas for calculating the distance thresholds:

The distance between the farthest nodes = D,

$$\text{First threshold } Q1 = \frac{D}{3}, \quad (1)$$

$$\text{Second threshold } Q2 = \frac{D}{1.5}.$$

In level 1, the first cluster will be formed depending on the threshold distance $Q1$. The nodes that are located before this threshold are members of cluster 1, and these nodes are considered to be the nearest nodes to one of the farthest nodes that define D. In level 2, the second cluster will be formed depending on threshold distance $Q1$ and threshold distance $Q2$. The nodes that are located between distance thresholds $Q1$ and $Q2$ are members of cluster 2. In level 3, cluster 3 is formed containing all the remaining nodes, of which locations are greater than the threshold $Q2$.

In Figure 2, we assume that the MS is in the first cluster and is the farthest node from the north and that node 14 is the farthest node from the south. This information is delivered from the GPS devices in all nodes. First, we calculate D as the difference between N14 and the MS. Second, we calculate the distance threshold $Q1$, which equals $(D/3)$, to form cluster 1, and finally, we calculate the distance threshold $Q2$, which equals $(D/1.5)$ to form cluster 2.

As a result, nodes MS, N1, N2, N3, N4, and N5 will form cluster 1. After that, we calculate the distance threshold $Q2$, which is equal to $(D/1.5)$. Then, the nodes which are located between $Q1$ and $Q2$ will form cluster 2; in this case, N6, N7, N8, N9, N10, and N11 are the members of cluster 2. Finally, all remaining nodes, which are greater than $Q2$, will form cluster 3. N11, N12, N13, N14, N15, and N16 are the members of cluster 3, and these members are considered the nearest nodes to the farthest node from the south, N14.

Once the distance thresholds are defined and the members of each cluster are known. Mobile nodes should send membership message to the MS or to the relative cluster head

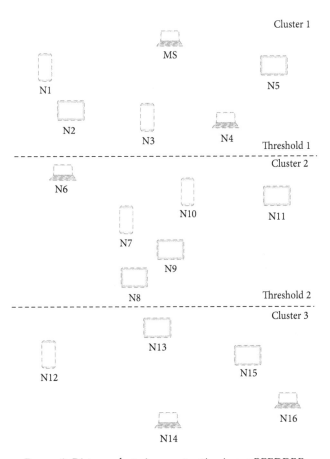

FIGURE 2: Distance clustering construction in our REEDDRE.

to inform these nodes with their locations and to be a part of a multicast tree happening in each cluster.

The cluster which includes the node which has the MS is called the home region cluster, because it will start multicasting the message. Each cluster member can be classified into the master sender, which has the original message; gateway nodes, which will forward the message to other clusters; and relay nodes, which will remulticast the message into their own clusters. This will be discussed in more detail in the next section.

By dividing the nodes into two distance thresholds, we can ensure that all clusters will have at least one member and that nonoverlapping clusters will form, but we cannot ensure that the distribution in all clusters will be even.

3.3. Calculating the Remaining Energy of Nodes. In mobile *ad hoc* networks, the stability is important. To increase the stability in MANETs, every node in the network should be power aware, meaning that each node must calculate its remaining energy and announce it periodically, which is done with the assistance of the physical layer in all nodes in the network. To announce the remaining energy of nodes, all mobile nodes should follow these equations as follows.

In transmission, the consumed power is calculated as

$$\text{Consumed Energy for Transmission} = T_e \times T, \quad (2)$$

where T_e is the needed energy for transmission and T is the time needed for this transmission.

In reception, the consumed power is calculated as

$$\text{Consumed Energy for Reception} = R_e \times T, \quad (3)$$

where R_e is the needed energy for reception and T is the time needed for reception operation.

Thus, from (2) and (3) the remaining energy of a node can be easily calculated as [1]

$$\text{Remaining Energy} = \text{Available Energy} - \text{Consumed Energy.} \quad (4)$$

After calculating the remaining energy, all nodes should announce the remaining energy by broadcasting these values in the network to help the MS to create general idea about the energy level in network for further actions.

After all nodes have announced their remaining energy and locations, classification of the nodes role is applied. Thus, in the home region cluster, the MS node will be defined, after which we sort nodes depending on their distance from the distance thresholds. We pick the nearest node to the distance threshold to serve as a gateway node, which will forward the message from one cluster to other clusters.

In the other clusters which are not the home region cluster, we also sort the nodes depending on their remaining energy and we pick the nodes with the maximum remaining energy to be the cluster heads and the relay nodes for further retransmission in their cluster.

To preserve the energy in the network, the nodes in the network may operate in different modes; that is, along with the transmission mode and the reception mode, we add the listen and sleep modes, which provide improvements to the stability of the network. Transmission mode means that the node is either the MS or a node that transmits to other nodes by unicast. Reception mode means that the node is a recipient of either our multicast member or a unicast transmission. Listen mode means that the node is ready to receive, which means that it has enough energy to do so, but it is not included in the multicast message and other nodes want to transmit to it. Sleep mode means that the node has a lack of energy; it

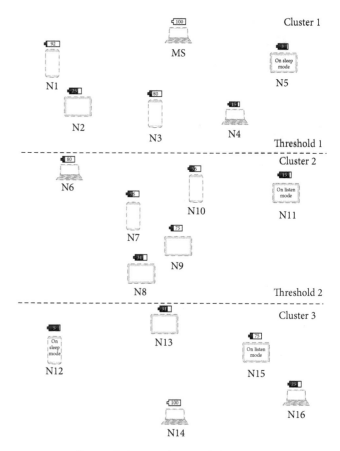

FIGURE 3: Announcing remaining energy.

thus turns on sleep mode until its battery is charged. In some cases, nodes in sleep mode may be involved in the multicast message; in this case, after charging the battery this node may ask the nearest node to unicast the message to it. In our tree-based design, we need to know which node has the maximum remaining energy in all clusters.

In the example shown in Figure 3, N3 (which is in cluster 1) and N8 (which is in cluster 2) will be gateway nodes and will forward the message from cluster 1 (the home region) to cluster 2 and from cluster 2 to cluster 3. Furthermore, after sorting the nodes depending on the remaining energy, N6 (which is in cluster 2) and N13 (which is cluster 3) will be relay nodes in their clusters (cluster head) because they have the maximum remaining energy in their cluster. In addition, we can see that N5 and N12 are in sleep mode because they have less energy than the threshold of energy permitted to be involved in communication where N11 and N15 are listen mode which means they have enough power to be a part of the multicast transmission.

After routes have been discovered, the network has been divided into clusters, and all nodes have announced their remaining energy, all nodes will be assigned with hybrid addresses containing a node ID, which may be a MAC address, and a cluster ID. If there is no transmission, joining or leaving cluster is permitted; however, if there is transmission, joining or leaving clusters is not allowed; this is to avoid misbehavior of the addressing technique. If the node enters a new cluster, which means that it passes one of the two distance thresholds, it will send an update message to inform the cluster head that it has become a member of the cluster. The update message will contain the new node address and its location.

3.4. Multicast Traffic Flow Adjustment in Our REERRDE Protocol. In this phase, we will adjust the typical flow of the multicast network to adopt MANET properties and clustering properties. In our REEDDRE protocol, once the MS picks up nodes of multicast tree, all nodes should be able to send an acceptance tone with a predefined duration (i.e., 35 microseconds) to inform the sender that it is a part of the multicast group. We assume that all nodes should be able to buffer the message for further retransmission if needed.

After we divide the network into three clusters according to distance, the MS will pick up all wanted nodes, and routes will be discovered in all three clusters by sending to the nodes a send synchronization packet (SSP) and expecting an acknowledgment acceptance tone (AT) from the nodes with enough energy.

The MS will multicast the message to nodes in cluster 1 (the home region cluster) to preserve as much energy as possible, and this will be multicast group 1. We assume that only the master sender and the gateway node will save the message in their buffers for further retransmission if needed and that all other nodes are not required to save the message. This will minimize the capacity overhead, leading to better results in the congestion status of these nodes.

After that, in cluster 2 we find which node has the maximum remaining energy, and this node announces itself as the cluster head in cluster 2. The closest node from cluster 1 (gateway node of the home region cluster) will retransmit the message by unicasting the message to the node which has the maximum remaining energy in cluster 2; then this node (the relay node or the cluster head node) will remulticast the message of the MS in cluster 2. This will be the multicast group 2, and again only the relay node and gateway node of this cluster will save the message in their buffers.

In cluster 3 the node which has the maximum remaining energy will announce itself as the cluster head, and the closest node from cluster 2 (the gateway node of cluster 2) will retransmit the message by unicasting the message of the MS to this node. Again, this node which has the maximum remaining energy in cluster 3 (relay node or the cluster head node) will remulticast the message in cluster 3, which will be considered as multicast group 3. Since in this cluster no gateway node is needed, only the relay node will save the message of the master sender in its buffer. By doing this we preserve the energy of the MS and try to optimize the consumed energy in the whole network.

Unicast links between the gateway nodes and the relay nodes must contain a high level of reliability and error detection and correction mechanisms, because this is an essential procedure that moves our message from one partition to another.

Our system may result in some delay at the beginning of initialization but overall it provides an efficient way of handling the consumption of energy. Nodes whose energy has run out will not cause a message to remain in one cluster and not move to the next partition because we use some kind of acknowledgment of reception which is needed in a reliable scheme of multicast transmissions, and this causes an endless loop in our network.

After this adjustment, we conclude the cluster formation of the multicast batch. There are only one master sender, which is located in home region cluster; two gateways nodes, located in the home region and in cluster 2; and two relay nodes or cluster head nodes, which will remulticast the original message and are located in cluster 2 and cluster 3. This structure will reduce the formation overhead because only a few roles of nodes are required to perform multicast in the network and to reduce the cluster construction complexity.

Figure 4 shows the traffic modification procedures. In home region cluster the MS multicast the message within its cluster boundaries, N3 is the gateway node of this cluster which will save the message and forward it by unicasting the message to cluster 2.

In cluster 2, N6 is the cluster head and N8 is the gateway node of this group. The cluster head will remulticast the message within the boundaries of cluster 2 and N8 will save and forward the message to cluster 3 by means of unicast transmissions.

In cluster 3, N14 is the cluster head of this group, which will remulticast the message after receiving it from N8. At this stage all multicast group receives the original message coming from the MS.

4. Reliable Multicast Based on Busy Tones in MANETs (RMBTM)

This is a similar system to the system proposed in IEEE 802.11 [3], but we modify it to be convenient for MANETs. When we have several receivers, multicast transmission is very useful compared to unicast transmission to each receiver. It can save time, reduce the redundancy of retransmission, and preserve the bandwidth of the network. Unfortunately, multicast transmission does not support reliability in the exchange of a packet, as there are no control packets that may support reliability, such as the three-way handshake send, receive, and acknowledgment, which are used in unicast transmissions.

Several protocols have been proposed to provide reliable multicast transmissions. However, they are not efficient for MANETs because of the nature of the MANET network or due to excessive use of control packets in error recovery, which may cause an unacceptable overhead. We propose a simple and effective scheme, called reliable multicast based on busy tone for MANET (RMBTM), which can be used in our model. The novel idea behind this model is that we combine two well-known methods for error detection or error recovery over the MAC layer, the ARQ (Automatic Repeat Request), and FEC (Forward Error Correction), with tone-based acknowledgments to reduce the retransmission number and to provide data reliability in the multicast environment.

The RMBTM may support multimedia transmission because it can support block transmission, which means the

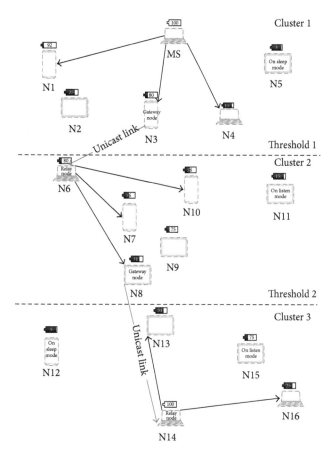

FIGURE 4: Multicast flow adjustment in our REEDDRE.

data stream into a number of blocks. In our RMBTM model, all mobile nodes are equipped with a tone-based system that uses short pulses of energy replacing the control packets; this increases the efficiency in MANETs by reducing the excessive usage of control packets.

These tones are categorized by different time durations to ensure good performance in the model. Tones are used as a replacement for acknowledgment in the handshake process. The first type of tone that we will use in our model is called the feedback request tone (FRT), which is sent from the MS to all involved multicast nodes to check whether the received data are correct or not; the duration of feedback request tones is fixed. The other types of tones used in our RMBTM model are packet request tones (PRTs) from the receiver to the MS, and the tone number of packet request is determined by how many packets must be recovered.

4.1. RMBTM Architecture.

Figure 5 shows the proposed system architecture for providing reliable multicast transmissions in the MANET. In the architecture, MS sends data packets to all multicast receivers, and these MS alternates between different receivers due to different scenarios in multicast transmissions and different messages.

All mobile nodes of the proposed RMBTM model are equipped with ARQ and FEC in their MAC layer to provide the error discovery and error recovery mechanisms. At receiver nodes, the FEC tries to recover any errors that

occurred in the packet. If it is unable to do so, the receiver will ask the MS or cluster head to retransmit via ARQ. The function of the FEC is, after receiving a number of packets of one block, to produce a parity check of packets for use in error recovery. The ARQ function is to retransmit the original message if the FEC fails to recover data.

First, the MS or the cluster head divides the original message into a number of blocks with the same size; then the MS or the cluster head sends each block individually, which contains a certain number of packets. After transmitting a number of packets of a block, the MS or the cluster head will send a feedback request tone (FRT) with a predefined duration (i.e., 45 microseconds) to all receivers involved. Second, at the receiving side, while the MS or cluster head sends its message, the receiving node generates a parity check packet from its own FEC to try to recover any errors that occurred in the transmission. If the parity check is not enough, then after receiving the feedback request tone (FRT), the receiving node will send a packet request tone (PRT) with a predefined duration (i.e., 50 microseconds) followed by the packet header of the lost packet. Third, when the MS or cluster head receives a PRT or a number of PRTs, its own ARQ will retransmit the needed number of packets. Fourth, this process of trying to recover errors by FEC and feedback and packet request and retransmission is repeated until the original block is recovered.

After that, the MS or cluster head continues sending other blocks with the same technique. The feedback request transmission is defined before the transmission based on the network congestion status; if the network status is excellent, it can be postponed to the end of the message to reduce the time needed for error recovery, while if the status of the network is not good, it is better to send a feedback request after a number of blocks have been transmitted [3]. This may cause extra time overhead compared to the original transmission of multicast without any method of providing reliability, but our proposal ensures a better level of reliability with an appropriate control overhead.

4.2. RMBTM Description.

To describe RMBTM we need a minor modification to three standard aspects, the packet header format, space frame, and handshake. Because our system is supporting block transmission and to allow our system to distinguish correctly where an error happened, we need to modify the standard packet header format of IEEE 802.11 as shown in Figure 6. We will add eight bytes of information (four-byte block number; four-byte packet index) in optional field of the standard packet header format; these modifications provide a way to identify precisely the error that happened in the packet in order to take an action. The packet size will not change, so as to prevent malfunction of our model and to avoid conflict with other systems. So our modification will not affect the packet header format since we use the optional field details.

In our RMBTM model, we will use the same standard spacing frame that we will use in the routing discovery method which is SIFS to utilize using tones and avoid the collisions of these tones [3].

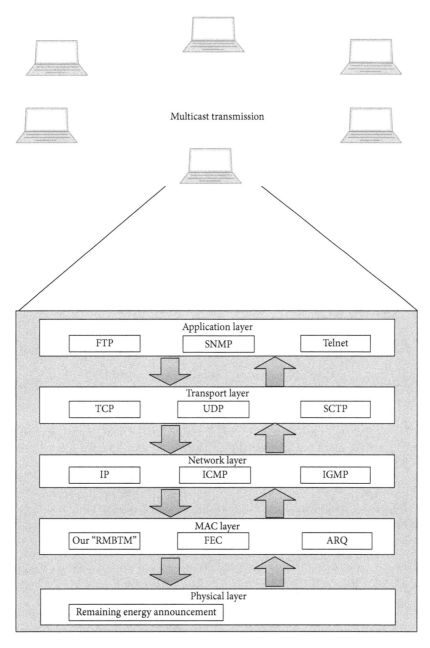

All mobile nodes should be at least equipped with these protocols

FIGURE 5: RMBTM architecture.

To provide reliability, the standard format of the three-way handshake is as follows: send, receive, and acknowledge (ACK); however, we will modify this format to be convenient to our tone-based system. We use a four-way handshake to ensure that all members of the multicast group are ready; this consists of the send synchronization packet (SSP), acceptance tone (AT) with a predetermined duration (i.e., 35 microseconds), and data feedback request tone (FRT), and finally we replace the ACK with FRT, which may result in a better performance because it is just a tone with no harm if it collides.

The acceptance tone (AT) could be considered as a replacement for the Clear to Send (CTS) packet, but it is just a busy tone, so it will not cause traffic overhead. It is sent in two situations; first, when the node wants to be a part of the multicast group and second, when the master want to send data to all multicast members. Moreover, FRT could be sent more than one time depending on the receiver's status; if the receiver asks for packets by sending a packet request tone (PRT), the FRT will be transmitted until all receivers get the original message correctly.

Transmitting a block which consists of a number of packets involves transmitting a number of different spacing frames and different packets. First, the node will wait for one standard frame space (i.e., the short interframe space, SIFS);

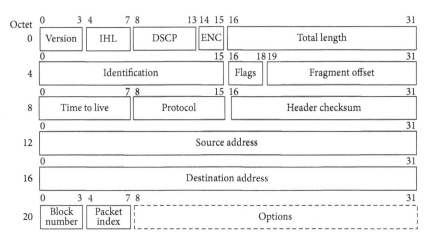

FIGURE 6: Data packet format in RMBTM.

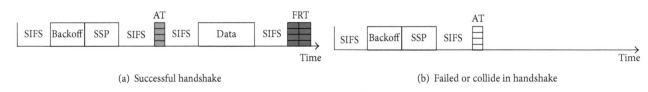

(a) Successful handshake

(b) Failed or collide in handshake

FIGURE 7: Handshake mechanism in our RMBTM.

after that, it uses the standard backoff algorithm used in DFC; then again it will wait for the SIFS. Next, it will send the synchronization packet (SSP) to all involved receivers, after which it will wait for one SIFS. After that, the sender will expect from all involved receivers an acceptance tone (AT) to inform the master sender that all multicast members are ready to receive and have enough power.

After the master sender receives the ATs, it will wait for one SIFS before sending the packets of the original block. Once it finishes, it will wait again for one SIFS; then it will send a feedback request tone (FRT) as depicted in Figure 7(a).

If the master sender does not receive the ATs, it will not send the packets but will instead try to send the synchronization packet again as shown in Figure 7(b). This may happen if the acceptance tones coming from multiple receivers collide, but it does not matter since it is just a tone and will not affect the network links.

From the ATs the master sender knows the involved nodes in the multicast transmission which is ready to receive from the MS.

After the master sender sends the original data it will wait for one space frame (SIFS); then it will send a feedback request tone to all involved receivers in the multicast transmission. If there is an error during the transmission that the FEC is not able to recover, the receiver will send back to the master sender a packet request tone (PRT) determined by the number of errors that occurred or send an AT telling the MS that the original message is received correctly.

This spacing frame procedure makes our multicast transmission operate like unicast because the master sender or relay node will wait and listen to ensure that the channel is free before sending the synchronization packet to all

receivers. If the channel is not free, then the backoff algorithm counter is zero, and the MS or cluster head will wait for a time defined by the backoff algorithm before trying again. The counter of the backoff algorithm is decreased by the MS when the channel is idling. This process is repeated until the master sender sends the SSP packet.

Block transmission by the master sender involves dividing the stream of data into a number of blocks of equal size; each block is composed of one standard space frame, backoff, send synchronization packet, acceptance tone, and data, which consists of a number of packets as shown in Figure 8.

The decision of the time to send the feedback request tone (FRT) is made based on network status; if the network connection is considered excellent, then the master sender will send FRT only after a number of blocks have been transmitted, to avoid delay and waste of network resources. Otherwise, it will consider making FRT more frequently during the transmission.

After the master sender sends its data, it will wait for one space frame (SIFS), and then it will send two-time slot feedback request tone (FRT) without any interframe spacing. After that, if the receiver decides that it could not recover all data by using FEC and want additional data from the master sender in order to recover the message, the receiver will wait for one space frame (SIFS) and then send a packet request tone (PRT) to the master sender based on the number of packets it wants followed by the packet header of these lost packets. For example, if a receiver has three errors and this receiver could not recover these errors via its FEC, it will send a three-time slot PRT without any interframe spacing to the master sender followed by the packet header of these three

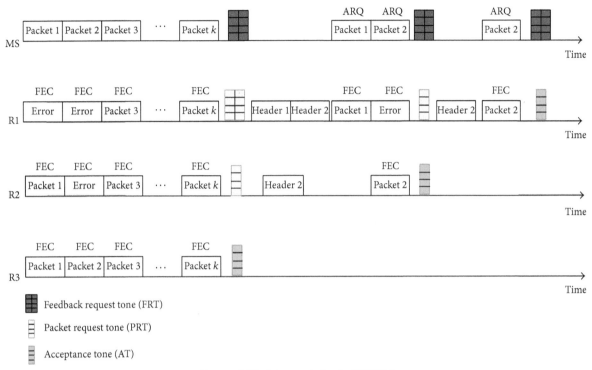

FIGURE 8: Block transmission in RMBTM.

lost packets to make the MS or cluster head send precisely these lost packets via its ARQ.

The master sender will make its own ARQ and will retransmit the needed additional data to this receiver, and then the master sender will send the two (FRT) again to this receiver to check whether this receiver has received the original message correctly. If not, again the receiver will send a number of PRTs to the master sender depending on the received data that could not be recovered also followed by the packet headers. This process is repeated until the receiver retrieves the original data. If the receiver node receives the data correctly, after the master sender sends two FRT, the receiver will send AT and wait for the next block to be transmitted. Upon transmission of the next block, the above process will repeat again.

Figure 8 gives an example of the procedures described above. The MS transmits k data packets. Receivers 1 receive two erroneous data packets (packet 1 and packet 2), receiver 2 receives one erroneous data packet (packet 2), and receiver 3 does not receive any error, all identified through our modification to packet header format. R3 will send an AT and will not do anything in whole correction procedure because it does not have any error.

To correct errors happening in the transmission, after receiving an FRT from the MS, R1 and R2 will transmit PRTs back to the MS followed by the packet header format of these erroneous packets, R1 will transmit PRT with two-time slot of duration, and R2 will transmit RPTs with one slot of duration due to the number of errors occurring in the transmission followed by packet header. From the PRTs and the packet headers, the MS knows the largest number of needed packets that could not be retrieved from the first attempt.

The master sender will retransmit these packets again to all nodes of interest and send again FRT. The involved receiver will receive the retransmitted packet again on the second attempt and do error correction by its own FEC. So after receiving the second FRT the R2 will send AT because it could retrieve the original data and R1 still suffer and still need one additional packet, so it will send one PRT to the MS with the packet header of this erroneous packet.

After receiving the second RPT, the MS will send this packet again to this receiver and it will perform error check. At this point all receivers recover all missing data and R3 will send an AT to tell the MS of the current status of these lost packets, so after the third FRT they do nothing and the MS will continue sending other blocks with the same procedures.

In our model, we use five different tones RRQT, RRPT, FRT, PRT, and AT. The duration of these tones should be different to avoid malfunction on the network. We assume that, for example, RRQT is 20 microseconds, RRPT 25 microseconds, FRT 45 microseconds, PRT 50 microseconds, and AT 35 microseconds to enable the system to distinguish between them. Also we assume the sender should send two FRT because it is essential part in our model and to enable the receiver in worst cases to receive at least one of these tones.

5. Simulation and Results

In this section, we will describe the procedure for the simulation of our proposal, for which we will use the OPNET simulator. Our proposal is simulated in various scenarios to evaluate its performance and efficiency. The simulation procedure of our proposal will follow these parameters:

(1) Consider a MANET = {N1, N2, ..., Nn}.

(2) The distance is measured by the GPS device for each node and the threshold value Q is defined.

(3) Create the partitions cluster 1, cluster 2, and cluster 3 and the involved nodes for cluster $1 = \{N1, \ldots, NQ1\}$, cluster $2 = \{NQ + 1, \ldots, NQ2\}$, and cluster $3 = \{NQ2 + 1, \ldots, Nn\}$, where Q1 and Q2 are the distance thresholds (as shown in Figure 2).

(4) All nodes in the network announce their remaining energy (as shown in Figure 3).

(5) The master sender defines the wanted nodes by using our handshake mechanism, that is, by sending a synchronization packet (SSP) and expecting from all nodes an acceptance tone (AT), excluding all nodes which are in sleep mode until they charge their batteries (as shown in Figure 7).

(6) Use our proposed scheme for route request and route reply (as described in Figure 1).

(7) Use our multicast modification (as shown in Figure 4).

(8) The master sender multicasts the message to cluster 1 and uses our RMBTM to provide more reliability.

(9) The closest node to cluster 2 will unicast the message to the node which has the maximum remaining energy in cluster 2 (cluster head), which will act as relay node 1.

(10) The cluster head in cluster 2 will remulticast the message to the nodes of interest in cluster 2 and will also use our RMBTM to provide more reliability.

(11) The closest node to cluster 3 will unicast the message to the node which has the maximum remaining energy in cluster 3 (cluster head), which will act as relay node 2.

(12) The cluster head in cluster 3 will remulticast the message to the nodes of interest in cluster 3 and will also use our RMBTM to provide more reliability.

(13) For more reliability, the master sender will ask the farthest node in our MANET to resend the message to it to ensure that the message has been received correctly through the whole network.

We will base our performance analysis on comparison with other protocols; this means that in our simulation we will build the same MANET network under the same conditions with different routing protocols. We compare our proposal with other well-known protocols supported by OPNET, such as AODV, DSR, and OLSR. This will allow us to show our enhancements in terms of delay, reliability, energy consumption, and throughput.

We conduct our simulation for all routing protocol in wireless environment using the network size of 10 × 10 km with 30 highly dynamic mobile nodes in a random deployment running for one hour. For our model, we build three trajectories to construct three clusters that depend on distance and remaining energy.

In routing discovery time, we compare our proposed model with the reactive routing protocol AODV as shown

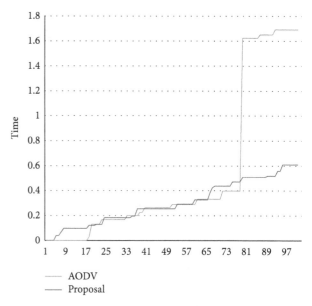

FIGURE 9: Comparison of route discovery time.

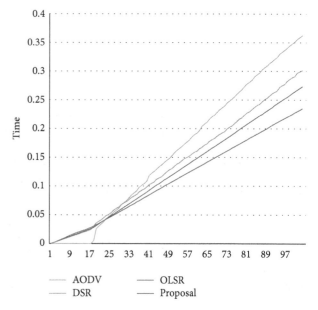

FIGURE 10: Comparison of delay factor.

in Figure 9. Our proposal shows more stable growth with acceptable delay, whereas the AODV route discovery time shows unpredicted growth. In the beginning of the simulation our model shows more delay caused by the initializing of RRQT and RRPT in routing discovery mechanism, but as time progresses our system produces better results since only successful interchanged tones will generate routing discovery packets, while in AODV protocol, the routing discovery packets could collide at the source causing more delay to retransmit these packets again.

In Figure 10, we show comparison results of our model against AODV, DSR, and OLSR in terms of delay factor happening in the entire network. Our model is the best performer in this comparison due to our proposed requirement

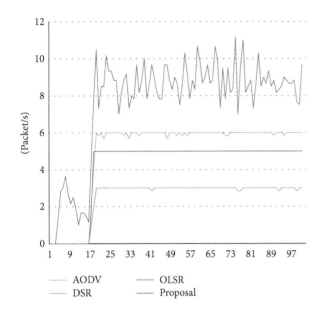

FIGURE 11: Comparison of reliability factor.

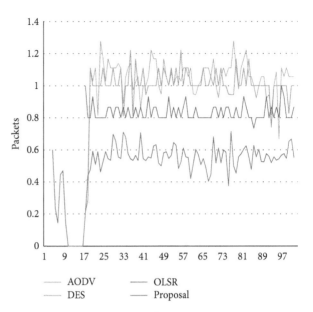

FIGURE 12: Comparison of retransmission attempts.

of initializing tones and adjusting the multicast flow; however, as time continues our model shows steady improvement with an overall acceptable delay.

The reliability factor results are shown in Figure 11; REEDDRE shows a great enhancement in received packets over dropped packets due to using our proposed handshake mechanism as described in Section 4.2. the corrugated shape of our model is caused by FRT and PRTs used to ensure the reliability in our model.

Figure 11 shows a comparison of retransmission attempts of all routing protocol used in the simulation; our model is the best performer in this comparison since it produces the lowest number of retransmission attempts, which means that REEDDRE is more reliable than others with less delay caused by these attempts.

As shown in Figures 11 and 12, the results support our proposed techniques to offer reliable scheme for multicast transmission in MANET. This is because we utilize the network resource with the assistance of short pluses of tones replacing the traditional routing protocols control packets.

Figure 13 shows the energy consumption results. Our model shows great enhancement in terms of preservation of the network energy. This enhancement is done with idea of our proposal to divide the network into three clusters based on distance and remaining energy and also with idea of role-based assignment such as gateway nodes.

We compare the network throughput among REEDDRE, AODV, DSR, and OLSR as shown in Figure 14. At the beginning, OLSR shows better throughput because of the MRP technique used in OLSR, but as the time advances, our REEDDRE demonstrates the highest throughput because of its reliability mechanism and clustering approach while OLSR will produce more overhead because of update MRP neighboring list.

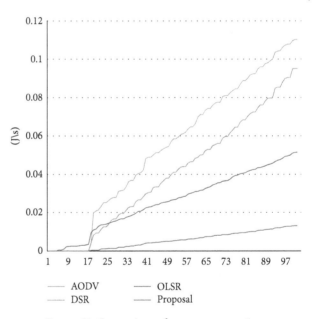

FIGURE 13: Comparison of energy consumption.

Finally, the overall comparison showed that our REED-DRE offers better results in every parameter, but it is important to note that REEDDRE does not demonstrate the best results at the beginning of the simulation. This is because of the model's initial requirements for initializing the tone system and modification, but as time progresses our system produces the best results.

6. Conclusion

In this paper, we propose the tone-based REEDDRE model as a means of overcoming the disadvantages of the huge consumption of energy relating to distance and to provide

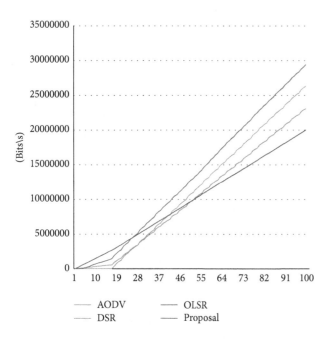

FIGURE 14: Comparison of throughput.

congestion control and reliability in multicast transmissions over mobile *ad hoc* networks (MANETs). Our model consists of a tree-based design where all nodes are divided into three partitions. Our proposal mandates that only the node with the maximum remaining energy will multicast because of the consumption of energy resulting from such a multicast. In addition, we propose for our REEDDRE model a reliable multicast transmission over the MAC layer. The proposed model uses RMBPM in combination with ARQ and FEC, using a tone-based system to provide data reliability and efficiency. We provide a short summary of the routing protocol in MANETs, the requirements for a reliable multicast over different topologies, and different approaches to provide congestion control. Our simulation results showed that the REEDDRE model produces better results in terms of delay, reliability, energy consumption, and throughput compared with well-known protocols such as AODV, OLSR, and DSR. These results support our proposed ideas regarding the use of tones and a clustering approach. These proposed techniques can all be implemented in one MANET without conflicting with others and will provide a level of service quality which is essential for services which depend on such networks.

Competing Interests

The authors declare that they have no competing interests regarding the publication of this paper.

Acknowledgments

The authors would like to extend their sincere appreciation to the Deanship of Scientific Research at King Saud University for funding this research group (no. RGP-1437-35).

References

[1] K. S. Rao, R. S. Kumar, P. Venkatesh, R. V. S. Naidu, and A. Ramesh, "Development of energy efficient and reliable congestion control protocol for multicasting in mobile adhoc networks compare with AODV based on receivers," *International Journal of Engineering Research and Applications*, vol. 2, no. 2, pp. 631–634, 2012.

[2] S. Arvind and G. Prasad, "Enhancement of network life time using binary tree based multicast routing protocol for mobile Ad Hoc network," *Global Journal of Computer Science and Technology Network*, vol. 13, no. 10, 2013.

[3] S. Kim and Y.-J. Cho, "Efficient multicast scheme based on hybrid ARQ and busy tone for multimedia traffic in wireless LANs," *Applied Mathematics and Information Sciences*, vol. 8, no. 1, pp. 171–180, 2014.

[4] M. Manjul, R. Mishra, Joytsna, and K. Singh, "Link utilization based multicast congestion control," *Communications and Network*, vol. 5, pp. 649–653, 2013.

[5] G. Li and Y. Xu, "A TCP-friendly congestion control scheme for multicast with network coding," *Journal of Computational Information Systems*, vol. 9, no. 21, pp. 8541–8548, 2013.

[6] R. Halloush, "HopCaster: a network coding-based hop-by-hop reliable multicast protocol," in *Proceedings of the Global Communications Conference (GLOBECOM '12)*, Anaheim, Calif, USA, 2013.

[7] L. Chen, T. Ho, M. Chiang, S. H. Low, and J. C. Doyle, "Congestion control for multicast flows with network coding," *IEEE Transactions on Information Theory*, vol. 58, no. 9, pp. 5908–5921, 2012.

[8] M. K. Marina and S. R. Das, "Ad hoc on-demand multipath distance vector routing," *ACM SIGMOBILE Mobile Computing and Communications Review*, vol. 6, no. 3, pp. 92–93, 2002.

[9] T. Lathies Bhasker, "A scope for MANET routing and security threats," *ICTACT Journal on Communication Technology*, vol. 4, no. 4, p. 840, 2013.

[10] T. Sasanth, S. Umar, and D. Bellam, "A study on data security in MANETS," *International Journal of Computer Science Engineering & Technology*, vol. 3, no. 11, pp. 408–415, 2013.

13

Developing an On-Demand Cloud-Based Sensing-as-a-Service System for Internet of Things

Mihui Kim,[1] Mihir Asthana,[2] Siddhartha Bhargava,[2] Kartik Krishnan Iyyer,[2] Rohan Tangadpalliwar,[2] and Jerry Gao[2,3]

[1]*Department of Computer Science & Engineering, Computer System Institute, Hankyong National University, 327 Jungang-ro, Anseong-si, Gyeonggi-do 456-749, Republic of Korea*
[2]*Computer Engineering Department, San Jose State University, One Washington Square, San Jose, CA 95192, USA*
[3]*Taiyuan University of Science and Technology, Taiyuan 030024, China*

Correspondence should be addressed to Jerry Gao; jerry.gao@sjsu.edu

Academic Editor: Jemal H. Abawajy

The increasing number of Internet of Things (IoT) devices with various sensors has resulted in a focus on Cloud-based sensing-as-a-service (CSaaS) as a new value-added service, for example, providing temperature-sensing data via a cloud computing system. However, the industry encounters various challenges in the dynamic provisioning of on-demand CSaaS on diverse sensor networks. We require a system that will provide users with standardized access to various sensor networks and a level of abstraction that hides the underlying complexity. In this study, we aim to develop a cloud-based solution to address the challenges mentioned earlier. Our solution, SenseCloud, includes a *sensor virtualization* mechanism that interfaces with diverse sensor networks, a *multitenancy* mechanism that grants multiple users access to virtualized sensor networks while sharing the same underlying infrastructure, and a *dynamic provisioning* mechanism to allow the users to leverage the vast pool of resources on demand and on a pay-per-use basis. We implement a prototype of SenseCloud by using real sensors and verify the feasibility of our system and its performance. SenseCloud bridges the gap between sensor providers and sensor data consumers who wish to utilize sensor data.

1. Introduction

As numerous devices and sensors get connected to the Internet, Internet of Things (IoT) is becoming a key topic of interest. Cisco predicts that 50 billion devices will be connected to the Internet by 2020. These devices and sensors will generate approximately 403 zetta bytes of data per year by 2018. In this fast-paced environment, the management of these devices, the networks, and the generated data is vital. The management and provisioning of such sensor devices and data opens doors to new business opportunities and poses new challenges. Industry and academia must manage these interconnected devices and exploit the opportunity presented by the extremely large amount of data generated. However, the huge investment and high maintenance cost of sensor network infrastructure prevents users from building their own IoT systems and web applications that utilize sensor data.

Thus, cloud-based sensing-as-a-service (CSaaS) appears as a new service paradigm; its system architecture is shown in Figure 1 [1, 2]. Sensor providers supply sensor data on mobile devices or on sensor networks through operations to subscribe to and publish sensing data. Big data are saved and processed on the CSaaS infrastructure. Sensor consumers utilize the sensing data from the cloud system on demand. The following important and specific challenges must be carefully addressed in the design and implementation of a CSaaS system [2]. First, the system must be generic and must hide the underlying complexity such that it can support various opportunistic and participatory sensing applications (which may even involve a large variety of sensors) and incurs very little overhead when launching a new sensing application and service. Second, the system can provide efficiency and sustainable scalability while using the same underlying infrastructure and ensuring the lowest cost-of-service

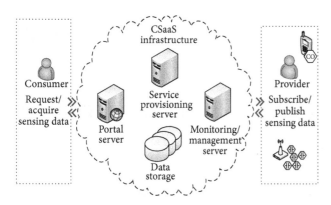

FIGURE 1: Service architecture on CSaaS infrastructure.

delivery for each incremental consumer. Third, the system can provide the service dynamically to allow consumers to leverage the vast pool of resources on demand.

Several models have been proposed in order to address some of these challenges in sensor networks. Service-oriented architecture (SOA) approaches [3–5] integrate wireless sensor networks (WSNs) and leverage the widespread use of WSNs. Service-centric models [6–11] focus on the services provided by a WSN as a service provider. Approaches using crowd-sourced mobile devices as sensors have been proposed [2, 12, 13]; they utilize the sensors of existing mobile devices to fulfil user requests. Integrated approaches to share the sensing data on existing sensor networks [14–16] provide efficient sharing mechanisms among multiple applications. However, these studies have not resolved the challenges related to the engagement and connectivity for diverse sensor networks, multitenancy considering both sensor providers and consumers in CSaaS, and on-demand big data sensing service. Further, these studies have not demonstrated a prototype implementation of the platform with real sensors.

In this study, we develop a CSaaS system called Sense-Cloud. The system aims to create a universal cloud platform with the following features: (1) It engages and manages various sensors on IoT devices by using the virtualization layer; (2) it gathers data from diverse sources such as sensors and sensor networks for useful and predictive analysis on a cloud system; (3) it provides access to real-time and historical data for analysis on an intuitive and feature-rich web interface; (4) it gives multiple users access to virtualized sensor networks while sharing the same underlying infrastructure; (5) it provides easy and standardized sensing data service for consumers and third-party applications dependent on data; and (6) it allows dynamic provisioning for users to leverage the vast pool of resources on demand. We implement a prototype of SenseCloud with real sensors. Then, we evaluate the operation and feasibility of our system and verify the system performance in terms of request time, load balancing, and scalability.

The contributions of this study are as follows:

(i) Design of a CSaaS platform with virtualization, multitenancy, and dynamic provisioning.

(ii) Sensor virtualization at two levels—that is, sensor level and consumer level—to enable multiple consumers to customize and control virtual sensors corresponding to a single physical sensor.

(iii) Two different multitenancy architectures, one for sensor consumers and another for sensor providers. The architecture for sensor consumers offers the highest degree of multitenancy to enable sharing of the same application for login, engagement, and management of sensors and sensor data. The architecture for providers provides instances dedicated to each sensor provider, taking into consideration security, failover mechanisms, high availability, and reliability.

(iv) Dynamic provisioning of CSaaS to allow consumers to leverage the vast pool of resources on demand and on a pay-per-use basis.

(v) Implementation of a SenseCloud prototype system with real sensors and evaluation to ensure the feasibility of the system and analyze its performance.

The remainder of this paper is organized as follows. Section 2 introduces existing works related to CSaaS or sensor data sharing approaches. Section 3 designs the Sense-Cloud architecture and explains the system design. Section 4 describes the experiment results for operation and performance. Finally, Section 5 provides concluding remarks with future work.

2. Related Work

Numerous devices around us generate an enormous amount of data. Devices with sensors to capture such data have existed for decades; however, recent developments in technology have enabled these devices to be equipped with energy-efficient and cost-effective wireless modules that allow the devices to transmit data wirelessly in real-time. This feature enables the measurement, inference, and understanding of environmental indicators, ranging from delicate ecologies and natural resources to urban environments. The proliferation of these devices in a communicating-actuating network creates IoT, in which sensors and actuators blend seamlessly with the environment around us, and the information is shared across platforms in order to develop a common operating picture [17]. IoT has been defined as object sensing, object identification, and communication of object-specific information. The information is the sensed data related to temperature, orientation, motion, vibration, acceleration, humidity, chemical changes in the air, and so forth, depending on the type of sensors. A combination of different sensors can be used for the design of smart services [18].

A multitude of these sensors connected wirelessly form a sensor network. These sensor networks can be leveraged for a variety of applications. Some of these applications, mentioned in [18], are natural-disaster prediction, industrial applications, water-scarcity monitoring, smart-homes design, medical applications, agricultural applications, intelligent transport system design, smart-cities design, smart metering and monitoring, and smart security [2, 12, 19, 20]. However, general users are deterred by the huge investments

TABLE 1: Comparison of sensor data sharing approaches based on cloud system.

	Scale mechanism	Load balancing	Sensor virtualization	Explicit multitenancy	Dynamic provisioning	System development
Sensing sharing [4]	√				√	√
IaaS [9]	√		√		√	
SIaaS [10]			√			
SCI [11]			√		√	√
PPSF [12]					√	
FSCI [14]			√		√	
VFSN [15]	√	√	√			√
SenseWeb [16]	√	√				√
SenseCloud	√	√	√	√	√	√

and high maintenance costs involved in sensor network infrastructure to utilize sensor data. Thus, the concept of CSaaS originated [1, 2], and it could be a value-added service to boost the expansion of IoT infrastructure.

The emergence of a plethora of applications for sensor networks is accompanied by several challenges and problems in the management of these networks. The IoT gateway acts as a bridge between WSNs with traditional communication networks or Internet, and it plays an important role in IoT applications; thus, it facilitates the seamless integration of WSNs and mobile communication networks or Internet and the management and control with WSNs [21, 22]. Some of the problems and challenges that arise are the standardization of governance and management models [3, 11, 18], complexity arising from heterogeneity [3, 21], virtualization, and monitoring [11].

As shown in Table 1, several models have been proposed in order to address these challenges in sensor networks. WSNs as a service [3–5] leverage the widespread use of WSNs and adopts a SOA approach based on the integration of WSNs. In particular, sensing sharing mechanism [4] provides a module to integrate industrial sensor information with the World Wide Web through the cloud in order to monitor and control the development process (e.g., nuclear plant management system). In the system, the integration controller and sensor node communicate through SOA to enable the services to be discovered and invoked by the sensor applications (client). Cloud computing is used to provide the extensibility of application servers and constant availability of data to users. However, the system does not address sensor virtualization, which would enable on-demand sharing of the physical sensors among users.

Service-centric models [6–11] focus on the services provided by a WSN and view a WSN as a service provider. Information as a service (IaaS) for WSNs [9] uses virtualization of WSNs to provide techniques for sensor provisioning and sharing for the large number of existing WSNs. However, IaaS leaves further scope for expansion in terms of load balancing and universal abstraction for all classes of sensors or sensor networks. A new service model called sensing instrument as a service (SIaaS) [10] provides virtualized sensing instruments to users and shares them as a common resource in a controlled manner. However, SIaaS does not

consider on-demand provisioning, which is important to users. Sensor-cloud infrastructure (SCI) [11] manages physical sensors by virtualizing them as virtual sensors on the cloud. SCI provides monitoring, automatic provisioning, and control for virtual sensors and virtual sensor groups, similar to our system; however, SCI does not explicitly design the scalability, load balancing, and multitenancy mechanisms to efficiently manage the infrastructure.

Approaches using crowd-sourced mobile devices as sensors have been proposed [2, 12, 13]; these approaches utilize the sensors of existing mobile devices and fulfil user requests. A priced public sensing framework (PPSF) [12] is designed for heterogeneous IoT architectures; this framework considers resource limitations in terms of delay, capacity, and lifetime from the perspective of the data provider and considers quality and trust requirements from the perspective of requesters. However, PPSF does not consider the service efficiency of the framework, that is, scalability or load balancing.

Integrated approaches to share the sensing data on existing sensor networks [14–16] provide efficient sharing mechanisms among multiple applications. A framework of sensor-cloud integration (FSCI) [14] utilizes the ever-expanding sensor data with a content-based pub/submodel. Virtual federated sensor network (VFSN) [15] enables multiple applications to share widely distributed sensor networks flexibly, preserving resource isolations. In VFSN, virtualized sinks are interconnected to achieve a dedicated federated sensor network; further, VFSN provides operations for multiple-sensor information to service providers. An infrastructure for shared sensing (SenseWeb) [16] enables applications to initiate and access sensor data streams from shared sensors across the entire Internet. The SenseWeb infrastructure helps ensure optimal sensor selection for each application and efficient sharing of sensor streams among multiple applications. However, these integration approaches do not address the multitenancy challenge that will enable each provider to exclusively and efficiently manage their own resources in a large integrated infrastructure.

In summary, none of the previous studies have developed a prototype of CSaaS with real sensors supporting all the following features: the scaling mechanism, load balancing, virtualization, multitenancy, and dynamic provisioning. In this study, we propose and demonstrate SenseCloud, a prototype

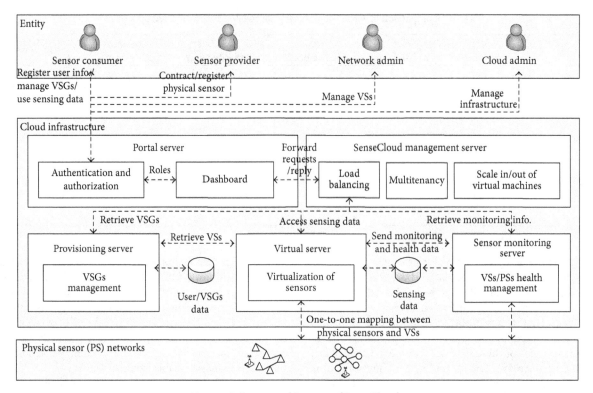

FIGURE 2: System architecture of SenseCloud.

that implements sensor system management and addresses the above mentioned challenges.

3. SenseCloud System

This section describes our proposed SenseCloud system according to a top-down approach: first, the overview and then, the detailed system design.

3.1. Overview of SenseCloud System Architecture. This subsection presents an overview of our SenseCloud system architecture, which consists of three main components— *Entity, Cloud Infrastructure,* and *Sensor Network*—as shown in Figure 2.

The four entities are *Sensor Consumer, Sensor Provider, Network Admin,* and *Cloud Admin.* The roles of each entity are described below. All entities perform their roles after authentication by the portal server.

(i) *Sensor Consumer.* First, sensor consumers register on the system and log in. After successful authentication, they subscribe to interesting sensors and create or modify sensor groups that include these sensors. Then, sensor consumers fetch the sensing data from sensors and view the analytical data. Further, they can download historical data and view their bills.

(ii) *Sensor Provider.* Sensor providers register on the system and log in. After successful authentication, they register their sensors on the system, manage the

sensors, and control them while checking their status. Sensor providers view the sensor usage statements.

(iii) *Network Admin.* After logging in to the system as a network admin, this entity monitors sensor health and manages virtual sensors. Further, a network admin manages the sensor provider accounts.

(iv) *Cloud Admin.* After logging in to the system as a cloud admin, this entity monitors virtual machines (VMs) and manages cloud infrastructure. A cloud admin manages the sensor consumer accounts and services.

The cloud infrastructure consists of the following servers and storage: *Portal Server, SenseCloud Management Server, Provisioning Server, Sensor Monitoring Server, Virtual Server,* and *Data Storage for User/Virtual Sensor Group (VSG)/Sensing Data.* The features of the main components and the roles of each entity are described below:

(i) *Portal Server.* When a user logs in to the SenseCloud portal, the user role, which can be sensor consumer, sensor provider, or admin, determines the operations. In the case of sensor consumers, the dashboard presented by the portal server allows the user to place a request to monitor their virtual sensors, to provision or terminate virtual sensor groups, and to control virtual sensors. In the case of sensor providers, the dashboard provided by the portal server allows the user to register or remove physical sensors. In the case of SenseCloud admins, the dashboard presented by the portal server allows the user to create, modify, and remove the VMs, virtual sensors, and virtual sensor groups. The portal server also forwards the requests to other servers when required.

(ii) *Provisioning Server.* The SenseCloud provisioning server creates the virtual sensor groups and manages them according to the requests that are received from the portal server. This task is achieved by the workflow engine and some predefined workflows in the system. The workflow is executed in the following order:

The provisioning server creates and reserves a VM (if not already created) when it receives the request for provisioning. After the VM is ready, a virtual sensor group is automatically provisioned by the provisioning server. The virtual sensor group is owned by a sensor consumer, and it has one or many virtual sensors. The provisioning server updates the records in the data storage for the virtual sensor groups created by consumers. The consumers can control the virtual sensors. For instance, they can activate or deactivate their subscribed virtual sensors, set the frequency of data, and check the status.

(iii) *Sensor Monitoring Server.* The sensor monitoring server receives the informational or health data about virtual sensors from the virtual servers and stores these data. This information about the virtual sensors is available to sensor consumers on the dashboard. Further, the sensor monitoring server monitors the health status of the physical sensors. This monitoring is important because live data provisioning is based on the live physical sensors. The admins can also monitor the status of the servers.

(iv) *SenseCloud Management Server.* This server provides the location-aware load balancing algorithm that attempts to select a VM instance that is closest to the request sender zone and that has the shortest pending list. This server provides a multitenant solution over the cloud to the registered sensor consumers and providers. It also performs scaling according to the policy engine. This policy engine is based on the network and system performance.

(v) *Virtual Server.* When requested by the provisioning server, the virtual server creates virtual sensors (VSs) on the VM. The VSs are controlled by the portal server. The virtual server provides health information about the sensors to the sensor monitoring server when requested and saves the information in data storage.

(vi) *Data Storage.* Data storage consists of databases for user, VSG, and sensing data.

3.2. System Design.

This subsection provides a detailed explanation of the operations of the sensor provider and consumer in SenseCloud by using sequence diagrams, state machine diagram, and active diagram. Then, this subsection presents the functional view of our system.

3.2.1. Operations of Provider and Consumer. Figure 3 depicts the sequence diagram for the workflows of an important entity, that is, the sensor provider. The sensor provider installs the sensors or sensor network at the corresponding locations. As shown in Figure 3, the sensor provider registers the sensors or sensor network with SenseCloud. After the sensors or sensor networks are registered (registerSensor()), the sensor providers can view them on the dashboard of the portal server, monitor their health (listSensor()), view the usage of their sensors (sensorUsageDetails()), and obtain the monthly usage statement (viewStatement()).

Figure 4 describes the state machine for registerSensor(). When a sensor provider registers for an account, the setup is executed in the cloud. This setup involves the creation of a VM for that sensor provider; the VM will hold all the virtual sensors for every physical sensor plugged in to the cloud by the sensor provider. This setup initiates a process on amazon web service (AWS) using AWS CloudFormation, creates a VM, and updates the database by recording the assignment of the newly created VM against the entry of the sensor provider. If the setup fails, or if the assignment of the VM to the sensor provider account fails, the process is stopped, and the sensor provider is notified. On de-registering the account, the VM is unassigned, and the user account is removed from the records.

Figure 5 shows the detailed flow of the sensor consumer operations in SenseCloud. The sensor consumer registers with SenseCloud. After registration, the consumers can view the list of available sensors on their dashboard of the portal server. They can subscribe to any interesting sensors. After subscription, the consumers can club multiple sensors in a group and can manage their groups through the dashboard. The end consumer can view the real-time analytics, download the archived data, and use the developer APIs to utilize the data in their own applications.

Figure 6 illustrates the activity flow of the sensor consumer who subscribes to the sensor, downloads the historical data, and views the analytics on the dashboard. The cloud infrastructure creates a virtual sensor for each physical sensor that the consumer subscribes to. After subscription to a sensor, the consumer can view and download the real-time and historical data in addition to the analytics on the dashboard.

3.2.2. Functional View of SenseCloud. Figure 7 shows the functional modules corresponding to each entity in SenseCloud; each module provides the following features:

(i) *Registration.* The registration module provides consumers with the login and registration capability to enable them to consume the services and data from the sensors via the dashboard. Further, the sensor providers can register their sensors, which will be authenticated by the admins.

(ii) *Virtualization.* The virtualization module virtualizes the sensor network in the cloud by virtually grouping the sensors and services requested by a consumer. Thus, each consumer can group the sensors and services and can configure, add, edit, and delete the virtualized sensors in the group.

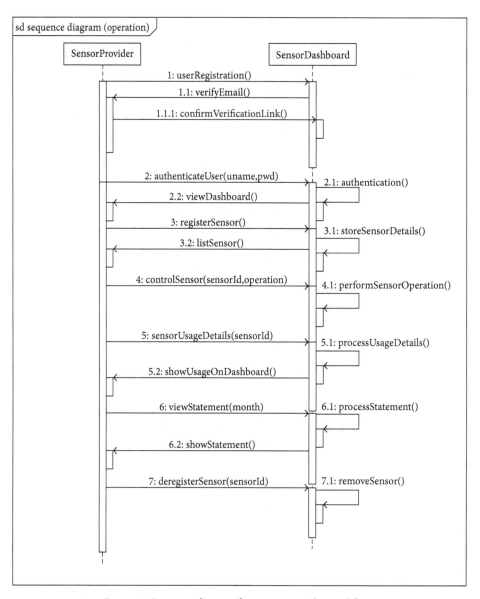

FIGURE 3: Sequence diagram for sensor provider workflow.

(iii) *Provisioning.* The provisioning module provides a sensor provisioning capability to consumers. The network admin should be able to provision the requested sensor resources to the consumers.

(iv) *Multitenancy.* The multitenancy module provides a multitenant solution over the cloud to the registered users (i.e., consumers and providers).

(v) *Scalability and Load Balancing.* The scalability and load balancing module provides easy scalability through an effective and efficient load balancing algorithm. The cloud admin can scale the cloud solution easily. The load balancing ensures the appropriate redirection of user requests to the multiple servers in order to handle the load efficiently.

(vi) *Security and Policy Engine.* The security and policy engine ensures authorization and user-level permissions for different types of users based on configurable

policies and security features. The cloud admin can apply and configure policies to restrict or provide different access control based on the user type.

(vii) *Monitor.* The monitor module provides monitoring capability to sensor providers, cloud admin, and network admin. It uses different metrics such as data bitrate, time, and sensor state to gauge bandwidth, performance, health, and billing. The sensor provider can monitor the actual physical state of the sensors to perform maintenance, provisioning, and de-provisioning of sensors. The cloud admin can monitor the VMs. The network admin can monitor the resource usage for billing and the sensor state for health.

(viii) *Control.* Similar to the monitor module, the control module provides controlling capability to the sensor

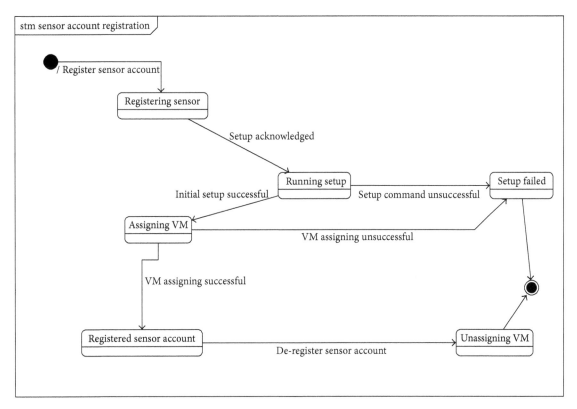

FIGURE 4: State machine diagram for registerSensor() in Figure 3.

provider and admins in order to control the users and sensor network services.

(ix) *Billing.* The billing module provides billing to the consumer according to the usage of data and services. The billing is based on a configurable cost model. The sensor providers can view the usage of their sensors and obtain the monthly usage statement.

(x) *Analytics.* Sensor consumers can access real-time sensor data analysis and archived sensor data analysis on the dashboard.

(xi) *Management.* The management module enables the network admin to manage the virtual sensors. The network admin can create virtual groups with virtual sensors. Further, this module provides user account management and cloud infrastructure management capabilities to the cloud admin.

We focus on the design of virtualization, multitenancy, and dynamic provisioning. We explain our solutions that address these aspects.

(1) Virtualization Solution. In order to obtain the typical benefits of virtualization and provide an abstraction and isolation to the consumers, the virtualization in SenseCloud is composed of two levels (similar to the model in [11]), as shown in Figure 8; these levels are *Sensor-Level Virtualization* and *Consumer-Level Virtualization. Sensor-Level Virtualization* refers to the actual virtualization of physical sensors to VMs. *Consumer-Level Virtualization* refers to the logical

grouping of virtual sensors, thus providing an abstraction and isolation to the consumers.

In *Sensor-Level Virtualization,* SenseCloud virtualizes physical sensors from providers to virtualized instances available to individual consumers. Besides sensor virtualization, we allocate a VM instance to each sensor provider to register, manage, and monitor their sensors and sensor networks, as shown in Figures 8 and 9. In *Consumer-Level Virtualization,* if a consumer subscribes to any of the sensors, the sensors are virtualized, and multiple virtualized sensors are grouped together. This process allows multiple consumers to customize and control virtual sensors corresponding to a single physical sensor. For example, a consumer C1 could group the temperature sensor (virtual sensor) and light sensor (virtual sensor) as virtual sensor group VSG1, and another consumer C2 could group the temperature sensor (virtual sensor) and pressure sensor (virtual sensor) as virtual sensor group VSG2. These two virtual groups (VSG1 and VSG2) are independent of each other and can be customized by the consumer.

Although our system consists of two levels of virtualization, the sensor data are not replicated by each virtual sensor, and the data from each sensor are stored in a common distributed database. Thus, instead of replication of data, the data are shared with consumers who subscribe to the sensors and own the virtual sensors in their virtual sensor group.

(2) Multitenancy Solution. As shown in Figure 10, SenseCloud has two different perspectives for multitenancy: perspective of sensor consumer and perspective of sensor provider.

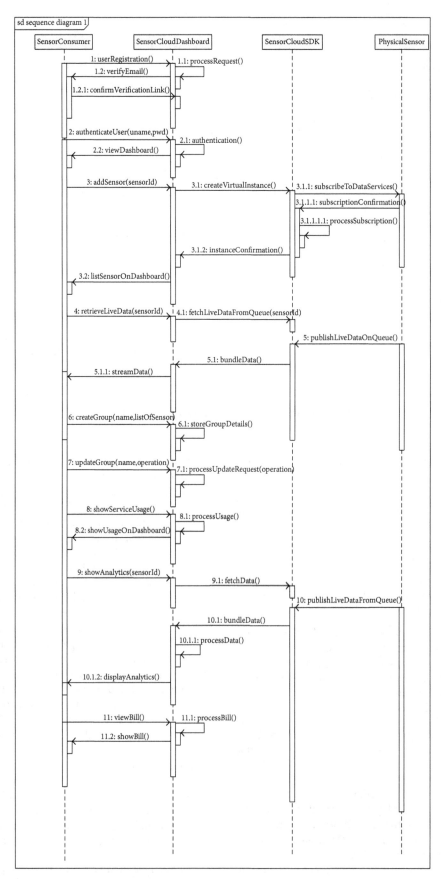

FIGURE 5: Sequence diagram for sensor consumer workflow.

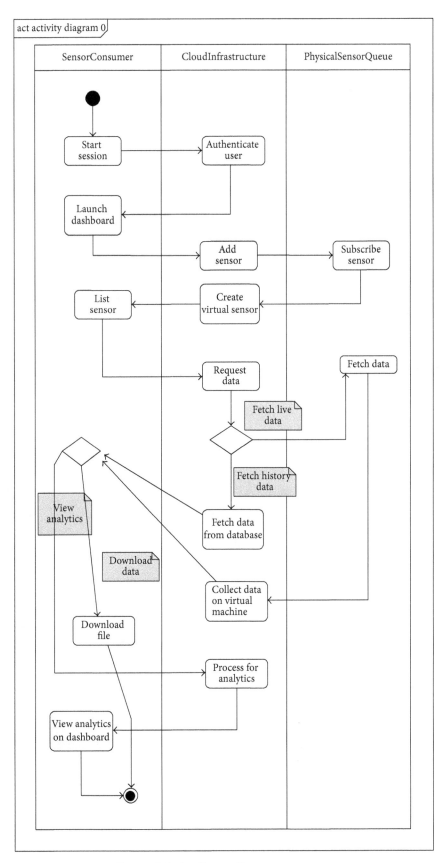

FIGURE 6: Active diagram for sensor consumer.

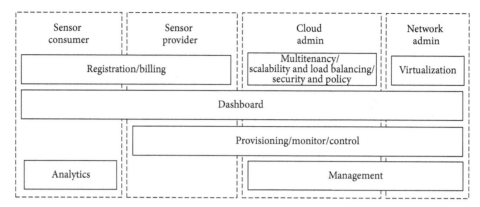

FIGURE 7: Functions of SenseCloud.

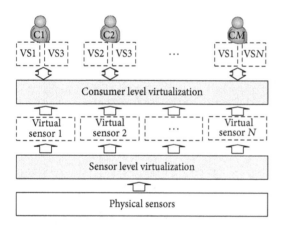

FIGURE 8: SenseCloud virtualization approach (*Ci* is the *i*th sensor consumer, and VS*j* is the *j*th virtual sensor).

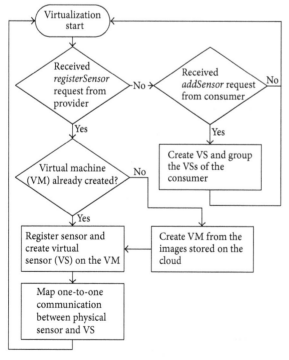

FIGURE 9: SenseCloud virtualization algorithm.

Let us consider SenseCloud from the perspective of the sensor consumer. SenseCloud has the highest degree of multitenancy from this perspective. Sensor consumers share the same application to log in, engage, and manage sensors and sensor data. The application servers (i.e., provisioning servers in the infrastructure) are also shared among various sensor consumers. These application server instances can scale out or in according to the policy engine (refer to (3) Dynamic Provisioning below). The data corresponding to the sensor consumers are stored in shared tables in a common database (i.e., MySQL).

Next, let us consider SenseCloud from the perspective of the sensor provider. Each sensor provider has dedicated infrastructure (i.e., VMs). Each of the instances dedicated to the sensor provider runs its own software stack exclusively for the particular sensor provider. This design considers the following important aspects: security, failover mechanisms, high availability, and reliability. For each sensor provider, several sensors can post data to their specific instances. In case of data corruption, failover, or deliberate attacks, the specific sensor provider can be isolated without affecting or compromising the entire application. However, the data collected from the sensors across sensor providers are stored in a shared database (i.e., Cassandra DB) after filtering and validation. This step is performed to enable analytics over the entire data set.

Further, the multitenancy solution in SenseCloud spans three levels: sensor level, sensor-data level, and sensor-service level. In the multitenancy view of the sensor level, SenseCloud provides diverse sensors and sensor networks to each tenant—that is, consumer—according to the individual demand. Our cloud infrastructure of sensors provides customized composition, provision, and schedule of sensors for each tenant. SenseCloud provides sensor-data level multitenancy—that is, customized data collection, data management, and data visualization—according to the demand of each tenant. Further, our system provides sensor-service level multitenancy, for example, real-time data service and historical data service. In addition, this feature could be enhanced to provide prediction and recommendation services through in-depth analysis of historical data.

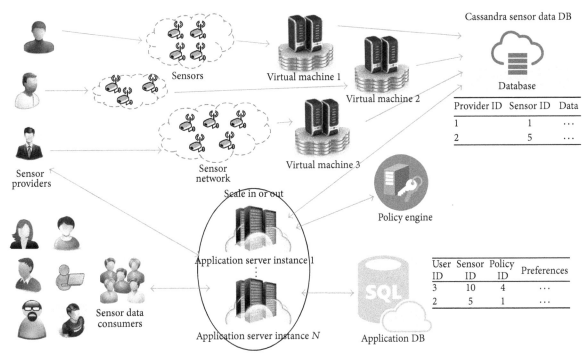

FIGURE 10: SenseCloud multitenancy solution.

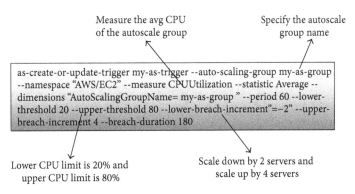

FIGURE 11: Example of SenseCloud scaling policy.

(3) Dynamic Provisioning. In order to allow the sensor consumers to efficiently leverage the vast pool of resources on demand and on a pay-per-use basis, we provide two solutions: scalability solution and load balancing solution.

Our scaling solution considers three parameters for scaling in and out. We consider the average incoming network traffic per instance, average outgoing network traffic per instance, and average CPU utilization per instance. As shown in Figure 11, we dynamically set thresholds for each of these parameters according to the usage patterns. When surpassed, these thresholds trigger the dynamic creation and deletion of instances to efficiently scale out and scale in, respectively.

The load balancing solution is shown in Figure 12. When an application server (e.g., provisioning server) receives the request, it selects a load balancer from the multiple load balancers by using the round robin algorithm. If only one load balancer exists, it is selected by default. The selected load balancer uses the location-aware load balancing algorithm in conjunction with the least outstanding request routing algorithm. Thus, the location-aware load balancing algorithm attempts to select an instance that is closest to the request sender zone and that has the shortest pending list. First, the load balancer selects the availability zone closest to the location where the request is sent. Then, the load balancer determines the application server instances that exist in the selected availability zone. If multiple application server instances exist, the load balancer selects an instance according to the least outstanding request routing algorithm; that is, it selects an instance that has the smallest queue size for outstanding requests.

4. Performance Evaluation

This section describes the implementation of a prototype of SenseCloud, thus demonstrating the feasibility of our system. Then, the prototype is evaluated in terms of the

TABLE 2: Tools and technologies.

Tools and technologies	Name	Version	Description
Development	Java, Python, Groovy, JS	NA	Independent programming language
API framework	Swagger	1.5	Representation of RESTful API
Operating system	Linux	14	Open-source operating system
White-box testing framework	JUnit	3.8.1	Dedicated testing framework for Java with native support
Black-box testing framework	Selenium	2	Automated testing framework for web applications
Integrated development environment	Eclipse	Luna	Widely used IDE with full support for Java and third-party plugins
Communication protocol	MQTT	2.3.1	Lightweight publish-subscribe broker communication protocol for IoT
Storage	Cassandra	2.1.7	Big data storage on clustered commodity hardware
	MySQL	5.1.36	SQL database to store dashboard-related information
Continuous integration framework	Jenkins	1	Continuous integration for software development. Also supports Git repository
UI	HTML	5	Fundamental and flexible Web UI language for web application
	CSS	3	Fundamental and flexible Web UI styling for web application
	JQuery	2	DOM manipulation library
Web	moris.js	0.5.1	Graphical data visualization Java Script library
	Bootstrap	3	Java Script framework to build responsive websites
Repository	Git	1.9	Open-source subversion repository. Powerful collaboration, management, and code review for projects
Cloud	AWS	NA	Amazon Web Services to build cloud infrastructure
Build tool	Maven	3.2.1	Build automation system to automate build, testing, publishing, and deployment activities
UML	Astah	6	Design UML diagrams
MQTT client	Eclipse Paho	0.4.0	Open-source client implementation of MQTT
Logging	Log4j	1.2.17	Library for logging in Java
Sensor kit	RasberryPi, Samsung SmartThings	NA	10 microcontrollers with sensors: RasberryPi has temperature sensor, pressure sensor, ambient light sensor, and LED; SmartThings has temperature sensor, contact sensor, humidity sensor, motion sensor, and orientation sensor

system response time and the performance of our functional algorithms.

4.1. Evaluation of Implementation. Table 2 shows the tools and technologies that we used to implement a prototype of SenseCloud and to test it.

We present some screenshots of our implemented prototype. Users type the SenseCloud index page URL in the browser. After successful registration, the users can log in to their account by entering their credentials. After successful login, the users are redirected to the main dashboard page, which shows the links to the functions that the users can perform, as shown in Figure 13(a).

Sensor providers can click the "Manage My Sensors" menu to view, edit, and delete the sensors that they have registered; Figure 13(b) shows the sensor list of a sensor provider. Sensor providers can add sensors by clicking the "Add a Sensor" menu. They can group their sensors and manage the groups through the "Manage Provider Groups" menu; further, they can add sensor hubs by selecting the "Add a Sensor Hub" menu in order to create a sensor network.

Sensor consumers can subscribe to interesting sensors through the "Subscribe Sensors" menu, view the list of available sensors, search for sensors, and subscribe to these sensors. Sensor consumers can manage their subscriptions and view the data of the subscribed sensors through the "Manage Subscribed Sensors" menu. The subscribed sensors can also be grouped together; then, the consumer can view, edit, manage, and visualize the data from the sensors of the created group by selecting the "Manage Subscriber Group" menu. Figure 13(c) shows the temperature sensor data for a subscribed sensor. The consumer can view the daily current, minimum, maximum, and average temperature and can also download the historical data in JSON format by selecting the date. Figure 13(d) shows the maximum and minimum temperatures of the current week for a subscribed sensor.

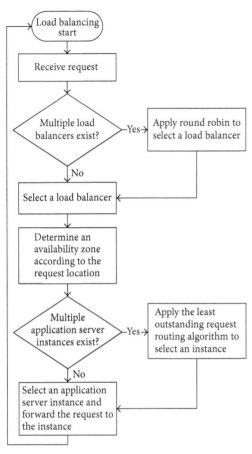

FIGURE 12: SenseCloud load balancing algorithm.

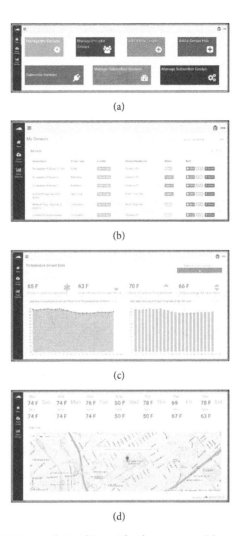

FIGURE 13: Screenshots of SenseCloud prototypes: (a) menu page; (b) sensors viewed through "Manage My Sensors" menu; (c) sensor historical data through "View" menu of each sensor; (d) view sensor data with map through "View on Map" menu of each subscribed sensor.

A map displays the current geo-location of the sensor. The implementation of the SenseCloud prototype confirms the feasibility of our system.

4.2. Performance Observation. In order to evaluate the performance of our prototype, we develop the servers of SenseCloud on AWS cloud infrastructure and generate client requests to the servers. We observe the system response time, varying the request types of each scenario, the number of requests, and applied performance-tuning mechanisms. Having many requests more than 1000 is statistically meaningful. Finally, we measure request distributions to show the performance of our functional algorithms (i.e., load balancing and scalability).

First, in order to evaluate the system response time, we create three scenarios by varying the number of requests to list the subscribed sensor and the number of requests to add sensors. Further, in a scenario, we increase the number of users from 1 to 100. The requests from a single user correspond to synchronous calls, and different users create simultaneous connections.

As shown in Tables 3 and 4, the performance remains the same even if we increase the number of synchronous requests from 1000 to 5000. This result is an effect of the multitenant architecture and load balancer algorithm running on the VMs; owing to this design, the incoming requests are handled

in parallel, and the same throughput is obtained. Further, when the number of simultaneous connections increases, we observe that even if the number of users increases, the performance deteriorates only by a small amount.

Next, we create eight scenarios, varying the number of requests to perform the following 13-page traverses and applying mechanisms for performance tuning (i.e., connection pooling, prepared statement, and object caching). A request includes traversals of the following 13 pages:

(1) Home page.

(2) Registration.

(3) Login.

(4) Add sensor to cloud.

(5) List provided sensors.

(6) Group of provided sensors.

(7) Consumer dashboard.

TABLE 3: System response time versus requests to list the subscribed sensors.

| Scenario | Number of requests | | | Average (deviation) response time (ms) |
	Requests to list the subscribed sensors per user	Users	Total requests	
1	1000	1	1000	6 (0)
2	5000	1	5000	6 (7)
3	1000	100	100000	27 (63)

TABLE 4: System response time versus requests to add sensors.

| Scenario | Number of requests | | | Average (deviation) response time (ms) |
	Requests to add sensors per user	Users	Total requests	
1	1000	1	1000	11 (2)
2	5000	1	5000	11 (0)
3	1000	100	100000	1177 (78)

(8) Subscribe sensors.

(9) My Sensors.

(10) My Groups.

(11) Dashboard for temperature sensor analysis.

(12) Dashboard for temperature and video sensor analysis in my group.

(13) Logout.

From the results in Table 5, the use of other performance-tuning mechanisms such as connection pooling, prepared statement, and object caching has significantly reduced the average time for a request response. Our system implements connection pooling by maintaining a connection pool of database connections and using the queue mechanism to dequeue or enqueue database connection objects. This process improves the performance significantly because the connection objects are reused. Instead of traditional statements, prepared statements are used for database querying. The prepared statements are precompiled. Object caching is also implemented in our system; the most frequently queried results are cached based on the time-to-live.

In order to evaluate the performance of our load balancing and scalability algorithms, we use a request generator that, at a given time, randomly generates 1000 requests across nine locations. Initially, each location has one instance. All instances have different configurations created in the Elastic Cloud Compute service of Amazon Web Services (AWS). The nine locations on AWS are as follows [23]:

(1) US East (N. Virginia).

(2) US West (Oregon).

(3) US West (N. California).

(4) EU (Ireland).

(5) Asia Pacific (Singapore).

(6) Asia Pacific (Tokyo).

(7) Asia Pacific (Sydney).

(8) Asia Pacific (Seoul).

(9) South America (Sao Paulo).

Figure 14 is a graphical representation of the request distribution results according to the applied algorithms. From the results shown in Figure 14(a), in the absence of the algorithms, all the 1000 requests were randomly distributed across all the locations. Thus, the result of request distribution is the most uneven in this case. In Figure 14(b), only the load balancing algorithm is applied; the load balancer attempts to distribute the requests originating from a particular location until the capacity of the server to serve requests reaches a maximum. If overload occurs, the requests are redirected to different locations randomly, using the least pending request algorithm. For example, location 1 received 121 requests, and according to the load balancing algorithm, the first 101 requests are handled by the instance at location 1. After the instance at location 1 reaches its threshold, the subsequent requests are directed to other locations by using the least outstanding request routing algorithm. In Figure 14(c), only the scalability algorithm is enabled. When a particular location experiences a surge in network traffic and high CPU usage that reaches the threshold values, our system scales the infrastructure for that location. For example, when the instance at location 1 reached its threshold, the infrastructure at location 1 scaled out, and the subsequent requests were handled by these instances at location 1. In Figure 14(d), both algorithms are enabled, and they work in conjunction to serve the requests. For example, location 1 received 202 requests. Based on the load balancing algorithm and these requests, location 1 scaled out to serve these requests. A similar trend is observed for the other locations.

5. Conclusions and Future Work

SenseCloud is a cloud platform that addresses the challenges of virtualization, multitenancy, and dynamic provisioning encountered by the IoT industry today. Our cloud infrastructure provides a layer that connects with different sensor networks, resolves the connectivity and engagement concerns, and efficiently provides CSaaS between sensor providers and consumers. SenseCloud provides a two-level virtualization mechanism. It virtualizes the physical sensors to enable the consumers to utilize them without apprehensions about the specification and location details. Further, it allows the

TABLE 5: System response time versus requests and applied mechanisms.

	Number of requests			Applied mechanisms			
Scenario	Requests per user	Users	Total requests	Connection pooling	Prepared statement	Caching	Average (deviation) response time (ms)
1	1000	1	1000				65 (86)
2	1000	1	1000	√			54 (73)
3	1000	1	1000	√	√		42 (66)
4	1000	1	1000	√	√	√	13 (17)
5	1000	10	10000				401 (392)
6	1000	10	10000	√			307 (502)
7	1000	10	10000	√	√		250 (417)
8	1000	10	10000	√	√	√	125 (84)

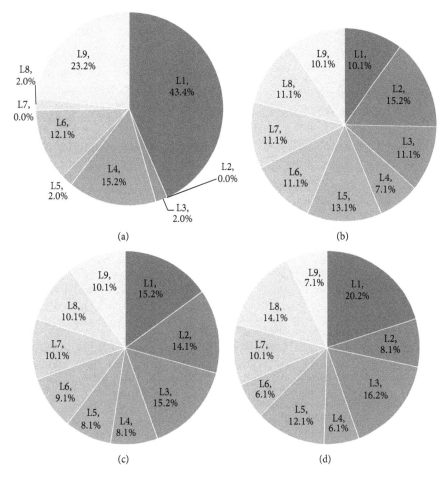

FIGURE 14: Request Distributions with/without our load balancing and scalability algorithms on AWS (L*i* denotes location *i*): (a) without algorithms; (b) with load balancing; (c) with scalability algorithm; (d) with load balancing and scalability algorithms.

consumers to place dynamic requests for virtual sensor groups and to customize the virtual sensor groups. Sense-Cloud provides different types of multitenancy to sensor providers and consumers: It provides a virtual instance dedicated to each provider to enable isolation without affecting the other providers in case of failover or attacks; further, it also provides common application server instances to all consumers for efficient sharing of resources. SenseCloud

provides dynamic provisioning to allow the consumers to leverage the vast pool of resources on demand and on a pay-per-use basis. The results from our prototype implementation and simulation have demonstrated the feasibility of Sense-Cloud and the achievement of our objectives.

In future work, we must consider the large number of IoT devices and the exponential growth of sensor manufacturers in the market. Instead of adopting a de facto standard, we must define a specific standard for communication, data format, and security between the devices and the cloud platform. The definition of such a standard will eliminate the necessity of frequent changes in the cloud implementation when a new manufacturer enters the market. Current security in SenseCloud is imposed by the role-based access control and provision policy and the two levels of virtualization. With advanced and proper security being the most important feature in the world of connected devices, further development and advancement is required to increase the trust in such cloud platforms among consumers.

Competing Interests

The authors declare that there is no conflict of interests regarding the publication of this paper.

Acknowledgments

This research was supported by Basic Science Research Program through the National Research Foundation of Korea (NRF) funded by the Ministry of Education (Grant no. 2015R1D1A1A01057362).

References

[1] A. Botta, W. De Donato, V. Persico, and A. Pescape, "On the integration of cloud computing and internet of things," in *Proceedings of the 2nd International Conference on Future Internet of Things and Cloud (FiCloud '14)*, pp. 23–30, Barcelona, Spain, August 2014.

[2] X. Sheng, J. Tang, X. Xiao, and G. Xue, "Sensing as a service: challenges, solutions and future directions," *IEEE Sensors Journal*, vol. 13, no. 10, pp. 3733–3741, 2013.

[3] F. C. Delicato, P. F. Pires, L. Pirmez, and T. Batista, "Wireless sensor networks as a service," in *Proceedings of the 17th IEEE International Conference and Workshops on the Engineering of Computer-Based Systems (ECBS '10)*, pp. 410–417, Oxford, UK, March 2010.

[4] V. Rajesh, O. Pandithurai, and S. Mageshkumar, "Wireless sensor node data on cloud," in *Proceedings of the IEEE International Conference on Communication Control and Computing Technologies (ICCCCT '10)*, pp. 476–481, IEEE, Ramanathapuram, India, October 2010.

[5] J. Ibbotson, C. Gibson, J. Wright et al., "Sensors as a service oriented architecture: middleware for sensor networks," in *Proceedings of the 6th International Conference on Intelligent Environments (IE '10)*, pp. 209–214, Kuala Lumpur, Malaysia, July 2010.

[6] A. Zaslavsky, C. Perera, and D. Georgakopoulos, "Sensing as a service and big data," in *Proceedings of the International Conference on Advances in Cloud Computing (ACC '12)*, pp. 21–29, Bangalore, India, July 2012.

[7] D. Gračanin, M. Eltoweissy, A. Wadaa, and L. A. DaSilva, "A service-centric model for wireless sensor networks," *IEEE Journal on Selected Areas in Communications*, vol. 23, no. 6, pp. 1159–1165, 2005.

[8] S. Distefano, G. Merlino, and A. Puliafito, "Sensing and actuation as a service: a new development for clouds," in *Proceedings of the IEEE 11th International Symposium on Network Computing*

and Applications (NCA '12)*, pp. 272–275, Cambridge, Mass, USA, August 2012.

[9] A. Deshwal, S. Kohli, and K. P. Chethan, "Information as a service based architectural solution for WSN," in *Proceedings of the 1st IEEE International Conference on Communications in China (ICCC '12)*, pp. 68–73, Beijing, China, August 2012.

[10] R. Di Lauro, F. Lucarelli, and R. Montella, "SIaaS—sensing instrument as a service using cloud computing to turn physical instrument into ubiquitous service," in *Proceedings of the 10th IEEE International Symposium on Parallel and Distributed Processing with Applications (ISPA '12)*, pp. 861–862, IEEE, Madrid, Spain, July 2012.

[11] M. Yuriyama and T. Kushida, "Sensor-cloud infrastructure—physical sensor management with virtualized sensors on cloud computing," in *Proceedings of the 13th International Conference on Network-Based Information Systems (NBiS '10)*, pp. 1–8, IEEE, Takayama, Japan, September 2010.

[12] M. A. E. Al-Fagih, F. M. Al-Turjman, W. M. Alsalih, and H. S. Hassanein, "Priced public sensing framework for heterogeneous IoT architectures," *IEEE Transactions on Emerging Topics in Computing*, vol. 1, no. 1, pp. 133–147, 2013.

[13] C. Perera, A. Zaslavsky, P. Christen, and D. Georgakopoulos, "Sensing as a service model for smart cities supported by Internet of Things," *European Transactions on Telecommunications*, vol. 25, no. 1, pp. 81–93, 2014.

[14] M. M. Hassan, B. Song, and E.-N. Huh, "A framework of sensor—cloud integration opportunities and challenges," in *Proceedings of the 3rd International Conference on Ubiquitous Information Management and Communication (ICUIMC '09)*, pp. 618–626, Suwon, Republic of Korea, January 2009.

[15] Y. Ishi, T. Kawakami, T. Yoshihisa, Y. Teranishi, K. Nakauchi, and N. Nishinaga, "Design and implementation of sensor data sharing platform for virtualized wide area sensor networks," in *Proceedings of the 7th International Conference on P2P, Parallel, Grid, Cloud and Internet Computing (3PGCIC '12)*, pp. 333–338, Victoria, Canada, November 2012.

[16] A. Kansal, S. Nath, J. Liu, and F. Zhao, "SenseWeb: an infrastructure for shared sensing," *IEEE MultiMedia*, vol. 14, no. 4, pp. 8–13, 2007.

[17] J. Gubbi, R. Buyya, S. Marusic, and M. Palaniswami, "Internet of Things (IoT): a vision, architectural elements, and future directions," *Future Generation Computer Systems*, vol. 29, no. 7, pp. 1645–1660, 2013.

[18] R. Khan, S. U. Khan, R. Zaheer, and S. Khan, "Future internet: the internet of things architecture, possible applications and key challenges," in *Proceedings of the 10th IEEE International Conference on Frontiers of Information Technology (FIT '12)*, pp. 257–260, Islamabad, Pakistan, December 2012.

[19] D. B. Hoang and L. Chen, "Mobile Cloud for Assistive Healthcare (MoCAsH)," in *Proceedings of the IEEE Asia-Pacific Services Computing Conference (APSCC '10)*, pp. 325–332, Hangzhou, China, December 2010.

[20] B. B. P. Rao, P. Saluia, N. Sharma, A. Mittal, and S. V. Sharma, "Cloud computing for Internet of Things & sensing based applications," in *Proceedings of the 6th International Conference on Sensing Technology (ICST '12)*, pp. 374–380, Kolkata, India, December 2012.

[21] Q. Zhu, R. Wang, Q. Chen, Y. Liu, and W. Qin, "IOT gateway: bridging wireless sensor networks into internet of things," in *Proceedings of the IEEE/IFIP 8th International Conference on Embedded and Ubiquitous Computing (EUC '10)*, pp. 347–352, Hong Kong, December 2010.

14

Cybercrimes: A Proposed Taxonomy and Challenges

Harmandeep Singh Brar ⑩[1] **and Gulshan Kumar** ⑩[2]

[1]*Department of Computer Applications, Maharaja Ranjit Singh Punjab Technical University, Bathinda, India*
[2]*Department of Computer Applications, Shaheed Bhagat Singh State Technical Campus, Ferozepur, India*

Correspondence should be addressed to Harmandeep Singh Brar; harmanbrar22@gmail.com

Academic Editor: Youyun Xu

Cybersecurity is one of the most important concepts of cyberworld which provides protection to the cyberspace from various types of cybercrimes. This paper provides an updated survey of cybersecurity. We conduct the survey of security of recent prominent researches and categorize the recent incidents in context to various fundamental principles of cybersecurity. We have proposed a new taxonomy of cybercrime which can cover all types of cyberattacks. We have analyzed various cyberattacks as per the updated cybercrime taxonomy to identify the challenges in the field of cybersecurity and highlight various research directions as future work in this field.

1. Introduction

In this modern age, the world is becoming more familiar and close to each other by means of Internet and new networking technologies. The networking infrastructure is the base for information sharing among individuals, private sectors, and military and government sectors. Approximately 50% of the world population has an Internet connection up to January 2017. There is a rise of 10% in the Internet users from January 2016 to January 2017 [1]. According to [2], in 2016, there are 6.4 billion connected devices and this will reach 20.8 billion by 2020. The present world technologies of hardware and software give new wings to the process of connecting various devices (mobiles and smartwatches) with Internet. Anybody can get, see, and share information on the Internet from any place in this world. There is a huge growth of Internet-connected devices from the past to the present which give rise to the area of the cyberspace. The growth of Internet users in the world and world population is shown in Figure 1.

During the last five years, we observed that an increasing number of data, devices, and clouds were forming a perfect security storm of threats. Some of the threat predictions became true which are leading significance of much bigger storm expected in the near future. The dynamicity in the

work place, highly mobile work strength, and frequently changing expectations of workers have changed the concept of network boundary. The flood of personal network devices has created an exponential growth of personal data on the Internet. According to [3], the number of devices will continue to grow in both volume and variety, and they predict that this number will reach 200 billion by 2020 and continue to grow in the future. So, the cyberspace is expanding everyday. This expansion has given rise to the various opportunities for cybercriminals to do malicious acts on the Internet and also given rise to the difficulty level for security professionals to put a security umbrella on the entire cyberspace. It is clear from the above discussion that the cyberspace has a huge volume of data and information that is available on the Internet and its resources must be protected from cybercriminals [3].

Every individual is doing some work to fulfill his/her objective. The objective may be to gain money, respect, revenge, or any other. Cyberattackers also have objectives for which they do cyberattacks/cybercrimes. Here, we will discuss the most common objectives of cyberattackers.

(1) Entertainment. Some cybercriminals perform their activities of cyberattack to test their hacking abilities. They feel proud and joy in their successful attempts.

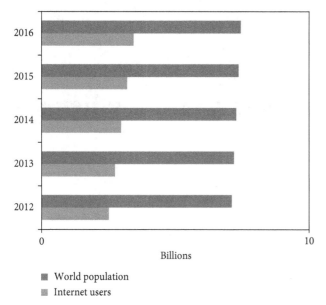

Billions

■ World population
■ Internet users

FIGURE 1: Internet users in the world.

They are willing to get fame in the world of cyber-criminals. They feel joy and proud when they make an attack which was not performed by any other attacker or other attackers failed to perform that attack.

(2) Hacktivists. These cyberattackers are motivated by political, religious, and social ends. Their motive is to preach their political and religious mottos and to discourage the people of other sets. They want to extend their religion or politics to make them popular among the masses. The current trend of 2016 and 2017 shows that hacktivists are exposing the individuals having secret affairs through social websites. The latest example is Ashley Madison dating whose users list was exposed by attackers in public domain.

(3) Financial gain. Most of the cyberattackers perform the cyberattacks for financial gain. They desire to become rich. The target of cyberattackers may be the banking system, big companies, organizations, rich individuals, or wealthy countries. Some of these cyberattackers are either hired by some country, organization, company, or individual.

(4) Spying. These types of cybercriminals attack the networks to steal the confidential information of specific country, organization, or individual. Spy hackers may use similar tactics as hacktivists, but their only agenda is to serve their client's goals and get paid in return.

(5) Revenge. These types of cybercriminals include the expelled, irritated, and humiliated employees. They knew the policies, secrets, and weak points of their company, organization, or country. They perform their activities of cyberattacks under the emotion of hate to take their revenge in the form of financial loss, tarnishing their social image, reputation, and so on.

In this paper, we conduct the survey of cybersecurity of recent prominent researches in context to various security principles, namely, confidentiality, integrity, and availability in the field. We categorize the recent incidents of cybersecurity on the basis of these fundamental principles and propose a new taxonomy of various cybercrimes. We have analyzed various security attacks as per the updated taxonomy to identify the challenges in the field and highlight various research directions as future work in the field.

To facilitate the discussion of cybersecurity, Section 2 introduces the cybersecurity and the fundamental principles of cybersecurity. In Section 3, the various types of environments affected by cybercrimes in the past few years have been discussed. Section 4 gives the introduction of various types of cybercrimes. The introduction about various types of cyberattacks is discussed according to the fundamental principles of cyberattacks and also classified according to cybercrimes in Section 5. In Section 6, the various challenges of cybercrimes are discussed. Section 7 concludes this paper.

2. Cybersecurity

Cybersecurity deals with the security of the cyberspace from cybercriminals. The cyberspace constitutes all those things (hardware, software, and data/information) that are connected to the Internet/network. It is important to implement the cybersecurity effectively to protect the Internet system and the trust of people on this system from various cyberattacks. A flaw in cybersecurity and an uncovered cyberspace will provide a chance to cyberattackers to disrupt the Internet system. The three basic fundamental principles of cybersecurity are confidentiality, integrity, and availability. The three basic fundamental principles are also known as the CIA triad. The elements of the triad are considered as the most crucial components of cybersecurity [4]. The cyberattacks on the information and data on the Internet can affect these three fundamental principles of cybersecurity. So, there is a great need to setup cybersecurity to preserve these fundamental principles. Cybersecurity that does not constitute these three fundamental principles is considered to be vulnerable to cyberattacks. The fundamental principles of cybersecurity are discussed below.

2.1. Confidentiality. In the present day, every person may have confidential information like login credentials (username and password), SSN, credit card information, and a soft copy of personal documents and work files which may be stored on the computer system or server or it may be on any device connected to the Internet which needs protection from cyberattacks. Access to confidential information must be restricted to an organization of authorized users only. The measure is to be taken according to the importance of data. The higher the importance of data, the higher the risk. So, serious measures are to be taken to protect the confidential information from cyberattacks to narrow down or eliminate the risk level. There are various methods which can be used to protect the confidentiality of information from the cyberattacks:

TABLE 1: Classification of recent cybercrimes on the basis of security fundamental principles.

Security goals	Objective	Recent incidents of cybercrimes in 2016-17
Confidentiality	Limits the data access to authorized users only	(1) Confidential information of users of nine password manager apps like Dashlane, My Passwords, Password manager, etc. was found to be leaked. Methods used by attackers were data residue attacks and clipboard sniffing [6] (2) 85 million user accounts have been stolen from Dailymotion on 20 October 2016 [7]
Integrity	Assures the accuracy of data	(1) Cyberattack on the Ukraine Kiev's power grid caused the power outage on December 17 near midnight in the northern part [8] (2) Two weeks before the Trump's presidency in America, a cyberattacker hacked the radio stations to play "F**k Donald Trump" across the country [9]
Availability	Makes sure that authorized users always access the network and its resources	(1) Cyberattack affected 900,000 customers of Deutsche Telekom by knocking a million routers offline in November 2016 [10] (2) DDoS attacks on five major Russian banks disrupted the services of the bank to their customers for two days in November 2016 [11] (3) The WannaCry attack locked 90,000 computers in 99 countries and was ready to release them for a ransom of $300–$500 bitcoins [12]

data encryption, biometric verification, using strong user id and password, and user awareness [4, 5].

2.2. Integrity. Integrity means protecting the information and data on the Internet from alteration by cybercriminals. Integrity provides the consistency and accuracy of information on the network. The integrity of the information and data on the cyberspace can be preserved by taking appropriate steps like file permissions, user access controls, and digital signature. The bigger attacks are always the main attraction of security professionals. But security professionals cannot underestimate the small cybercrimes, as the number of small integrity attacks on information can make a huge impact on the infrastructure of an organization, state, or country. The information on the Internet might include cryptographic checksums to ensure the integrity. Backup must be maintained to recover from any tampering in information and data on the Internet due to cyberattacks or any natural calamities (earthquakes and tsunami) [4, 5].

2.3. Availability. Availability is a security policy which ensures that any individual, employee of an organization (public or private), with authorized access can use information and data on the Internet according to the specified access level by its organization. Information which cannot be used by any authorized user is like waste in a dustbin. Server systems and computer systems must have sufficient capacity to satisfy user requests for access of information on the Internet. Availability of information can be disrupted by cyberattacks, natural calamities, and environmental factors [4, 5].

Here are some latest cybercrimes that are classified according to the cybersecurity fundamental principles shown in Table 1.

3. Literature Survey

To understand a concept in a better way, it is necessary to study its pattern that can be formed by learning its past and present. This section presents the various studies related to cybersecurity and cybercrimes in different platforms from 2012 to 2016.

Liu et al. raised the need for cybersecurity in the smart grid environment [13]. They had surveys about the various factors that show that the current security mechanisms are not enough to protect the smart grids from various cyberattacks. They stated that the security requirements of smart grids are just the reverse of requirements of IT networks. They focused on the need for some different kinds of mechanism needed for smart grids that can fulfill its security requirements.

von Solms and van Niekerk presented a paper in which they explained the difference and relation between information security and cybersecurity [14]. They stated that most of the people use the term "cybersecurity" instead of information security. But both the terms have a different meaning and effect in the cyberworld. They concluded that the cybersecurity is a broader term than information security which not only provides security to a specific area but also everything that constitutes the cyberspace.

Razzaq et al. presented a survey paper on cybersecurity of data and information on the cyberspace [15]. They analyzed that nothing is safe in the present scenario. They stated that the current cybersecurity techniques are not quite efficient for all kinds of attacks and focus on the need for new security mechanisms which are not based on previous cyberattack signatures but also can defend against future attacks.

Schneider presented a paper on the need for proper implementation of cybersecurity education in educational institutions or universities [16]. He stated that the lack of the cybersecurity education in universities is giving chance to outsiders like private sector and also public sector to offer cybersecurity training which makes the work of cybercriminals easy. There is a need for study and training of cybersecurity to make an environment that can defend against cyberthreats. The devices used by a person that are connected to the Internet are difficult to hack if he/she has basic knowledge of cybersecurity. So, cybersecurity training also decreases the number of cyberattack incidents to make the work of cybercriminals harder.

Kaster and Sen presented the study of cybersecurity of the world's largest power grid [17]. From various observations, they found that the cybersecurity at the present stage is not smart enough according to new technologies and new devices that are part of the cyberworld. They presented the need and importance of cybersecurity for power grid system by pointing out that cyberthreat is the topmost threat in the list of various threats to the power grid system.

Jang-Jaccard and Nepal presented a survey on the changing trends in threats to social media, cloud computing, smartphones, and so on and various types of vulnerabilities found in hardware, software, and network infrastructure [18]. They found that the traditional approaches make the cybersecurity system stronger against existing ones and new cyberthreats are not suitable to modern technology. They stated that unique identity and the traceback techniques are new hot future research topics.

Arlitsch and Edelman presented a survey on various data breaches in 2013 and 2014 [19]. They found out that confidential data of an individual and private and public sectors are one of the main targets of a cyberattacker. Their paper focused on the need for new mechanisms to enhance the current cybersecurity for information infrastructure on the Internet.

Rawat and Bajracharya presented a survey paper on the need for cybersecurity for smart grids [20]. They discussed the increased cybersurface of smart grids and various security challenges of this extended cybersurface of smart grids. They discussed the cybersecurity attacks and defense techniques in smart grid systems that are aimed at different networks and protocol layers. Their paper is well formed to understand the concepts of the smart grid and its security.

Ali et al. presented software-defined networking as a best possible solution to enhance the security of networks [21]. They presented various benefits of using SDN (like flexible policies, threat detection and remediation, and network verification) to protect the network system from various cyberthreats. They presented some issues of SDN (NFV, overlay networks, and OpenFlow) which are yet to be resolved in the near future to protect SDN from cyberthreats. They presented the need for more advanced security for the SDN to defend against cyberattacks.

Sadeghi et al. presented the need for more security and privacy in the IoT (Internet of Things) [22]. They stated that, with the invention of new types of computing devices in the IoT environment, the attack surface has grown to be very sharp and there is a need for new security mechanisms that can cover this increased cyberspace of IoT.

Singh et al. stated that, despite several advantages of cloud computing, its one disadvantage is its major challenge in its adoption [23]. That disadvantage is its vulnerability. In this paper, they discussed a scenario of cloud computing, various security issues, and threats in cloud computing. They proposed a new 3-tier security architecture to enhance the security of cloud computing by reviewing the old techniques.

Weber and Studer presented a paper in which they showed the need, change, and importance of legal aspects of cybersecurity in the Internet of Things [24]. They stated that IoT brings a lot of advantages but whenever a new device is connected to the Internet, it also faces the same threat level which previous devices were facing. They focused on the point that the cybersecurity should not be limited to a specific point or legal aspect or regulatory approaches.

Zou et al. described the various layers of the OSI model for wireless systems which follow a different approach than wired systems [25]. They discussed the vulnerabilities of all the layers of the OSI model, and their focus is on the exploration of physical layer security concepts due to its nature of securing the open communication environment. They briefly discussed the various attacks (eavesdropping and jamming attacks) and their countermeasures on the physical layer. Their paper contributes in terms that very good knowledge of wireless security concepts and techniques used in that OSI model are explained.

As per the findings of the literature survey cited above, it is clear that cybercrimes on the Internet are an emerging and dynamic concept. The types of cybercrimes and their effects are changing day by day. However, most of the researches have discussed cybersecurity from the viewpoint of a specific environment. No general taxonomy has been provided. So, the present study is focused on the brief knowledge of cybercrimes and cyberattacks that can affect the cybersecurity in general covering various aspects of cybersecurity in terms of security principles.

4. The Proposed Taxonomy of the Cybercrime

In the existing world of Internet, we can find a huge volume and a variety of cyberattacks. From the history of cyberattacks on the Internet, it is concluded that trends of attacks are continuously changing day by day. The crime which can take place with the help of the computer system and the Internet is known as *cybercrime*. It is malicious activity which can affect the three fundamental principles of network security, that is, confidentiality, integrity, and availability. The cybercrime includes the terms like fraud, stealing, fights, and world war. These terms are also used in real-life crimes, but in the world of Internet, these terms have almost the same meaning but with different techniques. Most of the crimes occurring in today's world are cybercrimes. Hackers are finding a new way to change their attack patterns which increases the difficulty for security professionals to defend the information and data on the Internet and its resources. Hackers are providing free attack tools on the Internet to increase the number of attack rates on the Internet system. The increasing numbers of e-services like online shopping, online banking, and social apps have given a huge rise to the number of Internet users which are easily targeted by the cybercriminals. So, the various types of cybercrimes

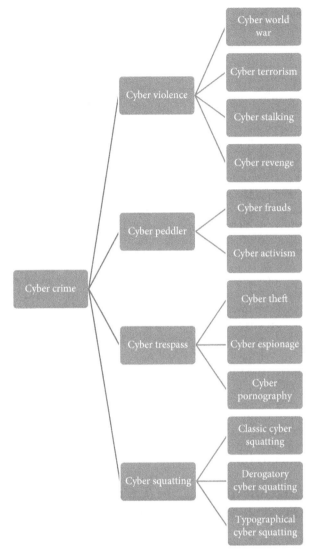

FIGURE 2: Taxonomy of the cybercrime.

to disable, or to destroy the infrastructure and resources based on the Internet system of rival or enemy country. In this war, every type of cyberattack is used to achieve victory over the target country.

4.1.2. Cyberterrorism. There are some people or groups which have only aim of destroying the humanity known as terrorists. They believe that they are doing this to make their religion more powerful in the world or they have only right to command over the world or no other can be stronger than them. The terrorism like this in the digital world is known as cyberterrorism. They have no emotions or sympathy. They are like machines whose aim is fed into them. They can use any type of cyberattack to fulfill their aim.

4.1.3. Cyberstalking. It is like for loop of C language in which termination condition is the harassment of your target. In this type of attack, attackers make use of electronic communication (email and instant messaging) to attack their target [28].

4.1.4. Cyberrevenge. Revenge means harming someone in response to one's previous action. The aim of cyberrevenge is to destroy the enemy by various ways like exposing their confidential information, destroying their computer-based infrastructure and resources, and making their false image on the Internet system. The aim of cyberrevenge is to steal and change the confidential information of enemy for his/her vested interests.

4.2. Cyberpeddler. Cyberpeddler is an act of doing something illegal or stealing someone's confidential data with the help of a computer system connected to the Internet. There are basically two types of cybercrimes in this category which are discussed below.

4.2.1. Cyberfraud. The act of making financial or personal gain by deception is known as cyberfraud. The main aim of fraud is to gain benefits in terms of money. Cyberfrauds include social engineering attacks like password guessing, spear phishing, and DNS redirecting in which the hacker manipulates the users to get their confidential information and then uses this information for his/her vested interests.

4.2.2. Cyberactivism. It is the latest type of crime. In this type of crime, Internet-based social and communication applications are used to create, operate, and manage the activism like faster communication with people or the distribution of information to a large audience in a few seconds. The communication technologies used in this activism are Twitter, Facebook, YouTube, LinkedIn, Whatsapp, Gmail, and so on. These technologies are made for good purposes like better connectivity with friends, colleagues, and employees and spreading the latest information easily to a vast geographical area. But some people use these technologies for spreading rumours to damage their rival image or spread

occurring in today's world are depicted in Figure 2 and discussed below.

4.1. Cyberviolence. The violence created in real world with the help of a computer system or any device (like mobile) connected to the Internet is known as cyberviolence. Where the word "violence" is present, its effect in terms of harm will be there. In the world of cybersystem, the components that can be harmed are devices connected to the Internet, data on servers, information on the Internet, and any individual or organization that can be ruined by cyberviolence. There are various forms of cyberviolence from which most common are discussed below [26, 27].

4.1.1. Cyberworld War. The cyberworld war has a maximum level of violence that acts among various countries of the world. The cyberworld war constitutes every individual, military, country, hackers, and government and private employees. The aim of the cyberworld war is to malfunction, false information about their organization or individuals to get various types of benefits [5].

4.3. Cybertrespass.

Trespass means crossing boundaries for which someone is not authorized. Cybertrespass is the crime in which cyberlaw is violated by hacking an authorized user system. This type of attack violates the confidentiality and integrity fundamental of cybersecurity. The various types of cybertrespass are as follows [26, 27].

4.3.1. Cybertheft.

Theft means there is a fear of something important that can be damaged or stolen. In real life, stealing or damaging is done by going physically into someone's house or organization and stealing something like file, television, gold, and so on. But in case of cyberworld, it is different from real world. Cybertheft in the cyberspace can be done by technically hacking someone's computer system connected to the Internet. In cyberworld, hackers have the aim of stealing/damaging information and data on the cyberspace for financial or personal gain. Basically, there are two types of thefts:

(i) Theft to cyberspace: Space is one of the important factors, which if not maintained properly leads to malfunction of the Internet. Cyberattackers aim to overflow the cyberspace to stop their target services or hack their targets.

(ii) Theft to data/information: Data/information constitutes the confidential record of an individual, organization, and country. The confidentiality, integrity, and availability of information on the Internet and servers must be maintained from cyberattackers.

4.3.2. Cyberespionage.

It is also known as cyberspying. It is the act of tracking the activity of individual, company, organization, country, enemy, or rival by performing malicious activities on the network. These are technically sound people who are difficult to detect. They analyze the network traffic illegally, or they can hack the security cameras and laptop cameras to obtain the information about their targets, that is, what type of information they are accessing, what type of work they are doing, and when they leave their workplace or home [5].

4.3.3. Cyberpornography.

It is the attack in which an attacker posts sexual or nude material of his/her target on public websites. The attacker can find the private material of his/her target by hacking the target computer system, mobile, security cameras, or tablet. This type of exposure of private pictures or videos makes shame to the target of the attacker, or even in some cases, the target commits suicide [26, 27].

4.4. Cybersquatting.

It is the cybercrime in which an attacker illegally registers the name of the trademark of others as domain name so that the owner of the trademark fails to register his/her trademark as domain name. The various types of cybersquatting are discussed below [29].

4.4.1. Classic Cybersquatting.

It is the same as cybersquatting, but the main aim of the cybersquatter is to get paid. When the cybersquatter gets ransom from his/her target, he/she sells off or deletes his/her domain name. But now, laws have been changed, so the trend of this type of attack is not very popular today [29].

4.4.2. Derogatory Cybersquatting.

In this type, the cybersquatter's main aim is to destroy the reputation of his/her target. A cybersquatter does this by various means like posting the pornographic material, hate speech, or violated contents on that domain name [29].

4.4.3. Typographical Cybersquatting.

In this type of attack, the attacker cannot use the same name as the trademark because the owner of the trademark had already registered for the domain name. So, in this case, the attacker registers with the name very similar to the original trademark name. For example, if the attacker registers a domain name of Gmail that is very similar to Gmail, then he/she may succeed to make loss to the original trademark owner [29].

Figure 2 represents the major categories of cybercrimes happening in today's world. According to us, any kind of cybercrime can be subcategorised in this taxonomy. Our taxonomy helps a reader to easily understand the similarities between the attacks.

5. Classification of Cyberattacks on the Basis of Fundamental Principles of Cybersecurity

Cyberattacks are the techniques used by cybercriminals to disrupt the fundamental principles (confidentiality, integrity, and availability) of cybersecurity. Cyberattacks are skills of a cyberattacker to do cybercrimes in the Internet system. Cybercrimes present the general form, whereas cyberattacks are the specific form of attacks/crimes on cybersecurity. Here, we will discuss the cyberattacks on the cybersecurity fundamental principles as shown in Figure 3.

5.1. Attacks on Confidentiality.

It is detected that there are many kinds of attacks on confidentiality of network information which are as follows.

5.1.1. Traffic Analysis.

In the traffic analysis attack, an attacker analyzes the information on the network between the sender and the receiver without any tampering in it. The attacker makes analysis of information on the network to find some new information to steal confidential information. It is a passive attack, and it only violates the confidentiality principle of network security [30].

5.1.2. Eavesdropping.

Eavesdropping means secretly listening to a confidential conversation on the network. An

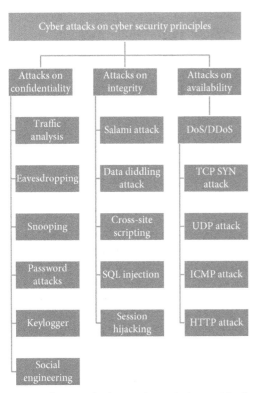

FIGURE 3: Classification of cyberattacks on the basis of fundamental principles of cybersecurity.

attacker can read and capture the information on the network between the sender and the receiver. This attack is similar to traffic analysis. But in this type of attack, an attacker can sniff and record the information and later listen or read this information for his/her vested interests [31].

5.1.3. Snooping. It is the passive form of attack where the attackers attempt to obtain confidential information about network users like login credentials of email, social apps, online banking, and so on or their personal records. The corporate sector or government officials use the snooping method to track their employees' activities for various purposes. Snooping is further divided into two types as discussed below [5].

(i) Digital snooping: Monitoring a private or public network for passwords or data is known as digital snooping. This attack is performed at the network layer. This snooping is done on the physical cable. Attackers may reprogram network switches or other devices to allow them to capture data off a network. Attackers can hack security cameras of an organization to get the username and password of employees so that they can access organization data like authorized users [5].

(ii) Shoulder snooping: This is a physical attack where someone tries to watch for typed passwords or see information on a monitor that they should not have access to [5].

5.1.4. Password Attacks. Password-based attacks are used to get the username and password of authorized users of an application, website, desktop computers, and laptops. These captured usernames and passwords are further used to get access to network services as authorized users and to do malicious act. The success of password attacks depends upon the user awareness on how to choose the password. If the user is aware about choosing passwords, it will add complexity for hackers to gain access to the authorized user's password. There are various types of password attacks as discussed below.

(i) Dictionary-based attack: In this attack, an attacker tries every combination of characters or words as defined in the dictionary to hack passwords of authorized users of Internet resources or applications. This type of attack result depends on the authorized user's password. If the user does not choose passwords similar to dictionary words, then it is almost impossible for the attacker to hack the password of the user with this attack.

(ii) Brute-force attack: In this attack, an attacker tries every single possible password combination using brute-force hacking tools to hack the user password. This technique is time-consuming but results in the hacking of the authorized user's password. This attack can take few seconds to few days or few months also according to the complexity of passwords.

(iii) Password-guessing attack: In the password-guessing attack, an attacker tries to guess the passwords of authorized users by using common words like date of birth, name, and religion.

5.1.5. Keylogger. Keylogger is a type of malware that runs in the background of a computer system in the hidden mode; that is, the user is not aware about the running of keylogger. It has no icon or entry on desktop, quick launch, all programs, or anywhere else in the computer system. All the information entered by the user is captured by keylogger and transmitted to the attacker without the knowledge of the authorized user of that computer system [32].

5.1.6. Social Engineering. Social engineering is a type of attack in which someone with very good interactive skills manipulates others into revealing information about the network that can be used to steal data of authorized users of an organization or an individual. Attackers carry out this attack by either influencing network users or through technical attack. It aims at small groups of Internet users. The various types of social engineering attacks are discussed below [33].

(i) Phishing: Phishing is an attempt to hack sensitive information (usually financial information like bank user id/password, credit card details, etc.) of network users by tricking them in various forms. These attacks use fake emails and websites which look almost the same as the original to fool the people. It aims at small groups to large groups of network users. The various types of phishing attacks are discussed below [34].

(a) DNS phishing: DNS phishing is a process in which an attacker alters host files on the victim's computer system or DNS database or at any access point so that legitimate web URLs point to a fraudulent URL of the attacker. Due to lack of awareness about phishing attacks, users enter their confidential information in the fraudulent website of the hacker. Sometimes, technically sound people also fail to differentiate between the fraudulent website and the authorized website [34].

(b) Spear phishing: It is a form of targeted attacks. At first, an attacker seeks available public information of its target through websites or social networking sites. On the basis of public information gathered, the attacker makes malware-contained email to gain the victim trust. Then, the attacker sends this email to some selected people whom he/she wants to target. If anyone receiving that email clicks on it, he/she will become the victim of the attacker and lose his/her confidential information to the attacker because the malware attached with email works automatically when email is opened [33].

(ii) Dumpster diving: It is an attack in which an attacker himself/herself finds confidential information of a network user or an organization without the use of the network system. For example, the attacker may look up trash of an organization to find sensitive information [33].

(iii) Baiting attack: In this approach, an attacker places the malware-infected storage device (CD, DVD, and pen drive) at that point where the future victim may see that device. The attacker adds more curiosity to the victim by labelling that storage device. When a person uses that storage media, his/her computer system gets infected and he/she will become a victim of the attacker's attack [33].

(iv) Waterholing: It is a form of targeted attack in which an attacker indirectly targets his/her victim. In this method, the attacker infects those websites which his/her target mostly visits so that the victim computer system may get affected and the attacker gains access to his/her confidential information [33].

(v) Reverse social engineering: In this attack, an attacker represents himself/herself as a trusted person to the victim. Then, the attacker creates a situation in which the victim believes that the attacker is a person who can solve his/her problem and trustworthy to share his/her confidential information [33].

5.2. Attacks on Integrity. A huge number of attacks can be found to disrupt the integrity of network information which are as follows.

5.2.1. Salami Attacks. Salami attacks are a series of minor data security attacks that together result in a larger attack. Example of this attack is a deduction of very small amount of money from bank account which is not noticeable. But when these deductions of very small amount from various numbers of accounts in the bank become a huge amount, it can damage the infrastructure of the bank [35].

5.2.2. Data Diddling Attacks. Data diddling is an illegal or unauthorized data alteration. For example, account executives can change the employee time sheet information of employees before entering to the HR payroll application [35].

5.2.3. Cross-Site Scripting (XSS). In this attack, an attacker uses vulnerable websites or applications. The hacker inserts his/her malicious script into that website or application that a target user visits. When the target visits that vulnerable website, the hacker's malicious code is transferred to the victim's browser. This malicious script can access sensitive information like cookies and session from the victim's browser [36, 37].

5.2.4. SQL Injection Attack. It is also an injection attack like cross-site scripting. But this attack uses the vulnerabilities of database SQL statements. This attack affects the web application database. It also affects websites and web applications that make use of databases. The attacker can gain access to the sensitive information of the database by bypassing the web application's authentication and authorization mechanism [36, 38].

5.2.5. Session Hijacking Attacks. Session hijacking is another type of network attack where the attacker alters session between two or more authorized users to gain authorized access to information or services used by authorized users. TCP session hijacking and man-in-the-middle attacks are examples of this type of attack [35].

5.3. Attacks on Availability. There are various methods that can be used to slow down or stop the availability of network resources to the authorized users of the Internet and its resources. Here are a few common attacks against availability that are discussed below.

5.3.1. DoS/DDoS. DoS (denial of service) is a very common attack that disrupts the availability of the network and its resources. An attacker can attack his/her target directly or indirectly or both. In direct attack, the attacker generates huge traffic by using his/her own computer system, and in indirect attack, the attacker uses bots (a system that is hacked by an attacker and is under his/her control) to generate huge traffic for his/her target. A large variant of the DoS attack is DDoS (distributed denial-of-service) attack in which a number of bots or even a server can be used to make an attack on the target to disrupt his/her network services.

TABLE 2: Classification of cyberattacks on the basis of cybercrimes.

Cyberviolence	Cyberpeddler	Cybertrespass	Cybersquatting
Denial of service/distributed denial of service	Keylogger and social engineering	Traffic analysis, eavesdropping, snooping, password attacks, SQL injection, salami attack, and data diddling	Session hijacking

DoS/DDoS attack can disrupt the network bandwidth, system resources, and application resources [39].

The consequences of a DoS attack are the following:

(i) Slow network performance

(ii) Unavailability of network services

The various types of Dos/DDoS attacks are discussed below.

(i) TCP SYN attack: In this type of attack, an attacker uses the flaw of the three-way handshake process during TCP (transmission control protocol) connection establishment. In the three-way handshake process, the client sends SYN (synchronization) request to the server. Then, in the second step, ACK (acknowledgement) is given by the server with SYN to the client. At the last step, the client sends the final ACK. The attacker sends too many SYN requests and never gives the final-step ACK which overflow the target capacity of request handling or memory which results in nonavailability of network services. The attacker can also use spoofed address to send requests so he/she does not get any response from his/her target which can also overwhelm his/her network [40].

(ii) UDP attack: TCP is the connection-oriented protocol and UDP (user datagram protocol) is the connectionless protocol, and both work on the transport layer of the TCP/IP model. The connectionless mechanism used packets for information exchange and is used where reliability can be compromised up to some extent. An attacker generates huge traffic of UDP packets to his/her target to overflow his/her response handling queue which results in nonavailability of network services to authorized users [40].

(iii) ICMP attack: ICMP (internet control message protocol) works on the network layer of the TCP/IP model. It is used by network devices (like routers) to generate an error report when there is problem in the delivery of IP packets. An attacker generates and sends a huge volume of ICMP traffic to the target host which will consume the bandwidth of the target network. ICMP can be performed by two ways, that is, ping of death and smurf attacks, discussed below [41].

(a) Ping of death attack: Ping is a mechanism used to check the availability of a particular IP address by using small packets. An attacker sends large-sized packets in a ping which has a range higher than the maximum limit of packet size that TCP/IP allows. So, the target is not configured for these large-sized packets because it may crash, freeze, or reboot [42].

(b) Smurf attack: Smurf attack basically uses the amplification approach. It targets the Internet broadcast address (IBA) that is built in the IP protocol. A hacker sends request by generating ICMP traffic with spoofed address (containing address of the target) to IBA of the intermediary site that will generate and send amplified response to the target host. All this process works on the network layer of the TCP/IP model, but the intermediary response is sent to all hosts on layer 2. An IBA can support a maximum of 255 hosts. So, a smurf attack amplifies a single ping 255 times [40, 43].

(iv) HTTP attack: HTTP (Hypertext Transfer Protocol) works on the application layer of the TCP/IP model. It targets all the web applications and services which use HTTP packets (GET and POST requests). This type of attack does not need high volume of traffic, so this attack needs less bandwidth. In this attack, an attacker sends a large volume of GET or POST requests to the target which results in overwhelm of target capabilities [40, 44].

Table 2 represents the various types of cyberattacks grouped on the basis of cybercrime categories. According to us, every type of cyberattack can be adjusted in Table 2. Our cybercrime taxonomy gives a way to uniquely distribute the cyberattacks. It helps to understand the similarity and differences between various types of cyberattacks. Table 2 helps the newcomers to decide what type of security technique is effective on what type of cyberattacks. Hence, classification of cyberattacks according to cybercrime categories in Table 2 provides a complete understanding of common types of cyberattacks. So, a security technique can be updated to protect the cyberspace from more than one cyberattack.

6. Challenges to Tackle Cybercrimes

The increasing technology of the Internet has provided various advancements in human beings' daily life. But this advancement of technology is facing various challenges that are discussed below.

6.1. Mixed Attacks. Various mechanisms are discovered by cybersecurity researchers to defend against cyberattacks. But there is no such single technique that can defend the data and information on the Internet from all the cybercrimes. Cybercriminals are very creative. They are always busy in making a new variant of existing cyberattack or forming a new cyberattack. This type of dynamic environment of cybercrimes gives a very hard challenge for security researchers to defend the data and information on the Internet from the various types of cyberattacks from cyberattackers [25].

6.2. Huge Increase in the Cybersurface. The increasing popularity of the Internet has given a steep rise to the cybersurface. The cybersurface basically constitutes desktops, laptops, mobiles, tablets, and smartwatches that can be connected to the Internet with the help of hardware and software. The Internet of Things (IoT) and cloud computing are major platforms that have extended the cybersurface to a large circumference as stated in [3]. The increased cybersurface provides various opportunities to cybercriminals for cyberattacks due to lack of proper implementation of cybersecurity. Some vendors have major focus on their product's quality and minor on cybersecurity. They do not implement the full-fledged cybersecurity mechanisms which give opportunities to the cyberattacker to enter an Internet or network system like an authenticated user. This increased cybersurface gives rise to the difficult level of defending data on the cybersurface by security professionals. Some new type of security standards is needed to implement properly the cybersecurity to save the cyberspace from cybercriminals [24].

6.3. Remote User Connectivity. In the present stage, government and private sectors have offered an opportunity to its employees to connect remotely from anywhere by deploying the Internet-based virtual private network (VPN). This facility has enhanced the working system of these sectors. But this system has brought the private information of these sectors to public networks. Remote user connectivity also provides opportunities for cybercriminals to hack the Internet-connected devices remotely. There is a challenge for network security professionals to provide security from cybercriminals to the corporate or government sectors' confidential information on public networks and those public devices who have such confidential information [45].

6.4. Network IP Address Infrastructure. The numbers of Internet-connected devices are proportionally larger than the numbers of Internet users as stated in [3]. A single user of the Internet can have a mobile, a laptop, or a desktop. Each device has a unique IP address on the Internet. The traditional methods of manually configuring IP addresses are no longer viable, and they also lack the scalability, reliability, and effectiveness of security methods needed by the today's networks. So, securely and effectively managing the IP addresses of these fast-growing networks is a big challenge for a network administrator as the forged IP address is used by the cyberattacker to disrupt the Internet system [45].

6.5. Unified Network Control. The technique SDN (software-defined networking) is widely adopted to control the Internet system easily and effectively than the traditional system. This technique provides various benefits like the centralized network approach, low cost, and reliability. But the flaws in

this technique have provided various opportunities for cybercriminals to hack the control of the network system. If security of the controller working in the control plane of SDN is compromised, then the complete architecture of the network system will be compromised where the SDN is installed. This will give the confidential information of many users, the control of various networking devices, and the integrity of applications installed on that network to cybercriminals. So, this is a big challenge for security professionals to protect the SDN from cybercriminals [21].

6.6. One Technique for All Layers. There are different techniques to protect all the layers of the OSI or TCP model. It is a complex task to advance all the techniques according to the latest cyberattacks at a time. It is also wastage of time and money to make many techniques for the previous known attacks. There is a need for a single technique that should protect all the layers of the ISO or TCP model from various known and unknown cyberattacks [25].

7. Conclusion

The increasing popularity of the Internet has given a sharp rise to the digital world which constitutes very large volume of information and data stored on the cyberspace. With the increase in cyberspace, the cyberattacks/cybercrimes are also increasing in numbers and their effect is also growing bigger. The existing security techniques are not enough to protect the current Internet system and its resources. Some new types of security techniques are required to defend the cyber space from cybercrimes that can never be cracked or require years to crack down, which are cost-effective and can defend against all types of cybercrimes. We cannot misguide the cybersecurity as information security or data security. Cybersecurity is a broader term which protects all the hardware (devices, routers, and switches), software, information, and data that are part of the Internet. On behalf of our study, the future work will constitute the following points:

(i) To propose a security technique that can defend against ever-changing attacks at different levels of network protocols

(ii) To propose an effective, accurate, and cost-efficient security technique for a specific environment (IoT, cloud computing, SDN, and smart grid)

(iii) To propose a technique for securing the information in remote user connectivity or BYOD (Bring Your Own Device) policy

References

[1] March 2017, https://wearesocial.com/special-reports/digital-in-2017-global-overview.

[2] March 2017, http://www.gartner.com/newsroom/id/3165317.

[3] *Report of McAfee Labs 2016 Threat Predictions by Intel Security*, November 2016.

[4] M. Haughn and S. Gibilisco, *Confidentiality, Integrity, and Availability (CIA Triad)*, March 2017, http://whatis.techtarget.com/definition/Confidentiality-integrity-and-availability-CIA.

[5] G. Kumar, A. Kaur, and S. Sethi, "Computer network attacks- a study," *International Journal of Computer Science and Mobile Applications*, vol. 2, no. 11, pp. 24–32, 2014.

[6] April 2017, http://thehackernews.com/2017/02/password-manager-apps.html.

[7] April 2017, http://thehackernews.com/2016/12/dailymotion-video-hacked.html.

[8] April 2017, http://thehackernews.com/2016/12/power-outage-ukraine.html.

[9] April 2017, http://thehackernews.com/2017/02/radio-station-trump-hack.html.

[10] April 2017, http://thehackernews.com/2016/11/mirai-router-offline.html.

[11] April 2017, http://thehackernews.com/2016/11/bank-ddos-attack.html.

[12] April 2017, http://thehackernews.com/2017/05/how-to-wannacry-ransomware.html.

[13] J. Liu, Y. Xiao, S. Li, W. Liang, and C. L. Philip Chen, "Cyber security and privacy issues in smart grids," *IEEE Communications Surveys & Tutorials*, vol. 14, no. 4, pp. 981–997, 2012.

[14] R. von Solms and J. van Niekerk, "From information security to cyber security," *Computers & Security*, vol. 38, pp. 97–102, 2013.

[15] A. Razzaq, A. Hur, H. Farooq Ahmad, and M. Masood, "Cyber security: threats, reasons, challenges, methodologies and state of the art solutions for industrial applications," in *Proceedings of the 2013 IEEE Eleventh International Symposium on Autonomous Decentralized Systems (ISADS)*, pp. 1–6, Mexico City, Mexico, March 2013.

[16] F. B. Schneider, "Cybersecurity education in universities," *IEEE Security & Privacy*, vol. 11, no. 4, pp. 3-4, 2013.

[17] P. Kaster and P. K. Sen, "Power grid cyber security: challenges and impacts," in *Proceedings of the 2014 North American Power Symposium (NAPS)*, pp. 1–6, Pullman, WA, USA, September 2014.

[18] J. Jang-Jaccard and S. Nepal, "A survey of emerging threats in cybersecurity," *Journal of Computer and System Sciences*, vol. 80, no. 5, pp. 973–993, 2014.

[19] K. Arlitsch and A. Edelman, "Staying safe: cyber security for people and organizations," *Journal of Library Administration*, vol. 54, no. 1, pp. 46–56, 2014.

[20] D. B. Rawat and C. Bajracharya, "Cyber security for smart grid systems: status, challenges and perspectives," in *Proceedings of the SoutheastCon 2015*, pp. 1–6, Fort Lauderdale, FL, USA, April 2015.

[21] S. T. Ali, V. Sivaraman, A. Radford, and S. Jha, "A survey of securing networks using software defined networking," *IEEE Transactions on Reliability*, vol. 64, no. 3, pp. 1086–1097, 2015.

[22] A. R. Sadeghi, C. Wachsmann, and M. Waidner, "Security and privacy challenges in industrial internet of things," in *Proceedings of the 2015 52nd ACM/EDAC/IEEE Design Automation Conference (DAC)*, pp. 1–6, San Francisco, CA, USA, June 2015.

[23] S. Singh, Y.-S. Jeong, and J. H. Park, "A survey on cloud computing security: issues, threats, and solutions," *Journal of Network and Computer Applications*, vol. 75, pp. 200–222, 2016.

[24] S. H. Weber and E. Studer, "Cybersecurity in the internet of things: legal aspects," *Computer Law & Security Review*, vol. 32, no. 5, pp. 715–728, 2016.

[25] Y. Zou, J. Zhu, X. Wang, and L. Hanzo, "A survey on wireless security: technical challenges, recent advances, and future trends," *Proceedings of the IEEE*, vol. 104, no. 9, pp. 1727–1765, 2016.

[26] M. Yar, *Cybercrime and Society*, SAGE Publications, Thousand Oaks, CA, USA, 2013.

[27] D. Wall, *Crime and the Internet*, Routledge, Abingdon, UK, 2003.

[28] April 2017, http://searchsecurity.techtarget.com/definition/cyberstalking.

[29] N. S. Sreenivasulu, *Law Relating to Intellectual Property*, Partridge Publishing, Gurugram, India, 2013.

[30] M. N. Mejri, J. Ben-Othman, and M. Hamdi, "Survey on VANET security challenges and possible cryptographic solutions," *Vehicular Communications*, vol. 1, no. 2, pp. 53–66, 2014.

[31] B. Mokhtar and M. Azab, "Survey on security issues in vehicular ad hoc networks," *Alexandria Engineering Journal*, vol. 54, no. 4, pp. 1115–1126, 2015.

[32] A. Solairaj, "Keyloggers software detection techniques," in *Proceedings of the 2016 10th International Conference on Intelligent Systems and Control (ISCO)*, pp. 1–6, Coimbatore, India, January 2016.

[33] K. Krombholz, H. Hobel, M. Huber, and E. Weippl, "Advanced social engineering attacks," *Journal of Information Security and Applications*, vol. 22, pp. 113–122, 2015.

[34] J. A. Chaudhry, S. A. Chaudhry, and R. G. Rittenhouse, "Phishing attacks and defenses," *International Journal of Security and Its Applications*, vol. 10, no. 1, pp. 247–256, 2016.

[35] April 2017, http://www.omnisecu.com/ccna-security/types-of-network-attacks.php.

[36] A. Kieyzun, P. J. Guo, K. Jayaraman, and M. D. Ernst, "Automatic creation of SQL injection and cross-site scripting attacks," in *Proceedings of the 31st International Conference on Software Engineering (ICSE 2009)*, pp. 199–209, Vancouver, BC, Canada, May 2009.

[37] April 2017, https://www.acunetix.com/websitesecurity/cross-site-scripting/.

[38] April 2017, https://www.acunetix.com/websitesecurity/sql-injection/.

[39] V. Zlomislic, K. Fertalj, and V. Sruk, "Denial of service attacks: an overview," in *Proceedings of the 2014 9th Iberian Conference on Information Systems and Technologies (CISTI)*, pp. 1–6, Barcelona, Spain, June 2014.

[40] O. Osanaiye, K.-K. Raymond Choo, and M. Dlodlo, "Distributed denial of service (DDoS) resilience in cloud: review and conceptual cloud DDoS mitigation framework," *Journal of Network and Computer Applications*, vol. 67, pp. 147–165, 2016.

[41] April 2017, http://www.webopedia.com/TERM/I/ICMP.html.

[42] April 2017, http://searchnetworking.techtarget.com/definition/ping.

[43] April 2017, http://www.techrepublic.com/article/understanding-a-smurf-attack-is-the-first-step-toward-thwarting-one/.

[44] April 2017, https://www.verisign.com/en_US/security-services/ddos-protection/ddos-attack/index.xhtml.

[45] S. Barnett, "Top 10 challenges to securing a network," *Network Security*, vol. 2000, no. 1, pp. 14–16, 2016.

15

Network Restoration for Next-Generation Communication and Computing Networks

B. S. Awoyemi ⓘ,[1] **A. S. Alfa,**[1,2] **and B. T. Maharaj**[1]

[1]*University of Pretoria, Pretoria, South Africa*
[2]*University of Manitoba, Winnipeg, MB, Canada R3T 2N2*

Correspondence should be addressed to B. S. Awoyemi; awoyemibabatunde@gmail.com

Academic Editor: Ignacio Soto

Network failures are undesirable but inevitable occurrences for most modern communication and computing networks. A good network design must be robust enough to handle sudden failures, maintain traffic flow, and restore failed parts of the network within a permissible time frame, at the lowest cost achievable and with as little extra complexity in the network as possible. Emerging next-generation (xG) communication and computing networks such as fifth-generation networks, software-defined networks, and internet-of-things networks have promises of fast speeds, impressive data rates, and remarkable reliability. To achieve these promises, these complex and dynamic xG networks must be built with low failure possibilities, high network restoration capacity, and quick failure recovery capabilities. Hence, improved network restoration models have to be developed and incorporated in their design. In this paper, a comprehensive study on network restoration mechanisms that are being developed for addressing network failures in current and emerging xG networks is carried out. Open-ended problems are identified, while invaluable ideas for better adaptation of network restoration to evolving xG communication and computing paradigms are discussed.

1. Introduction

Current and emerging communication and computing networks are expected to provide high reliability by achieving near-instantaneous restoration in the event that one or more network elements fail. This requires that network restoration plans be put in place such that in the event of failures, the network can immediately adjust, regroup, and/or revert to an alternative arrangement, usually in terms of a reroute, to continue and complete the given communication task [1]. Hence, developing network restoration models to cater for sudden failures, thereby improving the efficiency and reliability of our telecommunications and computing networks, is an imperative. Network (or routing) restoration (or recovery) is the field that describes the design and implementation of appropriate mechanisms and/or models for achieving desirable network reliability by creating proper backup plans for networks in the event of preconceived or unexpected failures [2].

The main goal of network restoration is to seek to instantaneously make available new routes once one or more network elements (e.g., links or nodes) fail, thereby avoiding disruption to network traffic. The new routes are usually either computed immediately at the point of failure or are usually preplanned even before such failure occurs. Generally, in research works that involve developing appropriate network restoration mechanisms for protection against failures, several factors have to be put into consideration. The most important factors are the cost of network infrastructure, length of rerouting paths, amount of the total capacity that has to be reserved for restoration or recovery from failure, and the time taken to achieve such network restoration. The design goal is always to achieve optimal productivity for the network with as much less resource and cost as possible over the shortest amount of time. Network restoration models are built around this goal. The restoration capacity problem, for instance, is designed to place the minimum amount of spare capacity needed in the network to restore a part of lost connections [3].

Several works have been carried out and more works are still being done in addressing network restoration problems, particularly for communication and computing networks. This paper provides a comprehensive study on common failures types and peculiar restoration mechanisms that are being developed for addressing both current and newly evolving next-generation (xG) communication and computing network paradigms.

The main contributions of this paper are summarised thus:

(i) An up-to-date analysis of network restoration solutions that are being developed and applied for current and emerging communication and computing networks is carried out.

(ii) An exploration of the key aspects of network restoration for xG communication and computing networks that still require further investigations is carried out. Furthermore, invaluable insights on how such investigations can be successfully achieved based on the peculiarities and promises of xG communication and computing networks are provided.

The remainder of this paper is organised as follows: Section 2 describes different failure types in communication and computing networks, Section 3 establishes the categorisation of the various network restoration mechanisms for communication and computing networks, Sections 4 and 5 provide a review of network restoration models being employed for addressing failures in both current and emerging communication and computing networks, Section 6 discusses some examples of practical models of network restoration for emerging communication and computing networks, Section 7 gives some observations and future directions of network restoration for emerging networks, and finally, Section 8 provides the concluding remarks.

2. Failures in Communication and Computing Networks

Modern communication and computing networks are designed using network models. A network model is an interconnectivity of active devices, switches, equipment, and so on developed to drive telecommunication and computing needs. In simple description, the devices and other equipment that make up the network are represented as nodes, while the connections between them (either wired or wireless) are referred to as links. The direction in which data transmission flows or in which traffic is routed is called a path. Figure 1 gives a general depiction of a network model for a typical communication or computing network. The nodes are labelled from A to G. Two paths are indicated; P_1 is a path from A to G and P_2 is a path from A to D.

One shared experience for all communication and computing networks is the possibility and/or occurrence of network failures. A network failure can be defined as a forced temporary modification of a network, usually as a result of disruption to actual design of flow or traffic, which results in the capacity of certain links in the network to decrease, possibly to zero [4]. Network failures in communication and

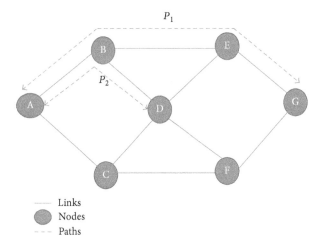

FIGURE 1: An architectural depiction of a communication or computing network model with 7 nodes, 10 links, and 2 paths shown.

computing networks are broadly classified into the following categories:

(i) Link failures: a link failure occurs when a link component in a network fails [5]. Solving a link failure problem can be achieved by adding a new link or by redirecting and redistributing the traffic of the failed link to other still functional links with enough capacity to carry the additional traffic from the failed link.

(ii) Node failures: a node failure occurs due to the failure of an equipment at the nodes of the network such as a switch or a router [6]. A node failure can also be considered as the simultaneous failure of all the adjacent links to a node. One way of protecting against node failure is by installing alongside one or more redundant equipment that can immediately replace an active equipment acting as a node.

(iii) Single failures: a single failure occurs in a network when only one equipment, node, or link fails at a time [7]. To protect networks from single failures, network restoration models are developed to offer protection for individual or single elements in the network, with the assumption that multiple, near-simultaneous failures are a rare and/or improbable event.

(iv) Multiple failures: multiple failures in a network can occur when more than one equipment, node, or link fail at the same time [8]. To protect networks from multiple failures, network restoration models are developed to offer protection for two or more elements in the network, with the understanding that such multiple, near-simultaneous failures, though rare, are not entirely impossible occurrence(s).

Good communication and computing networks are designed to quickly restore networks to full activity and/or capacity when failures occur. In the next section, the various types of network restoration mechanisms designed to

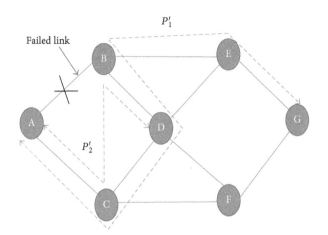

FIGURE 2: A depiction of a link failure and a corresponding line restoration.

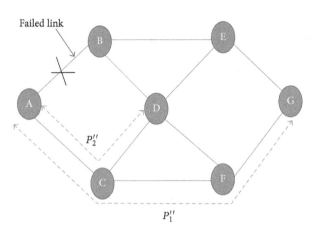

FIGURE 3: A depiction of a link failure and a corresponding path restoration.

address failures in modern communication and computing networks are discussed.

3. Types of Network Restoration for Communication and Computing Networks

Network restoration seeks to instantaneously find the best alternative route to transmit network traffic when a failure occurs. Network restoration in communication and computing networks can be classified into the following categories:

3.1. Line Restoration. In line restoration (also referred to as link restoration), the traffic carried on the failed link is rerouted from its tail node to its head node. Thus, the original route for traffic that uses the failed link is only slightly modified by replacing the failed link with an alternate route that connects its end nodes [9]. Usually, the end nodes of the failed link are made to participate in a distributed algorithm to dynamically discover a new route. The design of networks under line restoration requires limited information, that is, link loads and capacities, but it does not require source-destination traffic information. Moreover, restoration can be executed very quickly since there is no need to backtrack individual connections to their corresponding ingress nodes [10]. Figure 2 is a follow up on Figure 1 but now gives a pictorial representation of a link failure and a line restoration approach for recovering the network. In Figure 2, when link A-B fails, then

(i) link A-B is replaced by line A-C-D-B, and hence path P_1 is replaced with path P_1';

(ii) link A-B is replaced by line A-C-B, and hence path P_2 is replaced by P_2'.

3.2. Path Restoration. In path restoration, the traffic routed on a failed link is backtracked to its ingress nodes and new, perhaps totally disjoint, alternate routes are selected for restoring the traffic for all affected source-destination pairs. This implies that a completely new path is used as the alternate path [11]. Path restoration schemes have dedicated

backup reserves (spares) that are used as backup routes for particular demands. Path restoration often requires less restoration capacity resources than line restoration at the expense of more complex signalling and larger execution time. Path restoration was employed in [12], for example, in providing adequate spare capacity in a telecommunications network environment. Figure 3 is a follow up on Figure 1 but now gives a pictorial representation of a link failure and a path restoration approach for recovering the network. In Figure 3, when link A-B fails, then

(i) path P_1 is replaced with path P_1'';

(ii) path P_2 is replaced by P_2''.

3.3. Reactive Restoration. In reactive restoration schemes, alternate routes are only calculated after the actual failure has occurred [13]. In these schemes, data packets are flooded into the network after the occurrence of failure to look for free capacity and to setup the new path. These restoration schemes are also referred to as real-time restoration approaches and they are mostly applicable in scenarios where traffic changes very frequently in the network.

3.4. Proactive Restoration. In proactive restoration schemes, alternate routes are always precalculated way before the failure happens. In the event of a failure, the connection is simply rerouted to the previously designed route [14]. These schemes are also called preplanned restoration approaches and are faster in execution than the reactive or real-time restoration approaches, even though they usually give poorer capacity utilisation than the real-time approaches.

Network restoration models are most often classified into the abovementioned categories. Generally, communication and computing networks are designed using either the centralised or the distributed architecture. In some instances, therefore, restoration mechanisms are usually classified based on these architectural representations.

3.5. Centralised Restoration. In centralised schemes, there is usually a central controller that performs computations and sends information about the current state of the network as well as restoration decisions to all components of the network [15]. Centralised schemes are capacity efficient but have single points of failure. They may also have communication overhead and scalability issues.

3.6. Distributed Restoration. In distributed schemes, there is usually no central hub that directs network decisions and information dissemination but rather, individual components of the network are empowered to understand situations in the network and immediately make decisions to enhance network reliability and quick recovery after failures [16].

In the next two sections, we study the utilisation of the various types of network restoration mechanisms described in this section: first in current communication and computing networks, and then in emerging xG communication and computing networks.

4. Network Restoration in Current Communication and Computing Networks

In this section, a review of works in which the various types of network restoration have been developed and employed in addressing network failures in present-day communication and computing networks is carried out.

4.1. Path Restoration

4.1.1. Path Restoration for Teletraffic Networks. In [17], the authors developed a mathematical model for determining transmission network restoration capacity for wide area teletraffic networks. Two path restoration models were developed. The models were called connection-based restoration and load-directed restoration. The connection-based restoration model was designed to restore as many connections as possible in the transmission network for every affected or failed link based on the available built-in reconnection capacity. The idea behind the load-directed restoration model was to make even better use of the reconnection capacity depending on the time of failure, since loads vary from time to time in the course of the day. Network simulation showed that the load-directed approach outperformed the connection-based approach for network restoration when failure occurs in a dynamic call-routing teletraffic network.

The authors in [18] developed an on-line distributed multicommodity flow approximation algorithm for path restoration in circuit-switched telecommunication network. The restoration algorithm developed ran on a number of iterations. Each iteration consisted of two phases—an explore phase and a return phase. The explore phase was started by the source nodes of the disrupted paths. The return phase was started by the destination nodes of the disrupted paths. The return phase started after the explore phase ended. In the return phase, the paths traversed by the explore messages were retraced by the return messages. The return phase ended when the return messages have reached

the sources. The return phase helped to resolve the contention for spare capacity in the network.

4.1.2. Path Restoration for Optical Communication Networks. In [19], the authors proposed an adjacent shortest cycle backup path as the restoration method whenever a link in an optical communication network using wavelength division multiplexing (WDM) fails. The shortest path was calculated using an ant colony optimisation algorithm. Adjacent cycles were updated using the restoration method developed. The authors established that the proposed method can survive link failure and theoretically provide better performance than existing restoration methods.

4.1.3. Path Restoration for Mesh Networks. In [20], the authors argued that dual-failure availability is an important metric for a reliable network where the restoration of all single failures is fully satisfied. Hence, an algorithm to evaluate network dual-failure availability for shared backup path protection mesh networks with the existing multiflow design model was developed. The authors created four network families, while each network family has eleven networks. From the algorithm developed, it was revealed that the values of network dual-failure availability increase first and then drops mildly when the average nodal degree of network increases.

4.1.4. Path Restoration for Computing Networks. In [21], the authors proposed the allocation of a backup path as a restoration model for failure in a computing network. The proposed model addressed the problem of the possibility of the backup path being disjoint from the original path at the Internet protocol or overlay layer but sharing the same physical links on the physical layer, meaning that if the failure occurred on the physical link, the failure could affect both the original and the backup paths simultaneously. The proposed solution was to find a route for the backup path that minimised the joint path failure probability between the original and the backup paths.

4.2. Line Restoration

4.2.1. Line Restoration for Teletraffic Networks. In [22], the authors developed network restoration models for scenarios where there is uncertainty in the traffic matrix (i.e., traffic demands can change on varying time scales) and the network topology is also dynamic (i.e., network topology can change when links fail). The models investigated included a restoration strategy that allowed the traffic to be arbitrarily rerouted in order to obtain an optimal utilisation on the modified network, a restoration strategy that is end-to-end and which allowed all affected flow paths to be arbitrarily rerouted and finally, a restoration strategy that reroutes only the affected flows by bypassing around the failed link rather than end-to-end. The models developed provided useful performance

TABLE 1: Summary of network restoration models employed in current communication and computing networks.

Number	Type of network restoration model	Type of failures addressed	Applicable networks	References
(1)	Path restoration, for example, shortest cycle backup path, minimal joint failure probability, and end-to-end restoration.	Link failures (single and multiple links) and node failures	Teletraffic networks, optical communication networks, mesh networks, and computing networks	[17–21]
(2)	Link (or line) restoration	Link failures (single or multiple failures) and node failures	Teletraffic networks	[22]
(3)	Proactive restoration, for example, connection-based and load-directed restoration models	Node failures and joint link failures	Optical communication networks and computing networks	[23, 24]
(4)	Reactive restoration	Link failures and node failures	Mesh networks	[25]

guarantees both on the original network and on the network after one or more links failed.

4.3. Proactive Restoration

4.3.1. Proactive Restoration for Optical Communication Networks.
The authors in [23] considered the possibility of two links failing one after another in any given order in an optical WDM network and developed a restoration model for such occurrence. Three types of proactive restoration methods were developed and a heuristic was used to solve the recovery problems that ensued. A one hundred percent recovery from double link failures that occur immediately one after another was achieved with a slight increase in backup capacity.

4.3.2. Proactive Restoration for Computing Networks.
The authors in [24] established the need for routing mechanisms which describes how information is transferred between network nodes for one computer to find another in a network. A route was explained as the sequence of network nodes through which it is possible to transmit information from source node to destination node. To increase reliability in a computer network, the restoration model must establish sufficiently fast routes on or before a failure is detected in the network device. Furthermore, once data cannot be transferred on the main route due to a failure, the source node must immediately switch to the backup route without it taking time on the calculation of a new route. The authors therefore proposed a proactive backup scheme of routes for dynamic changes in the structure and configuration of the network which allowed reducing the recalculation time of optimal routes and thereby increasing the efficiency of the routing mechanism.

4.4. Reactive Restoration

4.4.1. Reactive Restoration for Mesh Networks.
The authors in [25] studied the relationship between failure localisation and the properties of available link restoration algorithms in a mesh network topology. From the study, it was discovered that the topological constraints on restoration paths required by algorithms that embed rings within mesh networks resulted in significant degradation in the ability to localise failures. Hence, the use of proactive restoration

schemes, as opposed to reactive restoration, had a negative impact, although not as significant as the topological effect. Algorithms that make use of the mesh topology and dynamically route around existing failures using reactive restoration came close to an inherent limit imposed by the complexity of additional algorithmic advances.

Table 1 gives a summary of the various types of network restoration that are being developed and employed for protecting networks against failures in present-day communication and computing networks, as discussed in this section.

5. Network Restoration for Emerging Communication and Computing Networks

Network restoration models are currently being developed for emerging xG communication and computing paradigms. A review of works in which the various types of network restoration models have been developed and employed for addressing network failures in emerging xG technologies is carried out in the following subsections.

5.1. Path Restoration

5.1.1. Path Restoration for Software-Defined Networks.
Software-defined networks (SDNs) are the immediate future of telecommunication networks [26]. In SDNs, the part that handles the decision-making process of network traffic (called the control plane) is separated from the part that transmits or relays the data traffic (called the data plane or physical plane) [27]. This makes it possible for intelligence to be carried out in the control plane, thereby easing network management while also enabling dynamic networks configuration. In [28], the authors developed a network failure recovery solution for software-defined optical networks using cognitive mechanisms for achieving the restoration. The authors established that SDN-based networks, in their architecture, enable administrators to simplify the network management and to efficiently detect network failure; hence, they are being considered for application in optical networks. The SDN-based solution developed had a centralised controller which allowed the network to make more efficient failure detection, effectively isolating the affected forwarding elements, and immediately remedying abnormal operations in optical networks.

5.1.2. Path Restoration for Wireless Sensor Networks. Wireless sensor networks (WSNs) are an example of an already developed technology but which is currently evolving for xG applications. Hence, network restoration for WSN is gaining attention. Particularly, occurrences of failure are more prominent in WSN than in most other communication technologies because of the adverse conditions in which those sensor nodes are deployed and for which they are intended to work. WSN nodes are also extremely resource-constrained. It is thus imperative to develop resourceful network restoration models for WSN. The authors in [29] developed a failure recovery model for WSN based on grade diffusion. The model also used the saved shortest path approach to figure out the best recovery path with minimal energy consumption for WSN. The grade diffusion method kept the sensors working for the longest period possible, thus increasing the lifetime of the network. The authors argued that the grade diffusion, enhanced by the shortest path approach which uses routing tables with saved shortest paths, was able to quickly identify faulty nodes and to recover the network in good time.

5.2. Line Restoration

5.2.1. Line Restoration for Mission-Critical or Emergency Networks. The authors in [30] developed a failure recovery model that deals with the problem of efficiently restoring sufficient resources in a communication network to support the demand of mission-critical services after a large-scale disruption like a natural disaster has occurred. The goal was to sufficiently recover the communication network infrastructure in the shortest time and with minimum interventions when massive disasters happen. The problem was modelled as a demand graph which takes into account the demand increase that occurs during such incidents. The graph defined a set of demand flows on the communication network of which a major disruption has made it unable to meet the capacity requirements of demand flows. The extra demand flows were to be accommodated by means of the recovery actions or by deploying new links and nodes. The recovery problem was developed as a mixed integer linear programming problem. The idea was to look for the best strategy that recovers the damaged infrastructure and deploys new links and nodes in order to minimise the cost of the recovery actions under the constraints on network capacity and demand flows satisfaction.

5.2.2. Line Restoration for Expansive Networks. In [31], the authors investigated a network recovery mechanism when a network has experienced massive failures from which recovery could take a long time and may involve several stages before the network can be fully back to its original state. The authors established that unlike in cases of minimal, predictable failures for which network can be quickly restored by preplanning redundant components and/or alternative paths, large-scale failures actually require gradual recovery of traffic. This can only be achieved by repairing failed components and reorganizing logical path connectivity over partial physical resources. It therefore has to be determined which physical components have to be repaired first and what logical paths should be reestablished over the partial recovered network components to realise a fast and effective restoration of traffic flow. The recovery model developed attempted to balance the requirement between maximising the total amount of traffic on all logical paths (i.e., the total network flow) and maximising traffic demand of each logical path. This problem was formulated as an optimisation problem and a heuristic algorithm called grouped-stage recovery (GSR) was introduced to solve the problem with a large number of damaged components in practical time.

5.3. Proactive Restoration

5.3.1. Proactive Restoration for Software-Defined Networks. The authors in [32] investigated a fast failure discovery and network recovery mechanism for dynamic networks using SDN. In the model, a central controller monitored the connectivity so that if a link got broken, the network is instantly reconfigured to restore the end-to-end connectivity for all paths and thus maintain connectivity between nodes. A failure detection scheme that used per-link bidirectional forwarding detection sessions was developed. The per-link detection was said to be better than per-path detection because it reduced detection time, decreased message complexity, and removed false-positive alarms. More so, its recovery time did not depend on the network size and path length. In the design, after detection of a failure, the controller selected a preconfigured backup path to restore the network. The proposed design was said to be a relatively simple way to reduce the recovery time in a dynamic network.

In [33], the authors developed a failure recovery model for data traffic in SDNs. In the model, a controller directs network flow around a failed link or node using preconfigured alternative paths. To significantly reduce recovery time, the developed model used virtual local area network tags to aggregate flow disruptions/failures, and based on the information gathered, a well-developed proactive recovery scheme was invoked to help recover the network from the failure.

The authors in [34] developed a failure recovery mechanism for a hybrid network where traditional Internet protocol routers coexisted and worked alongside SDN switches. In the recovery model, by redirecting traffic on a failed link to SDN switches through preconfigured Internet protocol tunnels, the proposed approach was able to react to failures very fast in order to guarantee traffic reachability in the presence of single link failures. Also, with the help of coordination among SDN switches, multiple backup paths were designed for the failure recovery. The proposed approach was said to avoid potential congestion in the post-recovery network by choosing proper backup paths.

5.3.2. Proactive Restoration for Fifth-Generation Networks. The design of fifth-generation (5G) wireless communication networks is currently evolving very rapidly. 5G is the soon-to-be wireless communication standard. In [35], the authors established that in carrier cloud, which is one major tool for driving and achieving the goals of this newly developing 5G technology, service resilience could be heavily impacted by a failure of any network function that runs on a virtual machine. Hence, a framework was built which used efficient and proactive restoration mechanisms to ensure service resilience in carrier cloud. Two mechanisms were proposed; the first mechanism was based on bulk signalling whereby only one single message was created to replace a certain number of signalling messages in a bulk, while the second one created message profile which reduced the signalling message header by replacing repetitive information element by a profile identification. An analytical model based on Markov chain was used to evaluate the performance of the mechanisms developed.

5.3.3. Proactive Restoration for Internet-of-Things Networks. Internet-of-things (IoT) network is the emerging computer networking paradigm that makes the interaction between humans and nonhuman elements or objects more realistic and provides the connection among different existing networks. In [36], the authors argued that the current fault detection algorithms, usually designed for specified networks, are not suited for the complex communication environment of IoT, whose transmission is usually through hierarchical networks. Hence, a layered fault management scheme was proposed for IoT, with uniform observation points set around. In order to distinguish between the real fault and false alarm, fuzzy cognitive maps theory was introduced to setup the monitoring model. By adjusting the weighting rules in the model, it was possible for different observing points to achieve flexible judgement of the link failure risk in their authorities. After locating the fault roots, original recovery methods for individual networks were then employed to rescue the broken transmission.

5.3.4. Proactive Restoration for Dependency Networks. The authors in [37] investigated a recovery mechanism for networks in which, when a node fails, other neighbouring nodes that depend on such failed node are adversely affected and they could fail too. Such networks are called dependency networks. In dependency networks, the recovery of a node depends on the state of its dependent nodes. For this kind of networks, the dependency model is that the nodes depending on each other form a dependency group. This dependency group fails only when more than a certain fraction of nodes in the group fails. Obviously, in this model, there exists a fraction of nodes whose failure has no effect on the function of dependency of the group and the failed nodes can be recovered due to dependency relations among nodes. This recovery mechanism is referred to as dependency recovery mechanism. The authors therefore proposed a cascading process model to investigate the failure propagation of such dependency networks with a recovery mechanism. In the work, a fraction of network nodes was chosen randomly to form the dependency groups, while all the other nodes in

the complementary fraction did not belong to any dependency group. By means of randomly removing a fraction of nodes and their links, the cascading failure on dependency networks was studied.

5.3.5. Proactive Restoration for Scalable Networks. In [38], the authors developed a coding-based failure recovery mechanism which used diversity coding to achieve quick network restoration over any type of arbitrarily large network. The authors established that coding-based recovery techniques improved capacity efficiency of proactive protection/restoration schemes by making the dedicated paths share the spare resources using coding operations. In the developed model, connection demands in each traffic vector were partitioned into coding groups and an advanced diversity coding technique was employed to achieve the recovery. It is also interesting to note that classical optimisation techniques (column generation and integer linear programming), and not the more generally used approach of developing heuristics, were used in solving the network restoration problem in this work.

5.4. Reactive Restoration

5.4.1. Reactive Restoration for Wireless Sensor Networks. In [39], the authors proposed a restoration method to deal with the failure of an articulation node (a node whose failure may result in the network being broken into different segments that are isolated from each other) in a multichannel WSN scenario. The problem was formulated as a multiobjective optimisation problem. In the centralised solution approach developed, the sink carried out the entire recovery procedure from failure detection to the reallocation of channels after the connectivity has been restored. The recovery solution developed used graph theory heuristics such as graph colouring and Steiner points to rearrange the nodes around the failed node and to recover from the network partitioning and restore network connectivity.

The authors in [40] proposed an energy-efficient failure recovery scheme for WSN. The model used a coverage preserving failure recovery mechanism to achieve energy-efficient network restoration when failure occurs. The authors argued that the proposed scheme was able to diagnose failures with very low false alarming rate and was also able to recover failures by maintaining coverage above a given acceptable threshold value.

5.4.2. Reactive Restoration for Fifth-Generation Networks. In [41], the authors proposed that 5G would have baseband units that are connected to remote radio heads via high-speed fronthaul links. Hence, failure of any 5G cell site fronthaul would imply the loss of hundreds of gigabits or even terabits of data. The authors therefore presented a novel cell outage compensation approach using new self-healing radios added to each cell site in the 5G network. The self-healing radios are being designed to operate only in cases of fronthaul/backhaul failures of any cell site in the network.

TABLE 2: Summary of network restoration models employed in emerging xG communication and computing networks.

Number	Type of network restoration model	Type of failures addressed	Applicable networks	References
(1)	Path restoration	Link and node failures, single and multiple links failures	Software-defined networks, wireless sensor networks	[26–29]
(2)	Link (or line) restoration	Link and node failures , single and multiple links failures	Mission-critical or emergency networks, expansive networks	[30, 31]
(3)	Proactive restoration	Link and node failures, single and multiple links failures	Software-defined networks, fifth-generation networks, internet-of-things networks, dependency networks, scalable networks	[32–38]
(4)	Reactive restoration	Link and node failures, single and multiple links failures	Wireless sensor networks, fifth-generation networks, internet-of-things networks	[39–43]

The authors then developed a new software-defined controller to handle the self-healing procedures. Finally, a high-level simulation study was carried out to assess the proposed approach. The simulation results confirmed the advantages of the proposed approach in terms of the degree of recovery from failures.

5.4.3. Reactive Restoration for Internet-of-Things Networks. In [42], the authors addressed the reliability of IoT under emergency situations. The authors argued that the reliability of IoT under such emergency or crisis situations could only be guaranteed when the network is self-adaptive and resilient to errors by providing efficient mechanisms for information distribution, especially in the multihop scenario. The restoration mechanism developed to achieve this reliability used the implicit acknowledgements that objects in the network usually receive to detect transmission errors. The mechanism then used a routing metric to designate the best link, thus minimising packet loss probability.

The authors in [43] developed a distributed and dynamic fault-tolerant mechanism for IoT whereby an object with a failed service could be taken over by another service peer without the involvement of other users, including developers and installers. The restoration mechanism used strips to store a list of duplicated services, with each service peer maintaining a consistent view of duplicated services in the strip. In combination with the heartbeat protocol, recovery from failure was achieved by manipulating strips in a distributed manner, and results obtained showed that failures could be recovered within few seconds without administrator or developers in the loop.

Table 2 gives a summary of the various types of network restoration that are being developed and employed for protecting networks against failures in emerging xG communication and computing networks, as discussed in this section.

6. Practical Examples of Network Restoration for Emerging Communication and Computing Networks

In this section, two practical examples where network restoration models have been employed for addressing failures in emerging xG communication networks are discussed. The first example describes a link failure scenario with a proactive restoration plan being designed to restore the network. The second example describes a node failure scenario with a reactive restoration plan being developed to achieve the network restoration.

6.1. An Example of Link Failure with Proactive Restoration Plan. The link failure recovery plan understudied in this section is the work carried out in [33]. The work is chosen because it describes a good model of link failure recovery in xG communication using an SDN platform. The outstanding characteristics of SDN that makes it a preferred network for the immediate future were highlighted as follows: SDN makes use of a centralised network intelligence platform, SDN separates its network data from its control planes, and finally, SDN abstracts network infrastructure from it general applications. In the developed network restoration model of [33], the goal was to investigate how SDN can be deployed for very high network reliability communication prototypes (otherwise referred to as carrier-grade networks (CGNs)). Failures at the data plane were introduced in the form of link or switch failures which could result in problems such as network instability, degrading quality of service, and packet loss. The aim of the proactive scheme developed was to achieve recovery without overwhelming the network with control traffic and dependence on the controller. The developed scheme relied on the protection mechanism to achieve rapid recovery of the data plane failures. Alternate backup paths were preconfigured for every link. Virtual local area network (VLAN) tagging was used to aggregate disrupted flows. The proactive scheme effectively reduced the dependence on the controller. The recovery scheme investigated is represented in a pictorial form in Figure 4.

In the model presented in Figure 4, nodes (switches) A, B, C, D, E, and F are interconnected through links AE, AB, AF, and so on. If one of the nodes or links (e.g., switch B or link AB in Figure 4) fails, switch A detects the failure, tags the flows with the ID of failed core switch, and autonomously detours the two disrupted flows from link AB to their destined 2-hop neighbours via the preconfigured alternate paths. The VLAN ID field of the detoured packets of various disrupted flows is matched against the preconfigured

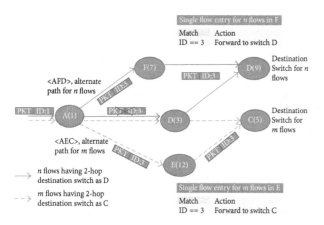

FIGURE 4: Link failure recovery model for SDN [33].

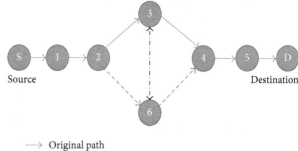

⟶ Original path
←·⟶ Local backup request and response
--⟶ Detour path for the moved data flow

FIGURE 5: An illustration of local traffic distribution for node failure recovery model in MCWNs [44].

alternate path flow rules from switch F which then forwards the packets to the alternate path's next switch. All the preconfigured alternate paths are identified by a unique identifier of the network component (core switch or an edge link) that it is protecting. In the case of a failure, the detoured flows on the alternate path are matched against the identifier of the failed network component and forwarded to the next switch of the backup path or destination 2-hop neighbour of the detour switch.

The developed model was experimented using the xG backbone network topology being developed by AT&T. The network contained 25 switches and 52 links with virtualised rings on the Mininet virtualisation environment. In the experiment, the total recovery time for the developed recovery scheme was calculated by varying the number of flow rules to recover. The aim was to study the total time required to recover from a core network component and edge link failure. Additionally, the experiment was carried out to examine the effect of a number of disrupted flows on the overall recovery time. The failure was triggered by shutting down a switch while the flows passing through it were rerouted to achieve the recovery. The overall failure recovery time was calculated as a time difference between the time that the last disrupted flow occurred and the time in which it was successfully detoured after each failure. The disrupted flows were aggregated into one single flow. With this single group entry modification, it was possible to redirect all disrupted flows to the backup path. The results obtained showed that with the proactive plan, the recovery time was completely unaffected by the number of disrupted flows. Furthermore, the recovery scheme successfully achieved the failure recovery of about 3-4 ms, which means that it successfully fulfilled the carrier-grade recovery requirement of 50 ms time interval.

6.2. An Example of Node Failure with Reactive Restoration Plan. The reference work for this example is [44]. It is a good example of how to address node failure in broadly general xG communications. The xG communication network that was employed in the work is called multichannel wireless networks (MCWNs). In MCWNs, wireless nodes are equipped with multiple wireless network cards or radios to take the advantage of channel diversity. This makes MCWNs

very useful in emerging technologies such as WSNs, IoT, and 5G because end-users are enabled to access the Internet at a low cost, with ease of deployment and configuration and flexibility of construction. The model investigated in [44] developed a recovery (backup) scheme that improved the robustness of MCWNs against random failures. At its core, the scheme was equipped with a local traffic load redistribution scheme that identified local traffic load changes in order to maximise the recovery possibility while also minimising the possibility of congestion generation.

In the model developed in [44], the recovery scheme searches for feasible local-to-end rerouting plans which generate new paths to avoid the faulty area, based on any given routing and channel assignment algorithm. Then, by considering current network settings as constraints, the scheme redistributes the traffic load in the local area to satisfy the quality of service requirement of each data flow. In the design for an efficient node failure backup scheme, the aim is to fully explore the capacity of the surviving network components in order to find new paths that do not overload the neighbours of the failed node which reduces the probability of generating congestion. The backup process involves failure testing/identification, deciding feasible routing plan, satisfying quality of service requirements, local traffic redistribution, and backup decision. An illustration of the local traffic distribution is provided in Figure 5.

In the analysis of the model, the achievable capacity (or throughput) of each link is affected by two factors—transmission capacity and channel occupancy ratio (COR). When a single link uses the entire capacity, COR is represented by α_i^r which was given as

$$\alpha_i^r = \frac{L_i^r}{\tau_i^r}, \tag{1}$$

while the aggregated COR when multiple links share the capacity of one channel, represented by β_i^r, was given as

$$\beta_i^r = \sum_j \left(\frac{L_j^r}{\tau_j^r} \right) \quad j = 1, 2, \ldots, \tag{2}$$

where L_i^r is the traffic load on radio r of router v_i and τ_i^r is the transmission capacity on radio r of router v_i. The achievable link capacity C_i^r was therefore

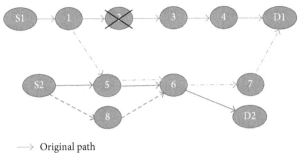

$\longrightarrow$ Original path
$\cdots\rightarrow$ Local-to-end rerouting path
$--\rightarrow$ Local rerouting path

FIGURE 6: Solution approach for node failure recovery in WSN [44].

$$C_i^r = \left(1 - \beta_i^r\right) \times \tau_i^r. \tag{3}$$

If the achievable capacity of the neighbour node C_i^r was enough for the requested backup stream C_{req} (i.e., if $C_{\text{req}} < C_i^r$), it accepts the backup stream. Otherwise, the local traffic redistribution will be triggered. In that case, a new capacity $C_i^{r'}$ was calculated thus:

$$C_i^{r'} = C_i^r + \left(R_i\right)^{(-l)} \times L_i^r, \tag{4}$$

where l is the level parameter and R_i is the number of radios of the node. If $C_i^{r'} > C_{\text{req}}$ and satisfied quality of service requirements, backup stream was accepted. Otherwise, the backup stream was dropped. After all the backup paths for the affected data flows have been built or refused, the backup process stops. This process is illustrated in Figure 6.

7. Observations and Future Directions for Network Restoration Solutions

From the study on failures and network restoration for current and emerging communication and computing networks, the following general observations are made:

(1) From the review of current literature on network restoration, it is observed that a lot more work has been done on link failure detection and restoration than on node failure detection and restoration, especially for emerging xG communication and computing networks. The reason for this, it seems, is that link failures are a lot easier to understand and analyse. Hence, it is easier to study and develop restoration models for link failures than for node failures. However, exploring node failure problems and developing restoration models for them are equally critical for emerging communication and computing networks. Therefore, a lot more attention has to be dedicated to addressing node failures, especially in xG communication and computing networks.

(2) It is also observed that most of the network restoration problems have been solved by the use of heuristics. While this, in itself, is not a bad idea, solutions through heuristics may not always be the best because they are usually problem-specific, suboptimal, and nontransferable. In other words, since heuristics are usually only based on logical reasoning and not on numerical or analytical basis, they therefore cannot be easily transferred to solving other problems or addressing similar or not-so-similar failure recovery problems. A lot more work has to be done in developing optimal, practicable, and transferable solutions for the failure and network restoration problems in xG communication and computing networks.

From the study and observations already provided, it is clear that there are some aspects of network restoration for emerging xG communication and computing networks that still require further investigation, if the expectations and promises of xG technologies are to be fully realised. The most important areas of network restoration that still requires further studies are highlighted.

7.1. Specific Adaptation of Network Restoration to WSN. While modern WSN is an integral part of emerging xG communication and computing networks, it has its own peculiar characteristics that network restoration can exploit. For instance, a good WSN design can still be effective even when a number of nodes have failed, as compared to most other emerging network paradigms where a single node failure may be catastrophic, and could possibly result in the near collapse of the entire system. More so, in modern WSN designs, some nodes are deliberately put to sleep in order to conserve energy and battery life. This, in some way, may be viewed as those nodes "failing," even though these sleeping nodes have not failed in reality and can still be employed in the network at some later time frame. Another important aspect of WSN is the speed with which data have to be transmitted, especially for xG networks such as in IoT applications. It is imperative therefore to develop network restoration models that specifically identify the peculiarities of WSN and that are built to cater for such peculiarities in their adaptation to and application for IoT and other xG network designs. The authors are currently working on some new network restoration models for practical WSN applications in IoT and other similar xG networks.

7.2. Need for Improved Network Restoration Models That Address Emerging xG Communication and Computing Peculiarities. xG communication and computing prototypes have high promises in terms of speed, reliability, coverage, and so on that would require the application of high-speed failure detection, isolation, and network restoration models for them to be adequately equipped to achieve their goals. Even though research work in this regard is currently on-going, as already established in this study, it is still very inadequate. There are lots of research gaps that still need to be filled, open-ended problems that are still up for investigation, and practical issues (such as scalability and computational complexity) that still require to be addressed. Therefore, there is need for more research work on network restoration for emerging xG communication and computing technologies if the research gaps are to be filled.

7.3. Experimental Implementation of Network Restoration Models in Emerging Technologies. Most recent works on network restoration for emerging xG technologies are still focussed on mathematical and simulation modelling and not on actual implementation of the ideas and models being developed, whether on experimental or deployment basis. The reason construed for this is that many of these emerging xG technologies are themselves still in their early stages of development and fine-tuning, making it difficult to find actual test-beds or experimental models for carrying out the necessary experimentation on network restoration. What we believe can be done in this regard is to create opportunities to implement the network restoration models being developed alongside the experimental developments for these emerging technologies as much and as quickly as possible.

7.4. Developing xG Network Restoration Models for Reliable Disaster Management and Emergency Services. The expectation of remarkable interconnectivity, fast speed, high data rates, wide coverage, and so on that xG networks promise is also its major albatross in case of large-scale disasters and emergency needs. This is because, the impact of such disasters on the network can be extreme, leading to massive numbers of equipment, nodes, links, and so on failing simultaneously. It is important to develop network restoration strategies for emerging xG networks that can provide an acceptable level of reliability and survivability of the network in times of network disruptions as a result of sudden colossal disasters, either natural or man-made.

7.5. Improving Network Security of Emerging Technologies through Network Restoration. One important aspect of emerging xG networks where network restoration can be very useful is in improving network security. A good example is the use of network restoration in tracking down malicious activities by intruders or detecting compromised elements in a network. In such a case, by developing and incorporating the right network restoration models in the system, the activities of malicious nodes can be minimised, if not completely eliminated. More so, reports provided through the network restoration models can be used in identifying and isolating already compromised nodes. However, not much work has been done in this regard yet, making it an important area for active research.

8. Conclusion

Current and emerging xG communication and computing networks, in their design, must be robust against failures and be built with swift network restoration capacities in order to achieve their promises in terms of capacity, latency, speed, and so on. While failures are inevitable, it is important to study existing network restoration models so as to discern the applicability of these models to both present and emerging technology paradigms. In this study, the most impressive network restoration types and models that have been and/or are being developed for recent and xG com-

munication and computing technologies are identified, with their properties and proficiencies also investigated. Important observations on network restoration for xG communication and computing networks are made, and suggestions on improvement and practical adaptation are discussed. Finally, directions for further work in the area of developing network restoration models that meet the needs and peculiarities of emerging xG communication and computing networks are provided.

Acknowledgments

This research is funded by the Advanced Sensor Networks SARChI Chair program, cohosted by the University of Pretoria (UP) and Council for Scientific and Industrial Research (CSIR), through the National Research Foundation (NRF) of South Africa.

References

[1] W. Lau and S. Jha, "Failure-oriented path restoration algorithm for survivable networks," *IEEE Transactions on Network and Service Management*, vol. 1, no. 1, pp. 11–20, 2004.

[2] R. Dighe, Q. Ren, and B. Sengupta, "A link based alternative routing scheme for network restoration under failure," in *Proceedings of the Global Telecommunications Conference*, vol. 3, pp. 2118–2123, Singapore, November 1995.

[3] G. Shen and W. Grover, "Capacity requirements for network recovery from node failure with dynamic path restoration," in *Proceedings of the OFC 2003 Optical Fiber Communications Conference*, pp. 775–777, Atlanta, GA, USA, March 2003.

[4] P. H. Franklin, I. Tavrovsky, and R. Ames, "A strategy for optimal management of spares," in *Proceedings of the 2016 Annual Reliability and Maintainability Symposium (RAMS)*, pp. 1–6, Reno, NV, USA, January 2016.

[5] X. Zhang and Z. Zhang, "Link fault identification using dependent failure in wireless communication networks," *Electronics Letters*, vol. 52, no. 2, pp. 163–165, 2016.

[6] W. P. Tay, J. N. Tsitsiklis, and M. Z. Win, "On the impact of node failures and unreliable communications in dense sensor networks," *IEEE Transactions on Signal Processing*, vol. 56, no. 6, pp. 2535–2546, 2008.

[7] W. Grote, A. Arenas, and A. Zapata, "Netfailpac: a single failure protection algorithm with QoS provision for optical WDM networks," in *Proceedings of the Third International Conference on Systems (icons 2008)*, pp. 226–229, Cancun, Mexico, April 2008.

[8] S. Yin, S. Huang, B. Guo et al., "Shared-protection survivable multipath scheme in flexible-grid optical networks against multiple failures," *Journal of Lightwave Technology*, vol. 35, no. 2, pp. 201–211, 2017.

[9] R. Shenai, C. Maciocco, M. Mishra, and K. Sivalingam, "Threshold based selective link restoration for optical wdm mesh networks," in *Proceedings of the Fourth International Workshop on Design of Reliable Communication Networks, 2003 (DRCN 2003)*, pp. 31–38, Banff, AB, Canada, October 2003.

[10] H. Luss and R. T. Wong, "Survivable telecommunications network design under different types of failures," *IEEE*

Transactions on Systems, Man, and Cybernetics–Part A: Systems and Humans, vol. 34, no. 4, pp. 521–530, 2004.

[11] S. Hegde, S. G. Koolagudi, and S. Bhattacharya, "Path restoration in source routed software defined networks," in *Proceedings of the 2017 Ninth International Conference on Ubiquitous and Future Networks (ICUFN)*, pp. 720–725, Milan, Italy, July 2017.

[12] J. Veerasamy, S. Venkatesan, and J. C. Shah, "Spare capacity assignment in telecom networks using path restoration," in *Proceedings of the 3rd Modeling, Analysis, and Simulation of Computer and Telecommunication Systems (MASCOTS '95)*, pp. 370–374, Durham, NC, USA, January 1995.

[13] N. Haider, M. Imran, N. M. Saad, and M. A. Zakariya, "Performance analysis of reactive connectivity restoration algorithms for wireless sensor and actor networks," in *Proceedings of the 2013 IEEE 11th Malaysia International Conference on Communications (MICC)*, pp. 490–495, Kuala Lumpur, Malaysia, November 2013.

[14] M. Dzida, M. Zagozdzon, M. Zotkiewicz, and M. Pioro, "Flow optimization in ip networks with fast proactive recovery," in *Proceedings of the Networks 2008-The 13th International Telecommunications Network Strategy and Planning Symposium*, pp. 1–15, Budapest, Hungary, September 2008.

[15] J. Perell, S. Spadaro, F. Agraz et al., "Experimental evaluation of centralized failure restoration in a dynamic impairment-aware all-optical network," in *Proceedings of the 2011 Optical Fiber Communication Conference and Exposition and the National Fiber Optic Engineers Conference*, pp. 1–3, Piscataway, NJ, USA, March 2011.

[16] G. Li, D. Wang, C. Kalmanek, and R. Doverspike, "Efficient distributed restoration path selection for shared mesh restoration," *IEEE/ACM Transactions on Networking*, vol. 11, no. 5, pp. 761–771, 2003.

[17] D. Medhi and R. Khurana, "Optimization and performance of network restoration schemes for wide-area teletraffic networks," *Journal of Network and Systems Manangement*, vol. 3, no. 3, pp. 265–294, 1995.

[18] S. Venkatesan, M. Patel, and N. Mittal, "A distributed algorithm for path restoration in circuit switched communication networks," in *Proceedings of the 24th IEEE Symposium on Reliable Distributed Systems (SRDS'05)*, pp. 226–235, Orlando, FL, USA, October 2005.

[19] Mallika and N. Mohan, "Link failure recovery in WDM networks," *International Journal of Computer Science and Electronics Engineering*, vol. 1, no. 5, pp. 1–4, 2013.

[20] W. Wang and J. Doucette, "Dual-failure availability analysis for multi-flow shared backup path protected mesh networks," in *Proceedings of the 2016 8th International Workshop on Resilient Networks Design and Modeling (RNDM)*, pp. 127–133, Halmstad, Sweden, September 2016.

[21] W. Cui, I. Stoica, and R. H. Katz, "Backup path allocation based on a correlated link failure probability model in overlay networks," in *Proceedings of the 10th IEEE International Conference on Network Protocols*, pp. 236–245, Paris, France, November 2002.

[22] D. Applegate, L. Breslau, and E. Cohen, "Coping with network failures: routing strategies for optimal demand oblivious restoration," *ACM SIGMETRICS Performance Evaluation Review*, vol. 32, no. 1, pp. 270–281, 2004.

[23] H. Choi, S. Subramaniam, and H.-A. Choi, "On double-link failure recovery in WDM optical networks," in *Proceedings of the Twenty-First Annual Joint Conference of the IEEE Computer and Communications Societies*, vol. 2, pp. 808–816, New York, NY, USA, June 2002.

[24] P. D. Alexandrovich and T. I. Yurievich, "Proactive backup scheme of routes in distributed computer networks," in *Proceedings of the 2016 International Siberian Conference on Control and Communications (SIBCON)*, pp. 1–4, Moscow, Russia, May 2016.

[25] S. S. Lumetta and M. Medard, "Towards a deeper understanding of link restoration algorithms for mesh networks," in *Proceedings of the Twentieth Annual Joint Conference of the IEEE Computer and Communications Society (Cat. No. 01CH37213)*, vol. 1, pp. 367–375, Anchorage, AK, USA, April 2001.

[26] F. Hao, M. Kodialam, and T. V. Lakshman, "Optimizing restoration with segment routing," in *Proceedings of the IEEE INFOCOM 2016-The 35th Annual IEEE International Conference on Computer Communications*, pp. 1–9, San Francisco, CA, USA, April 2016.

[27] A. Ghannami and C. Shao, "Efficient fast recovery mechanism in software-defined networks: multipath routing approach," in *Proceedings of the 2016 11th International Conference for Internet Technology and Secured Transactions (ICITST)*, pp. 432–435, Barcelona, Spain, December 2016.

[28] X. Zhang, W. Hou, L. Guo, S. Wang, Y. Sun, and X. Yang, "Failure recovery solutions using cognitive mechanisms for software defined optical networks," in *Proceedings of the 2016 15th International Conference on Optical Communications and Networks (ICOCN)*, pp. 1–3, Hangzhou, China, September 2016.

[29] S. Abuelenin, S. Dawood, and A. Atwan, "Enhancing failure recovery in wireless sensor network based on grade diffusion," in *Proceedings of the 2016 11th International Conference on Computer Engineering Systems (ICCES)*, pp. 334–339, Cairo, Egypt, December 2016.

[30] N. Bartolini, S. Ciavarella, T. F. L. Porta, and S. Silvestri, "Network recovery after massive failures," in *Proceedings of the 2016 46th Annual IEEE/IFIP International Conference on Dependable Systems and Networks (DSN)*, pp. 97–108, Toulouse, France, June 2016.

[31] K. Genda and S. Kamamura, "Multi-stage network recovery considering traffic demand after a large-scale failure," in *Proceedings of the 2016 IEEE International Conference on Communications (ICC)*, pp. 1–6, Kuala Lumpur, Malaysia, May 2016.

[32] R. Ahmed, E. Alfaki, and M. Nawari, "Fast failure detection and recovery mechanism for dynamic networks using software-defined networking," in *Proceedings of the 2016 Conference of Basic Sciences and Engineering Studies (SGCAC)*, pp. 167–170, Khartoum, Sudan, February 2016.

[33] P. Thorat, R. Challa, S. M. Raza, D. S. Kim, and H. Choo, "Proactive failure recovery scheme for data traffic in software defined networks," in *Proceedings of the 2016 IEEE NetSoft Conference and Workshops (NetSoft)*, pp. 219–225, Seoul, Republic of Korea, June 2016.

[34] C. Y. Chu, K. Xi, M. Luo, and H. J. Chao, "Congestion-aware single link failure recovery in hybrid SDN networks," in *Proceedings of the 2015 IEEE Conference on Computer Communications (INFOCOM)*, pp. 1086–1094, Hong Kong, China, April 2015.

[35] T. Taleb, A. Ksentini, and B. Sericola, "On service resilience in cloud-native 5G mobile systems," *IEEE Journal on Selected Areas in Communications*, vol. 34, no. 3, pp. 483–496, 2016.

[36] X. Li, H. Ji, and Y. Li, "Layered fault management scheme for end-to-end transmission in internet of things," in *Proceedings of the 2011 6th International ICST Conference on Communications and Networking in China (CHINACOM)*, pp. 1021–1025, Harbin, China, August 2011.

[37] Y. N. Bai, N. Huang, L. N. Sun, and Y. Zhang, "Failure propagation of dependency networks with recovery mechanism," in *Proceedings of the 2017 Annual Reliability and Maintainability Symposium (RAMS)*, pp. 1-6, Orlando, FL, USA, January 2017.

[38] S. N. Avci and E. Ayanoglu, "Link failure recovery over large arbitrary networks: the case of coding," *IEEE Transactions on Communications*, vol. 63, no. 5, pp. 1726–1740, 2015.

[39] S. Chouikhi, I. E. Korbi, Y. Ghamri-Doudane, and L. A. Saidane, "Articulation node failure recovery for multichannel wireless sensor networks," in *Proceedings of the 2015 IEEE Global Communications Conference (GLOBECOM)*, pp. 1-7, San Diego, CA, USA, December 2015.

[40] K. P. Sharma and T. P. Sharma, "CPFR: coverage preserving failure recovery in wireless sensor networks," in *Proceedings of the 2015 International Conference on Advances in Computer Engineering and Applications*, pp. 284–289, Ghaziabad, India, March 2015.

[41] M. Selim, A. E. Kamal, K. Elsayed, H. M. Abdel-Atty, and M. Alnuem, "Fronthaul cell outage compensation for 5G networks," *IEEE Communications Magazine*, vol. 54, no. 8, pp. 169–175, 2016.

[42] N. Maalel, E. Natalizio, A. Bouabdallah, P. Roux, and M. Kellil, "Reliability for emergency applications in internet of things," in *Proceedings of the 2013 IEEE International Conference on Distributed Computing in Sensor Systems*, pp. 361–366, Cambridge, MA, USA, May 2013.

[43] P. H. Su, C. S. Shih, J. Y. J. Hsu, K. J. Lin, and Y. C. Wang, "Decentralized fault tolerance mechanism for intelligent IoT/M2M middleware," in *Proceedings of the 2014 IEEE World Forum on Internet of Things (WF-IoT)*, pp. 45–50, Seoul, Republic of Korea, March 2014.

[44] P. Sun and N. Samaan, "Random node failures and wireless networks connectivity: a novel recovery scheme," in *Proceedings of the 2016 IEEE Canadian Conference on Electrical and Computer Engineering (CCECE)*, pp. 1–6, Vancouver, BC, Canada, May 2016.

Permissions

List of Contributors

Istikmal, Adit Kurniawan and Hendrawan
School of Electrical Engineering and Informatics, Institut Teknologi Bandung, Jl. Ganesha 10, Bandung 40132, Indonesia

Zhiyi Fang
College of Computer Science and Technology, Jilin University, Changchun, China

Hongyu Sun and Zheng Lu
College of Computer Science and Technology, Jilin University, Changchun, China
Computer Science and Electrical Engineering, University of Maryland, Baltimore, MD, USA

Ting Zhu
Computer Science and Electrical Engineering, University of Maryland, Baltimore, MD, USA

Qun Liu
Network Center, Jilin University, Changchun, China

Santosh V. Purkar
Department of Electronics and Telecommunication Engineering, Matoshri College of Engineering and Research Center, Nashik Eklahare odhagaon, Affiliated to Savitribai Phule Pune University, Pune, India

R. S. Deshpande
S. C. S. M. CO. E, Ahmednagar Nepti, Affiliated to Savitribai Phule Pune University, Pune, India

Saswati Mukherjee, Matangini Chattopadhyay and Pragma Kar
School of Education Technology, Jadavpur University, Kolkata, India

Samiran Chattopadhyay
Department of Information Technology, Jadavpur University, Kolkata, India

Riku Luostarinen and Jukka Manner
Aalto University School of Electrical Engineering, Department of Communications and Networking, Espoo, Finland

Partha Pratim Ray
Department of Computer Applications, Sikkim University, 6th Mile, Gangtok, Sikkim 737102, India

Ahmad Jalal and Daijin Kim
Pohang University of Science and Technology (POSTECH), Pohang, Republic of Korea

Shaharyar Kamal
KyungHee University, Suwon, Republic of Korea

Mahadev A. Gawas and Lucy J. Gudino
Department of Computer Science and Information System, BITS-Pilani K K Birla, Goa Campus, Goa, India

K. R. Anupama
Department of Elecrical, Electronics and Instrumentation Engineering, BITS-Pilani K K Birla, Goa Campus, Goa, India

Zhaoming Lu, Chunlei Sun, Jinqian Cheng and Xiangming Wen
School of Information and Communication Engineering, Beijing University of Posts and Telecommunications, Beijing 100876, China
Beijing Laboratory of Advanced Information Networks, Beijing 100876, China

Yang Li
China Electric Power Research Institute, Beijing 100192, China

Yong Li
Department of Electronic Engineering, Tsinghua University, Beijing 100084, China

A. Charif, N. Zergainoh and R. Velazco
Université Grenoble-Alpes, INPG, TIMA Laboratoires, Grenoble, France

J. A. Fraire
Université Grenoble-Alpes, INPG, TIMA Laboratoires, Grenoble, France
Universidad Nacional de Córdoba-CONICET, Laboratorios LCD, Córdoba, Argentina

P. Madoery and J. Finochietto
Universidad Nacional de Córdoba-CONICET, Laboratorios LCD, Córdoba, Argentina

S. Burleigh
Jet Propulsion Laboratory, California Institute of Technology, Pasadena, CA, USA

M. Feldmann
Faculty of Computer Science, Technische Universität Dresden, Dresden, Germany

Ahmed Helmy and Amiya Nayak
School of Electrical Engineering and Computer Science, University of Ottawa, Ottawa, Canada

Modhawi Alotaibi
School of Electrical Engineering and Computer Science, University of Ottawa, Ottawa, Canada
College of Computer Science and Engineering, Taibah University, Medina, Saudi Arabia

Bander H. AlQarni and Ahmad S. AlMogren
Computer Science Department, College of Computer and Information Sciences, King Saud University, Riyadh 11543, Saudi Arabia

Mihui Kim
Department of Computer Science & Engineering, Computer System Institute, Hankyong National University, 327 Jungang-ro, Anseong-si, Gyeonggi-do 456-749, Republic of Korea

Mihir Asthana, Siddhartha Bhargava, Kartik Krishnan Iyyer and Rohan Tangadpalliwar
Computer Engineering Department, San Jose State University, OneWashington Square, San Jose, CA 95192, USA

Jerry Gao
Computer Engineering Department, San Jose State University, OneWashington Square, San Jose, CA 95192, USA
Taiyuan University of Science and Technology, Taiyuan 030024, China

Harmandeep Singh Brar
Department of Computer Applications, Maharaja Ranjit Singh Punjab Technical University, Bathinda, India

Gulshan Kumar
Department of Computer Applications, Shaheed Bhagat Singh State Technical Campus, Ferozepur, India

B. S. Awoyemi and B. T. Maharaj
University of Pretoria, Pretoria, South Africa

A. S. Alfa
University of Pretoria, Pretoria, South Africa
University of Manitoba, Winnipeg, MB, Canada R3T 2N2

Index

Printed in the USA
CPSIA information can be obtained
at www.ICGtesting.com
JSHW052023301024
72690JS00004B/150

9 781682 85766